THE CONVERT CARDINALS

BY THE SAME AUTHOR

A HISTORY OF WELLINGTON COLLEGE

GODLINESS AND GOOD LEARNING
Four Studies on a Victorian Ideal

THE PARTING OF FRIENDS
A Study of the Wilberforces and Henry Manning

TWO CLASSES OF MEN
Platonism and English Romantic Thought

ON THE EDGE OF PARADISE
A. C. Benson: The Diarist

EDWARDIAN EXCURSIONS
From the Diaries of A. C. Benson 1898–1904

The Convert Cardinals

JOHN HENRY NEWMAN

AND

HENRY EDWARD MANNING

David Newsome

JOHN MURRAY

First published in 1993
by John Murray (Publishers) Ltd,
50 Albemarle Street, London W1X 4BD

A catalogue record for this book is available from the British Library

ISBN 0–7195–4635–4

Typeset in 11/13pt Baskerville by Wearset, Boldon, Tyne and Wear

Printed and bound in Great Britain at
the University Press, Cambridge

Contents

Illustrations

ACKNOWLEDGEMENTS

Plate 1, from Shane Leslie's biography of Manning; Plates 4, 8, 10 and 11, The Oratory, Birmingham; 5, 16 and 19, Archbishop's House, Westminster; Plate 6, Christ Church, Oxford; Plate 7, National Portrait Gallery, London; Plate 12, from R. Chapman, *Father Faber*; Plates 3 and 13, Westminster Diocesan Archive; Plate 14, from B. Ward, *Sequel to Catholic Emancipation*; Plate 15, from Butler's *Life of Ullathorne*; Plate 17, P. A. F. Fenn; Plate 18, from E. E. Y. Hales, *Pio Nono*.

Acknowledgements

MR STUART PROFFITT (of HarperCollins) must come first among my acknowledgements. Without his persistent efforts to overcome my diffidence at the prospect of re-entering the dauntingly well-worked field of nineteenth-century ecclesiastical history after twenty years as a headmaster, I should never have embarked upon this project. Then John Murray, who has published all my books, applied the sort of friendly pressure which those who know him will appreciate cannot easily be resisted. Thereafter he, Roger Hudson and Grant McIntyre have been a constant source of help and encouragement, not least in their insistence that although the recent Newman centenary produced a whole crop of new publications, no one had ever before ventured upon a study in depth of the relationship between Newman and the other great Anglican convert to be raised to the cardinalate – his one-time friend, but more often rival, Henry Edward Manning.

My researches have been greatly assisted by the kindly help of Mr Gerard Tracey, archivist and librarian at the Birmingham Oratory. He not only allowed me to take copies of the originals of the Manning–Newman correspondence, covering the years between 1839 and 1845 (the four-volume gap in the monumental published collection of Newman's *Letters and Diaries*), but also ransacked the vast Newman library for useful articles and pamphlet material. I also received much help from Dr Peter Nockles, on the staff of the John Rylands University Library of Manchester, in locating rare books for me at both Oxford Road and the original Deansgate branch of that fine library. The staff of Keswick Public Library deserve a word of thanks, too. For three years I plagued them with requests for titles which caused them mounting amusement because of their recondite nature; and – through the good offices of the British Library – they never failed eventually to track them down. Father Dickie, at the Westminster diocesan archives, has also been a great help in my quest for suitable illustrations.

One of the greatest pleasures in my return to nineteenth-century studies, after a long absence, has been the renewal of old friendships with fellow-workers in the same field – Dr Geoffrey Rowell, Fellow of Keble, Professor Alan McClelland of the University of Hull and Dr Sheridan Gilley, Senior Lecturer in Ecclesiastical History at the University of Durham. These last two scholars kindly agreed to read the whole of my typescript and both made a number of very useful suggestions as well as correcting the occasional error and guiding me to material that I had overlooked. Notwithstanding their kindness, which went far beyond the claims of old friendship, I must still take full responsibility for any imperfections that remain.

Thornthwaite, Cumbria   David Newsome

Prologue

THE LIVES of the two central characters of this book spanned the length, if not quite the breadth, of the nineteenth century: they were both born in its first decade and died in its last. Inevitably, then, their lives and their attitudes – their thoughts and hopes and fears – reflected the movements and tensions of a century in British history abounding in so many contrasting features that never yet has a wholly satisfactory label been devised to describe it. It was an 'Age of Reform' (E. L. Woodward); an 'Age of Improvement' (Asa Briggs); the first half of the century has been described by Boyd Hilton as the 'Age of Atonement', and its central years, by W. L. Burn, as an 'Age of Equipoise'. All these descriptions are apt in their way, and all are equally inadequate. In the space of a hundred years a transformation was taking place in almost every aspect of life. As G. M. Young observed in his review of Victoria's reign, only two fundamental assumptions remained inviolate from the assaults of critics and reformers: belief in the essential rightness of representative institutions, and respect for the Family as the primary social unit.[1]

The Christian faith and the Established Church survived, it is true. But neither was immune from attack, either intellectually or politically. After all, if the nineteenth century might seem, in comparison with the century preceding it and the indifference and materialism of modern times, an 'Age of Faith', it was also witnessing the ominous beginnings of what has been described as 'the Secularization of the European Mind'. What, however, is incontestable is that religion was taken deadly seriously. Whatever the individual standpoint might be – Christian of this denomination or that, or honest doubter or convinced atheist – religion was seen to be something that *mattered*. It mattered so much that differences or deviations of belief could promote a bitterness of strife barely credible to the children of the children who lived through these conflicts; it mattered so much that a Government

could be toppled by such a seemingly trumpery issue as the
granting of an endowment to a Catholic university in Ireland. It
mattered so much that the Chancellor of the Exchequer (Gladstone), on the very eve of the Crimean War, could put all else
aside in order to write a letter of voluminous length to a friend
whose faith in the credentials of the Anglican Church was on the
point of breaking.[2] It mattered so much that, as George Kitson
Clark put it: 'Probably in no other century, except the seventeenth
and perhaps the twelfth, did the claims of religion occupy so large
a part in the nation's life, or did men speaking in the name of
religion contrive to exercise so much power.'[3]

How had this come about? G. K. Chesterton offered a typical
paradox to explain it: 'The most important event in English
history happened in France.'[4] For decades the nineteenth century
– on the Continent as well as in England – was haunted by the
spectre of the French Revolution which, in its wild excesses, had
demonstrated what could happen to the social stability of a nation
when Reason was elevated to the status of a Goddess and when
the established order, of which the Christian Church was so
generally-accepted a part, was subverted by violent means. Fear
that such a disaster could befall England led to two wholly
different responses. The disciples of Jeremy Bentham (the Utilitarians) – on the whole, in alliance with the Whig party – felt that
the sooner one put one's own house in order the better, and
pressed for major legislative reforms. The more immediately
dominant response, however, after the restoration of the Bourbon monarchy in France, was a staunch conservative reaction,
witnessed throughout Europe, taking the form of a strengthening
of the bulwarks against agitators and a reaffirmation of respect
for traditional rights, values and institutions, the chief beneficiary
of which tended to be the Church.

In the Catholic countries of Europe, this meant an unprecedented revival in the fortunes and prestige of the Papacy, not
least because of Pius VII's resolute stand against Napoleon. One
could hardly expect fiercely Protestant England to share in this
enthusiasm, but a pietistic revival which had long antedated the
cataclysm in France (heralded by the Wesleys and Whitefield in
the middle years of the eighteenth century) was now to experience its full flowering. The Evangelical revival had originally been
a self-conscious reaction against the – at least superficially – cold,
unenthusiastic, unemotional, over-rational religious temper of

the Hanoverian establishment. The events of the French Revolution, exhibiting so starkly the neglected truth of the natural depravity of man, supplied fresh momentum. Curiously, since the Evangelical message was inclined to play down ecclesiasticism, the post-Revolution Evangelicals tended to emphasize the importance of Church order and decorum in worship, partly because they came to see that unbridled passion – even in religious enthusiasm – was a dangerous force to unleash.

The revolutionary years and the religious revival of their aftermath coincided with a cultural and intellectual reaction against the rationalism of the Enlightenment. The genesis of Romanticism was really a coming to the surface of the never-dying, esoteric Platonic tradition which, both in its Continental expression and in its English equivalent, conveyed in the writings of Blake and Coleridge, spoke a language in total harmony with the mood of the period. How could those who had witnessed the horrors of the Paris streets continue to subscribe to the naïvely optimistic notion that the universe was the product of Design, the artefact of a benevolent divine lawmaker? William Paley's *Evidences of Christianity* seemed a very insipid brew after tasting the richness of the Romantic world-picture. The Romantics took men back to the wisdom of the ancients; extolled the authenticating qualities of imagination and feeling in the quest for truth; and their picture of nature, its mysteries and its hidden secrets, was awe-inspiring and brought men to their knees.

The flight from Reason, the appeal to the heart rather than to the head, the seductive attraction of the mysterious and the insights of sages long ago, all served to nourish a yearning for the spiritual, which was not a word much used by the Enlightenment. With the exception of figures like William Law and Thomas Wilson, it is not the word that first comes to mind in describing the Hanoverian Church. Another word – 'Gothic' – came into currency with the Romantics; in its earliest usage, redolent of darkness and the supernatural, a creepy sort of medievalism. The romance and drama of the Middle Ages, however, were popularized in the novels of Walter Scott. Soon, one age of faith would begin to emulate certain features of another, in the first place in the architecture of the hundreds of new churches to be built in nineteenth-century England; then, in later decades, fascination with all things medieval would be the inspiration of a new movement in art – the Pre-Raphaelites. Such fancies or enthu-

siasms would have no meaning to the advocates of Useful Knowledge, but to churchmen of a conservative disposition, and to
those who craved to serve a Church rather than an Establishment,
the recovery of the ethos of the centuries that antedated the
Reformation came as an inspiration.

It was in this period of transition and reaction that Newman
and Manning passed their formative years; and in their manhood
they bore the marks of the influences of their times. They were
introduced to the reality of the Christian faith by Evangelical
mentors; they both soon fell victim to the allurement of a vision of
the Church as it once had been and therefore could and should
become again. They never ceased to distrust Utilitarianism, and
they never threw off their dread of revolution. In their maturer
years, they both upheld the dogmatic principle against free-
thinkers and sceptics as strenuously as they had rejected the
questioning of the fundamentals of the Christian faith by the
so-called 'Latitudinarians' of their youth.

They both lived long lives, so that the world of their old age was
almost unrecognizable as the England into which they had been
born: government which was still predominantly aristocratic had
given way to democracy; a primarily agrarian economy was
becoming increasingly an industrial one; and the evil of indifference to Christian truth seemed to have spread unchecked. Not
surprisingly, they themselves changed less than the world they
lived in. It was a strange experience for Manning to find himself,
in the Metaphysical Society, listening politely to T. H. Huxley
attempting to prove the spurious credentials of the Christian
revelation. It did not worry him much, because the rock on which
his faith was based was solid and sure. Newman's faith was equally
unshaken, but he had one sadness to acknowledge in the last year
of his life, when he read *Lux Mundi*, the restatement of Anglican
incarnationalism by those who regarded themselves as his true
successors in the Church of his baptism. 'It is the end of
Tractarianism,' he said. 'They are giving up everything.'[5]

INTRODUCTION

Abuse and Panegyric

'Abuse is as great a mistake in controversy, as panegyric in biography.' J. H. Newman to H. J. Coleridge, 13 April 1866

I

JOHN HENRY NEWMAN and Henry Edward Manning were the two most prominent and influential figures in the history of the Roman Catholic Church in England during the second half of the nineteenth century. The nature of their influence was such that both men, in their different ways and for different reasons, commanded respect, sometimes amounting to veneration, among their contemporaries both within and outside the Roman communion. Their careers, too, had followed a remarkably parallel course. Both of them had been Anglican churchmen of eminence before their conversion to Rome, in 1845 and 1851 respectively, which happened to coincide with the half-way point of each of their lives. They died within two years of each other (Newman aged 89 and Manning 83), having been elevated to the Sacred College of Cardinals, the first two Anglican converts to have received that accolade. Similarities, however, do not necessarily signify harmonious relations; and when their names are coupled together, the historical record tells time and time again of personal conflict and mutual misunderstanding. Ignatius Ryder, who knew them both, being Manning's nephew and Newman's successor as Superior at the Birmingham Oratory, expressed the difference between them in a colourful metaphor. They were 'radically different . . . Like the sea, and the rocks confronting it, they might, while the storm lasted, combine against a hostile armada; but their eventual condition was ever one of settled opposition of sentiments, method, aspiration.'[1] In J. E. C. Bodley's assessment, 'their mutual antipathy was, I think, primarily due to the conflict of an objective mind with a subjective mind.'[2]

Differences may certainly divide, but not necessarily so, given the disposition to accommodate or to seek some workable compromise. Both Newman and Manning, however, were men of firmness of principle, to whom compromise never came easily. They were, in this respect, too like each other for comfort or for amicable co-operation. Neither could accept, without intense frustration, the propensity of others to think or to act differently from themselves. Although occasionally in private and sometimes even in public, the one was prepared to acknowledge the gifts and achievements of the other, circumstances – especially in later life – seemed increasingly to oblige them to adopt a contrary stance, so that there gathered about them ever-thickening clouds of mutual distrust. Each had admirers and disciples who, out of a sense of misplaced loyalty, tended to exaggerate and exacerbate the differences between them. Inevitably, then, since their careers coincided with stirring and controversial times, their personal conflicts soon began to assume the proportion of unseemly faction fights. Wilfrid Ward, the son of the exuberant and impetuous W. G. Ward, whose nature it was ever to turn a difference into a conflict, recalled 'through the refracting medium of a child's mind that controversies were going on between the party of Newman and the party of Manning and my father. But more than this, we thought of the world that really mattered somewhat as of a great battlefield with two camps – which we always called "the right side" and "the wrong side", the former consisting of all who took my father's general views on matters ecclesiastical, the latter of those who opposed them.'[3]

In an age when polemicists, and the press in particular, were as little solicitous of the privacies and sensitivities of those in high places as they are today, spiteful innuendo and malicious gossip were gleefully disseminated, thereby exacerbating both vulnerabilities and tensions. The butler at Archbishop House happened to be called Newman. Ill-disposed persons smiled knowingly, as they insinuated that Manning had deliberately employed a servant of that name to give himself the rare satisfaction of ordering 'Newman' about. It was conveniently forgotten that this faithful retainer had been inherited from Cardinal Wiseman. When the news was leaked, allegedly by Manning, that the famous Oratorian had declined the offer of the cardinalate in 1879 (a misunderstanding, as it turned out), *Punch* was not slow in publishing a lampoon:

> A Cardinal's Hat! Fancy Newman in *that*,
> For the crown o'er his grey temples spread!
> 'Tis the good and great head would honour the hat,
> Not the hat that would honour the head.

> There's many a priest craves it: no wonder he waives it,
> Or that we, the soiled head-cover scanning,
> Exclaim with one breath, *sans* distinction of faith,
> Would they wish Newman ranked with old Manning?[4]

Time would appear to have done very little to heal the wounds. Indeed, their posterity has tended, if anything, to magnify the differences and conflicts which divided their respective lives, almost as if the story of the one or of the other must have a hero to make it a proper story, and if a hero, then somewhere there must lurk also a villain. Not surprisingly, in view of recent developments in the Roman Catholic Church leading up to, and consequent upon, the second Vatican Council, and also in the context of the sincere endeavours to promote the cause of Newman's canonization, the tendency has been to cast Newman in the role of hero, thereby – at least implicitly – allocating to Manning an altogether lowlier part. Eighty years ago, J. E. C. Bodley expressed his concern about the way in which posterity had chosen to memorialize two great men by seeking to elevate the one by the process of denigrating the other. Because of his intimate association with Manning, in the Cardinal's later years, he expressed it thus: 'It has always been incomprehensible to me why Manning's hostility to Newman should be imputed to him as a sin, while Newman's hostility to Manning is held to be a virtue.'[5]

Perhaps the fairness of such a judgement will become clearer as this study unfolds. It is, however, indisputable that the biographical treatment of the two Cardinals has played a major role in fostering the notion that – as Shane Leslie once put it – every good Catholic, at some stage or another, has to pose to himself the first question of the Anglican catechism – 'What is your name?' Answer: 'N or M'.[6]

II

Both men were well aware that they would become the subjects of biography, whatever strictures or explicit wishes they might hope to impose. 'I don't wish my life written,' Newman stated categorically in November 1872, adding somewhat naïvely, 'because there is so little to say.'[1] He must have realized, however, that this was a vain wish. Even during his own lifetime he had to witness, with varying degrees of discomfort, early attempts to appraise his career and influence. He disowned as 'inaccurate and fulsome' an article by E. S. Purcell in *Celebrities of the Day* in the autumn of 1881,[2] and refused to read the proofs of an unauthorized 'Story of his Life' by Henry Jennings, published in the same year.[3] He was outraged by the treatment of his family background in an article by Wilfrid Meynell, under the pseudonym 'John Oldcastle', which appeared in *Merry England* in 1885,[4] and squirmed over the many inaccuracies in his brother-in-law Tom Mozley's *Reminiscences chiefly of Oriel College and the Oxford Movement*, published in 1882, taking particular exception to 'its miserable *half* truths which he said of my dear Father' (relating to the 'failure' of his bank).[5] On the other hand, he was appreciative of J. A. Froude's memorial of him in his article on 'The Oxford Counter-Reformation',[6] and deeply moved by the sensitivity and fidelity of Dean Church's account of Hurrell Froude, later to appear in his history of the Oxford Movement.[7]

There were three things which caused him apprehension about any future biography. In the first place, he feared the efforts of well-intentioned devotees who might try to portray him as a sort of saint. 'I don't want a panegyric written of me, which would be sickening,' he recorded in October 1876, 'but a real fair downright account of me according to the best ability and judgment of the writer.'[8] Ten years earlier he had made a similar observation to H. J. Coleridge. 'Abuse is as great a mistake in controversy, as panegyric in biography';[9] and he warned Anne Mozley in February 1885, very shrewdly, that she must 'beware of panegyric, for this reason if no other, that it would provoke a reaction'.[10] Secondly, biographers seem unable to resist the temptation to impute motives. They 'varnish; they assign motives; they conjecture feelings'.[11] In two passages of his published works, Newman developed this theme. In an essay on John Keble, he deplored the tendency of writers to search out motives (and if not motives, then 'faulty tendencies' or 'hypothetical failings') to account for the fact of a man's conversion, seeking to explain even the operations of the Holy Spirit.[12] When writing of St Chrysostom in his *Historical Sketches*, he pointed to the difficulty of apprehending a man's interior life from 'mere biographies'. They may be 'true to the letter, as far as they record facts and acts', but 'the actions themselves seldom carry the motives along with them. In consequence, they are often supplied simply by the biographer out of his own head ... The biographer in that case is no longer a mere witness and reporter; he has become a commentator.'[13] Thirdly, Newman had the gravest doubts about anyone's ability to handle the issues of his Catholic career. In February 1884 he wrote: 'No account of my *Catholic* life can ever be given, for it would involve the saying things which would be disadvantageous to the reputation of men who for their writings (and or) their works are in merited esteem.'[14] Doubtless, Manning was one of them.

So what did this leave? In an ideal world, Newman sometimes seemed to be saying, the subject should be left to write his own life, because only he can truly understand 'the whole man'. Perhaps, too, only he – if the subject happened to be Newman himself – could command the delicacy of touch and subtle nuance of expression to describe the conflicts of his life without causing pain or offence to others. This, after all, is precisely what Newman had tried to do in the major part of the *Apologia*, in charting the history of his own mind, and of his religious opinions. There are autobiographical allusions in both his novels – *Loss and Gain* and *Callista*; and in practically nothing that he published are the personal and subjective elements absent. Just occasionally, he concedes that autobiography does not necessarily guarantee a truthful picture. He poses the question in the *Apologia*, 'For who can know himself, and the multitude of subtle influences which act upon him?',[15] and his own letters supply – understandably enough – the odd instance of faulty self-analysis. He frequently denied, for instance, any qualification to be a theologian. Perhaps, too, one can picture Manning smiling wryly to himself, in later years, if he recalled a letter written by Newman to the *Tablet* in September 1852, where he stated: 'If there be a man in the whole Church, who from faith, obedience, and love towards her would rejoice and exult in sacrificing any opinion of his own at the bidding of his Ecclesiastical superiors (if I dare speak of myself), I am the man.'[16]

It is entirely in character, too, that Newman regarded theological commentaries, as opposed to the plain scriptural text, especially the simplicity of the Gospel stories, as misleading rather than helpful. Translated into biography, this meant letting a man's life speak through his letters. He had, after all, himself memorialized Hurrell Froude in this way in the four volumes of his *Remains*, forgetting that he would have served the memory of his friend better by more judicious selection and by recognizing that some of the more startling and disturbing sentiments in Froude's letters and journals cried out for a sympathetic commentary. Nevertheless his conclusion was that 'a volume of "Letters" is the only true life.'[17]

As early as the winter of 1860 he began preparing for this eventuality, making transcriptions of a number of autograph letters, which he then destroyed, preserving especially those which contained 'the records of misunderstandings or personal collisions', so that answers were readily available should other parties in a dispute publish material to substantiate their own point of view.[18] Towards the end of his life, he decided to set in motion a compilation of his Anglican letters and journals, determined that they should, in the first place, be edited by an Anglican, and that, secondly, he should himself select the editor. Having strongly approved of Anne Mozley's collected letters of her brother, J. B. Mozley, in 1884, he decided to entrust her with the task, notwithstanding the fact that she was herself nearing the end of her days. Although he had assured his sister Jemima, twenty years or so earlier, that 'I detest suppression',[19] when it came to the point he found it impossible to give Anne Mozley an entirely free hand. He frequently offered advice; decided that her work should be submitted to Dean Church and Lord Blachford as 'monitors' whom he could trust; and even went so far as to warn her to avoid editorial footnotes. Edward Kelly, in recent years, has commented on the extent to which 'Newman defends Newman by appealing to Newman'. The personal interest which he took in Anne Mozley's collection is an example. 'In view of modern developments in philosophy, psychology and literary theory,' he writes, 'Newman's view appears very conservative and unenlightened. But it is even more amazing that modern Newman scholars do not question his view.'[20]

III

In one respect, Manning agreed with Newman over the writing of his own biography. It needed an Anglican to comprehend his Anglican life. He told Wilfrid Meynell that actually three different writers would be required to cover the three different aspects of his career – the Anglican, the Roman Catholic and the civic.[1] During the 1880s, however, his acquaintance with J. E. C. Bodley, whom he first met as a member of the Royal Commission on the Housing of the Working Classes (of which Bodley was secretary), prospered into a close and trusting friendship. Bodley, although much younger than Manning and also a non-Catholic, could share memories of Oxford and Balliol with the Cardinal, who – partly from his position but also from his temperamental predilections – found it difficult to relax with his co-religionists. In 1886, he decided to invite Bodley to undertake the writing of the 'Protestant' (as he himself put it) phase of his life. A year later, so close was the bond between them, that he resolved to widen the commission. 'No one', he wrote to Bodley, 'will understand me as a man of the world and as a politician better than you, and if you take that side of me I shall have a good and safe biographer. But when it comes to dogmas and canons and censures, on the rule of "set a thief to catch a thief" a priest will be needed. Of all this we can talk.' Bodley readily agreed, the more so because Manning included within the political definition – therefore to be covered by Bodley with an entirely free hand – the historic role that he had played at the Vatican Council.[2]

Alas – it was not to be. If anyone deserves to be cast as villain of this piece, Edmund Sheridan Purcell's claims must surely go unchallenged. In the same year that Bodley received his verbal commission from Manning, Purcell's machinations to secure the right to publish the Cardinal's official biography had already begun. The story must rank as one of the most extraordinary scandals in literary history. Briefly, the facts are these.[3] E. S. Purcell, of Irish extraction, educated mainly in Germany, was a Catholic journalist whose allegience to one party or another veered according to the winds of fortune. In the mid-1860s he was sufficiently in sympathy with Manning's views to secure from the new Archbishop of Westminster the editorship of the *Westminster Gazette*, founded by Manning to advance the causes dearest to his heart. It did not have a long life. By the late 1870s, partly because the Catholic hierarchy withdrew its support (for which Purcell blamed Manning), the *Gazette*'s circulation had slumped to such an extent that Purcell found himself in straitened circumstances, and began increasingly to identify himself with personalities and issues known to be at variance with official Catholic policy. Furthermore, his eulogy of Newman in *Celebrities of the Day*, which had been so ill-received by the subject of his fulsome praise, can hardly have pleased Manning by its references to the 'fanatical' nature of Newman's opponents. Nevertheless, Purcell believed that he had some sort of claim on Manning, because of the failure of the *Westminster Gazette*, and in 1887 visited the Cardinal, with the request that he should be given some materials for writing a biographical sketch to be published during Manning's lifetime.

Manning was notorious for his prodigality in charity and may have raised Purcell's hopes by some vague promise of some future major commission. Nothing, however, was put in writing.[4] In the light of what he had said to Bodley, and from the suspicions that he must have harboured even then of a personal animus against him, it is difficult to conceive that he would have been so imprudent. It is known, however, that Manning lent Purcell one of his journals (relating to his travels in Italy in 1847 and 1848, and therefore comparatively innocuous in terms of confidential or sensitive disclosures), from which he could prepare an article. But armed with this, as some sort of earnest of his credentials, Purcell approached Gladstone with the request for reminiscences and then for Gladstone's letters to Manning, giving him to understand that the Cardinal had raised no objection to Purcell having access to his own side of the correspondence. Gladstone's suspicions were aroused, and Manning at once assured him that 'no letter of yours to me, or of mine to you, has been or will be in Mr Purcell's hands.' In an earlier letter, he warned Gladstone that 'My friend Mr Purcell is a bolter.'[5]

There followed a series of misfortunes, the significance of which was not foreseen at the time. In the first place, Manning changed the executors of his will, removing the name of Herbert Vaughan, his successor as Archbishop, following an altercation over Vaughan's public refusal to support Manning's Temperance activities. As Vaughan himself conceded later: 'If I had been his executor, his private papers would never have fallen into the hands of Mr Purcell.'[6] Secondly, Bodley, who had been horrified

at the time, when he heard that Purcell had interviewed Gladstone and done his best to 'pump him dry', was abroad when
Manning died suddenly in January 1892. Purcell acted at once. In
an article on Manning's Anglican career, which appeared in the
Dublin Review in April 1892, he published his claims to be
Manning's official biographer. On the strength of this, and the
alleged agreement of Herbert Vaughan, he succeeded in nego-
tiating a contract with Macmillan's; and then the three executors
of Manning's will, all of them members of his own foundation, the
Congregation of the Oblates of St Charles Borromeo, made the
greatest mistake of all. Showing remarkably little concern for the
memory of the late Cardinal, they accepted Purcell's claims at
their face value (he had, indeed, nothing in writing to substantiate
them), and made the fatal error themselves of authorizing Purcell
by letter to make such use of the Cardinal's papers as he thought
fit. Purcell duly turned up at St Mary of the Angels in Bayswater,
in a four-wheeler, having been invited 'to make an afternoon's
search' of the materials that were housed there. By the end of the
afternoon, 'before Dr Butler [the senior executor] could realize
what was happening', half the contents of Manning's archives had
been packed into the four-wheeler, and Purcell drove off in
triumph. 'If it had been a hansom cab,' Shane Leslie was later to
lament, 'the damage might not have been so irremediable.'[7]

Purcell had already overstepped the mark in helping himself to
the archives indiscriminately; and when he returned to collect the
remaining half of the papers, the Oblates refused to surrender
them. But the damage was done; and just how much damage was
speedily perceived by both Wilfrid Ward and Baron von Hügel, to
whom Purcell showed portions of the draft of the first volume of
his work, in the hope that they would be sympathetic to the line
that he was adopting. They were frankly horrified. They enlisted
Herbert Vaughan's assistance, and a combined effort was made to
persuade Purcell to accept some form of censorship, and – when
that failed – to press the Oblate-executors to withdraw their
permission. Litigation was threatened; the Duke of Norfolk
added his voice to protect Manning's reputation against Purcell's
insinuations (Lady Margaret Howard described him as a 'clever
villain').[8] But it was all to no avail. The Oblates were reluctant to
engage in a lawsuit; and, in any case, their own written permission
to Purcell rendered a favourable outcome unlikely.

What was so damaging about Purcell's *succès de scandale* (for such it rapidly became)? Quite apart from the misdating of letters and passages in Manning's diaries, several instances of incorrect transcription (Purcell clearly found Manning's handwriting not always easy to read), and false assertions about the non-existence of papers which – if consulted – could have thrown a different light upon some of Purcell's assumptions, the hostile animus of the author is exhibited by the way in which he consistently puts the worst interpretations upon Manning's actions, reflections and motives. As Ignatius Ryder expressed it, in the course of a shrewd analysis of Purcell's innuendoes and misunderstandings, he 'never manifests the slightest sympathy with anything Manning says or does'.[9] Purcell accuses him of being the victim of ruthless ambition, of exhibiting calculated duplicity in his last years within the Anglican Church, speaking time and time again with what he describes as a 'double-voice'. He insinuates that silences in his diaries, especially during his visit to Rome in 1848 and his first audience with Pius IX, could be of sinister significance.[10] He suggests, when all the evidence was to the contrary, that Manning would never support a losing cause ('His nature instinctively shrank from those that were failing, or were down'),[11] and – worst of all – totally misrepresents Manning's role in the conflict between Cardinal Wiseman and Archbishop George Errington by explicitly stating that Manning was responsible for securing Errington's removal from his coadjutorship with right of succession to Westminster in order to smooth his own way to the archiepiscopal see. 'The hand which struck the fatal blow was the hand of Manning.'[12]

One must not underrate, however, Purcell's skill and command of his craft. With the liberties that he took with the documents at his disposal, he presented a convincing, if damning, case. Even Gladstone, who knew Manning so intimately during his Anglican career, and who maintained an intermittent relationship with him thereafter, could write to Purcell in eulogistic terms. 'You have produced, I think, by far the most extraordinary biography I ever read, and have executed a work of (I think) unparalleled difficulty with singular success. I have not been interested in it, I have been fascinated and entranced.'[13] Gladstone wrote this letter, however, in January 1896, a year before the true story of the notorious Errington affair was given to the world in Wilfrid Ward's *Life of Cardinal Wiseman*, effectively exposing the injustice of Purcell's accusations.[14] In his researches, Ward had been assisted by the archivist of the Oblates, William Kent, who resolved to put the record straight by himself producing a biography of Manning. Its imminent publication was announced by Ward in 1906. Inexplicably, the book never appeared, nor has there survived any record of Kent's intended riposte.[15]

Purcell's work in tarnishing Manning's reputation was compounded, in some ways even more culpably, by Lytton Strachey in 1918, with the publication of his *Eminent Victorians*, in which Manning appeared as the first, and substantially the longest, of the four biographical studies, selected by their gifted author for their potential for witty and irreverent exposure of Victorian over-earnestness and hypocrisy. In fact, it was through reading Purcell's biography, in a moment of boredom, that Strachey conceived the idea of writing the book which, perhaps more than any other, established his literary reputation. What made Strachey's caricature so unpardonable was that in using Purcell's volumes as 'the great ocean of material' into which he dipped his notorious 'little bucket',[16] he dredged up charges that he must have known were untrue. His bibliography lists the titles of books in which the charges were refuted. Strachey's technique was clever, however, as F. A. Simpson observed, in one of his rare excursions into print in the *Cambridge Review* in 1943. Here was something new in the art of mockery. 'You did not condemn your victims; you made them condemn themselves. You did not ridicule them; you made them make themselves ridiculous. With considered and calculated cunning you selected from the wealth of their writings ... just the half-page or half-sentence which, quoted in isolation, would sound supremely ludicrous; and having done so you almost audibly refrained from laughter.'[17]

Purcell and Strachey between them did their work so well that their calumnies live on, despite the various efforts made in recent decades to redress the image. Shane Leslie was one of the first in the field in 1921 with his *Henry Edward Manning: His Life and Labours*, followed – with more scholarly apparatus – by Professor V. A. McClelland's study of Manning's public and political influence during the period of his archiepiscopate. A definitive biography, however, has still to appear, largely because of the chequered history of the Manning archives. To begin with, some of the papers that Purcell took from Bayswater were never returned, and a certain mystery hangs over their consequent fate. Some, it appears, were offered for private sale, but no trace has been found of their purchasers. It has also to be admitted that the Oblates of St Charles, over the years, have shown markedly less reverence for their founder than – for instance – the Oratorians at Birmingham for theirs. During the Second World War, Manning's papers were left to languish in a sort of damp cellar at St Mary of the Angels, imperfectly secured from outside access by a piece of corrugated iron. It was not long before the local *gamins* discovered a useful den for questionable purposes, and precious documents were subjected to a variety of indignities – some converted into paper aeroplanes, others used to light a bonfire; a large bundle was discovered rotting away in a pool of water. This was their condition, as described to the present writer by a French priest, Alphonse Chapeau, who – on first witnessing this scene of mayhem – was so outraged by the neglect of valuable archives that he set about the monumental task of rescuing and cataloguing them. Determined that never again should such depredations be repeated, and that materials that he was himself using for a doctoral thesis at the Sorbonne should be reserved for himself exclusively, he imposed such strict security against access that the Manning archives at Bayswater were transformed into a miniature Fort Knox. Since Chapeau's recent death the papers have become dispersed (between Oxford, Atlanta in the USA and Angers in France), but it is hoped that the bulk of the Catholic papers will find their ultimate home in the Westminster archives.

Until such a time, the world must wait for as thorough a reappraisal of Manning's life and work as has been accorded to the great Oratorian at Birmingham. The most recent study to appear is Robert Gray's biography, published in 1985: eminently readable, jauntily critical – even Stracheyesque – at times. But the whole ethos of the Victorian religious scene and temper is an alien world to him, and this seriously impairs his understanding of his central character. In his conclusion, however, he delivers one emphatic riposte to Purcell: 'If Henry Manning is not saved seventy times seven times, God help the rest of us.'[18]

IV

It should not be thought that it was only Manning who was subjected to hostile treatment by ill-disposed critics in the years following his death. Newman had his fair share of detractors as well. In 1891, in addition to the Anne Mozley selected Anglican letters, three books appeared, two of which were firmly appreciative, and one about as sour as could be imagined. R. H. Hutton, editor of the *Spectator*, whose passage from Unitarianism to Anglicanism had coincided with his growing admiration for Newman as a thinker and a writer, produced a short, perceptive memoir, but barely touching upon his Catholic career for the simple reason that the materials were not yet to hand. (Interestingly, his namesake, who was no relation, A. W. Hutton, produced a companion memoir on Manning for the same publishers in the year after his death.) R. W. Church's classic study of the Oxford Movement (posthumously published) depicted Newman as the undoubted hero of an absorbing story, lovingly told by – in Owen Chadwick's words – 'the literary equivalent of the artist George Richmond, who painted the Victorians with a far-seeing refined spirituality in their faces; the aesthetic antidote to Lytton Strachey.'[1]

The sour offering was from Francis Newman in his *Contributions chiefly to the Early History of the late Cardinal Newman*. Here was brother sniping at brother with a vengeance, written by the strange, sad, brilliantly talented yet curiously wayward youngest of the three Newman brothers, whose spiritual journey had led him from extreme Evangelicalism, via membership of the Plymouth Brothers, into becoming a sort of humanist social crusader, with great love for his fellow men, but painfully little for his eldest brother. It leaves a very unpleasant taste in most mouths, but was savoured with relish by the second of Newman's detractors – Edwin Abbott.

Abbott was a man of some standing, by all accounts a brilliant Headmaster of the City of London School and a gifted mathematician, the author of what has been described as 'a minor mathematical classic' entitled *Flatland*, published under the pseudonym 'A. Square'.[2] He had a strictly logical mind and his religious views were as liberal in sympathy as Newman's were dogmatic. They could never have talked the same language. Abbott's antipathy to Newman was provoked by his reading of the second of Newman's essays on miracles, written in his last years as an Anglican, in which he defended the veracity of ecclesiastical miracles as strongly as he had repudiated them in an earlier essay dating from 1825. This second essay exhibited, to Abbott's mind, a degree of credulity so far-fetched that he was prompted to write in 1891 a voluminous exposure of the unhistorical and gullible nature of Newman's mind in a book entitled *Philomythus: An Antidote against Credulity*. Having then persuaded himself that a man who could seriously defend the historical legitimacy of such improbable miracles as the Thundering Legion of the Emperor Marcus Aurelius and the change of the course of the river Lycus by St Gregory, on the principle that 'a fact is not disproved because it is not proved',[3] must be of flawed mind, he resolved to write a fuller exposure of Newman's enormities in a detailed study of his Anglican career.

In this two-volume work, published in 1892, Abbott certainly weakened the force of his attack by the extravagance of his language and the fancifulness of some of his imagery, and by too-obvious exaggeration. No one doubts that Newman sincerely maintained that it was better to believe too much than too little, but it is surely hyperbole to describe the *Essay on Ecclesiastical Miracles* as 'an utterance of delirium';[4] and whether one is inspired or repelled by the severity with which Newman could preach the Law rather than the Gospel and defend questionable positions by sophistications and skilful rhetoric, the simple conclusion that he can be summed up as a 'Judaizer'[5] is absurdly inadequate.

While the world was still waiting for the appearance of the first official biography of Newman from the pen of Wilfrid Ward, a French Jesuit of far greater consequence than Edwin Abbott – Henri Bremond – produced his controversial psychological study, translated into English in 1907 under the title *The Mystery of Newman*. It was bound to cause a stir, not least because Bremond's orthodoxy was suspect, and he had narrowly escaped having one of his most recent writings placed on the Index. He was known, too, to be sympathetically disposed towards Modernism, a movement especially vigorous in his home country, encouraging the abandonment of traditional scholastic theology and advocating advanced liberal views on biblical criticism, which was so little to the liking of Pius X that it was officially condemned by the decree *Lamentabili* and the encyclical *Pascendi* in 1907, the very year that Bremond's book on Newman appeared in its English format. It was known that the Modernists were inclined to take shelter from censure by arguing, not altogether convincingly, that their views would have received the posthumous imprimatur of Newman; and Bremond did nothing to dispel the anxieties of the Oratorians at Birmingham by entrusting the writing of the introduction to his book to George Tyrrell, who had in 1906 been expelled from the Society of Jesus for his unrepentant Modernist views. Certainly, the opening sentences of Tyrrell's contribution were hardly calculated to ease their minds: 'That a man's worst enemies are those of his own household is true in more senses than one. It may be taken to mean that a hero should dread none so much as his worshippers, that a prophet should tremble for the day when the descendants of his persecutors shall build up his sepulchre.'[6]

Bremond was fascinated by Newman and did not write the book with any hostile intent. He described Abbott's work, for instance, as 'the heaviest, most finical, most merciless, and most irritating of cases for the prosecution'.[7] But his is a book full of personal idiosyncrasies – a sort of exploration into Newman's inner personality, revealing perhaps as much about Bremond's own unquiet state of mind as about Newman's. Furthermore, such limited study as he makes of Newman's writings focuses on works such as the *Essays on Miracles* and his series of *Historical Sketches*, rather than on the far more significant *Oxford University Sermons* and the *Essay on Development* – in the course of which he arrives at judgements not dissimilar to Abbott's. Newman is represented as basing proofs on sheer hypothesis,[8] of writing history suggestive of sermonizing.[9] It is observed that, notwithstanding his genuine love of souls, his sermons are relentlessly severe.[10] Like Abbott, Bremond is fascinated by the seeming contradictions and antinomies in Newman's character and attitudes. The book enraged Wilfrid Ward, who described it as 'very impertinent . . . Here then is a writer dealing with a great man, belittling while professing to admire him (as Purcell did Manning) and making it quite clear that that great man's chief work is simply beyond his comprehension.'[11]

Wilfrid Ward's exasperation is quite understandable. He was longing to launch into print himself, and enduring constant frustrations. He was not quite fair, however; Bremond's book has certain insights and qualities which give it an enduring value. He writes of Newman's '*autocentrisme*', for instance, which – in the French – does not quite carry the pejorative connotation of the English rendering 'self-centredness'.[12] Bremond was trying to convey both Newman's natural solitariness of disposition (he was a 'man who can and will remain alone')[13] and the recurrent note of personalism in his thought and writings. Then again, although

Bremond was not the first to perceive 'the extraordinary ease with which Newman identifies himself with the thought and mind of some one else' (paying due acknowledgement to Newman's contemporary, Isaac Williams),[14] he develops this facet into the very striking paradox that 'at any stage of his life, it is always easy to tell what saint he wishes to be like. He is ever changing, and always remains the same.'[15]

At last, in 1912, Wilfrid Ward's two-volume biography was published, over twenty years after the death of the Cardinal. There were two main reasons for the delay, the first being the vacillations of Father William Neville, Newman's sole literary executor, who for fifteen years refused to allow Ward access to the Oratory archives, mainly because he had disapproved of his treatment of Newman in his biography of Cardinal Wiseman. Neville 'judges everything simply by the amount of butter which Newman personally receives', Ward said in disgust, deploring instructions that there should be a 'total absence of any shade of criticism of him'.[16] Neville's successor, following his death in 1905, was Father John Norris, who was inclined to be very much more supportive, until fresh anxieties arose over the possible implications to Newman's reputation of the Papal condemnation of Modernism,[17] there being some suspicions at the Oratory that Ward, instead of completely exonerating Newman, might try to defend him. Only very gradually, as Ward submitted drafts for inspection, was he given a freer hand and cautiously supervised access.

To have doubted either Ward's ability or his sympathies was very foolish. He had already proved himself as a biographer of consummate skill, not only in his sensitive and meticulously thorough biography of Wiseman, but also in his rare accomplishment of filial detachment in the brilliantly-researched two-volume *Life* of his own father, W. G. 'Ideal' Ward. He was incapable of writing a biography of any figure with whom he did not sympathize;[18] and for Newman himself he felt the deepest love and respect, dating from his first encounter with him, in 1877, when as young men he and his brother, Bernard, made a long cycle-ride together to meet a friend at the Oratory School at Edgbaston and were prevailed upon to pay their respects to the eminent man with whom their father had waged so many theological battles.[19]

There have been dozens of studies of Newman since Ward

produced his masterpiece, but few biographies to compare with it in terms of the mastery of his subject and its sympathetic detachment. Its only flaw is its lack of balance, in that Ward gave such scanty treatment to Newman's Anglican career (on the assumption that it had been adequately covered already), in comparison with his study of the Catholic years. He may not, however, have been an entirely free agent in coming to this decision, because it has been suggested that the Oratory were unwilling to allow Ward to use any Anglican material that had not already been published.[20] For the first time, however, Ward was able to tell the full story of Newman's Catholic life, and no better tribute to his achievement has been made than the beautiful letter that he received from Canon Barry (who had himself written an earlier study of Newman) in the same month that the biography was published.

> I think you have been especially fortunate in showing, without argument, how the Divine elements – Revelation, Mass, Sacraments and the Vita Devota corresponding – enabled the most sensitive, the most individual soul that ever put on the Catholic yoke, to be more than conqueror, though wounded again and again in the house of his friends . . . Well, you have succeeded grandly . . . J.H.N. is safe; he is at rest . . . The problem, too, has been resolved; I mean, how to reconcile intellect and originality with a tradition largely stereotyped and a regime so panic-stricken as to be afraid of its most capable defender.[21]

Nevertheless, the fathers of the Birmingham Oratory have never been entirely happy about Wilfrid Ward's biography. They were jumpy while Ward was writing it and they have been jumpy ever since. Immediately after Ward had completed his book, he asked to be allowed to produce a supplementary volume of letters, but was refused. The Oratory wanted an 'in-house' production, and themselves published a volume of letters, covering the last six years of Newman's Anglican period, complete with lengthy commentary (*The Correspondence of John Henry Newman with John Keble and Others, 1839–1845*). They had taken particular exception to Ward's chapter entitled 'Sad Days', when Newman was at his lowest ebb in the early 1860s, pointing out that the anguished comments in his journals 'were not meant for public eyes and were addressed to God to relieve his feelings'.[22]

When, in 1961, Charles Stephen Dessain published his first volume of the complete Newman *Letters and Diaries* (volume XI, covering the first eighteen months of Newman's life in the

Catholic Church), he returned to this charge. Ward had given a false impression of 'the natural, energetic, humorous and practical man' the Oratorians had known, calling Abbot Butler as witness of the mistake in depicting Newman as a 'hyper-sensitive, a *souffre-douleur*'. Dessain claimed, however, that he was confident that this type of misrepresentation was 'on the wane', there being 'enough material at hand for judgments independent of it to be formed'.[23] He was himself to play the major role in editing 21 of the 27 volumes of this massively-impressive material (there are still four volumes due to appear), and they are a model of careful and scholarly editing. Some reservations, however, have been expressed about the degree of impartiality, both in the selection of additional material and in some of the editorial comments, one of his collaborators expressing some concern when Dessain stated his intention 'to cook Manning's goose'.[24]

Dessain, in his remarks about misinterpretation being on the wane, had also in mind the phenomenon known as 'the Rediscovery of Newman', which effectively dates from the years immediately following the end of the Second World War, at least in this country, although the impetus to a revival of Newman studies in depth had actually begun in Germany and France during the inter-war years. From Germany and France it spread over the Continent and to the USA until it reached the proportions of what is sometimes described as a 'Newman industry', marked – *inter alia* – by the series of symposium volumes of *Newman Studien*, and a number of specialist publications associated with the University of Louvain.

During these inter-war years, in Britain, few works of comparable significance appeared, with the exception of Cuthbert Butler's two-volume biography of Bishop Ullathorne (Newman's diocesan bishop during his Catholic career), which still stands as one of the most balanced accounts of the major Catholic figures during the second half of the nineteenth century, especially in his treatment of the conflicts which divided Newman and Manning. In 1933, however, Geoffrey Faber caused a slight fluttering in the dovecotes with his book *Oxford Apostles*, which ventured on to the delicate territory of the hot-house atmosphere of what he described as 'the cult of virginity' in Tractarian Oxford, and this was not exactly the corrected image of Newman that the pioneers of 'rediscovery' had in mind.

The immediate post-war years saw a flood of new publications, especially on Newman's Anglican career – by Maisie Ward ('the best of his biographers, excepting only her father' in Sheridan Gilley's opinion),[25] and by R. D. Middleton; a rather less reverential note, however, being sounded by Seán O'Faoláin in his breezy but perceptive study, focusing largely on Newman's family background and relationships. But the major influences behind the 'rediscovery' movement were undoubtedly Stephen Dessain at Birmingham, and John Coulson at Downside. Dessain was anxious to procure a biographer of his own choosing, effectively to replace Wilfrid Ward's *magnum opus* as the new definitive 'Life'. His choice fell upon Meriol Trevor, whose two volumes – *Newman: The Pillar of the Cloud* and *Newman: Light in Winter* – were published in 1962.

This was a labour of love, indeed; but it missed its mark. Miss Trevor failed at exactly the point where Wilfrid Ward had succeeded. The particular quality of Ward's biography was – in A. O. J. Cockshut's estimate – 'his power of empathy' which 'does not inhibit the judicious balance of his historical account. This ability to *vary the distance* from the subject is both rare and valuable ... Newman is always surrounded by living, breathing men, acting on principles of their own, often wrong as against Newman, but sometimes right.'[26] With Meriol Trevor, Newman is always right (a phenomenon surely unknown to history). The determination to defend him on every issue and against every critical comment 'effected the opposite of what she intended. She revealed too much and conceded too little.'[27]

George Tyrrell's shrewd comment in his introduction to Bremond's study appears to have been forgotten, as also Newman's own unease at being made the subject of a panegyric. As the centenary of Newman's death approached, and among the celebratory offerings that it called forth, one book, however, exactly fulfilled one of Newman's expressed desiderata. This was Ian Ker's substantial biography, based almost entirely on Newman's own letters, telling his own story in his own words, sympathetic to the point of being defensive at times, and keeping critical comment to a minimum. Two years later, the balance was restored in Sheridan Gilley's masterly *Newman and his Age*, which with its combination of empathy and critical detachment has succeeded in presenting a figure of flesh and blood as opposed to a two-dimensional image in stained glass.

What lies behind the 'rediscovery of Newman'? It has really two objectives, both related. The first is to exhibit the extent to which Newman is a 'man for our times', demonstrating his prophetic vision, so often inadequately appreciated in his own day. The second is to advance the cause of his canonization. Both may be laudable objectives in their way, but – as Josef Altholz points out in his study of Victorian religious biography, with special reference to Newman and Manning – 'the frankly uncritical approach of hagiography, which would be rejected in any other field of history, not only survives but is rewarded in religious biography.' Writing admittedly some years before the publications that coincided with Newman's centenary, he continued: 'There is no life of Newman which is at once comprehensive and critical. Perhaps there never will be. The present atmosphere of impending canonization is hardly conducive to critical biography. Newman deserves a better fate than that.'[28]

V

Owen Chadwick, in his biography of Michael Ramsey, recalls how Harold Macmillan was subjected to some criticism for his decision to recommend to the Queen that Ramsey should succeed Geoffrey Fisher as Archbishop of Canterbury in 1961. His reputed reply was, 'I thought we had had enough of Martha and it was time for some Mary.'[1] Martha and Mary represent two different types of the Christian character, as Newman himself expounded in a sermon in October 1834, to show how 'both of them glorify [God] in their own line, whether of labour or of quiet.' He had scriptural authority in observing, however, that 'Mary's portion' was 'the better of the two'.[2]

Newman and Manning were each shining exemplars of these different Christian characters, living lives of total commitment to their Saviour and rock-like fidelity to the Church whose communion they had chosen to join. We can but speculate how grievous would have been the loss to that Church had Newman not made the decision that he did in 1845 and had not Manning made the same decision six years later; how greatly weakened, too, would the Roman Church have been had Pope Pius IX been inspired to nominate any other English ecclesiastic, in preference to Manning, to the See of Westminster as Cardinal Wiseman's successor in 1865. When their respective achievements are assessed, and the contribution that each made within the reponsibilities to which they were called, few will take exception to the judgement of Archbishop David Mathew, that 'in the development of Catholicism in England, Cardinal Newman and Cardinal Manning were complementary'.[3] The sadness is that neither has been treated well or fairly by their posterity, and this because of a curious paradox. The abuse of his original biographer has saddled Manning with a reputation too bad to be wholly credible, while the tendency to panegyric in the biographical treatment of Newman over the last fifty years has served to make of him a figure rather too good to be true.

CHAPTER 1

Vocations

'I should say that it is difficult to realize or imagine the identity of the boy before and after August 1816.' J. H. Newman to Anne Mozley, 9 February 1885

'I fear he will occasion his friends to lead an unquiet life.' Favell Bevan on H. E. Manning, 1832

I

THE FIRST recorded meeting between Newman and Manning was at Oxford on Sunday, 12 September 1830. Newman had been preaching at St Mary's and dined afterwards at Oriel with his friend, S. F. Wood. They were joined by the two Wilberforce brothers, Robert and Henry, T. D. Acland, and Manning. His diary states the occasion, noting only the names of his companions; nothing more.[1] Newman was at that time a Fellow of Oriel; Manning, who was seven years his junior, was in his final undergraduate year at Balliol, somewhat keyed-up before his Final Honours Schools at the end of November. Whether Manning had been in Newman's congregation that afternoon is not certain, but sixty years later he recalled his frequent attendance at St Mary's over this period ('I never willingly failed to be there'),[2] so it may be safely assumed that he was. He also suggests that it was 'during that last long vacation' at Oxford 'I became first at all intimate with Newman',[3] which would appear a somewhat exaggerated description of their relationship, since no further reference occurs in either of their papers to any subsequent meeting or correspondence until two years later, when Manning had recently been elected to a Fellowship at Merton. Then, indeed, shortly before Newman was due to leave the country for a voyage in the Mediterranean, he both paid a call on Manning (on 19 September 1832) and a few days later went out walking with him.[4] Effectively, then, until Newman was in his early thirties, and Manning in his middle twenties, they lived their lives entirely apart.

On the face of it, however, the circumstances and experiences of these early years of their lives exhibit some remarkable similarities. Their families were both engaged in commerce and banking; both men had to endure the experience of the collapse of their family fortunes at impressionable stages of their life. Both lost their fathers when they were only in their twenties (Newman aged 23, and Manning 27), and were profoundly affected by further close personal bereavement, Newman by the death of his favourite sister Mary in January 1828, and Manning by the death in 1826 of Harriet, the sister closest to him in age as well as affection. Each discovered his religious vocation through the experience of an Evangelical conversion. Shortly after their respective ordinations each, in their different circumstances, through their first experience of parochial ministry, came to the conviction that Evangelicalism simply did not answer, either in its doctrines or in its methods, the needs of their parishioners, so that they found themselves growing ever more in sympathy with both the teaching and the temper of its rival tradition; and so far did these sympathies grow, as the years passed, that they both, after a period of anguished spiritual torment, abandoned the Church of their baptism to join the Roman communion at practically the same stage of their lives, Newman at the age of 44 and Manning at the age of 43. Very significantly, too, both were stricken with illness serious enough to induce genuine *timor mortis*, Newman in Sicily in 1833, and Manning in 1847, recovery from which persuaded both men that providence had ordained for them some further work to do, and had endowed them with the sense of purpose to accomplish it.

Closer examination, however, reveals differences more fundamental than these strange coincidences or superficial similarities suggest. It is true that both the Newman and the Manning families were engaged in commercial and banking enterprises at the time that the two future Cardinals were born – but at very different levels. Newman's mother – Jemima Fourdrinier – came from a wealthy background, her family being successful paper-manufacturers based in Lombard Street and boasting both a town house and a country residence. On her marriage to Newman's father she brought with her a dowry of £5,000, a not inconsiderable sum in those days. There is little doubt that she was the social superior of her husband (John Newman), who was the son of a London grocer but had bettered himself sufficiently to enter the banking world, and – at the time of the birth of their eldest son, John Henry, on 21 February 1801 – was a partner in the Ramsbottom bank, also with premises in Lombard Street. This sounds well enough, but it has to be remembered that very little capital was required to establish a private banking firm, and that – as Seán O'Faoláin has put it – 'under the last two Georges banks rose like mushrooms and went down like ninepins'.[5] In short, it was a risky enterprise. There could be good moments and bad, and since there are indications that Mrs Newman's memories of relative affluence led her at least not to discourage her husband from living rather above his means, this meant that the bad moments could become very bad indeed.

In 1801, however, one of the good moments seemed to be growing markedly better; and a sure register of mounting fortunes was the changing of residence, a little further from the centre of business in the City. So from 80 Old Broad Street, the Newmans moved to 17 Southampton Street (in Bloomsbury) in 1802, and then – in 1804 – they established a further mark of rising prosperity by acquiring a country residence, Grey Court House at Ham, near Richmond. This marked the peak of their good fortunes.

But what was a peak for the Newmans was little more than a molehill to the Mannings. Theirs was a family which belonged to the mercantile aristocracy, prospering greatly on the profits of the West Indian sugar trade, and acquiring through marriage the entrée into one of the most influential circles of late eighteenth-century England. Manning's father's first wife, who died in 1789 leaving two children, was the daughter of Abel Smith, sister of the first Lord Carrington, and related to the Wilberforces, the Spooners and the Sumners, some of the weightiest names of the Anglican Evangelical revival. Mary Hunter, William Manning's second wife and the mother of eight children (of whom the future Cardinal was the youngest, born on 15 July 1808), was distantly related to Sir Hans Sloane, and her brother – Claudius – was Lord Mayor of London in 1811. Money and powerful connections brought to William Manning a seat in Parliament (he was Tory MP successively for Plympton Earle, Evesham and Penrhyn over a period of 39 years), offices of prestige within the City and eventually, in 1812, the Governorship of the Bank of England. The family became accustomed to living in a style commensurate with their father's position; first at Copped Hall in Totteridge, an elegant mansion set in the midst of a substantial estate with parkland and an ornamental lake, and finally (from 1815) at Coombe Bank, an estate purchased from the Argyll family, at Sundridge, near Sevenoaks. They also possessed a town house in New Street, Spring Gardens. The children were brought up with every advantage of powerful potential patronage. One of Manning's brothers, Charles, was a page at the Court of the Prince Regent; one of his godfathers was an ex-Prime Minister, Viscount Sidmouth, and he was baptized by the Bishop of Bath and Wells. All this was a different milieu from the world in which Newman was brought up. Not surprisingly, William Manning's children became accustomed to moving easily and naturally within the governing classes of England.

Possibly because their social status was lower than that of the Mannings, the Newman family appear to have been a rather more closely-knit community. Nevertheless, both the future Cardinals retained vivid memories of their early years, recalled with warmth and nostalgia. For Newman, their house at Ham was a place of the happiest memories. 'I know more about it', he wrote in later years, 'than any house I have been in since, and could pass an examination in it. It has ever been in my dreams.'[6] Just occasionally, after they left, he revisited it; once, in 1813, on a walk with his father, they peeped into their old garden and stopped to talk with the gardener, who offered the boy three apricots. He chose the largest – 'a thing which still distresses me', he wrote forty years later, 'whenever I think of it.'[7]

Manning returned to Copped Hall for the first time in 1881, sixty-six years after leaving the house for good. He noted all the changes. Memories came flooding back. He recalled how a labourer had fallen from one of the elm trees and broken a leg while trying to reach a young owlet in its nest. There was a small stained-glass window, painted by his brother William, still in 'the little boudoir between the library and the conservatory'. He pointed out the exact spot in the Tapestry Room where his uncle had read out to the family the list of officers killed and wounded at the Battle of Waterloo.[8]

With both of them, relations with their mother appear to have been closer than with their father. Although Newman inherited his considerable musical gifts from his father (he was a talented violinist, while Manning was practically tone-deaf), they had very little else in common. Francis Newman, who seems to have been more his father's boy than his mother's, described him as 'an unpretending, firm-minded Englishman, who had learned his morality more from Shakespeare than from his Bible'.[9] He was bluff and sociable; a Freemason, a member of the Beefsteak Club, proud of his talented eldest son but also puzzled by him and occasionally greatly irritated by his tendency to dogmatize and to take High Tory views. In one such quarrel between them, when John Henry was stoutly defending George IV's treatment of Princess Caroline, his father lost all patience with him, and cried out: 'Go on! . . . Always stand up for men in power, and in time you will get promotion.'[10] John Newman senior, however, was no fool, and was capable of giving his headstrong son some sound advice. 'Take care,' he once wrote to him at Oxford, when the young man was displaying aggressive Evangelical views:

> you are encouraging a morbid sensibility and irritability of mind, which may be very serious. Religion, when carried too far, induces a mental softness. No one's principles can be established at twenty. Your opinions in two or three years will certainly, certainly, change. I have seen many instances of the same kind. You are on dangerous ground. The temper you are encouraging may lead to something alarming. Weak minds are carried into superstition, and strong minds into infidelity; do not commit yourself, do nothing ultra.[11]

The ladies of the family, perhaps, rather spoiled him at times. He was certainly a great favourite of his paternal grandmother, Elizabeth Newman, and kept in regular communication with his father's sister, Aunt Elizabeth, until her death in 1852 (partly because in later years she was in such continual need of financial help in maintaining a not very successful establishment for the education of young ladies). How much influence his mother actually exercised over him is less easy to gauge. J. B. Mozley once commented on her special quality of 'simplicity of mind', adding, 'I cannot help thinking that she must have had considerable influence on Newman's character on this point; though one is greatly disposed to think his a case where the maternal influence has been but slight in forming the man.'[12]

In later years, when Mrs Newman as a widow moved to Nuneham Courtenay to be nearer her eldest son at Oriel, her close proximity seems not always to have been as warmly appreciated as she cared to think. There is no doubt, however, that Newman's was a happy childhood, although relations with his brothers and sisters became severely strained when the family broke up and the children – as adults – went their separate ways. With Charles, the middle of the three brothers, relations were effectively severed in 1825, when he lost his faith entirely and embarked upon the drift into a life of pathetic impotence, profligacy and wasted opportunities (propped up from time to time by such financial help as Newman and his mother could afford). With Francis ('Frank'), the youngest, religious differences, first exhibited seriously in 1826, led gradually to a complete inability to communicate with each other without sourness and misunderstanding. After the death of his beloved sister Mary, in 1828, Newman found himself increasingly estranged from Harriet, in exact proportion to the advance of his Catholic sympathies; and only with Jemima was regular contact maintained, sometimes at a rather cool level, during his Catholic career.

The circumstances of Manning's boyhood were somewhat different. There is no doubt that he had the deepest admiration for his distinguished father – 'one of the justest, most benevolent, most generous men I ever knew'.[13] But because he was so distinguished and so preoccupied with public life, his youngest son actually saw very little of him. His mother, however, adored him. As Robert Gray has put it, she 'would, indeed, have had to be quite other than human not to have doted on her youngest son, with his wide-set eyes and curling blonde [*sic*] locks, especially as he so resembled his mother'.[14] Manning's physical appearance was always a factor to be reckoned with in estimating his subsequent success. He was a beautiful child, a very good-looking young man; handsomely dignified in his maturity, and austerely noble, with an air of frail dignity, in his old age. Until Manning went to school, at the age of eight, his mother took complete charge of his education, both secular and religious. Years later the Cardinal acknowledged one lesson that she had taught him that he never forgot, which was actually more an assessment of character than any specific instruction. When, as a young man, he despaired of gaining high honours at Oxford, his mother said to him, 'I never knew you undertake anything you did not do.'[15] Others were to make the same observation about him, when they got to know him well. It sums up a facet of Manning's character precisely.

Such was the age difference between Manning and his other brothers and sisters (fifteen years divided Henry Edward from the eldest boy, William, who died at the age of nineteen, and thirteen years from the eldest surviving brother, Frederick), that his natural companion at home was Harriet, only two years his senior, and she died at the age of twenty. Thereafter his closest family associate was his brother-in-law, John Anderdon, who had married his sister Anna Maria. With another sister, Caroline, who married a Colonel Austen, he maintained friendly relations until his death. She was the only member of the family to survive him, dying at the age of 92.

The schooldays of Newman and Manning brought out more strongly their differences in character, and perhaps in circumstance too. Manning attended two private schools – the first at Streatham, from which he was removed because of the dangerous influence of 'a bad boy ... who left a trail of immorality behind him',[16] and the second near his former home, under the austere discipline of the curate of Totteridge. At the age of fourteen, he joined the sons of the governing classes at Harrow, and – for one of the rare occasions in his life – discovered that he was inferior to many of his contemporaries, at least in classical learning, mainly as a result of being taught at home and then having to change schools. This was not to his liking, and he therefore rectified the deficiency during the holidays by rising regularly at 5 a.m., reading until 8, and then riding over to Sundridge for private tuition with the local curate. Even so, his Harrow career was not marked by any particular academic distinction. He seems to have been a thoroughly normal schoolboy, keener on sport than on studies, displaying sufficient ability at cricket to gain a place in the Harrow XI for two successive years. In the Winchester–Harrow match at Lords in 1825, he was dismissed for a duck in the second innings, caught by his friend Christopher Wordsworth, the future Bishop of Lincoln,[17] whose father had been Rector of Sundridge when the Mannings moved to Coombe Bank.

Manning rather magnified his cricketing prowess when reminiscing in old age (a not uncommon characteristic of the elderly), mainly – one suspects – because he was not a natural games player. His slim build enabled him to exhibit remarkable agility into advanced middle age, however. Wilfrid Ward recalled an occasion when Manning, as Provost of Westminster, was visiting his father at St Edmund's, Ware, and took the whole family by surprise by suddenly vaulting a locked five-barred gate in order to pick a flower which one of their company had admired.[18] This was not the first time that Manning's vaulting ability was recorded. When he was a boy at Harrow, he and Charles Wordsworth (also a future Bishop) narrowly avoided detection by their headmaster, who had seen them entering a local hostelry. They escaped by vaulting a hedge.[19] But health problems prevented him from becoming a proper 'blood'. He was a chronic asthmatic; and this may explain his habit of punctuating his conversation with occasional loud sniffs, which in later years developed into something of an affectation, employed when parrying an uncalled-for remark, or sometimes, in the course of a speech, to give him time to reflect on what he wanted to say next.

Manning's schooldays certainly offered no expectations of future greatness, and least of all in the field in which it was subsequently displayed. He seemed to some of his contemporaries a rather affected boy, both in his dress and in his manners, and he cultivated a sort of arrogant aloofness, which earned him the nickname of 'the general' (which he preferred, it is interesting to note, to the other nickname which accompanied him from home – 'the parson'). He was not the first eminent Victorian to state early in life that his motto was *aut Caesar aut nullus*.[20] At roughly the same time, though several years senior in age, Thomas Arnold in 1823 had vouchsafed the same sentiment.[21] But it has a somewhat pretentious ring in a schoolboy. As for a career in the Church, Harrow offered virtually no religious instruction at all. In those days, it did not even have a chapel, and boys were expected to attend the local parish church. 'Good learning', if by that is meant a sound education in the Classics, was firmly inculcated by Manning's headmaster, George Butler, but 'godliness' hardly at all, which makes it all the more surprising that so many future princes of the church could be counted among his contemporaries. The scorecard of a house match of the period included in the two opposing XIs the names of three future bishops and two archbishops.[22]

Newman's entire schooling was conducted, from the age of seven until he left to matriculate at Oxford at the end of 1816, at a private school in Ealing, under the headmastership of the Revd George Nicholas. Although its numbers were actually slightly higher than those of Harrow, it was an altogether humbler establishment, set in an extraordinary conglomeration of ramshackle buildings. But its achievements, and the alumni that it could boast, were not negligible. Over the years Sir Henry Lawrence, Thomas Huxley, Captain Marryat, W. S. Gilbert, and William Makepeace Thackeray, as well as the three Newman brothers, were pupils there, although not of course at the same time. As with most schools of the period, a nucleus of resident masters was supplemented by part-time visiting teachers; one such (to teach French) happened to be, somewhat improbably, the future 'Citizen King', Louis-Philippe, although perhaps not while Newman was a pupil.

Nevertheless Ealing, in terms of its tuition, was certainly not Harrow; nor remotely the equal of Winchester, where Newman was apparently intended to proceed, and only did not do so through his own wishes and the entreaties of his mother and headmaster.[23] Later he was to realize that there was a price to pay for his pleas to remain at Ealing, when he discovered, during his first year at Oxford, how far behind the products of the great public schools he was in classical learning.[24] But after initial timidity, and a tearful introduction, he settled down at Ealing and soon began to make his mark, if not quite as a conventional schoolboy. Although Louis Bouyer has suggested that he rapidly began to display 'those qualities of leadership and charm which never left him',[25] there seems little evidence to support this. He was precocious; a loner who wrote verses in preference to playing games, and even composed – when he was not quite ten years old – a miniature opera. In his teens, according to his brother Francis, he displeased several of his contemporaries by producing a sort of 'in-house' newspaper entitled 'Spy', and he took a delight in founding an exclusive society over which he presided as Grandmaster.[26]

So at least he had this in common with Manning at the same stage of his life – a certain aloofness from his companions, exacerbated no doubt by his distaste for rough and tumble and his preference for his own company. This was not only a reflection of his disposition. Like Manning, he had his share of health problems. His eyesight was never good; he also suffered from chronic indigestion. In his middle age, after he became a Catholic, his language sometimes gives one the impression that his change of communion added about twenty-five years to his life. 'I am now getting to a great age,' he explained to his sister Jemima on 26 September 1850, when he was still short of his fiftieth birthday.[27] Perhaps he was always inclined to add, mentally or temperament-ally, a few extra years to his actual age. A poem of his Ealing years begins as follows:

> Here as we sit, and view the boys at play
> Rejoicing in their sunbright holiday,
> While some at fives attack the patient wall,
> And others glory in the bat and ball,
> Be our employ in philosophic ease . . .[28]

One has to admit that for a boy under sixteen to write such lines as these reveals more than a touch of middle age. This was written, however, before 1 August 1816. On that day, and during the six months that followed, Newman's life underwent a change; a change so complete, in his own estimation, that everything that had gone before it was as if it had never been.

II

Two things happened in 1816 to constitute a watershed in Newman's life. The first was a dramatic change in his family circumstances; the second was a revelation so powerful within his spiritual life that he looked upon it ever afterwards as the moment of his true conversion to Christianity. The two events are not unrelated. It was in March of that year that the blow fell upon the Newman family. The bank of Ramsbottom, Newman and Rams-bottom was forced to close its doors. The aftermath of the final defeat of Napoleon at Waterloo was a grim time for banks generally, and Newman's bank was by no means the first to fail, as depositors sought to withdraw their money more quickly than the banks could find funds to meet their demands. John Newman and his junior partner were honourable men (not so, however, the senior partner) and did their utmost to pay their creditors in full, but with near disastrous effect upon their private resources. Bankruptcy was averted for a while. The house in Southampton

Street was initially put out to let, and the Newman family squeezed into Vine Cottage in Norwood, where their grand-mother and Aunt Elizabeth were living (although it was only to be – as they suspected – on borrowed time). John Newman eventu-ally secured a position as manager of a brewery in Alton, where he was joined by his family in the autumn of 1817. This was only the prelude to further disasters. The brewery business failed to prosper; John Newman fell steadily into debt and was already mortgaged up to the hilt. In November 1819 the family moved again to London, where their unfortunate father struggled bravely on as, effectively, a tavern-keeper in Clerkenwell. The house in Southampton Street and Vine Cottage were put on the market. A small property at Strand-on-the-Green, near Kew Bridge, was secured for the grandmother and Aunt Elizabeth, where they tried to make ends meet by opening a Finishing School for Young Ladies. The final blow fell at the end of 1821, when bankruptcy proceedings began, concluded in the autumn of 1822. Thereafter the family moved from a succession of lodgings into meaner and meaner quarters until John Newman's death in 1824.

At the onset of the disaster, with the closure of the bank, Newman was only fifteen and still at school. Everything possible was done to protect him from the inevitable disruption. Dr Nicholas would not hear of the boy being removed, and even allowed him to stay on at the school during the summer holidays while the family were trying to solve their immediate accommoda-tion problems. So it was that the boy came under the influence of one of the resident classical masters, the Revd Walter Mayers, who not only took care of him during these months but – in Newman's words – also proved to be 'the human means of the beginning of divine faith in me', by long talks together and by guiding his reading to books which had been the source of his own Calvinist convictions. 'I fell under the influence of a definite creed,' Newman wrote years later, acknowledging the influence of his first spiritual mentor, 'and received into my intellect impressions of dogma, which, through God's mercy, have never been effaced or obscured.'[1] They were tough books for a fifteen-year old to master – works of William Romaine, Thomas Scott's *The Force of Truth*, Joseph Milner's Church History and, finally, in December 1816, as a leaving present from Walter Mayers, confident that the great change had been effected in his protégé, the *Private Thoughts* of Bishop Beveridge.[2]

In such a way was Newman introduced to the great classical expositions of Evangelical doctrines, particularly treasured by those inclined to the Calvinist wing of that party. This needs a little elucidation. Although within the Evangelical camp, as within all church parties, there could be found both extremists and moderates, there was sufficient common ground between them for the label to embrace both branches. The basic standpoint of the Evangelicals was a simple one; and, indeed, this quality of simplicity was itself part of that common ground. They had no time for mysteries; no truck with priesthood of any kind or any suggestion that between God and the individual soul there could or should be any intermediary. They looked simply to the Word of God in the Scriptures, wherein was contained all things necessary for salvation, every part of which, being held to be equally inspired, was therefore to be understood and accepted in its literal sense. This was the starting point. As for the all-important question 'What shall I do to be saved?', the answer was most succinctly supplied in the third stanza of A. M. Toplady's famous hymn, 'Rock of Ages':

> Nothing in my hand I bring
> Simply to thy cross I cling;
> Naked, come to thee for dress;
> Helpless, look to thee for grace;
> Foul, I to the fountain fly;
> Wash me, Saviour, or I die.

That is to say, since the whole of mankind without exception is in a state of natural depravity, there is nothing that any one of us can do to merit justifying grace. All that is asked of us is Faith – faith in the redemptive power of the Atonement, whereby ransom was paid once and for all for our sins by Christ Crucified. Faith alone justifies, and it is God's act, by His accounting us righteous (not by any good works of our own) that grants us salvation.

Up to this point, all well and good. But then problems arise. Where does Baptism fit in? Are we not regenerated in being made children of God through the grace of this first of the sacraments? The more moderate Evangelicals were prepared to concede a conditional regeneration; others explained the gift imparted by the sacrament in different ways, according to the differing views of Luther, Zwingli and Calvin in the sixteenth century, the Calvinists maintaining that the assurance of pardon was efficacious only for the Elect, and that it is God who chooses His Elect. Whom, then, does He select for this greatest of gifts? The Evangelicals answered, 'Have faith and you will discover'. You will also *know*. This is what they meant by 'the great change' – the moment that God invests you with the quality of 'seriousness', an inward (and sometimes outward as well) token of His gracious blessing, bestowed upon you totally unearned. This could be a dramatic revelation, such as Paul experienced on the Damascus Road; or it might be a gradual awakening to the awareness of God's gift.

One of the favourite texts of the Evangelicals was the concluding passage of the parable of the marriage feast in St Matthew's Gospel (22:14), 'For many are called, but few are chosen', and there developed among Evangelicals a sort of freemasonry, whereby the 'few' could be distinguished from the 'many'. There were the 'real' Christians as opposed to 'nominal' Christians (i.e., those who counted themselves as members of the Church but lacked the quality of seriousness). Real Christians bore the marks of their privileged position upon their persons and their characters. One of those marks was 'enthusiasm', whereby you were seen to live a life of 'vital religion'. 'Seriousness' did not necessarily involve outward austerity or any form of world-renunciation; its identifying mark was a change of attitude, whereby all things worldly came to be seen in a different perspective as your thoughts were directed heavenwards; frivolous pursuits would therefore be naturally shunned; but you would radiate Christian joy, by praising your Saviour on every possible occasion for His beneficent goodness, and you would continually look for signs of His 'Providences', whereby God guided or warned, or even chastised, His Elect. Providences, however, could sometimes be visited upon the reprobate, by striking down with disturbing celerity those who blasphemed His name, and cautionary tales about such wrathful divine interventions were widely publicized for the edification of the young. It follows from all this that the ministry of the Evangelicals concentrated on preaching the Word rather than administering the sacraments, for by the Word conversions would be achieved, especially when the polar opposites of the bliss of Heaven and the agonizing torments of Hell were vividly and luridly displayed. Sacramentalism, to the Evangelicals, suggested emphasis on priesthood as opposed to ministry, and the most manifest exhibition of sacerdotalism was found in the Roman Church, regarded as the dominion of the Man of Sin, or Antichrist.

Divisions arose, however, primarily over two interpretations of the Protestant or Evangelical canon. The first was over the Calvinist understanding of the word 'predestination' (used by St Paul and St Augustine, in particular), and its relation to the text 'Many called, few chosen'. One might accept that the Elect knew that they had been predestinated to salvation, and perhaps even granted the gift of final perseverance to maintain or to gain (opinions differed here) sanctification to fit themselves for Heaven. Did that also mean that the mass of men, not chosen, had been predestinated to eternal damnation? It was on this question that George Whitefield and John Wesley, the pioneers of Methodism, had divided, and on which Evangelicals continued to hold opposing views. The second difference concerned the limits (if indeed there were any) of 'enthusiasm'. When this attribute led to extravagant claims of the direct inspiration of the Holy Spirit into a sort of Pentacostalism, and consequent fanatical behaviour, many of the moderates felt profoundly uneasy, and began to show a greater respect for Church order, sobriety, deference to the Establishment and to episcopal authority than the rugged pioneers of the Evangelical Revival could ever have countenanced. In consequence, leading Anglican Evangelicals of the early decades of the nineteenth century – notably Charles Simeon at Cambridge, Daniel Wilson (Vicar of Islington and later Bishop of Calcutta) and the highly influential members of William Wilberforce's circle, the Clapham Sect – deliberately began to distance themselves from 'ranters' and 'noisy professors', the devotees of extremists like Edward Irving and Henry Drummond.[3]

Now the excellent Walter Mayers, who was far from being a noisy professor, sympathized none the less with the Calvinist wing of the Evangelicals. But Newman did not simply absorb all that he was given like a sponge. Louis Bouyer suggests that, on the contrary, Mayers was frequently disconcerted by his pupil's precociousness in dialectic.[4] For instance, he found that he could not accept the 'detestable doctrine' that those not chosen to be of the Elect were predestined to eternal death. They were 'simply passed over'.[5] But he knew that he himself was safe. Although he was later to abandon belief in the doctrine of final perseverance, he recalled in the *Apologia* that 'I ... believed that the inward conversion of which I was conscious (and of which I still am more certain than that I have hands and feet) would last until the next life, and that I was elected to eternal glory.'[6] Four years later, he recorded in a private journal 'the reality of conversion . . . I know I am right. How do you know it? I know I know. How? I know I know I know, etc., etc.'[7] In the exhilaration of his converted state he began to make collections of scriptural proofs of the doctrine of the Trinity, and then of each verse of the Athanasian Creed. Only one of Calvin's tenets took firm root in his mind, however: 'the fact of heaven and hell, divine favour and divine wrath, of the justified and the unjustified . . . From this time I have given a full inward assent and belief to the doctrine of eternal punishment, as delivered by our Lord Himself, in as true a sense as I hold that of eternal happiness; though I have tried in various ways to make that truth less terrible to the reason.'[8]

Three important questions now suggest themselves. First, how accurate was Newman in his statement to Anne Mozley in 1885 that 'I should say that it is difficult to realize or imagine the boy before and after August 1816 . . . I can look back at the end of 70 years as if on another person.'?[9] Stephen Dessain does not presume to question this. 'Allow him to speak for and interpret himself', he writes. 'Newman *sui-ipsius interpres*, and let us not forget that he was a man passionately devoted to the truth.'[10] Doubtless this is exactly what Newman thought, but the self-analysis may well be faulty, especially as the statement falls within the area where self-analysis is most likely to become distorted. It is easy enough to identify the moments of profound change in one's thinking and the re-orientation of one's whole approach to life. What is less easy to recognize are the elements in one's character and make-up which remain the same.

Newman had never encountered Calvinism in any shape or form before he met Walter Mayers. Shortly before he experienced his crisis of faith, he had been going through an early adolescent phase of dipping into irreverent and sceptical writings – Tom Paine, Hume and Voltaire – and musing over their plausibility. But Newman the man, even Newman the Cardinal, was still unmistakably the rather lonely boy who before he had ever come under Walter Mayers' influence 'used to wish the Arabian Tales were true', and who 'thought life might be a dream, or I an Angel, and all this world a deception, my fellow-angels by a playful device concealing themselves from me, and deceiving me with the semblance of a material world'.[11] He himself conceded, in the *Apologia*, that 'for some time previous to my conversion' he was very superstitious, and 'used constantly to cross myself in going into the dark'.[12] His Evangelical conversion, in clarifying his vision of 'two and two only supremely and luminously self-evident beings, myself and my Creator',[13] was actually only the confirmation of what he had been groping towards during his childhood, if he had not been able then to articulate the relationship quite so starkly. There was never a time in his life when he had thought otherwise. He defended his faith as a Catholic in these words:

> I am a Catholic by virtue of my believing in a God; and if I am asked why I believe in a God, I answer that it is because I believe in myself, for I feel it impossible to believe in my own existence ... without believing also in the existence of Him, who lives as a Personal, All-seeing, All-judging Being in my conscience.[14]

This personalism, this way of looking at the world wholly subjectively (or this *autocentrisme*, as Bremond put it), this understanding of the crucial role of conscience, are all constant features in Newman's life and thought.[15] What happened in 1816 was not so much that he changed as that he found direction.

The second pertinent question to pose is, how much of this Evangelicalism that he so deeply imbibed in 1816 was to survive through all the changes that were to come? Many of the peculiar (in its literal sense) tenets of Evangelicalism were abandoned during the next two decades, the first to be jettisoned being the doctrine of final perseverance. The notion of the Pope as Antichrist followed it, although Newman gives no precise date.[16]

Once an Evangelical, however, always an Evangelical. Newman bore many of the marks for the rest of his life: a certain puritanical streak in his character was one; another, more central to his religious thinking, was an unswerving adhesion to the dogmatic principle in religion. From Thomas Scott he learnt, and never forgot, that 'unhumbled reason' was the root of all heresy, and that once a man embarked upon that downward path his ultimate destination would be infidelity.[17] The influence upon him of his reading of Joseph Milner was also enduring, predisposing him not only to interpret the course of Christian history as an unending conflict between those on the right side and those on the wrong, but also – almost obsessively – to search for historical analogies to illustrate the issues of his own day.[18] Although there is no evidence that Newman ever read Calvin, he was never able to discard (as Stephen Thomas puts it) 'that Calvinist sense of the Satanic significance of contemporary events',[19] an apocalyptic world-picture which was also an enduring attribute of Manning's Evangelicalism.

Newman never lost his conviction of the force of special providences. He was always looking for signs and interpreting external events as directions from on high. In the *Grammar of Assent* he defends his firm belief in such providences in the same terms as he defended miracles. 'If logic finds fault with it, so much the worse for logic',[20] and later supplies the example of Napoleon's reaction to his excommunication by Pius VII in 1809.[21] The death of a close friend or near relative was instantly interpreted as a direct 'providential intimation' to himself.[22]

Finally, Newman returned time and time again, in his Anglican sermons, to the text 'many called, few chosen'. As R. C. Selby has pointed out, sometimes Newman gave a very unevangelical twist to the text, linking it to the Tractarian doctrine of Reserve, whereby God 'dispenses religious knowledge first to a chosen few'.[23] This was the way of Jesus in His teaching. 'He showed Himself openly, not to all the people, but unto witnesses chosen before of God.'[24] Newman preached on the text as a Catholic, changing its meaning from the customary Evangelical interpretation, pointing out that the 'many' are those who show complacency in the slack fulfilment of their Christian duties.[25] The emphasis had now fallen on the duty of obedience, which had been so marked a feature of his Anglican sermons. Frederick Borsch has explained this fusion of Tractarian and Calvinist teaching by pointing out that, to Newman, 'one can only know election by God's grace if one manifests that grace and not just to others but to oneself. Therefore one must show forth and experience within oneself the obedience and character of God's chosen.'[26] In 1857, Newman discussed the problem of death-bed repentance with W. G. Ward, prefacing his remarks with the observation, 'You know *I* do not feel the intellectual and moral difficulty of predestination which you do.'[27]

Nevertheless, although Newman's first conversion, the influence of Walter Mayers and the impressions left upon him from his early study of Evangelical writers made indelible marks, it is still reasonable to pose the third question – was he ever a genuine

Evangelical at all? The precision of dating his conversion in August 1816 (if not quite as precise as John Wesley, who actually consulted a timepiece, so that he could register that it was 'about a quarter to nine' on 24 May 1738 when he truly discovered that his sins had been forgiven)[28] has a definite Evangelical flavour about it. But Newman himself conceded that he used the word 'conversion with great diffidence, being obliged to adopt the language of books'.[29] His actual experience seemed to be wholly different from accounts of 'the great change' that he had read about elsewhere. It was certainly far from being his personal equivalent of events on the Damascus road. It is interesting, too, that his sense of greatest debt, among the authors that he was given to read, was to Thomas Scott, who had himself shied away from the Calvinist understanding of the doctrine of predestination. Furthermore, the two most enduring lessons that he learnt from Scott – according to his own testimony – were hardly exclusive Evangelical doctrines: 'Holiness before peace' and 'Growth is the only evidence of life'.[30]

Temperamentally, Newman could never have remained an Evangelical, heart and soul, for long. As Owen Chadwick has observed, he was an intensely emotional person, but the one area in which he found emotionalism distasteful was religion.[31] Religious enthusiasm, as displayed by the new generation of Evangelicals, who had abandoned the studied decorum of their forerunners of the Clapham Sect, repelled him. It was disrespectful and vulgar, the absolute antithesis of the reverential awe with which all holy things should be approached and spoken of. This was partly an expression of his personal fastidiousness and delicacy of taste, so beautifully conveyed in his own writings; but it went far deeper than that. Reserved by nature, the young Newman of 1816 knew nothing at that stage of the doctrine of Reserve in communicating religious knowledge, which he would find in his studies of the Fathers. As soon as he encountered this, and as soon as he met the living embodiment of the doctrine of Reserve in John Keble, he would discover the theology that spoke personally to him in a way that Evangelicalism never could. When that happened, he would never count himself truly an Evangelical again.

III

If Newman discovered 'seriousness', in the Evangelical sense of the word, in his last few months at Ealing, Manning also, as he was about to leave Harrow exactly ten years later (December 1826), came to the conclusion that seriousness, in its more widely-accepted meaning, was what had been lacking in his life so far, and that it was a virtue to be cultivated if he were to make any sort of mark in the world. What that mark should be was uncertain. As far as his father was concerned, his youngest son should enter the Church, a decision – one suspects – based more on conventional thinking than on any deep religious conviction, because a career in the Church was the time-honoured occupation for the youngest son. The Manning family was no more than respectably religious, showing few signs (except for Harriet, whom Manning once described teasingly as a Methodist)[1] of the seriousness that denoted Evangelical zeal. In fact, at Coombe Bank, the emphasis was rather the other way, partly because of the influence of the Wordsworths, their neighbours at Sundridge. Manning noted in later years, 'my family was strictly Church of England of the old High school of Dr Wordsworth, Mant and D'Oyly. The first and the last were Rectors of Sundridge, and behold they were very dry. But we always went regularly to church; never missing in the morning, often going in the afternoon, and going also to communion at times. My father read prayers and a sermon on Sunday nights ... I never heard or saw anything irreligious.'[2]

Such Christian convictions as Manning himself possessed at this stage harked back to the early teaching of his mother before he ever went to school. He had childhood memories of his horror at hearing that all one's sins were recorded by the Almighty in a book (indeed, he never rid himself quite of the terrors of this image, believing – as he looked back – that 'it has been a great grace to me, and kept me from the greatest dangers').[3] In his Bible-reading, he was especially fascinated by the Apocalypse, which he first 'devoured' (as he himself put it) at the age of eight, 'and I never all through my life forgot the "lake that burneth with fire and brimstone". That verse has kept me like an audible voice through all my life.'[4] This happens to be an exceptionally revealing observation. The consistent feature of Manning's sermons, whether as an Anglican or as a Catholic, was his love of apocalyptic imagery; and it is no exaggeration to say that he tended to see the great European conflicts in which he became involved as Archbishop of Westminster in starkly apocalyptic terms.

The newly-discovered sense of seriousness, which one can date fairly precisely between the closing months of 1826 and his entry at Oxford in the Michaelmas term of 1827, had two causes. The first was the impact upon him of his sister Harriet's death; the second was the close association he then formed with the first of the mentors in his life, his brother-in-law, John Anderdon. Here was no Walter Mayers; in fact, in some ways, Anderdon's influence was in the opposite direction, because it was he who first cast doubts in Manning's mind over whether a career in the Church was really the one most suited to his talents and disposition. He had higher aspirations for him. Anderdon himself was an Old Harrovian, several years Manning's senior, and had recently become a business partner of William Manning. Perceiving accurately that here was a youngster of limitless potential, idling and frittering away his opportunities, he decided to take him in hand; and Manning, who did not dispute for one moment that mountains were there to be climbed and that, given the right direction, he was perfectly capable of climbing them, happily submitted himself to Anderdon's guidance.

Letters in abundance passed between them, some didactic in tone from Anderdon, whom Robert Gray has aptly described as 'a natural pedagogue, ready with advice and information on every subject under the sun, to the point of stuffiness and way beyond';[5] some (especially Manning's) couched in the rather ponderous banter, bordering on facetiousness, occasionally affected by the early nineteenth-century clerisy in their lighter moments, which makes for somewhat painful reading to modern eyes. Manning wanted Anderdon as an ally to put pressure on his father, first of all, to enable him to live at Oxford in reasonable style, for which he would need a substantially increased allowance; and secondly, and more laudably, to meet the expenses of a private tutor to remedy some of the deficiencies of his Harrow education, for which he was certainly more to blame than the school. He succeeded on both counts. In 1827, for a spell of about nine months, he went to reside at Poulshot with Canon William Fisher, a scholar with an established reputation for working wonders with high-born private pupils who had hitherto squandered their gifts. Lord Ashley (later Earl of Shaftesbury) had been one such, an idle boy at Harrow who proceeded to take a First at Oxford. This was the treatment that Manning now sought for himself.

If John Anderdon was a mentor to Manning, Canon Fisher was a slave-driver; and never could he have found a more willing slave. 'I can say I never lost a moment,' Manning recalled. 'Up early and very late to bed. It was the turn of my life, and the beginning of my second or self-education.'[6] Each and every suggestion for improving his ultimate prospects was taken up on the instant. He worked assiduously, for instance, under John Anderdon's epistolary directions, to sharpen up his writing style, abandoning the pompous and affected grandiloquence which he had hitherto supposed to be the mark of a cultivated mind, and aspiring instead to the lucid and logical crispness which was to become such a distinctive feature of his later polemical writings. Encouraged to gain fluency in modern languages at Oxford, he subjected himself to a rigid discipline, making a chart, for instance, of Italian irregular verbs, and posting it up over his wash-basin, so that he could test himself each morning while shaving.[7] Little did he realize at the time what an enormous advantage this would give him during his Catholic years, especially at Rome, where he would be able to converse effortlessly with people of consequence in their native tongue.

So it was an altogether more purposeful Henry Manning who entered Balliol in 1827 than the seemingly rather feckless Harrovian of a year before. Some of the old features remained, at least at first. There was a touch of the dandy still, in the eyes of some of his contemporaries, as they observed him resplendent in his pink silk riding breeches; he took up rowing and boxing, the latter being a handy accomplishment for emerging honourably from the occasional skirmishes between Town and Gown. He seemed to move easily and naturally between the two rival sets at Balliol, the rowing men and the reading set, according to his disposition of the moment. But although he kept up good relations with the Christ Church circle that radiated around his Harrovian and family friend, Charles Wordsworth (thereby making the acquaintance of Gladstone for the first time), and became deeply attached to his tutor at Balliol, Herman Merivale, he appears to have had no very close friends. This was in part a reflection of his reserved nature, which always made him seem slightly aloof, but also a consequence of his indifferent health. His asthma frequently led to chest infections, so that his doctor eventually advised him to refrain from dining in hall, thereby inevitably restricting his social activities. One cannot picture many companions choosing to join Manning in his awesomely frugal diet of cold meat and bread, which was all that was permitted to sustain him for the rest of his undergraduate career.[8]

For the sake of his health he was taken abroad in the Long Vacation of 1828, in the company of his father and Herman Merivale, crossing the Channel for the first time in his life. The new seriousness was beginning to take on a tinge of 'the great change', it seems, as an incipient puritanism led him to resolve, after a single visit to the Paris Opera, 'never to put my foot into a theatre again'.[9] This may have been provoked by some edifying reading recommended to him, in his semi-invalid state, by the indefatigable John Anderdon – John Foster's *Essay on Decision of Character* – surely one of the most improbable prescriptions for bolstering the spirits of a sick man that could be conceived. It is a singularly dreary book of 'stern, unbending puritanism based upon complete confidence in personal judgment'.[10] Manning, curiously, rather liked it; and it certainly seems to have strengthened his resolve to be even stricter in eschewing all self-indulgence and to make even more strenuous efforts to aspire to university distinction. Shortly after entering Balliol, he had written to John Anderdon on the earlier theme of *aut Caesar aut nullus*.

> Hang me, Jack [he wrote], if I do anything by halves hereafter. I will endeavour to be Caesar, I know I can be *nullus*. But never will I be *Nullocaesar*, which is an amalgam of craving ambition and yielding softness, inadequate exertion and harrassed tranquillity. Just enough of one to make one miserable, and too little of the other to succeed in any attempt. Read the 40th chap of Ecclus.[11]

In 1829 he found the perfect arena for establishing his character of Caesar among his contemporaries: the Oxford Union. It is true that the Union was of recent creation, thanks largely to the initiative of Manning's future brother-in-law, Samuel Wilberforce, who was the first to exhibit to an admiring audience undergraduate eloquence at its most masterly. Gladstone was to achieve equal esteem there in due course. In the years between them, Manning established for himself a reputation quite as legendary. On the occasion of his maiden speech on 12 March 1829, he recalled that 'I was half-dead with fright, and when I got up saw nothing but the President's head out of a white mist.'[12] He must have sensed at once, however, that he was scoring a brilliant

success. Thereafter he spoke often, and with increasing confidence, fluency and enjoyment. 'There are occasions that seem to
defy eloquence,' Thomas Mozley wrote in his *Recollections*, 'but
Manning was more than equal to them.'[13] Sir Francis Doyle
recalled:

> Before Mr Gladstone paid much attention to the Debating Society, the
> leader of our house was Manning ... He would always have been in
> the ascendant, but his greater maturity ... increased that ascendancy.
> He possessed a fine presence, and his delivery was effective. These
> qualities, joined to an impressive and somewhat imposing manner,
> enabled him to speak as one having authority, and drew into his orbit
> a certain number of satellites who revolved round him, and looked up
> to him, with as much reverence as if he had been the actual Pope,
> instead of only an embryo Cardinal.

He could not resist adding, however, as people so often tend to do
when assessing a contemporary in the light of his later accom-
plishments, 'Their innocent adulation led him into his most
obvious weakness, an assumption of omniscience which now and
then overshot itself.' He could as pertinently have been writing of
Samuel Wilberforce.[14]

This meteoric success at the Union had two immediate effects
on Manning. The first was an enduring one. Having discovered
the art and the exhilaration of being able to hold an audience in
thrall by extempore public speaking, he used the gift to the full,
and with never-diminishing effect, for the rest of his life. The
second only proved to be a temporary phase – his decision to
abandon thoughts of proceeding to Anglican orders, and to
aspire to a career in politics. 'My whole mind was drawn that way,'
he wrote; 'I began reading Burke and political economy ... I had
always disliked the thought of being a clergyman, and this,
political aspiration finished.'[15] Gladstone's ambitions at the same
time, it may be noted, were in precisely the opposite direction. He
yearned for a life of service in the Church, but the contrary views
of his father eventually prevailed.[16] Since both men were destined
for greatness (their Oxford contemporaries never had any doubt
on that score), it is interesting to speculate on what might have
been had circumstances allowed them to adhere to their original
aims, with Manning as Prime Minister and Gladstone as
Archbishop (presumably of Canterbury, not Westminster).

It seemed just for a moment, in 1829, that the sun was shining
on Manning from out of a cloudless sky. That, however, was a

delusion, because already the fortunes of his father had taken a serious turn for the worse. From being a highly lucrative business, the West Indian sugar trade became steadily more precarious in the face of French and American competition, and consequently prices tumbled. A warning came from his father, with his 21st birthday present of £700 in Consols to his youngest son: 'I cannot at present do more for you ... Your future success in life must depend entirely upon your own exertion.'[17] As a serious situation plunged into irretrievable disaster Manning, if he could not fully comprehend the implications of impending bankruptcy, at least responded to the plea for self-help. He refused the Presidency of the Union, and devoted himself to the quest for the highest honours. He had his moments of anxiety but, a month before his Day of Judgement, he was able to assure Anderdon that he was quietly confident. 'I deem my present trial more one of moral courage and presence of mind. In neither of these WILL I be wanting. I fear it not, I await it not with dread or anxiety.'[18] He had clearly been imbibing copious draughts from John Foster's homiletic tome on the force of will power. Then came the intervention of a providence. In Balliol chapel, a week before he embarked upon his Schools, as the senior undergraduate present he was required to read one of the lessons. The passage appointed was from the Apocrypha, the eighth chapter of the Wisdom of Solomon, and when he came to verses 8 to 11, he read them as if in a dream, because he sensed that they contained a message addressed directly to himself. 'I shall be found of a quick conceit when I give judgment, and in the presence of princes I shall be admired.'[19] Six Firsts were awarded in Greats that year. Manning was one of them, in the company of another future brother-in-law, Henry Wilberforce, and W. K. Hamilton, later Bishop of Salisbury.

All the will-power and resolution in the world, however, would not help him to a parliamentary career without money and powerful patronage; and by this time his father's plight was desperate. The collapse came in 1831, and his youngest son accompanied him to the Guildhall to witness the humiliating spectacle of a former Governor of the Bank of England handing over his gold watch, chain and seals, the symbolic last possessions of a bankrupt. The experience was shattering; more so for the Mannings than the Newmans, for here was a fall into comparative penury from a state of opulence. William Manning never recov-

ered from the disgrace. 'I have belonged to men with whom
bankruptcy was synonymous with death,' he told his son;[20] and
his own death was not long in coming. He was left with a tiny
income resulting from the purchase by friends of the life interest
in Mrs Manning's marriage settlement, and his last years were
spent at 12 Gower Street, where he died in 1835.

So what was Manning to do? His academic distinction held out
high hopes of a Fellowship, perhaps at Merton; but this would
require at the very least a declaration of a commitment to proceed
to Orders, and he was not prepared all at once to abandon his
ambitions for a political career. The best, however, that his
friends could procure for him was a supernumerary clerkship in
the Colonial Office at a salary of £80 a year, and although his
mother was able to make him an allowance of £100, he was now
obliged to reduce his standard of living dramatically from the
carefree days of Balliol. The year 1831, Purcell has written,
proved to be 'the only idle year in Manning's busy life'.[21] He spent
it, first of all, by inundating John Anderdon with importunate
letters, both to while away his time and to urge him to continue to
support him in his ambitions, seemingly forgetting that Anderdon, having been his father's business partner, had plenty of
worries of his own. Indeed, it is difficult to resist the impression
that at this unhappy stage of his life, Manning was rather more
solicitous of his own interests than of the circumstances of others.
But life seemed full of frustrations for him. On top of everything
else, he had fallen in love, the object of his affection being a Miss
Deffell, the sister of two of Manning's fellow Harrovians. The
romance, which came to naught, is shrouded in mystery, because
Manning was ever after reluctant to talk of it, but there is no
evidence that his love was not reciprocated; rather, it seems that
strong objections were registered by her parents who, being
wealthy enough to have a residence in Grosvenor Street, regarded
the prospects of their daughter's suitor as too unpromising for a
match to be contemplated.

Another woman, however, had already been figuring in Manning's life. This was Favell Bevan, the sister of another Harrow
contemporary. She was six years older than Manning, a lady full
of good works, and strong Evangelical piety, and with – there
seems little doubt – some fluttering of the heart when in the
presence of the handsome young man who came to stay from time
to time with the Bevan family, as her brother Robert's friend. She

quickly discerned that he was much in need of sympathy and succour in his troublous times. Manning seems to have been unaware that Miss Bevan looked upon him as a possible future husband; indeed, from all accounts, she was a difficult, possessive woman of unattractive appearance, whose desperate attempts to gain a husband eventually persuaded her to elope with an equally unprepossessing Evangelical minister, Robert Mortimer, a man apparently so obese that it required the efforts of two attendants to squeeze him into his wedding carriage.[22] While Manning valued Miss Bevan's counsel, and allowed her to become some-thing of a spiritual guide for a short period, recent research by Christopher O'Gorman suggests that her influence, made so much of by Shane Leslie, has been greatly exaggerated.[23] She was not a Walter Mayers, however close she was to Newman's spiritual mentor in her Calvinist views. At any rate, a correspondence began between them during Manning's Oxford days, and from time to time he allowed himself to accompany her to open-air meetings, and Favell Bevan became every day more hopeful. 'I think a work of grace is going on in his heart,' she recorded on an occasion in 1831, after Manning had dined with the Bevans at their house at Belmont in Hertfordshire. 'He is deeply convinced of the vanity of the world and the sinfulness of sin. He is much interested in the Scriptures, from which he has formed a very high standard of religion.' However, 'he looks very poorly, and is not happy. He remains at the gate knocking; reflecting on his conversation, I perceive he is in bondage to the law.'[24]

Towards the end of November of that year, Favell Bevan was sufficiently confident that the claims of the Gospel had triumphed and that 'the great change' had been effected. To put it as strongly as this suggests an element of wishful thinking. In one respect, however, she spoke truth: 'Who knows but that after being tempest-tossed for a season he may seek the service of his Master?'[25] Which is precisely what Manning did. He put his name forward for the Merton Fellowship and was duly elected in April 1832. Before proceeding to ordination he set himself to study theology – interestingly, not the classics of Evangelical doctrine, but primarily the writings of the Caroline Divines and the early Church Fathers.[26] On 23 December 1832, he was ordained deacon by the Bishop of Rochester.

Miss Bevan had certainly not succeeded, if this had ever been her intention, in converting him to Calvinism. Years later, Manning was to declare that he 'never in his life accepted Calvinism, even in its most mitigated form'.[27] In an autobiographical note in his journals, recalling his religious beliefs in 1833, he described that he had found 'Evangelicalism illogical' and that he had no doubts about baptismal regeneration or 'in a spiritual, but real, receiving of Our Lord in Holy Communion'.[28] It may well be that, as with Newman's attempts to recall early religious views at any particular time, his memory cannot be wholly relied upon. Bodley, who knew him so well, emphatically believed that 'the evangelical training of [Manning's] youth was the basis of his Christianity',[29] and traces of Miss Bevan's mentorship survived to the end of his life. Although he conscientiously avoided the term 'enthusiasm', something of that essential Evangelical temper was discerned by the old English Catholics, who disliked this particular facet of the Anglican converts, most of whom had come via Tractarianism from the Evangelical ranks, more than any other of their peculiarities. They simply did not understand it. Newman, the least patently 'enthusiastic' of them all, was distrusted by John Lingard as having 'too much fancy or enthusiasm'[30] about him, and – even before the influx of Anglican converts – Bishop Baines had complained that 'Enthusiasts were damaging the Catholic cause'.[31] Manning, for his part, frequently accused his fellow Catholics of lukewarmness. If our Lord 'loved us so as to consume Himself for us in the fire of His charity,' he wrote in 1866, 'how without great personal sin can we be lukewarm towards Him? Cold returns for warm friendship are intolerable among men.'[32] In *The Eternal Priesthood*, he advises those who would be priests that one of the greatest dangers to their calling is 'lukewarmness'. 'Holiness consists not in doing uncommon things, but in doing all common things with an uncommon fervour.'[33] William Wilberforce would have said 'Amen' to that.

As with Newman, Manning maintained a belief in predestination, although never in the Calvinist sense, and felt that none should ever forget the implications of Jesus' words, 'many called, but few chosen'. Shortly after Pope Pius IX had nominated him as Wiseman's successor as Archbishop of Westminster, Manning wrote in his diary: 'May 29, 1865. It has impressed itself vividly upon me that God has predestinated me to Eternal Life, but that the way is by conformity to His Son.'[34] In *Religio Viatoris*, his miniature apologia for the Catholic faith, a very Evangelical passage is intruded: 'History shows that there ever has been a remnant according to the election of grace.'[35]

Shortly before Manning's ordination, Favell Bevan recorded her assessment of his character. 'I know of no power in which he is deficient. His imagination is warm, his taste refined, his memory retentive and accurate in no common degree; yet judgment holds her rightful supremacy, and gives an air of precocity to his mind ... Pride is the natural accompaniment of talent. This is the ruling passion of H.E.M. One characteristic, however, of a truly great mind is also his – namely, an ardent love of truth.' In words reminiscent of what his mother had said to him during his Oxford days, with faint echoes too of what he had taken so much to heart from the ponderous pages of John Foster, Miss Bevan continued: 'He has courage sufficient to enable him to face the world in arms against him.' Then, in conclusion, a truly prophetic comment: 'He is a complicated creature, and calculated to disappoint expectations in some respects and in some seasons. Yet he may take a flight beyond the warmest hopes of those who wish him well. I fear that he will occasion his friends to lead an unquiet life.'[36]

Manning's career was now set. There would be no looking back. Both his mother and Favell Bevan recognized that he would never undertake anything that 'he did not do'; and one thing is quite sure from the character that had been moulded in these formative years. Nothing that he ever did would be done in half measure.

IV

When Newman entered Trinity College, Oxford in 1817, Manning had barely started school at Streatham; ten years were to elapse before he proceeded to Balliol, somewhat older than his contemporaries (he was nearly twenty). By contrast, Newman was only sixteen, and acutely self-conscious of his lack of years. He had clearly outgrown Dr Nicholas' establishment at Ealing, however, and because of the financial anxieties at home, the sooner he embarked upon his university career the better. Why Oxford, it may be asked, in preference to Cambridge, still the acknowledged breeding-ground of Evangelicals, where Charles Simeon had held sway, together with the Milners and the Venns, the founding-fathers of the Anglican Evangelical revival? The actual decision turned out to be purely fortuitous. Although

Newman himself doubtless felt drawn to Oxford, where Walter
Mayers had received his education, his father happily left the final
choice to his friend, the Revd John Mullens, curate of St James's,
Piccadilly (himself a graduate of Exeter College), who happened
to call at the Newman household as the post-chaise arrived at the
door, its destination still in doubt.[1] Dr Nicholas, on hearing that
his brightest pupil had been matriculated at Trinity, heartily
approved; and Newman himself, looking back years later at one
of the many curious providences that punctuated his career,
described the event as 'the greatest turning-point in his life'.[2]

His first experiences, however, were not all that happy. He was
gauche, and knew that he was. 'Whenever I go out,' he wrote to
his father in June 1817, 'I am stared at, and the other day there
was a party of people laughing at my dress.'[3] He felt himself at a
disadvantage socially and academically; and he was painfully shy
in company. But at least he was honest enough to admit his
distaste for parties, his contempt for the hard-drinking gentlemen-commoners, and his own natural lack of conviviality, which
must have made him seem very priggish to most of his contemporaries. But not to his tutor Thomas Short who, seeing his
promise and admiring his strength of character, helped to build
up his confidence and encouraged him, while still under age, to
aspire to his first academic distinction, a Trinity Scholarship, in
May 1818. The other supremely redeeming feature of what
would otherwise have been an unhappy and lonely undergraduate career was the forging, practically on first acquaintance, of a
deep and lasting friendship with his contemporary, John Bowden. It was in Newman's nature, then and ever afterwards, to
draw strength and confidence from an intimacy of understanding
with one close friend; acquaintances, by comparison, hardly
mattered. In a scholar's gown, and with the companionship of
Bowden, he could now embark upon ventures reminiscent of his
later years at Ealing – producing a periodical called *The Undergraduate*, and even proposing in its pages the establishment of a
university debating club (the Union had not yet been founded). It
came to nothing, and one cannot believe that Newman would
have wished it long life, because debating was actually anathema
to him. He never found it easy to think on his feet, and – as a don
– strongly disapproved of undergraduate debating. Such societies
were 'spouting clubs', he thought, in which Oxonians aped the
habits of German students.[4]

Newman's undergraduate career, then, was almost as different from Manning's as could be conceived – even to the ironically cruel fate that overtook him in his Schools in December 1820, when he was unclassed in mathematics and placed 'under the line' (the lower division of the second class, there being no 'thirds' and 'fourths' in those days) in Classics. It was a result grossly unjust to his actual abilities and to his prodigious efforts of preparation. He had overworked, of course; and viva-voce examinations, which formed the major part of the ordeal, never saw him at his best, so that he became tongue-tied and confused.[5] In retrospect, he put part of the blame on the Trinity tutorial system for its failure to emulate the coaching methods of some of the other colleges, and notably Oriel.[6] Nevertheless, it was a bitter pill to swallow. Plans for his future had to be re-thought. His father had hoped that his eldest son would in time be called to the Bar (his name had been entered in the books for Lincoln's Inn in 1819). Quite apart from the fact that such a career was about the least suited to his disposition and particular gifts, academic failure scotched it for good and all. In any event, Newman's own thoughts had been moving towards taking holy orders, on the title of a college Fellowship. That also seemed unrealistic at the time.

Outwardly, Newman took his disappointment nobly, avoiding any indulgence in self-pity. He wrote to his mother, 'a man has just left me, and his last words were "Well, Newman, I would rather have your philosophy, than the high honours to which you have been aspiring".'[7] Inwardly, however, he refused to accept defeat. He could still remain at Oxford, for the Trinity scholarship had some years to run; he could eke out some sort of living by taking private pupils; and there was still open to him just one way by which the disastrous collapse in Schools could be overcome. He could enter the lists for a Fellowship at Oriel, the one and only college in Oxford that might be prepared to overlook a candidate's poor showing in Schools, just because its own competitive examination was so notoriously tough that success in it was reckoned to atone for all. As the world knows, this is exactly what he did, and – not without the timely interposition of a comforting providence (when he spotted the motto on a coat of arms in a window in Oriel hall which read *Pie repone te*, taking it as addressed to himself to calm his nerves)[8] – he wonderfully succeeded. The three bells of Trinity rang out through Oxford to proclaim the triumph. The date was 12 April 1822, the second 'turning-point of his life', he recorded in his journal; 'and of all days most memorable'.[9]

Oriel was, by general esteem, the first college in Oxford during the 1820s, although not all its rivals respected the means by which it had become so. The formidable competition for its prize Fellowships was one reason, especially when the College so perversely ignored the credentials of the Class Lists by selecting the modestly-placed in preference to those with Firsts. The other was the reputation of the Fellowship body itself. Certainly Thomas Arnold and John Keble were recognized as brilliant individual scholars, but both had settled out of Oxford at the time that Newman was elected. Still in the ascendancy, however, as the resident group of Fellows, were those who were labelled within the university as the 'Noetics' – moderate High Churchmen with a reputation for disputatiousness and a determination to employ the tools of logic to think things through to their first principles. Such were Edward Copleston, the Provost; the bluff and iconoclastic Richard Whately, later Archbishop of Dublin; Edward Hawkins, soon to succeed Copleston as Provost; and Joseph Blanco White (not actually a Fellow, but a member of the Senior Common Room), a former Catholic priest who had fallen foul of the hierarchy in Spain and had come to England to be ordained as an Anglican – a quiet, persuasive scholar whom H. P. Liddon described as 'the real founder of the modern latitudinarian school in the English Church'.[10] As an influence within Oxford, the heyday of the Noetics was passing, and the men whom they elected to join them as Fellows during the 1820s were to be the instrument of their effective demise. It is sufficient merely to mention some of their names: John Henry Newman, Edward Bouverie Pusey, Richard Hurrell Froude and Robert Isaac Wilberforce.

But this was in the future; and Newman, as a probationary Fellow without dividend for his first year, knew that his election had been a close-run thing. His examiners – according to Copleston – had not rated him 'even a good classical scholar', while deeming him 'in mind and powers of composition, and in taste and knowledge . . . decidedly superior to some competitors'.[11] He had, therefore, to prove himself, and he was profoundly over-awed by the company that he joined. It was ever so with Newman. On a change of situation, or in the company of people he had not met before, he was overcome with apprehensions. So it had been when he first went to school; he had suffered similar qualms on entering Trinity; the same was to happen when he first became a Roman Catholic, and even more so on his first visit, as a convert, to Rome. His confidence evaporated. It was a weakness that his mother had noticed when he was considering competing for the Oriel Fellowship. 'Your fault is want of self-confidence, and a dissatisfaction with yourself, that you cannot exceed the bounds of human nature.'[12] Mrs Manning had seen in *her* son exactly the opposite, and this difference between the two men was to assume a significant proportion in their respective careers in the Catholic Church.

On his reception into the Oriel Common Room, Newman met John Keble for the first time; indeed, he sat next to him at dinner that evening. He nearly sank into the ground with nerves, but the great man did his best to put him at his ease. Then there came the dreadful moment when he had to sit in the company of the other senior and eminent men and try to hold his own intelligently among them. Newman recalled: 'It disconcerted them to find that with all their best efforts they could not draw him out or get him to converse. He shrank into himself, when his duty was to meet their advances.' When he steeled himself to speak, he 'had a near escape of being a stutterer'. He agonized over his gaucheness afterwards, conscious of having committed solecisms 'whether actual or imagined'.[13]

What was to be done with him? The Fellows, realizing that he had to be taken in hand, passed him over to the tutelage of Richard Whately, a man who prided himself on penetrating the barriers of 'raw' and 'bashful youths'.[14] As Sheridan Gilley has written, 'there was no way of being shy with Whately'.[15] He liked nothing better than a good listener; and his talk was shrewdly directed to finding some common ground which would in time evoke a response. Whately's kindness to Newman seemed limitless. He liked the young man, and his affection was speedily and gratefully reciprocated. They went out for walks and talks together; Whately began finding helpful tasks for the younger man to undertake jointly with him, such as assisting him with an article on logic for the *Encyclopaedia Metropolitana*, thereby providing Newman with his first instruction in a tool that he was to use with devastating effect in years to come. He enabled him to earn some money, too, by writing articles for the *Encyclopaedia*, which paid the princely sum of five guineas a page. Soon Whately was able to assure Copleston and his colleagues that they had made no mistake in electing Newman to a Fellowship; indeed, he had proved to be 'the clearest-headed man he knew'.[16] Although Whately went out of residence in the summer of 1822, on the occasion of his marriage, they kept in touch with each other, and on his return in 1825 to become Principal of St Alban Hall, he further showed his respect for Newman by inviting him to join him as Vice-Principal.

By this time Newman had been ordained (to deacon's orders on Trinity Sunday, 1824, and to priest's orders on the same occasion a year later). He had accepted the curacy of St Clement's, a rapidly expanding parish beyond Magdalen Bridge, over which he had effectively to take sole charge because of the infirmity of the Rector. He had to face up to another access of nerves over preaching for the first time, the more so because he received complaints that he was inaudible, which became a constant worry to him thereafter;[17] he had to conquer his shyness over parish visiting, which he undertook assiduously, earning a reputation, both from his sermons and from his individual admonitions, for strictness and severity. Pusey passed on to him a comment from Charles Lloyd, Regius Professor of Divinity, whose lectures they were both attending at the time, that his parishioners liked him very much but thought that 'I damned them too much'.[18] Newman's reply to those who accused him of preaching a harsh doctrine was 'Comfort is a cordial, but no one drinks cordials from morning to night.'[19]

In September 1824 his father died, which made Newman not only the breadwinner of the family (he had effectively been so since his election at Oriel) but also their guide and counsellor, not the easiest of tasks with such wayward brothers as Charles and Francis, as it was to turn out. Contemplating the passing of his father, Newman reiterated a conviction which was first borne in upon him at the time of his conversion in 1816, that 'it was the will of God that I should lead a single life ... that my calling in life would require such a sacrifice as celibacy involved.'[20] He mused again: 'When I die, shall I be followed to the grave by my children? My mother said the other day she hoped to live to see me married, but *I* think I shall either die within College walls, or a Missionary in a foreign land – no matter where, so that I die in Christ.'[21]

His religious views were in a state of flux when he wrote this. In the course of his diaconate he admitted that he had been forced to think again about the Evangelical distinction between 'real' and 'nominal' Christians, and also about the doctrine of baptismal regeneration.

> My feelings as to those ordained with me [he recorded in his journal on 29 May 1825] was somewhat different from those I had this time [last] year. I hope I was not exactly uncharitable then; still I certainly thought that there might be some among them who were coming to the Bishop out of their own heads and without the Spirit of God. But when I looked round today, I could hope and trust that none was altogether destitute of divine influence, and, tho' there was difference of spirituality, yet all might be in some degree spiritual ... Then, I thought the *onus probandi* lay with those who asserted an individual to be a *real* Christian; and now I think it lies with those who deny it. Yet I do not even now actually maintain that the Spirit always or generally accompanies the very act of baptism, only that the sacrament brings them into the kingdom of grace, where the Spirit will certainly meet them with His influences.[22]

Almost from the date of his election as a Fellow, his colleagues had been gently undermining the Evangelical views he had imbibed from Walter Mayers. One, William James, in 1823, had disturbed him greatly by impressing upon him the doctrine of the Apostolical Succession. Whately pointed him to the *Letters on the Church by an Episcopalian* (anonymously published, but actually the work of Whately himself) to wean him away from overmuch respect for the Establishment, asserting the independence of the Church from the State, which had no right to interfere in spiritual concerns; but the major personal influence during the period of Whately's absence, and especially during Newman's short period at St Clement's, was Edward Hawkins. It was Hawkins who continued the work initiated by Whately, encouraging Newman to emerge from his shell, especially during the many talks they had together during the Long Vacation of 1824, when they happened to be practically the only Fellows in residence. 'He was the first who taught me to weigh my words, and to be cautious in my statements,' Newman later acknowledged.[23] Hawkins was a true precisian, and a stern critic of Newman's early sermons. He sent him off to read J. B. Sumner's *Treatise on Apostolical Preaching* with the intention that he should obtain a clearer understanding of the doctrine of baptismal regeneration. Most important of all, he impressed upon him the primary importance of the formularies of the Church – the Catechism and the Creeds – as the surest guide to Christian doctrine. From Hawkins, Newman first took to heart that it was the Church's role to teach, and that the Scriptures verified or confirmed the Church's teaching, and that this relationship was itself based on scriptural authority (Thess. 2:15), where the oral apostolical tradition receives such sanctification that we must accept that 'scripture can never be fully intelligible without aid and guidance'.[24] This, Newman conceded, 'was to strike at the root of the principle on which the Bible Society was set up':[25] as a good Evangelical, he had dutifully enrolled himself in its Oxford Association.

Over the same period, Newman had discovered the writings of Bishop Butler. He first read Butler's *Analogy of Religion* in June 1825; and for him, as for so many of those who were to make their mark in the cultural and theological life of Victorian England, once read, never forgotten, and never spoken of thereafter save in a tone of hushed reverence. So total became Newman's discipleship that he was later to argue, in an article for the *British Critic* on 'The Catholicity of the Anglican Church' (in January 1840), that the fact that Butler was and remained an Anglican was a sufficient credential in itself: 'What a Note of the Church is the mere production of a man like Butler, a pregnant fact much to be meditated upon.'[26]

Butler's teaching that 'probability is the very guide of life' was to be developed by Newman in almost every philosophical and theological work that he wrote. In 1825, however, Newman was struggling, for the first of many times in his life, to define the relationship between Faith and Reason, provoked by insistent letters from his brother Charles, who had recently plunged into unbelief and was pressing his clerical brother to defend his corner. Poor Charles – perhaps the only contribution of consequence that this unfortunate man made during his whole life was to force his extraordinarily patient brother to work out on paper the grounds of his belief. In these letters, for instance, occur the germs of Newman's later Oxford University Sermons and the *Grammar of Assent*. 'I consider the rejection of Christianity to arise from a fault of the *heart*, not of the *intellect*,' he wrote to Charles on 24 March 1825; and then, in the course of a series of questions, he asks him 'If there is a moral Governor of the world, is there any great antecedent improbability in his revealing his will to man?' and, 'Is there any great antecedent improbability of miracles being wrought?'[27] This letter to Charles was written just before Newman embarked upon his reading of Butler's *Analogy*. It is little wonder that he felt that he had struck gold.

Delving deeper, he found yet more gold: a new rationale of the role of sacraments within the Christian Church; and this, as Dr Härdelin was the first to point out, required digging very deep into the *Analogy* because, on the face of it, the book 'is a work of apologetics and of moral philosophy, but definitely not of ecclesiology'.[28] What appealed to Newman in the *Analogy* was 'its inculcation of a visible Church, the oracle of truth and a pattern of sanctity, of the duties of external religion, and of the historical character of Revelation',[29] and he found this in Butler because – in a sense – this was precisely what he was looking for: the relationship between religion as 'an inward principle seated in the heart' and 'the use of outward rites and observances', which Newman developed more fully in an early sermon 'On the Sacraments', preached for the first time in September 1826.[30] Furthermore, in the second part of the *Analogy* Butler supplied strong arguments, based on analogy, to support the 'notion of a mediator between God and man'.[31]

Add all these doctrinal ingredients together and there would seem to be precious little left of the original Evangelical deposit that Newman had gained from Walter Mayers. But he had not yet fallen under the spell of John Keble. In 1826 and 1827, as he was casting off more and more of his Evangelical notions, he was, according to his own analysis, beginning to look more like the last of the Noetics than a pioneer of a revitalized High Churchmanship. In a sermon preached in Oriel chapel in May 1827, 'On the Mediatorial Kingdom of Christ', he caused something of a stir by the 'freedom of language' he employed about the Athanasian Creed, prompting Whately to describe him as an Arian because of his depreciation of the divinity of Christ.[32] If this gave him furiously to think, he was then severely jolted out of this transitory flirtation with theological liberalism by the intervention, yet again, of providence. Two providences, in fact.

Dwight Culler has commented on the series of 'acute psychological crises' that occurred from time to time during Newman's life,[33] the first of which, when aged 15, coinciding with his experience of conversion. The second took place on 26 November 1827, when he was overcome by nervous illness while officiating for the first time as an examiner in Schools, so that he completely collapsed in the course of conducting a viva with one of the candidates and had to withdraw from the rest of the examination. He described his symptoms as 'not pain, but a twisting of the brain, of the eyes. I felt my head inside was made up of parts . . . I once or twice tried to count my pulse, but found it quite impossible; before I had got to 30, my eyes turned round and inside out, all of a sudden.'[34] Some six weeks later, on 5 January 1828, he was summoned to the death-bed of his beloved sister Mary. Not for the last time, Newman interpreted the death of someone dear to him as a personal providence. He had loved her so much, he told Robert Wilberforce, that he had 'almost antici-pated her death . . . Yet I rejoice, . . . because whom God loveth He chastiseth, and because I feel I am especially honoured by him and cared for, and that he is assuredly training me for usefulness here, and glory hereafter.'[35] (So cast down was Newman when he wrote this that – very rarely for him – he omitted to use capital letters in the pronouns standing for the Almighty.)

Geoffrey Faber has some rather cutting things to say about Newman's possibly exaggerated grief over Mary's death, espe-cially the egotistical strain in his meditations and reflections.[36] This is neither fair nor sensitive. To look upon the loss of a loved one as a personal chastening was not at all unusual among those who doubted not for a second that the departed was safely in the arms of God, so that the suffering of death fell upon those who were bereaved. Many of the people who figure in this story were to endure similar afflictions – Keble, Pusey, Samuel and Robert Wilberforce, and, perhaps most significantly of all, Henry Man-ning – and each in his way interpreted the loss, however bitter, as the fulfilment of a divine purpose to which it was his duty to respond. Perhaps Faber's comments have this degree of truth in them, that Newman's reaction to bereavement was exceptional even in an age which felt no inhibitions about outward express-ions of grief. Father Marvin O'Connell's treatment of this episode is rather more sympathetic: 'Somehow Newman's sorrows seemed to have a depth, an almost cosmic character to them, which other men could not reach . . . Or maybe [his] immense self-awareness made him feel such things with an intensity which most men escape. More likely the whole subject is something for the mystics to unravel.'[37]

The immediate effect of Mary's death on Newman was to induce a sense of shame over his recent exhibitions of intellectual pride. If Evangelicalism had failed to answer and Noeticism had threatened to imperil his orthodoxy, to whom should he now turn as a spiritual guide? Could it have been yet another providence that Mary, during her short illness, had found consolation in Keble's recently-published set of poems, *The Christian Year*?[38]

Although Newman had met the 'sweet singer in our Israel' several times during his early years at Oriel, it was not until August 1828, when he went to stay with Keble at Fairford, that he acknowledged their growing intimacy. By this time, however, his sympathies for both the substance and the tone of the traditional Anglican High Churchmanship which Keble represented had been steadily growing. The seed had actually been sown when he attended the lectures of Charles Lloyd during 1823 and 1824, although he did not recognize it fully at the time. Lloyd, who was described by Frederick Oakeley as a divine 'considerably in advance of the high churchmen of his time',[39] served to confirm, in his bluff but kindly teasing of the young Evangelical in his class, the lessons that Newman was already receiving during his walks and talks with Whately and Hawkins. In 1824 he was studying the annotated edition of the Book of Common Prayer, compiled by the 'Evangelical-baiter',[40] Richard Mant, which aroused an interest in the writings of the Caroline Divines and of the early Church Fathers. In May 1826 he wrote to his sister Jemima that he was considering embarking upon a detailed study of the vast field of patristic literature,[41] for which – a few months later – he invoked the help of Pusey, who was studying at the time in Germany and was handily placed to obtain the particular works that Newman required.[42]

Not that Pusey, at this stage of his life, was even a fellow-traveller along the road that Newman was taking. Elected to an Oriel Fellowship a year later than Newman, he had caused his senior colleague a little puzzlement at first. As Newman recalled years later to Pusey's biographer, H. P. Liddon, 'he struck me so much as being the first good man I had come very near who was not an Evangelical'.[43] But Pusey's determination to become a proficient Orientalist, which was to earn him the Regius Professorship of Hebrew in 1828, had led him for a while to appear as the disciple of the German biblical critics whose researches were as uncongenial to High Churchmen as they were to Evangelicals. No one could have supposed in the 1820s that this was the man who would later give his name, if not at his own wish, as the popular label for latter-day Tractarianism.

The man who led Newman to Keble was Richard Hurrell Froude, elected Fellow of Oriel in March 1826. With Froude, Newman established the second close friendship of his life, and of all his intimacies the most intense and the most significant. It was also both improbable and unique. Their temperaments were wholly different, as indeed were their backgrounds. Froude was the son of the Archdeacon of Totnes, whose household was untouched by Evangelical influences. He was volatile and flamboyant, yet also introspective and subject to fits of deep melancholia, a compound, as a recent biographer has described him, of 'godliness, manliness, Toryism and Romanticism'.[44] Although he was deeply religious and could be morbidly superstitious, he had no taste for theology, and his religious views, which were always passionately embraced, were governed largely by sentiment or ethos rather than by serious study. He was capable of veneration for causes and figures near to his heart, and of dismissive contempt for anything alien to him. He had found in Keble a father-figure and loved him dearly; conversely, a sentimental rather than informed attachment to all things medieval and Gothic led him to deplore the Anglican Reformers, and he therefore despised them.

Meeting Newman for the first time, he could make nothing of him. He was so shy, for one thing. 'I . . . have got far enough to see that he is not my sort,' he declared.[45] But gradually the barriers were broken down. They discovered certain sentiments in common – the disposition to believe too much rather than too little, their shared fascination with Keble's sober and reserved religiosity (Froude taking the credit for encouraging Newman to acquaint himself better with all that Keble had to teach); above all, their belief that a vocation to holy orders required a commitment to the celibate life. Newman needed some working on, Froude admitted; not over celibacy, but over his undue lingering respect for the Anglican Reformers. He had done his best to wean Keble away from Cranmer and was determined to do the same with Newman.[46]

It is in this respect – the enduring resolve of Froude to mould Newman's mind in conformity with his own way of thinking – that the uniqueness of this particular friendship consisted. Writing in the *Apologia* about these years, Newman made the enigmatic observation that 'my habitual feeling then and since has been, that it was not I who sought friends, but friends who sought me'.[47] This is surely open to question, bearing in mind his need at various stages of his life for close intimacy. He had enjoyed such a friendship with John Bowden, and this appears to have been an equal friendship. After Froude's early death in 1836, there would be other intimacies, the closest and longest-lasting being his relationship with Ambrose St John. But in all these subsequent friendships Newman was to be the dominant partner. Only once in his life did he allow a friend to exercise a superior influence over him – and that was in his relationship with Hurrell Froude.

Not until 1829 was the transformation in Newman virtually complete. His sister Harriet observed the change in a letter dated 14 November 1829; 'We have long since read your two Sermons,' she wrote. 'They are very high church. I do not think I am near so high, and do not quite understand them yet.'[48] On 8 June 1830 Newman withdrew his name from the Bible Society, almost a symbolical act of severance from the Evangelical party, because – as he explained later – only 'shreds and tatters' of that earliest affiliation had survived in his preaching since his ordination.[49] By 1830, however, his circumstances had greatly changed. He had been appointed to a College tutorship in 1826. Within two years he was actively involved in the election of a new Provost, on the appointment of Edward Copleston to the bishopric of Llandaff. There were only two possible successors to Copleston – Edward Hawkins, then Vicar of St Mary's, and John Keble. At least Newman was not at that stage and on this issue willing to be influenced by Froude, whose championship of Keble was both ardent and immediate, supported also – for a short while – by another of the Oriel tutors, Robert Wilberforce. Pusey and Newman, however, both doubted (perhaps wrongly) Keble's firmness on matters of College discipline, and Newman in particular had high hopes that Hawkins, who was a stern disciplinarian, would support him in his own tutorial battles with the rowdy and idle gentlemen-commoners, for whom he had as great a distaste now as when he was a Trinity undergraduate. On hearing the views of Newman and Pusey, Keble withdrew his candidature, and Hawkins was duly elected in January 1828. What might have been! Pusey lamented in after years. 'The whole of the later history of our Church might have been changed had we been wiser. . .To us it became a sorrow of our lives.'[50]

The immediate result for Newman, however, was that he

succeeded Hawkins as Vicar of St Mary's in March 1828; another turning-point in his life, because the church of St Mary the Virgin, centrally situated in the middle of the High, was the customary setting for the University Sermon, and from its pulpit over the next fifteen years (and in his afternoon lectures in the Adam de Brome chapel) the new incumbent was to exercise an influence over the resident members of the University quite as great as the effect he was to achieve in his polemical writings addressed to the wider audience throughout the Anglican Church. Newman himself believed that the appointment to St Mary's had more significance still. It marked the completion of his education in self-confidence. 'It was to me like the feeling of spring weather after winter: and, if I may so speak, I came out of my shell.'[51]

As he emerged from his shell, however, the reserve and deference of earlier years turned only too swiftly to a somewhat unbecoming belligerence. It is understandable, in a way. For years Newman had held himself back, out of shyness and also out of a genuine recognition that he had much still to learn. But now he had an acknowledged position. He had discovered in himself the confidence that he could more than hold his own in company and in front of an audience, so that, given a cause worth fighting for, he could prove to the world that he was a force to be reckoned with, especially perhaps seeking to prove it to those who had been so conscious of his former inadequacies. He was about to bite the very hands of those who had fed him.

The first such cause was the issue of the re-election of Sir Robert Peel as Member for the University in 1829, following his honourable resignation when he changed his stance over Catholic Emancipation, a measure which he had been elected to resist but which he had come to realize was both expedient and inevitable. Newman, with Keble and Froude, took up the cudgels against him, agitating vigorously within the College and the University on behalf of the rival Tory candidate, Sir Robert Inglis. It was almost as if Newman seized upon this issue to demonstrate that his future now lay with his new friends, and that he had need no longer of the friendship and support of Whately, Hawkins and Blanco White, all strong supporters of Peel. It was a typical young man's error, to view the contest in starkly contrasting colours. This was more than the question of Peel's volte-face; Church was opposed to State; indifferentism was challenging orthodoxy. The forces of latitudinarianism, among whom he counted – somewhat unjustly – the Noetics who had patiently guided him in former years, were now to be exposed, defeated and trodden under foot. His language became wildly intemperate. In February 1829 he wrote to his friend, Samuel Rickards, 'it is not pro dignitate nostra to have a Rat our member';[52] Hawkins, to whom he owed so much, was airily dismissed, in a letter to Harriet, as 'our meddling Provost'.[53] And when victory was gained, and Peel defeated, he fairly crowed in triumph. 'We have achieved a glorious victory,' he reported to his mother, '. . . We have proved the independence of the Church and of Oxford.' As to the opposition party, 'their insolence has been intolerable; not that we have done more than laugh at it.'[54] In defending his stance to Jemima, he declared, 'Oxford has never turned with the turn of fortune. Mistaken we may have been, but never inconstant. We kept to the Stuarts in misfortune. Better be bigoted than time-serving.' Then, to explain his own principles more explicitly:

> I am in principle Anti-Catholic – i.e., I think there is a grand attack on the Church in progress from the Utilitarians and Schismatics – and the first step in a long train of events is *accidentally* the granting these claims . . . If granted, something fresh will be asked; say, the unestablishing of the Irish Protestant Church.[55]

Prophetic words, indeed. Dr Peter Nockles, in reviewing this event in its wider context, has rightly observed that 'the rejection of Peel in 1829 marks . . . the origin of the [Oxford] Movement more accurately' than Keble's Assize Sermon in 1833. He also points out that it was a 'body-blow' to the Noetics from which they never really recovered.[56] Sadly, it led to the severance of Newman's friendship with Whately, shortly to leave Oxford to become Archbishop of Dublin. (Newman seems to have expected an invitation from Whately to accompany him there, and made out a list of reasons why he should decline; but in fact no offer was forthcoming.)[57] The man who was most wounded by Newman's actions, however, was Hawkins, who had perhaps rashly assumed that the Fellows of Oriel would follow his lead in supporting Peel, and then discovered that the most active agitator on behalf of Inglis, who had divided the College and caused him personal embarrassment, was one of his College tutors.

This was a factor, although not the principal one, in the second major issue which caused an enduring breach between Newman

and Hawkins: the conflict over the introduction by three of the
Oriel tutors – Newman, Robert Wilberforce and Hurrell Froude –
of a new system of organizing tutorial duties. As with most issues
that divide intelligent men, there was a degree of right on both
sides. It all began with a discussion between Robert Wilberforce
and Newman, when they were together at Brighton in the
summer of 1828 and discovered that they shared certain reservations about the existing tutorial arrangements at Oriel. They
disliked, for instance, the admission of freshmen at different
stages of the year; they felt that, as things stood, the College tutor
was regarded more as a disciplinary officer and lecturer than an
individual tutor to undergraduates with a pastoral responsibility
towards those in their charge. Such pastoral care was surely a
fulfilment of their ordination vows. They therefore favoured a
system whereby each tutor should be able to have a limited
number of pupils assigned to him and that they themselves should
determine the selection, choosing those whom they knew to be
conscientious 'reading men', and over whom they would exercise
both academic and moral supervision. This would have the
double advantage of avoiding teaching in large classes, at which
were present idle gentlemen-commoners, who were not interested in seeking the highest honours (they would be looked
after separately by lectures), and it would also mean that serious
students would be spared from having to pay privately for special
tuition.

Thus described, the suggestions seemed eminently reasonable;
and later that year, when Hawkins was staying with the Wilberforce family at Highwood, Robert Wilberforce put these proposals to him. At the time, Hawkins seemed quite favourably
disposed.[58] After mature reflection, however, he began to see
objections. The first was that it was an invitation to indulge in
favouritism. Tutors would pick the men they wanted to encourage, and leave others – less favoured – to fend for themselves; and
the Provost had a responsibility to the parents of all undergraduates to ensure that their sons received equal treatment.[59] No
doubt he also feared that the moral supervision, conceived as the
fulfilment of an ordination vow, would lead to excessive pressure
on the part of individual tutors to inculcate in the impressionable
young specific religious views, which could amount to proselytism.

His fears were not groundless. Newman, in particular, had
decided to accept a College tutorship on the understanding (given

to him by Keble) that the role was primarily a pastoral one.[60] He certainly took endless pains on behalf of his individual pupils; he could be exacting in his demands, blunt in his moral censures, and emphatic in the advice he offered, always mindful of their spiritual welfare as well as their subsequent performance in Schools. With some he developed close relationships: Tom Mozley (his future brother-in-law), and then, with greater and more lasting intimacy, Samuel Wood (younger brother of the 1st Viscount Halifax), Frederic Rogers (later Lord Blachford) and – closest of all – Henry Wilberforce, the youngest of the three sons of the Emancipator to come to Oriel. There is no doubt that all this was immensely appreciated by the recipients; and when Newman's tutorship had perforce to come to an end, they expressed their appreciation by presenting him with 36 volumes of the writings of the early Church Fathers,[61] and also by maintaining their friendship with him. Nevertheless, as Mark Pattison reflected, when the crisis was over and all three tutors had resigned, Oriel's academic reputation undoubtedly suffered; but at least another fate was averted. If Newman had had his way, Oriel might well have become 'a mere priestly seminary, and not an agent of a university'.[62]

The issue turned into a bitter conflict because it was so ineptly handled. The grossest blunder was the decision of the tutors to introduce their 'reforms' without consulting Hawkins, so that in effect they presented him with a *fait accompli*. This was quite deliberate, too. As Newman was later to explain in his *Autobiographical Memoir*:

> They knew him well enough to be sure that if, instead of acting on their own right ... they proceeded to consult him, he would put his veto upon it, however unnecessarily, and there would be a deadlock in the College administration. They determined then to let the matter take its course, and to leave the Provost to object, if he wished.[63]

And indeed he objected, as he was bound to do. After all, he had only recently become Provost, and the action of the tutors was a direct affront to his authority; and because they had acted in an underhand way, he was the more likely to suspect their motives. He was not alone in taking this view. He consulted his predecessor, the Bishop of Llandaff. Copleston's reaction was emphatic. He entirely rejected the tutors' plea that they were acting 'on their right', i.e., that they were answerable to the University and not to the College in their tutorial capacity. Furthermore, if the tutors persisted in their defiance, the Provost would be entirely within his rights to refuse to offer them any further pupils. He continued: 'From what you say of Newman's religious views, I fear he is impracticable,' adding, in a later letter, 'Newman ought to acknowledge that he has been wrong in practising this reserve towards you. It is utterly inconsistent with every liberal view of the relation in which he stands to the Head of his College.'[64]

Doubtless animosities had been exacerbated by the affair of the Peel re-election. But Newman did not help his cause by the somewhat imperious and aloof tone of his letters. Hawkins tried, by return, to be more friendly and conciliatory, but felt bound to reprove him for expressions in his communications 'which did not become a Fellow writing to the Provost, much less one friend addressing another'.[65] Unfortunately, in the heat of the conflict Newman seemed to forget all claims of friendship towards Hawkins. Later he was to protest that his love for him had never diminished, and – to his credit – on his sick-bed in Sicily, in May 1833, he looked back upon the whole episode with a sense of shame. 'I bitterly blamed myself, as disrespectful and insulting to the Provost, my superior.'[66]

But the damage was done. In the conflict itself, neither side was prepared to give way. Newman was young and obstinate; Hawkins stood on his dignity and on his rights. As Dean Church reflected, when he himself resigned his Oriel tutorship following the fracas in the University over the publication of Tract 90, Hawkins 'is rather a trying person to have to deal with'.[67] The Provost simply followed Copleston's advice, and refused to assign to the three tutors any fresh pupils. The significant result, however, was that Newman was now free to turn to other concerns: to his study of the Fathers, to his writing of the *History of the Arians*, and – in due course – to a notoriously active role in responding to the cry of 'the Church in danger'.

V

He also, in the same year, met Manning for the first time. Within their respective formative years there had been at least superficial parallels in their development, but also evidence of differences in their temperamental dispositions which would be likely to become more pronounced as circumstances gradually drew them closer together.

One common feature, however, suggests itself from a review of their early careers. The closing years of the 1820s saw neither man at his best. Newman, flushed with early success, became for a while bellicose and bossy; also painfully insensitive to the feelings of his former friends. Manning, for his part, before he became a Fellow of Merton, showed similar insensitivity to those to whom he owed the greatest debt, notably John Anderdon, when his hopes for a political career were dashed and he came face to face, for the first time in his life, with adversity. Their relative youthfulness goes some way to explain their reactions; perhaps also, in part, to excuse them. In the next two decades of their lives, however, success and adversity would confront them both; and they would be put more fully to the test.

CHAPTER 2

The Tractarian and the Churchman

'Manning . . . is exceedingly improved since he left Oxford
. . . A year and a half ago he did not know there was such a
thing as a Church.' Henry Wilberforce to J. H. Newman,
1 August 1834

'I am very much convinced that we must be more decidedly
Anglican. I am growing a stiff Anglican.' H. E. Manning to
J. H. Newman, 25 January 1839

I

ON 20 DECEMBER 1869, at the height of the speculations
over the definition of Papal Infallibility at the first Vatican
Council, in which Manning played such an influential role,
Gladstone wrote to Odo Russell, England's unaccredited agent at
Rome: 'It is curious that Manning has so greatly changed his
character; when he was archdeacon with us all his strength was
thought to lie in a governing faculty, and in its wise moderation.
Now he is ever quoted as the Ultra of ultras.'[1] Equally curious,
although Gladstone failed to note it, was the role-reversal, in the
opposite direction, by Newman. In his Anglican days he had
moved to extremes in his attempts to demonstrate the catholicity
of the Church of England, which had led him further and further
away from his original allies, while as a Catholic he became the
major spokesman of the moderate party, doing his utmost to tone
down or to correct the more extravagant claims of the Ultramontanes. What makes this the more remarkable is that, in actual fact,
the characters of the two men hardly changed at all; nor, in

essence, did they change their theological emphases or their sense of priorities. Manning, as Cardinal Archbishop of Westminster, in both his writings and his policies, was still identifiably the former Archdeacon of Chichester; and the Superior of the Birmingham Oratory was unmistakably the same man who had held his congregation in thrall at the church of St Mary the Virgin at Oxford.

Right through the years of excitement and controversy at Oxford in the 1830s and early 1840s, Newman moved at a faster pace than Manning, even to the extent of anticipating his conversion to Rome by six years. This can be seen in each phase of the Oxford Movement, there being three fairly well-defined stages through which the movement passed, each marked by a change in the nature of Newman's personal involvement before he finally accepted that he was being called to forsake the Church of his baptism. In the first phase, Newman was fighting an offensive–defensive action in response to specific dangers faced by the Church, in which he could count as allies both the traditional High Churchmen and at least the more respectable and influential wing of the Evangelicals. It coincided with the publication of the first and most hard-hitting, pithy and polemical of the *Tracts for the Times*, and ended with the furore within the University over Lord Melbourne's appointment of the allegedly heterodox R. D. Hampden to the Regius Professorship of Divinity in February 1836.

In the second phase, Newman attempted a scholarly rationale of the Anglican Church as the *via media* between the corruptions of Rome and the heresies of continental Protestantism, both in terms of ecclesiology and by an exploration into opposing theologies of grace in his *Lectures on Justification* in 1838, by which time the alliance with both the High Church party and the Evangelicals was beginning to disintegrate – the final dissolution taking place following the publication of Froude's *Remains*, also in 1838. During the third phase, Newman changed tack after losing confidence in the validity, and indeed the reality, of the *via media*, and began to seek, sometimes rather desperately, for evidence within the Church of England of such 'notes' of the true Church as seemed to be only too disturbingly manifested within the time-honoured Roman communion. This attempt reached its climax with the publication of the last of the *Tracts for the Times*, the notorious Tract 90 in 1841, the convulsions consequent upon which forced him to retire from the fray and eventually to work out a very different rationale of the true Church, based on the recognition of the essential principle of doctrinal development, exemplified uniquely in the Roman Church.

It had all started with the cry 'the Church in danger'. In the late 1820s and the opening years of the following decade, there seemed to be dangerous foes on every side. The long period of Tory domination was coming to an end, and the Church of England, which could so easily be represented as little better than the Tory party at prayer, was clearly going to be the prime target when the Whigs came to power, drawing strength from what appeared to be an infamous alliance with those whom Newman described as 'Utilitarians and Schismatics'.[2] The Whigs duly won the election of 1830 with a specific mandate to reform the Church. That it was in urgent need of reform, few could honestly doubt; it was riddled with corrupt and uncanonical practices, such as plurality of livings, non-residence, nepotism, simony and grotesque inequalities of income. To the defenders of the Church, however, reform was going to be undertaken by untrustworthy agents. The State would put the Church in order; and the State meant Parliament; and Parliament meant a mixed assemblage of laymen among whom – through recent legislation abolishing the Test and Corporation Acts and emancipating the Roman Catholics – would be dissenters of every creed, all of whom had been sharpening their knives against the privileged body now rendered hopelessly vulnerable to such drastic surgery as Parliament determined.

To make matters worse, the dominant philosophy of the age was against them – the Utilitarianism of Jeremy Bentham, which tested all things and institutions by the criterion of 'usefulness'. Subjected to such a test as this, the unreformed Anglican Church would clearly fail lamentably. In addition, there was an ugly mood abroad among the poorer and deprived classes, taking the form of riots, vandalism and arson. No wonder that churchmen trembled for the dual cause of Church and King as they looked across the waters to France, where revolution had broken out yet again, with the barricades raised in Paris and the Bourbon monarchy expelled. Nor could they count on a united front. Within their own ranks were Whig supporters who seemed little better than apostates – those whose views of the Church were so 'low' or so 'broad' (hence the term 'latitudinarian') that they were prepared to show excessive sympathy to dissenters and a seemingly treacherous willingness to join forces with the reformers. The worst of these was the recently-appointed Headmaster of Rugby School, Thomas Arnold, who in 1833 produced his own blueprint of a restructured and revitalized Church of England, entitled *Principles of Church Reform*. The title was bad enough; the contents, advocating *inter alia* what amounted to a general repudiation of all exclusiveness directed against dissenters (with the exception of Quakers and Roman Catholics), were outrageous.

Suddenly a settled world seemed to have gone mad. In the jeremiads of the clergy and churchmen all these horrors were lumped together as some iniquitous conspiracy – Whigs, Benthamites, schismatics, latitudinarians, the undisciplined populace, progressive ideas (described contemptuously as 'the march of mind'), even disturbing technological advances such as the coming of the railways, which somehow seemed to symbolize the acceleration of these forces of destruction; all these things stood for change, and almost certainly a change for the worse. These fears cut across the not-too-precisely-defined barriers of churchmanship of the times. The Evangelical H. F. Lyte could lament in his hymn 'Abide with me' that 'change and decay in all around I see', and offer up the prayer, 'O Thou who changest not, abide with me'. William Wilberforce viewed with dismay the Reform Bill of 1832: 'I almost tremble for the consequences', he said.[3] His son Samuel wrote to his friend Charles Anderson in 1837:

> For modern liberalism, I abhor it. I think it is the Devil's creed; a heartless steam-engine, unchristian, low, sensual, utilitarian creed which would put down all that is really good and high and noble ... and multiply such miserable comforts as going very fast through the air on a rail-road – and for this purpose it would overturn the Church, that is Christianity, and worship the very Devil if his horns were gold and his tail were a steam engine.[4]

This goes far to explain why, in the early stages of the Oxford Movement, the counter-attack launched against state interference in the affairs of the Church (Erastianism) and against latitudinarianism received so much support from the Evangelicals. Not to a man, of course. There was one wing of the party, known as the 'Recordites' (from their official organ the *Record*), whose admiration for historical puritanism and whose reservations about the scriptural foundation of episcopacy made them very wary of the

Oxford men.[5] But in the early 1830s, as George Landon has put it, 'when Evangelicals were not stressing the need for personal conversion, nor Tractarians the Apostolic succession and corporate holiness, then the two groups sounded much the same'.[6]

It was one of the traditional High Church party, however, who gave classic expression to the fears that lay behind the militant protest that emanated from Oxford. In William Palmer's words:

> We knew not to what quarter to look for support. A Prelacy threatened, and apparently intimidated; a Government making its powers subservient to agitators who avowedly sought the destruction of the Church. The State, so long the guardian of that Church, now becoming its enemy and its tyrant. Enemies within the Church seeking the subversion of its essential characteristics. And what was worst of all, *no principle in the public mind to which we could appeal*.[7]

William Palmer belonged to that class of churchmen whom its critics were wont to describe as 'High and Dry', and to whom Newman and Froude would refer to in their letters under the symbol 'Z', as opposed to the 'X's (the Evangelicals). The chosen label for themselves, with whom they would include Keble (who, if High, was certainly not Dry) was 'apostolical'. The 'Z's were the heirs of those who had kept alight the flame of the Caroline Divines and the Non-Jurors during the eighteenth century, the age – as Newman once described it – 'when love was cold', because so totally rejecting of the mysterious element in religion and so preoccupied with rationalism and the exposition of 'evidences'.[8] The doctrinal content of their teaching was almost indistinguishable from what Newman and Froude derived from Keble: profound respect for the teaching of the early Church Fathers as interpreted by what is called the Vincentian Canon, i.e., the test applied by St Vincent of Lérins in the fifth century to establish the claim to the catholicity of any particular doctrine, that it should have been believed everywhere, always and by all (*Quod ubique, quod semper, quod ab omnibus creditum est*). To this was added a reverential acceptance of the divine authority of the historic episcopate, through the doctrine of Apostolical succession, and – following from this – the strong emphasis in their teaching on the role of the sacraments and a devout acknowledgement of scriptural truths as interpreted by the formularies of the Church, in the Prayer Book, the catechism and the creeds.

The pedigree of the 'Z's can be traced back into the eighteenth century to divines such as William Jones of Nayland and a group known as the Hutchinsonians; but their identity as a party became more marked during the conservative reaction in the aftermath of the French Revolution, especially in a group known as the Hackney Phalanx (or sometimes the Clapton Sect). Their most prominent member was Joshua Watson, himself greatly influenced by the writings of Alexander Knox and John Jebb, Bishop of Limerick, whose anticipation of the doctrines so confidently proclaimed in the early numbers of the *Tracts for the Times* is so striking that the assumption can easily be made that the Tractarians found in this treasury of High Church views all the ammunition that they needed for their campaign.

This was not an influence that either Newman or Froude acknowledged. Knox's writings are quoted only twice in Newman's works;[9] and his references to him in his letters tend to be dismissive. 'I do not know enough of Knox to speak,' he wrote to Robert Wilberforce in June 1838. 'He seems to say dangerous things . . . I should be unwilling to think him more than eclectic, though that is bad enough. Froude did not like him.'[10] He was even stronger in his repudiation of any influence, in a later letter to R. W. Church. 'He had no more to do with us', he wrote, 'than Hampden and Arnold.'[11] It is perhaps significant that in Newman's extensive library, only a single work of Knox found its place.[12] Because their original mentor was Keble, and because they greatly valued their own independence, Newman and Froude were always inclined to distance themselves from the 'Z's – men such as William Palmer, Hugh James Rose, Benjamin Harrison and A. P. Perceval – and there was always a slight undercurrent of misunderstanding between them.

The first 'Z' with whom Newman had any close contact was H. J. Rose, a Cambridge man and one of the most distinguished New Testament scholars of his age. He was also a personal friend of Joshua Watson. In March 1831 Rose launched the *British Magazine*, with the intention that it should become the organ of High Church principles, called into being by the specific perils of the time. In taking this initiative, according to Dean Burgon, Rose has the strongest claim to be regarded as 'the true moving cause of that stirring of the waters' which posterity has tended to count to the credit of Oxford[13] and – because of the combined witness of two Oxonians, Newman and R. W. Church – to John Keble's Assize Sermon of 1833, in particular. The second initiative taken by Rose was to host the conference at his vicarage at Hadleigh in July 1833 (attended by Froude, Palmer, R. C. Trench and Perceval, but not by Newman, who had only just returned from his sick-bed in Sicily) at which the first steps in the campaign to defend the Church were discussed. It was not, however, in this connection at all that Newman first came to know Rose. Unforeseen by either man at the time, an invitation from Rose to Newman in March 1831 to embark upon a history of the early Church Councils was to prove a turning-point in Newman's career of immense significance to the history of the Church. What Newman produced was a history of the Arian controversy in the fourth century: not the subject that Rose had actually asked for, so that he and his co-editor, Archdeacon Lyall, had regretfully to decline it on the grounds that it was too narrow in its scope. Lyall also voiced the objection that there was an incipient Romanist flavour in the handling by Newman of the patristic doctrine of the *disciplina arcani*, the discipline of the secret, or – more explicitly – the doctrine of Reserve in communicating religious knowledge.[14] The book was therefore passed to Rivingtons, who published it in 1833.

Newman's *Arians of the Fourth Century* is probably, nowadays, the least read and studied of all his works. Indeed, he himself expressed dissatisfaction with its imperfections of form in later years.[15] Nevertheless, it is a landmark in the development of Newman's mind and theological understanding. In the first place, he discovered the treasures of the Alexandrian Platonists. 'The broad philosophy of Clement and Origen carried me away,' he wrote in the *Apologia*. 'Some portions of their teaching came like music to my inward ear, as if the response to ideas, which, with little external to encourage them, I had cherished so long.' Everything that he had learnt, studied and felt from his previous experience, and from the personal influences on his life, began to fall into place. 'The exterior world, physical and historical, was but the outward manifestation to our senses of realities greater than itself.' Had he not always felt this, even as a boy, discovering the first confirmation that he was not alone in so regarding material phenomena from his reading of Bishop Butler? 'I suppose it was to the Alexandrian school and to the early Church that I owe in particular what I definitely felt about the Angels ... as carrying on ... the Economy of the Visible World.'[16] This, again, was something he had sensed even in boyhood. He had been instinctively drawn, by temperament, to the doctrine of Reserve. In the writings of the Alexandrian Fathers, he began fully to understand how 'all these so-called Economies or dispensations ... are but condescensions to the infirmity and peculiarity of our minds, shadowy representations of realities which are incomprehensible to creatures such as ourselves.'[17] In the figures and the contests of the great issues that divided Alexandria and Antioch, Athanasius and Arius, Newman could not fail to discern parallels with the times in which he was living. Indeed, as Stephen Thomas has shown in his masterly analysis of Newman's first serious study of the phenomenon of early Christian heresy, it suited his rhetorical purposes to search for analogies. Much of the narrative of the bitter debates culminating in the Council of Nicaea in 325 was 'also an oblique satire upon liberalism of his own age'. He was deliberately 'trying to persuade his contemporaries of present dangers by a skilful comparison with Christian Antiquity.'[18] In his study of the Arians, Newman also made his first deep acquaintance with the figure who was to become his archetypal hero and saint – Athanasius. He had, however, met one saint in the flesh – John Keble – a man who, once roused, might be for the Church of England a 'second Ambrose'.[19]

Keble – so like the 'Z's in some respects, yet so unlike in others. Wherein lay the difference? It has been customary to represent Keble as the static element in the Oxford Movement, standing always in the ancient ways, offering nothing original or creative of his own. Yet no one contributed more to what Christopher Dawson has described as 'the moral ideal of Tractarianism', which 'is neither the mystical spirituality of the Catholic tradition, nor the lush emotional pietism of Evangelicalism, but a via media of sanctity which has a severe beauty of its own'.[20] Then again, the doctrine of Reserve was central to everything he said, wrote and did. It would appear from some of his early unpublished sermons, preached at St Clement's, that Newman did not actually learn this patristic doctrine from Keble himself;[21] nevertheless, there was something in the very ethos of the man that captivated him, most especially his shrinking from anything remotely irreverent or vulgar in speaking of sacred things, the temper and tone of his religious poetry, and his understanding of the relationship between the religious and the poetic, all of which in their way were manifestations of the doctrine itself.

'Reserve', or the *disciplina arcani*, embraces two different but related attributes of the communication of divine truths. The first is the actual deliberate holding back of certain aspects of the revelation, on the principle that some of the Christian mysteries are too sacred to be conveyed to those who are in no fit state to receive them. Meat is not offered to infants who require to be nourished on milk. As Newman himself expressed it, in his study of the Arians, with reference to St Paul in his first epistle to the Corinthians, he

> speaks of the difference of doctrine suited respectively to neophytes and confirmed Christians, under the analogy of the difference of food proper for the old and young; which arises, not from the arbitrary will of the Dispenser, but from the necessity of the case, the more sublime truths of revelation affording no nourishment to the souls of the unbelieving or unstable.[22]

The second meaning of 'reserve' is best expressed by the word 'economy', and this, R. C. Selby argues, becomes more prominent in Newman's writings during the 1830s[23] – the notion that a truth may have to be conveyed by the process of accommodation out of respect for the 'feelings and prejudices of the hearer, in leading him to the reception of a novel or unacceptable doctrine'.[24] A physician would do the same, in deference to the condition of his patient, vouchsafing what may only actually be a half-truth.[25] Newman was aware that this could be open to abuse and the accusation of priestcraft, and it was precisely this device of priestly accommodation that inspired Kingsley's later attack on Newman for giving credence to the unmanly notion that 'truth, for its own sake, was no virtue'.

It can be seen from this how naturally poetry could become the vehicle for conveying religious truth in a veiled, mysterious and accommodating form. As Walter Lock has expressed it, to Keble,

> poetry and religion are at one, and they demand one and the same temper of mind ... Poetry, like religion, hides its deepest truths and reveals them only to the pure in heart, to those who love them enough to press into their secrets. Thus poetry rises almost to the dignity of a Sacrament, with its outward visible words and inward spiritual truth.[26]

It is no coincidence that the three Tractarians who were most influenced by the doctrine of Reserve in communicating religious knowledge were John Keble, Isaac Williams (who wrote two tracts under that title) and Newman himself; and that the first two of them were respected, both by their contemporaries and by posterity, chiefly as religious poets, and that Newman was the major contributor to the *Lyra Apostolica*, a collection of poems, originally offered for publication in Rose's *British Magazine*, the purpose of which was – in Newman's words – 'to bring out certain truths and facts, moral, ecclesiastical and religious'. While Newman hoped that the poems, if they did not rival *The Christian Year* in terms of the beauty of the poetry, would exhibit a 'greater freedom and clearness' than Keble's,[27] nevertheless the genre was exactly the same, as was their religious temper.

The phenomenal success of Keble's *The Christian Year* was one of several influences abroad (the writings of Coleridge were another) which encouraged Newman in his belief that the Whigs, the Utilitarians and the latitudinarians were not by any means assured of success when they turned their weapons against the Church; and that the time was ripe for appealing to some indefinite yearning in the hearts of many who craved for something at once richer and warmer than the cold conceits of the 'Age of Reason'; that which spoke of mystery, the transcendental and the arcane; quests and sentiments that the eighteenth century had seemed so much to undervalue, to its great loss. This, of course, is the language of the Romantic Movement, and if one wishes to find it put into words by one who lived through it at its height, one need look no further than Newman's own attempt to describe how, in the early 1830s, there had arisen 'a growing tendency towards the character of mind and feeling of which Catholic doctrines are the just expression'.[28] In this delicately-expressed passage, the prose is almost as elusive as the idea that he is endeavouring to explain:

Of course every event in human affairs has a beginning; and a beginning implies a when, and a where, and a by whom, and a how. But except in these necessary circumstances, the phenomenon in question is in a manner quite independent of things visible and historical. It is not here or there; really it has no progress, no causes, no fortunes; it is not a movement, it is a spirit, it is a spirit afloat, neither 'in the secret chambers' nor 'in the desert', but everywhere. It is within us, rising up in the heart where it was least expected, and working its way, though not in secret, yet so subtly and so impalpably, as hardly to admit of precaution or encounter, on any ordinary human rules of opposition. It is an adversary in the air, a something one and entire, a whole wherever it is, unapproachable and incapable of being grasped, as being the result of causes far deeper than political or other visible agencies, – the spiritual awakening of spiritual wants.[29]

So, in December 1832, when Newman, having completed his book on the Arians, set sail for a Mediterranean tour with Hurrell Froude, who had been advised by his doctor to seek warmer climes for a while, all the pieces were on the board in preparation for the conflict to come. As they made their way to Gibraltar, Malta, Corfu, Sicily, Naples and Rome over the next three months, various bulletins reached them to arouse their militant spirit. The Whigs, they were told, were proposing to introduce legislation to reform the Irish Church by suppressing two archiepiscopal and eight episcopal sees (and, in so doing, addressing themselves to the greatest scandal of the unreformed Church, in its retention of an extensive and well-endowed hierarchy to minister to a tiny minority of Protestants within that predominantly Catholic land). 'Well done, my blind Premier', Newman fulminated in a letter to his mother. 'Confiscate and rob, till, like Samson, you pull down the political structure on your own head, tho' without his deliberate purpose and his good cause!'[30] To his ex-pupil, George Ryder, he declared that the only good to arise from 'the accursed Whig spoliation bill' was that it would precipitate a crisis, and then, anticipating his own words in the first of the *Tracts for the Times*, he wrote: 'The time is coming when every one must choose his side.'[31]

He was sent details of Arnold's *Principles of Church Reform*, and his response to this reveals well the true polarization of issues behind the Oxford Movement. Certainly Arnold's proposals for a union with the Dissenters seemed radical at the time. As Whately observed, 'the chief difference, as it seems to me, between Arnold and the rest is, that our older divines and politicians were for driving the flock by force into the fold, and he for building the fold round the whole of the scattered flock.'[32] That is to say, the principle of inclusiveness was ranged against exclusiveness. But the opposition went deeper than this. As Terence Kenny has observed, Arnold's proposed reforms 'struck at the roots of Newman's whole religious and political system'.[33] Arnold had no sympathy with dogma; to Newman, dogma, and the dogmatic principle, lay at the very heart of religion; Arnold abhorred the 'wickedness' of Toryism;[34] Newman dismissed the Whigs as 'vile vermin'.[35] What Arnold appeared to be saying was that the main function of the Church within the State was to make men good members of society; to Newman, this smacked of Utilitarianism, judging the Church by the criterion of usefulness. Apart from the high moral tone in the preaching and writing of both men, it is difficult to find any principle on which they could have stood together.

Samuel Rickards, Rector of Ulcombe, and a good friend of the Newman family, prided himself on his skills as a graphologist; and on one occasion made a review of the character of Newman's brother Francis from a specimen of his handwriting. There was much talent there, but some marked weaknesses as well, among them a closed mind through his unwillingness to listen to the opinions of others. 'In consequence of this defect he has many crude notions,' Newman related to his mother. '. . . The hand bears a considerable resemblance to Arnold's, a resemblance which I have made much of in giving his character.'[36]

Newman certainly made much of *The Principles of Church Reform*, even though he had never actually read the pamphlet. 'The contents . . . seem to be so atrocious that I am quite unable to talk calmly about it,' he wrote to Jemima from Rome in March 1833.[37] 'That precious Dr Arnold is for making us pig three in a bed with the Baptists and Socinians!' he commented a month later.[38] Then, unfortunately, some words let slip in a conversation at Rome in the company of Froude and his father and two Oriel friends, Edward Neale and Anthony Grant, reached Arnold's ears in the roundabout way casual and unguarded comments sometimes do. The German historian Niebuhr had been mentioned, Neale pointing out that 'Arnold considered him to be a Christian'; to which Newman had replied, 'but Arnold must first show (or prove . . .) that he is one himself'.[39] Not surprisingly, Arnold was profoundly hurt. He wrote to his informant (Anthony Grant),

> I cannot allow a calumny of this nature to proceed from a member of my own College without strong and direct remonstrance . . . My feelings towards N. are those of respect for his general character, and of kindliness for the sake of our common ties. But we must not throw about fire carelessly; and whether he or I are right in our opinion is a question; but it is no question at all, whether evil speaking, imputations of motives, and claiming a monopoly of Christian knowledge and Christian humility, be or be not offences against Christian charity.[40]

Newman did not handle the situation well. A letter of apology, acknowledging a jest in bad taste, might well have settled the matter. He made two mistakes. In the first place, he never wrote to Arnold himself; in the second, in his reply to Anthony Grant he tried to defend himself by shifting some of the blame, in pointing out 'that there are questions which it is as unbecoming to ask as it is unmanly not to answer'. One suspects, too, that Arnold would not have thought any more highly of Newman for saying, in the same letter, that 'I have no recollection of the words attributed to me', when clearly, from his ensuing defence of them, he remembered very well indeed.[41] Ian Ker has described this response as 'the first of many superb snubs Newman was to administer in his long career as a controversialist'.[42] That is as may be; at the same time, Newman then, and on other occasions thereafter, did not always serve his cause well by needlessly provoking resentment and thereby creating powerful enemies.

With all this evidence that events were fast moving to some sort of climax at home, Newman was anxious to return. He had seen enough of Rome not to like it; nevertheless, he came away with those mingled feelings of admiration and distaste that seemed to be the stock response of Anglicans to their first encounter with Roman Catholicism at its very fount. He was determined, however, to return to Sicily alone, drawn by the beauty of the landscape, which had seemed to him the nearest place in his imagination to the garden of Eden.[43] There he fell desperately ill. On what might well have proved to be his death-bed, he reviewed his life so far, not without a sense of shame and guilt, but the overriding message that returned to him again and again was the consciousness that 'I have a work to do in England'.[44]

What shape that work would take was not entirely clear at first. 'I do not ask to see, The distant scene – one step enough for me', he wrote as the closing lines of the first verse of his celebrated poem 'The Pillar of the Cloud', beginning with the words 'Lead, kindly light', composed on his return journey by sea to Marseilles, *en route* for England. Although he arrived back with no hair on his head, so that he had to wear a wig, his spirits were high. 'He was like a man reborn,' Christopher Dawson has written, 'with all his powers released and with such exuberant confidence and energy that his friends at Oxford actually failed to recognize him.'[45] He arrived in Oxford just five days before Keble mounted the pulpit in St Mary's to preach the Assize Sermon on the theme of 'National Apostasy'. The Oxford Movement had officially begun.

II

Keble's sermon was not heard by Manning. He had left Oxford, following his ordination, while Newman was abroad; and in the course of a matter of months, by a remarkable chain of circumstances, found himself placed in a Sussex curacy and engaged to be married. It had happened this way. Off and on during his quiet period at Merton, assimilating the theological profundities of 'acres of Anglican writers',[1] he had discussed with various friends the advantages and disadvantages of obtaining a suitable curacy, rather favouring a return to London on the somewhat surprising grounds that his asthma would be less troublesome there.[2] He considered, and then rejected, a possible opening in the diocese of Chester; and then Henry Wilberforce, with whom he had struck up a friendship through their joint activities in the Oxford Union, came up with an attractive proposition.

Although toying with the idea of a career in the law, Henry had finally decided to become ordained, and had been offered a curacy by the Rector of Graffham and Lavington, John Sargent, who needed an assistant to serve the tiny church of Upwaltham, a hamlet about two miles from Graffham. That John Sargent should have approached the youngest of the Wilberforce sons came as no surprise. Not only were the Sargents and the Wilberforces related by marriage (Mary Sargent being the daughter of Abel Smith the banker, who was first cousin to the Emancipator and also the brother of the first Mrs Manning), but their Evangelical churchmanship partook of an identical hue: eminently respectable, combining an ardent love of souls with such deference to the principles of Church order as befitted two highly prosperous families, united in friendship with at least two of the leading figures of the Anglican Evangelical revival, Charles Simeon and the revered missionary, Henry Martyn. Furthermore, already close connections had been forged between the offspring of their two families. As a boy Henry Wilberforce had been tutored by John Sargent at Graffham Rectory, and he and the youngest of the Sargent sons, Harry, had become almost inseparable. A further marriage had strengthened the links. In 1828, Samuel Wilberforce married Emily Sargent who, following the death of her elder sister Charlotte in 1818, was now the senior of four very beautiful Sargent girls.

Indeed, it was because the ties were so close that Henry

dithered over the offer. Could he conscientiously serve the beloved Rector of Graffham, whose standing within the Evangelical clergy was comparable to that of Keble within the High Church party, when his own views were beginning to reflect so closely those of his even more beloved tutor at Oriel, John Henry Newman? And Newman was not at all happy at the prospect of Henry, as a susceptible young bachelor curate, living in such close proximity to the three exceedingly attractive unmarried Sargent daughters, Caroline, Mary and Sophia. He expressed his views very plainly to Henry.

> I fear the ladies of the house will make you idle. You will be lounging and idling with them all day. There is this mischief attends all familiar society between us and the fair sex. We cannot talk without being idle, but ladies are employing their fingers in a thousand ways while they encourage idleness in us.[3]

Poor Henry; he knew himself well enough to perceive the likelihood of the distraction; and he also knew that Newman held strong views on clerical celibacy. He therefore decided to hold his decision until Easter 1833; but – as he told his brother Robert – since John Sargent needed assistance at once, perhaps there was a temporary solution to the problem. 'I had thought that possibly they might take a *locum tenens* till Easter, and it occurred to me that *Manning* would be a very fit man if he would accept it.'[4] The temporary nature of the charge appealed to Manning, and John Sargent heartily approved. So to Lavington he went on 3 January 1833, and stayed there for nearly eighteen years.

Two events determined that decision. The first was that he speedily fell victim to the charms of one of the 'ladies of the house' – Caroline; and by Easter that year they were engaged to be married. No record survives of this rapid courtship, only an irreverent legend, invented by W. G. Ward, whose first acquaintance with Manning was as a widower of some years' standing and already a rather solemn dignitary, that it would have been in character for the proposal to have taken the form, not of a lover on bended knee, but simply the seven words 'Caroline, I have spoken to your mother'.[5] This was typical of Ward's humour, but he can hardly have been wider of the mark. Manning was certainly reserved by nature; but the reserve that he displayed about his passionate love for Caroline, which never abated during the long years of his life, was that reticence which restrains a man from speaking of the things most precious to his heart, save to a select few who totally understand. The Sargent family, and his brother-in-law Samuel Wilberforce, together with those who joined the circle by their marriages to Mary (Henry Wilberforce) and Sophia (George Dudley Ryder), were of that privileged company. They knew what the relationship meant to Manning and the extent to which it transformed his whole life.

The second event, which put a completely different complexion upon his future, was the sudden death on 3 May 1833 of John Sargent. As a consequence Manning, after a curacy of only four months, became Rector of Graffham and Lavington, the presentation of the living being in the gift of Caroline's grandmother, the widow of John Sargent senior, the squire of the Lavington estate, who had died only two years earlier. Death, indeed, seemed to be the tragic portion of a family otherwise blessed with every circumstance of happiness, prosperity and security. The male line of the family seemed to have been especially blighted, some said as the result of a curse placed upon an infamous ancestor, Garton Orme, so that inheritance was never to pass through the male line (nor did it until 1873, in fact). Within the space of four years (1829 to 1833), the eldest son (John), his father and his grandfather had died; and the surviving son, Harry, died in 1836. The female line fared hardly better. Following the death of the eldest of the five girls in 1818, only one of the remaining daughters (Mary) lived to anything approaching a natural span of years. Caroline died aged only 25 in 1837, Emily aged 34 in 1841, and Sophia aged 36 in 1850. All the girls were renowned for their beauty, causing hearts to throb wherever they went. It was a beauty 'of no ordinary kind', recalled one of George Ryder's sons.

> Bishop Wilberforce used to say the most perfect likeness of his wife was the face of St Catharine of Alexandria in the beautiful picture representing her as borne by angels after her martyrdom for burial on Mount Sinai. As to my mother [Sophia] by far the most perfect likeness of her was Our Lady in Leonardo da Vinci's beautiful picture *La Madonna del lago*.[6]

It was as if the heaviest of prices was exacted for the gift of such loveliness, the delicacy of their complexion signifying a frailty of constitution rendering them all vulnerable to one of the commonest causes of fatality in the nineteenth century, consumption.

Manning was inducted to the Rectorship of Lavington in June 1833 (his brother-in-law, Samuel Wilberforce, officiating), having been ordained priest earlier that month. Samuel again officiated at the marriage to Caroline on 7 November. They had a long honeymoon, at the house of one of Manning's married sisters near Sevenoaks, stopping on the way at the home of one of his brothers, near Belgrave Square. Manning wrote to his mother-in-law the day after the wedding.

> My dearest Mrs Sargent, I can send you an account of dearest Caroline, which you will hardly believe. She is at the moment playing and singing, without a single evidence of fatigue, or indisposition . . . How I wish you could see her . . . Indeed we have to thank God most unfeignedly . . . I have thought of you all – an affectionate recollection in all I would express, for I do not feel any separation to have arisen between you and her you so love. May it please Him to unite us in one family; and give you the comfort and support of Caroline's affection. There is much I would say to you, but had rather you should gather it from your future observation. I cannot forget the intimate relation that was sealed between us yesterday, and I believe you will never want an evidence of this conviction hereafter. I know we have your constant prayers. Ask for us that our union may comprehend both time and eternity, and that our sincere, our single, aim in all things may be the glory of God in our holy and devoted life.[7]

Events in Oxford were far from his mind during these happy months. Of course he was not unaware of manifestations of that ugly mood within the country which was one of the causes of the militant reaction from that centre of orthodoxy. Caroline had memories of a rising of agricultural workers in the Graffham area, only three years before, when her father had boldly confronted a party of rick-burners and dispersed them with a stern lecture before they could do any damage; and how the military had been called out to defend Petworth jail against an attempt to release the prisoners.[8] Pass a few years, and Manning himself would take up the cause of the disaffected agricultural labourers, to do his utmost to obtain for them a fairer deal.[9]

His own churchmanship is difficult to define in these early years. He had not shared Henry Wilberforce's reservations about working in harmony with an Evangelical rector, but John Sargent was no Calvinist and his ministry was not likely to cause any embarrassment to a curate whose views on such matters were still in a state of flux. His studies at Merton, before ordination, had not been confined to the Caroline Divines and the Fathers. The record of his borrowings during that period includes Strype's *Memoir of Cranmer*, a work of Martin Bucer, and also – on two occasions – the works of John Calvin.[10] From his own recollections, one of the first problems that exercised his mind was his own credentials as a priest. What authority did ordination actually convey? 'By what authority do you lift the latch of a poor man's door and enter and sit down and begin to instruct or to correct him? ... If I was not a messenger sent from God, I was an intruder and impertinent.'[11] It would appear that he soon answered that question to his own satisfaction, because he showed no compunction over exercising a stern ecclesiastical discipline over his rural flock, rebuking irreverence, exhibiting daunting displeasure at late-comers, and drawing attention to his special status by wearing his cassock as he made his daily rounds (an unusual practice for those times). He even had to admit on one occasion, to Samuel Wilberforce, that he had overstepped the mark by entering the house of a local gentleman, Holford by name, without seeking his prior permission, in order to rebuke two of his servants for unseemly behaviour in church.

'I am provoked with myself,' he reflected. '... I was very incautious in doing so, and am truly sorry that I did give a goose a plea for misrepresentation.' Nevertheless, putting aside the discourtesy, he was still within his rights, he maintained.

> As to the *interference*, I feel that my obligations to all my people make it my duty to *admonish* etc ... It is a doctrine wholly unXtian and unecclesiastical that anyone can draw a circle round his household and forbid the ministry of Christ to reprove, and admonish. He and all his are under our ministry.[12]

In these early years, in so far as he was influenced by anybody in particular, Manning seems to have learnt most from Samuel Wilberforce. They were in close touch with each other through obvious family ties, and they were both acquiring increasingly strong Church views, while retaining a respect for the Evangelical spirit and an unquestioning acceptance of the gifts peculiar to the Church of England as a result of the Reformation. Nearly twenty years later, he acknowledged his debt to Samuel. 'When I came to Lavington in 1833,' he wrote to him, 'I believed, as I always did, in baptismal regeneration: I had no view on the sacrament of the Body and Blood of Christ; and no idea of the Church. You sent me in the year 1834 to Hooker to learn the doctrine of the Real Presence.'[13] There is no reason to question the accuracy of this. Gladstone recalled that Manning at this time occasionally found Henry Wilberforce's totally uncritical veneration for everything that emanated from Oxford, and from Newman in particular, irritating and vexatious, and how he advised Henry that the best cure would be for him to turn his back on Oxford and to work among the poor and sick.[14] Nevertheless, through his reading of Jeremy Taylor on Confirmation and Bishop Bull's *Condition of Man before the Fall*, he was becoming more convinced of the centrality of the sacramental principle, and more prepared to give the Tract writers more open, if still cautious, support.

Events had moved apace at Oxford; mainly because Newman, with Froude to goad him on, had taken over the leadership of affairs. Right from the start there had been a difference of opinion with the 'Z's. William Palmer was advocating the formation of an Association of the Church on a national basis, with the object of defending 'the Church's best interests against the immediate difficulties of the present day'.[15] Coincident with this should be an Address to the Archbishop of Canterbury, supported by as many signatories as possible, urging him to take a stand in defence of the 'Apostolical Doctrine and Polity of the Church over which you preside', and pledging 'their cheerful co-operation and dutiful support'.[16] Palmer wanted organization and a presiding committee to approve and monitor such tracts as might be issued.

This was not at all to the liking of Newman and Froude. They believed that the opposition to Erastianism and latitudinarianism should be Oxford-based, as befitting the bastion of orthodoxy. They were even prepared to agitate for disestablishment. But, most important of all, they wanted no interfering, editorial committee. The trouble with societies and committees, Newman wrote to Palmer in October 1833, is that 'second rate men with low views get the upper hand'.[17] By that time he had taken his own initiative, the first three of the *Tracts for the Times* having already been published (on 9 September 1833), all from his own pen, and all short, masterly, uncompromising declarations of the principles that were at stake and of the causes on which the clergy must unite – notably their apostolic commission, through the sacrament of ordination as administered by the successors of the Apostles, their rights to denounce unwarrantable intrusions by the State, and their absolute obligation to resist any attempt by Parliament to tamper with the Church's liturgy in any form whatever.

The success of the early tracts, and the exhilaration that they gave to Newman in the writing of them, as he explained to the cautious and rather pedestrian A. P. Perceval, confirmed that 'no great work was done by a system ... Luther was an individual. The very faults of an individual excite attention – he loses, but his cause (if good and he powerful minded) gains.'[18] So he gave expression to a conviction that time and time again throughout his life he was to reiterate. He had first enunciated it in a University Sermon preached in 1832 on the subject of 'Personal Influence the Means of propagating the Truth', when he posed the question: who are the 'high Christians' who 'carry on God's noiseless work'? He answered: 'A few highly-endowed men will rescue the world for centuries to come.'[19] Later that year he expressed the same idea in one of his verses of the poem 'The Course of Truth', written on Christmas Eve.

> Still is the might of Truth, as it has been:
> Lodged in the few, obey'd, and yet unseen.[20]

The heroine of his novel *Callista*, written in his Roman Catholic days, observes to her mentor Caecilius, 'a new religion begins by appealing to what is peculiar in the minds of a few'.[21] Then, in the *Apologia*, the same conviction received classic expression in the words, 'Deliverance is wrought, not by the many, but by the few, not by bodies, but by persons.'[22] One of the most fascinating features of Newman's life was the way in which he actually lived both his theology and his philosophy (or, conversely, devised a theology and a philosophy out of his own personal experience). He was always prepared, if need be, to take a solitary stance, even as did the greatest saints of old. 'All great things', he told Edward Churton in 1837, 'are done by calculation and individuality. They have been ruined by coalitions.'[23]

In these early optimistic days of unrestrained militancy, both Newman and Froude preferred to err on the side of extremism rather than moderation. Newman explained the tactical success of this to Samuel Rickards as early as November 1833, when Rickards had expressed uneasiness over a reference to the doctrine of transubstantiation as one of the gifts of the ministers of Christ. 'We are as men climbing a rock,' Newman observed, 'who tear clothes and flesh, and slip now and then, and yet make progress.' He continued: 'Surely it is energy gives edge to any undertaking, and energy is ever incautious and exaggerated.'[24] The principle, then, on which the early tracts were composed seems sometimes to have been – if in doubt, shout it out and, if the proclamation might seem a highly questionable one, thunder it out the louder. Almost certainly, behind such an approach lay the influence of Hurrell Froude. As Piers Brendon has written, 'Froude acted as agitator; he had the ideas; but he lacked the stamina to do much more than incite his friends to put them into practice.'[25] While Newman was still in Sicily, Froude declared the objective of the apostolicals to Isaac Williams, in the course of a walk through Trinity College garden. 'Isaac,' he said, 'we must make a row in the world.'[26]

Between 1833 and 1835, Froude did his utmost to incite Newman to be even bolder. He admitted as much in September 1834. 'I mean to ally myself to him in a close league,' he wrote, 'and put as much mischief into his head as I can.'[27] He himself had come to nourish an increasing dislike of the Reformers, ever since reading a life of 'Wickcliffe' in October 1831.[28] At that time Newman was wont to make a distinction between the 'foreign party', whom he was prepared to regard as heretics, and the English Reformers, for whom he had a lingering respect. Froude set out to disabuse Newman of such a notion.[29] He was also the prime mover in encouraging in Newman emphatic anti-Erastian views.[30] But most of all, he resolved to tone down Newman's hostile comments about the Roman Church. He reproved him for anti-Romanist remarks in 'Home Thoughts Abroad', singing the praises of monasticism.[31] At the beginning of 1835, he told Newman in a long letter that the Protestant doctrine of the Eucharist was frankly heretical. For himself, 'I shall never call the holy Eucharist "the Lord's supper"'. Nor would he ever again abuse the Roman Church 'for anything except excommunicating us'.[32] As for the uneasy alliance between the Tractarians and the old High Church party, as early as November 1833 Froude had advised Newman that he could see no good purpose in trying to maintain an amicable working relationship with William Palmer. 'We must throw the Zs overboard,' he wrote.[33]

Froude, because of his worsening health, necessitating a long sojourn in Barbados, had to work behind the scenes. Newman, however, was the consummate publicist; and needless to say his writings caused increasing concern within the ranks of both the

'X's and the 'Z's. The *Record* began to attack the Tracts from the Evangelical standpoint, and Newman, who had valued their earlier cautious sympathy and support, attempted to calm their fears by pointing to the many crucial doctrines that Tractarians and Evangelicals held in common. Not that he seemed to be particularly discountenanced by their hostility. He compared the apostolicals to the 'Davids' in conflict with the Evangelical 'Goliaths'. 'We will show these Midianites what Gideon can do.'[34]

The 'Z's took great exception to the hot-headed impetuosity of the Oxford men. Joshua Watson deplored their tendency 'to fight before they scarcely knew the weapons wherewith they should arm themselves'.[35] William Palmer became increasingly aware of another danger. Their novelties were attracting the wrong sort of discipleship, threatening to turn into a personality cult, centering on the figure of the Vicar of St Mary's. Such a following, and such a tendency to hero-worship, would be profitable to neither of them, and it would foster a perilously arrogant party spirit.

> We beheld every peculiarity and novelty of doctrine, everything that was startling and perplexing to sober-minded men, instantly caught up, disseminated, created into an article of *Catholic* faith, by young and ardent spirits ... an influence most dangerous to the Church, a disposition to create human leaders.[36]

Henry Manning was, on the whole, a sober-minded man during the 1830s; and he was certainly not disposed to hero-worship. Apart from being a fellow-member with Newman on the Oxford committee of the SPCK during 1834, he saw little of him. Manning's cautious advance into the Tractarian camp still remains a little bit of a mystery. E. S. Purcell was certainly in error in stating that Manning did not begin reading the Tracts earlier than October 1836.[37] Both he and Samuel Wilberforce were clearly aware of, and reasonably sympathetic to, their contents, as was a mutual friend, William Dodsworth, then minister of the Margaret Street Chapel in Cavendish Square, whose advance into strong Church views was greeted with approval by the two brothers-in-law. Then, Henry Wilberforce was for ever sending gleeful accounts to both of them of Newman's latest triumphs. Not that these would have necessarily moved Manning at all, because he was always a little suspicious of Henry's enthusiasms.

Probably Henry slightly exaggerated his confident reports back to Newman about the Rector of Lavington's progress towards discipleship. 'Manning has reviewed his opinions,' he told New-man in November 1833, 'and adopts the Apostolical Succession.'[38] Two days later, he announced that Manning was prepared to play his part as one of the distributors of the Tracts in Sussex.[39] In August 1834, there was better news still. Manning had come out strongly in support of Newman's controversial action in refusing to solemnize the marriage at St Mary's of the hapless Miss Jubber, who was discovered to have been unbaptized. 'Manning ... is *exceedingly* improved since he left Oxford,' Henry wrote; '... I am glad to say, that the improvement is most remarkable. He is aware of it himself; for he says that a year and a half ago he did not know there was such a thing as a Church.'[40] In January 1835 Newman visited Manning in London, where he introduced him to John Bowden, who had become one of the contributors to the Tracts. He then wrote to Froude to pass on the good news. 'Manning of Merton has quite come round, and preaches in all the synagogues.'[41]

Chichester Cathedral was hardly a synagogue, but Manning's first major sermon there, on the occasion of a Visitation, in the summer of 1835, gave substance to Newman's enthusiasm. He published it under the title *The English Church, its Succession and Witness for Christ*. Although it did not attract wide attention at the time, it was actually a highly significant landmark in his develop-ment. In the first place, he elaborated, and without qualification, some of the leading themes of the early Tracts: the high office of the priesthood, 'how peculiar to itself; to which no other office of moral teacher or labourer in God's service can bear affinity', echoing Newman's appeal to the clergy, in the first of the Tracts, to 'magnify your office'.[42] But if the dignity was high, so also was the awful responsibility that accompanied it, because the higher the privilege, the greater must be the burden of discharging it as responsible witnesses of Christ.[43] The doctrine of the Apostolical Succession within the Anglican Church was boldly asserted against the 'futile objections of the Papists'.[44] And then, in words which could as well be taken straight from his devotional manual on the nature of the priesthood, written as Cardinal Archbishop of Westminster in 1883 (*The Eternal Priesthood*), he expressed with great eloquence the necessity of conformity to the mind and character of Christ.

> The mind of Christ must be transfused into our own. There must be somewhat of the same intense love of perishing sinners, of the same

patient endurance of moral evil, and unwearied striving to bring the impenitent to God: a portion of the same holy boldness and fearless inflexibility of purpose; a measure of that perpetual self-denial and self-sacrifice to the service and glory of His Father: of that acute, affectionate, and universal sympathy with the sick, the suffering, the tempted, and without partaking of their contamination, even with the sinful: and somewhat also of that intuitive penetration of heart and character, which His omniscience apprehended at a glance, but we can gather only by keen observation, strict analysis, and rigid search, under the guidance of the Holy Ghost, into all the depths and windings of our own. What a mission, Brethren, is ours![45]

This remarkable passage was written less than three years after his ordination. In 1831 he was still a rather self-important, self-centred young man, fussing about the political career that might have been his. It is almost as if he had grown up overnight. In this first published sermon, some of the major preoccupations of his priesthood until the very end of his days were dwelt upon as being as all-important then as they were to be ever after: the obligation of the priest to be ready to be crucified with Christ; the mission of the Holy Ghost; the love of Jesus to penitents; the imperative duty to minister to the deprived, the suffering and those whom society counts worthless; the unity and authority of the Church. Even some of his favourite imagery appears for the first time, such as the command to the ministers of the church in Ephesus from him 'that walketh in the midst of the seven golden candlesticks' (Rev. 2:1).[46]

How can this be explained? There is nothing here that he had derived from Favell Bevan; much, clearly, that had impressed him from his reading of the Tracts. The deepening of his spirituality may well have come through his close contact with the Sargent family circle, and Caroline in particular; and there is evidence (from Gladstone's recollections) that Manning had not abandoned the Evangelical party completely at this stage. Glad-stone had met him in London in 1835, on his way to attend an SPCK meeting, resolved to defend the Evangelical cause, apparently 'against the Archbishop'.[47] Manning himself rarely intimated any specific individual influence upon his spiritual development, giving the impression that, on the whole, he worked out his own position quite privately from his own studies.

To a certain extent this is true. He prided himself on being his own man. Recent evidence, however, suggests that the closest approximation to a mentor in Manning's life, at this stage, was not Newman, or any of the Wilberforces, or William Dodsworth, but S. F. Wood. Samuel Francis Wood was the younger brother of Charles Wood, later 1st Viscount Halifax. From Eton he had proceeded to Oriel, where he became Newman's pupil and devoted disciple. He was also Manning's contemporary as an undergraduate, and within his circle of friends. It is curious how the careers of all three men overlapped in such a way that, but for two strange twists of fortune, S. F. Wood could well have become the colleague of either one or the other. His First in Classics in 1831, and his wish to take Orders, made him an admirable candidate for an Oriel Fellowship. Indeed, he would have secured this prize if the electors had judged on merit alone. In the end, however, their choice fell on C. P. Eden, who was of near equal merit but whose circumstances were less favourable than those of the son of a baronet. Newman wrote to Wood to express his personal sorrow. 'I consider you are the greatest loss to us the College has sustained in my time.'[48] He was encouraged to apply to Merton, where – if successful – he would have joined Manning, with whom the ties of friendship were strengthening. The fates, or more likely parental influence, decreed otherwise. Wood gave up his plans for ordination, turned to the study of law, and was duly called to the Bar. Theology, however, remained his principal interest, and his own passage from Evangelicalism to more Catholic sympathies slightly antedated that of Manning. In February 1832, Newman noted with satisfaction to Robert Wilberforce that 'you would be as much surprised as I could be by the great change in Wood'.[49]

S. F. Wood has been described by James Pereiro as one of that 'supporting cast of secondary figures' within the drama of the Oxford Movement 'which have remained in relative darkness'.[50] It might have been otherwise had he not died so young (in 1843) and had not his letters, at his own wish, been burnt by his elder brother following his death.[51] Some letters escaped the conflagration, however, and among those that survived is a scattered collection, only partially complete, of a three-way correspondence between Newman, Manning and Wood, dating from November 1835 to January 1836, which reveals that Wood's theological enquiries had led him along paths as yet untrodden by the other two, namely a tentative exploration into the question of doctrinal development.

It is true that a hint of what was to come in Newman's *Essay on Development* had appeared in his work on the Arians, but what is striking about Wood's hypothesis is his attempt to argue a doctrine of progressive revelation in which he comes to the conclusion that the Church, as a teacher of truth, must have within its power, through divine guidance, the 'right of authoritatively exhibiting' such truths, which are to be received by faith.[52] This went beyond anything that either Newman or Manning had even considered, preoccupied as they both were at the time with defining the role of Tradition (Newman in controversy with the Abbé Jager, and Manning in working out what are the 'Rules of Faith', which would be the subject of his second Visitation Sermon, in 1838). It is clear from the exchange of letters that Newman, who stayed for a fortnight in London in January 1836, lodging in Wood's chambers, talked this idea through with him and that, in the end, they agreed amicably to differ.[53] One revealing aspect of this correspondence, however, is the evidence it supplies of the extent to which Manning respected Wood's judgement on theological questions. Indeed, the correspondence was actually initiated by Manning, who had written to Wood in order to obtain confirmation from the other that his studies on apostolical tradition were following the right lines.[54]

Both men would soon become active collaborators together on behalf of the National Society for Promotion of the Education of the Poor, and they never ceased to correspond with each other on theological matters; nor did they always agree. In 1836, Manning felt sufficiently confident as a defender of Catholic principles to pick up the gauntlet thrown down by a truly formidable adversary, Dr Nicholas Wiseman, the future Cardinal Archbishop of Westminster, then Rector of the English College at Rome, who had been lecturing to packed audiences at St Mary Moorfields on the subject of the differences between the Roman communion and Protestantism. Wiseman gave great offence to the Tractarians by describing Anglicans as Protestants, confessing that he saw no difference between them and the heretical successors of Luther and Calvin. Manning published his riposte in Rose's *British Magazine*, sheltering – it is true – under anonymity by signing himself very pointedly 'A Catholic Priest'. Wood mildly remonstrated with him, accusing him of over-stating his case. 'Dr Wiseman had a right as a *controversialist*, with his principles etc., to group [our Church] with Biblical Protestants,' he wrote, offering to supply Manning with a catena of '*low* people in *high* places' within the Church of England since the Reformation to substantiate Wiseman's claim. He could have wished it otherwise, but the fact had to be faced.[55]

With these credentials Manning now seemed to Newman safely within the ranks of the apostolicals, and they began to correspond very much as allies in a common cause. Manning offered to become 'a patron of the Tracts', suggesting also that the recent change in their nature, since Pusey had joined the fold with his learned and lengthy treatise on Baptism, was not necessarily an improvement.[56] He also warned him that, in the course of circulating the Tracts in Sussex, he had sensed that 'the scent of Popery is thought to hang about them'.[57] Nevertheless, he offered to become a contributor himself in October 1836, suggesting the compilation of a *catena Patrum* (a collection of apposite quotations from the works of the Fathers) on the subject of Catholic Tradition, which Newman was happy to accept.[58] It duly appeared as Tract 78 in 1837, Manning having secured the assistance of Charles Marriott. He also contemplated offering a translation of Justin Martyr for Pusey's projected *Library of the Fathers*. In informing Newman of his plans, he was able to assure him that 'I find true Church principles spreading everywhere; and among laymen too.'[59]

In 1836 the party seemed strong enough to go to war, given an issue provocative enough to cause them to stand up and be counted; and just such an occasion occurred, causing so mighty a furore throughout the Church that – at least for a moment – the bickerings between the apostolicals and the 'Z's, and even the growing alienation from the Evangelicals, were forgotten. On 17 February, on the recommendation of the Premier, Lord Melbourne, Renn Dickson Hampden was gazetted as Regius Professor of Divinity in the University of Oxford. A battle royal was about to commence.

III

It was R. D. Hampden's misfortune to have been the subject of three major controversies, affecting profoundly the lives of three men far more eminent than himself; and in only one of these conflicts can it be said that he himself did anything to provoke the storm that raged around him. The first two issues, in 1834 and 1836, brought Newman to centre-stage, while Manning was only a peripheral figure. The final conflict, in 1847, when Hampden became Bishop of Hereford, proved to be the occasion of Manning's first serious unsettlement as an Anglican and probably cost Samuel Wilberforce, then Bishop of Oxford, his chances and expectations of proceeding to the highest ecclesiastical dignity in the land. As for Hampden himself, he was a figure of no consequence until he appeared on the Oxford scene to deliver the Bampton Lectures of 1832, and after 1847 his career as Bishop of Hereford made not the slightest impression upon the history of the Church, except for the fact that he earned for himself the questionable distinction of having sat in the House of Lords for eighteen years without making a single speech.

Hampden was by nature a scholar; a learned man of no charisma and little charm; short, rotund, of swarthy complexion. Someone, we are told, casting around in desperation for a compliment to pay him, could do no better than to recall that he had nicely shaped feet.[1] He had, for a short while, been a Fellow of Oriel (in 1814), and a colleague of Arnold and Whately while Newman was still a schoolboy. He had the highest academic honours, and on his marriage retired to country curacies and thence to London to bury himself in his books. He became something of an expert on the theology of the medieval school-men, and then learnt more about this relatively unexplored field by picking the brains of Blanco White, when he returned to Oxford for a brief period to act as public examiner in 1829. When invited to deliver the Bampton Lectures in 1832, he published some of the fruits of these researches under the title *Scholastic Philosophy considered in its relation to Christian Theology*. They caused no stir at the time because Oxford in general, and Newman in particular, knew little and cared less about such a recondite subject and – but for the events that followed – the lectures might well have remained buried in obscurity and forgotten.

In 1833, however, Hampden returned to Oxford as Principal of St Mary Hall, one of the lesser Heads of Houses with, nevertheless, a seat on the Hebdomadal Board. In the following year he put Newman's nose somewhat out of joint by securing the chair of Moral Philosophy, which Newman had been so sure of gaining himself that he had actually rashly instructed his publisher (Rivingtons) to leave a space on the title page of his first published volume of sermons, so that his prestigious office could be inserted once the announcement had been made.[2] Then Hampden committed his one highly provocative act.

Already the issue of the abolition of subscription to the Thirty-nine Articles (before matriculation at Oxford) had been raised in Parliament, and orthodox Oxford had, especially in the persons of the leading Tractarians, begun to bristle with anger and alarm at another attempt by the Whigs to invade the prerogatives of their exclusively Anglican citadel. Into the fray stepped Hampden with his pamphlet 'Observations on Religious Dissent', making so strong a plea for the rights of Dissenters that it seemed to Newman and Froude and the supporters of the Tracts that they now had to face an enemy within their own camp, who was tainted with both the latitudinarianism of Arnold and the Noeticism of Whately. To protect himself from the accusation of sour grapes (over the Moral Philosophy chair), Newman encouraged others – and notably Henry Wilberforce – to publish a blistering riposte to Hampden's pamphlet, trying not very convincingly to preserve his own editorial anonymity. The issue was debated at both national and local level. Successive bills to abolish subscription were defeated in the House of Lords. At Oxford, the conflict came increasingly to take on the aspect of a revolt by the more junior of the resident MAs against the oligarchy of the Heads of Houses, who were swayed by the wishes of the new Chancellor, the Duke of Wellington, to agree, by a majority of one in the Hebdomadal Board, to substitute for subscription a new declaration couched in innocuous terms, that all those matriculating at Oxford should pledge conformity to the discipline and worship of the University.

On 20 May 1835, the proposal of the Hebdomadal Board came before Convocation, where it was thrown out by a massive majority. Round One had been won by the Tractarians. The Heads of Houses had been publicly humiliated, as their juniors demonstrated where the *de facto* rule of the University lay. It recalled memories of Newman's first triumph in the defeat of Peel in 1829; and just as that victory had led to his estrangement from Hawkins and Whately, so now this second rebuff rendered the breach irreparable, while also adding a third implacable opponent who would not easily forget the virulence of the attacks upon him. In an exchange of frigid letters, Hampden accused Newman of 'malignity, because you have no other ground of your assault on me but a fanatical persecuting spirit'.[3] The episode was not without its irony. Six years later the militant defender of subscription in 1835 was to become himself the subject of censure by both the Hebdomadal Board and Convocation, for the liberties that he had presumed to take with the interpretation of the Thirty-nine Articles in his notorious Tract 90.

In 1836, Newman was to seize the initiative yet again, when Hampden's appointment to the Regius Professorship became public knowledge. A man who could indulge in such liberal conceits as to try to undermine Oxford's historic claim to be the bastion of orthodoxy was likely to hold heterodox views of his own. Indeed, there was sufficient evidence in his 'Observations on Religious Dissent' to arouse Newman's suspicions. Had not Hampden presumed to write: 'No conclusions of human reasoning, however correctly deduced, however logically sound, are properly religious truths'?[4] Newman therefore turned his attention to the text of the neglected Bampton Lectures of 1832, found what he suspected, and on 10 February 1836 rattled off in the course of an all-night sitting a pamphlet of 47 pages entitled 'Elucidations of Dr Hampden's Statements', in which he demonstrated under nine separate headings the extent to which the new Regius Professor had committed doctrinal error. Polemically, it was a *tour de force*, and tactically extremely effective. Few people would be conscientious enough to check the accuracy of Newman's *exposé*, when it entailed wading through several hundred pages of a somewhat obscure treatise. Newman's pamphlet, by comparison, could be read in bed; which is precisely how Lord Melbourne read it, dismissing it as 'abstruse'.[5] Not that it cost Melbourne a minute's sleep. When the fracas was over and Hampden felt it proper to thank the Premier for his refusal to listen to the clamour against him, Melbourne took him by the arm and said, 'Be easy. I like an easy man.'[6]

Since the King had already approved Melbourne's recommendation, and Hampden was extraordinarily quick off the mark in delivering his Inaugural, exactly a month after the gazetting of his appointment, his opponents were presented with a *fait accompli*. The only course left open to them was to try to inflict some sort of public humiliation upon Hampden by securing a vote in Convocation to deprive him of his right to have any voice in the appointment of Select Preachers before the University. A first attempt failed, being vetoed by the Proctors. On 5 May 1836, however, the proposal was raised a second time in Convocation and was carried by the huge majority of 474 votes to 94.

In terms of damaging Hampden's position, this was really little more than a pinprick, although the insult rankled for years. Hampden's supporters were furious. Thomas Arnold described the whole proceedings as an exhibition of 'lynch law',[7] and let fly at the Tractarians in an article in the *Edinburgh Review*, under a title supplied by the editors, 'The Oxford Malignants and Dr Hampden'. Whately put his finger very accurately on the vindictive character of their action. The forces against whom Hampden was battling were a group of

> enraged men, influenced by religious and political enthusiasm ... at once exulting and mortified; exulting in a local and temporary triumph and at the same time bitterly mortified by finding themselves defeated generally, and on their main object. It is observed that soldiers are usually the most cruel when, after having been beaten, they fall in with some small detachment which they can overpower. [8]

Those who came up to Oxford to vote, however, exhibited more of a carnival mood. Samuel Wilberforce was one, moved by Newman's pamphlet, but totally ignorant of the actual contents of Hampden's lectures, as he was later to discover with much embarrassment and chagrin. Henry Manning and Caroline made the journey from Lavington to witness the proceedings, and there is no evidence that Manning, in casting his vote against Hampden, was any better informed about the Bampton Lectures than his brother-in-law. They all gloried in the triumph of the size of the majority, proclaiming to the world at large the strength of sound Church views. Some took it all as a bit of a joke, Samuel Wilberforce suggesting that a further impediment should be imposed on Hampden – that he should be compelled to deliver all his lectures in Hebrew.[9]

But it was no joke to Newman. To him, a crucial point of principle was at stake. The primary heresy of Hampden was to have maintained, as he understood him, that the one and only binding obligation upon Christians was to accept the truth of the divine facts contained in Scripture, and that all human interpretations of these facts, whether in creeds or formularies or patristic writings, could not be held as binding because they partook of that fallibility to which all productions of human intelligence must be prone. As Newman subsequently explained, the distinction was between Hampden's assertion that 'Tradition is *nothing more* than expositions of Scripture, *reasoned out* by the Church, and embodied in a code of doctrine' and his own statement of the Catholic conviction that 'Had Scripture never been written, Tradition would have existed still; it has an intrinsic, substantive, authority, and a use collateral to Scripture'. Hampden, then, was guilty of an outrageous debasement, his teaching being 'but the gold and silver of inspired writers taken out in coppers'.[10]

This was not a view, of course, held by Newman alone. Pusey was horrified by Hampden's conclusions. Keble delivered one of the Latin speeches against him at the May Convocation. C. P. Golightly (later to be the scourge of the Tractarians) was equally vehement against him. As J. B. Mozley reported to his sister, Maria, on hearing the news of Hampden's elevation:

> It is astonishing how strongly men feel on the subject. Greswell of Corpus said he should consider himself guilty of an act of apostasy from the Christian religion if he did not protest against the appointment. Dr Gilbert of Brasenose declared the same thing. Dr Cardwell, Principal of St Alban Hall, was going about for two or three days quite furiously, with a passage from Hampden's moral philosophy lectures in his pocket, and declaring that he ought to be turned out of professorship and hall, and house and home, and everything. It must be strong feeling which could raise the Heads of Houses.[11]

In retrospect, it is difficult to resist the conclusion that everyone involved in these proceedings behaved rather badly. It was sheer perversity on Melbourne's part to select Hampden in the first place. His credentials for a professorial chair were certainly impressive, and as Professor Chadwick has observed, the latitudinarian thought of the time received, in his Bampton Lectures, its 'most interesting, able and attractive expression'.[12] But to thrust Hampden upon Oxford, of all places, was both a political blunder and a deliberate insult. Arnold's angry defence of Hampden was altogether too sweeping in its condemnation; and some of the jokes cracked at Hampden's expense were hardly in the best of taste. Nor can Newman be exonerated from the charge of vindictiveness. Did he quote Hampden out of context? Roderick Strange has recently maintained that such a criticism is unfair, while conceding that he failed to give his opponent any credit for 'positive views'.[13] The device of *reductio ad absurdum*, which Newman also employed, was of doubtful propriety, especially his exaggerating by implication what Hampden wrote, by the insertion of words that he never actually used.[14]

At the time of the troubles, Hampden acted with admirable dignity; and perhaps some of his audience at his Inaugural felt a little ashamed, when he closed by making a moving appeal for fair play:

> That I labour under very great disadvantages in commencing the duties of my office is known to you all . . . I come before you under a cloud of prejudice and clamour which, however easy for the feeblest among us to raise and diffuse, it is the hardest thing in the world to remove or even diminish, but to misrepresentation and clamour and violence, with God's help, I will never yield. I pray God to forgive those who have employed such weapons against me, and to turn their hearts, and to grant them more of that mind which was in Christ Jesus.[15]

It was only when it was all over that he began himself to resort to pettiness and peevishness. He refused to give up any of his existing preferments, despite friendly pressure to persuade him to clear himself from accusations of pluralism; and when the chance came to him to exact a little revenge in examining a Tractarian extremist, Richard MacMullen, for the BD degree, he imposed upon him such unreasonable demands that it took two years of unsavoury academic litigation before the degree could be awarded.

Within the Anglican Church, Hampden was expressing views very much out of season; and here again the situation was not without its irony. With complete sincerity Newman took issue with him because he genuinely feared the direction in which latitudinarianism could be driving the Church, and – in the end – he convinced himself that he was fighting a losing battle. Similarly Manning, in 1847, when Lord John Russell acted with even greater perversity than Melbourne in thrusting Hampden upon an affronted diocese and a scandalized Church, had to concede that his own vision of what a true Church, within the Catholic tradition, ought to be, was utterly at variance with the ugly reality of Erastianism. During his Catholic career, however, Newman was to discover some of the frustrations of holding views that jarred in the ears of authority, and the penalties that one sometimes has to pay.

The events of 1836 marked 'the zenith of Tractarian power within Oxford', a recent historian has commented.[16] They would never experience such a success again, perhaps for the very reason, paradoxically, that they had succeeded too well. Real and lasting animosities had been aroused; the methods of warfare employed – whipping up support within and without the University; writing pamphlets, as Newman freely admitted to Froude in June 1834, in order 'to irritate' and to do so 'as rhetorically and vehemently as I can';[17] using Convocation as a punitive body – all these things in time would rebound against the Tractarians. A mixture of animosity and adulation within a closed community is a potentially explosive compound. Dean Church recaptured the new mood of Oxford at the time of the Hampden crisis by comparing it with Florence in the days of Savonarola. In the city-state atmosphere of early nineteenth-century Oxford,

> feelings were apt to be more keen and intense and personal than in the larger scenes of life . . . And these feelings passed from individuals into parties: the small factions of a limited area. Men struck blows and loved and hated in those days in Oxford as they hardly did on the wider stage of London politics or general religious controversy.[18]

Love and hate. Over the relatively inoffensive R. D. Hampden, the knives had been sharpened; they would not settle easily back into their sheaths. The alliance that had brought the Tractarians victory had always been a fragile one. It needed only the slightest overstepping of the mark, in a mood of exuberant self-confidence, to shatter it, and then bitter internecine conflict would again break out. In 1835 the Hebdomadal Board had suffered humiliation at the hands of the more junior ranks within the hierarchy; and the hounding of a Regius Professor, especially one who had none of the charisma of the man who master-minded the attack upon him, was bound to make a deep impression upon the undergraduate body too.

Benjamin Jowett, looking back on those heady days, reflected years later to Wilfrid Ward that 'it was the age of young men'.[19] If indeed it was so more than any other, especially within the setting of a university, it was because it seemed to so many of the young, both undergraduates and the younger dons, that there had arisen within their midst and at that time someone whom they could admire as a hero. In casting the Vicar of St Mary's in that role, they looked up to him, not only because he appeared to be a champion of an exciting and uplifting cause, but also because he had achieved a reputation as a preacher of quite extraordinary depth and power. Something that William Palmer had feared might happen had turned out to be only too disturbingly true: a form of personal discipleship perilous both to the object of admiration and to the cause that he represented. Oxford was falling victim to an infectious disease; it was something called 'Newmania'.

IV

Some infections defy precise definition of their source. With 'Newmania', however, the centre in which it was most catching was undoubtedly the church of St Mary the Virgin, where practically every Sunday at 4 p.m. Newman was to be heard, according to Lord Coleridge, 'by as remarkable a congregation, as I should think, was ever gathered together to hear regularly a single preacher'.[1] Dean Church testified to the power of these sermons from his own recollections:

> None but those who remember them can adequately estimate the effect ... The world knows them, has heard a great deal about them, has passed its various judgments on them. But it hardly realises that without these sermons the movement might never have gone on, certainly would never have been what it was ... Since 1828 this preaching had been going on at St Mary's, growing in purpose and directness as the years went on ... While men were reading and talking about the Tracts, they were hearing the sermons; and in the sermons they heard the living meaning, and reason, and bearing of the Tracts, their ethical affinities, their moral standard. The sermons created a moral atmosphere, in which men judged the questions in debate.[2]

Newman once observed to F. W. Faber that 'I *do* think that my influence among persons who have *not* seen me has been indefinitely greater than among those who have',[3] which would suggest that he thought that his sermons in their published form would make a greater impact than his delivery of them from the pulpit. Certainly they made an immediate impact upon his reading public, Jemima assuring him in 1841, after reading volume V of the *Parochial Sermons*, that 'they are more read than any of your writings ... it is nothing intellectual; it is a sort of spiritual perception.'[4] But Newman underrated the effect of his presence and of his voice. He eschewed any emotional appeal;

never indulged in histrionics of any sort; his sermons (as an Anglican at least) were always read from a text.

> It is impossible to say whether on the whole he spoke quickly or slowly [one of the Oratorians later recalled], for there was no appearance either of haste or deliberation. His manner of speaking was the same in the pulpit as on ordinary occasions; in fact, he was not preaching but conversing, very thoughtfully and earnestly ... From time to time [a hearer] might almost be startled at some change in the preacher's voice and the words which accompanied it ... These little outbreaks came and went like a flash of lightning. They seemed like a momentary loss of the perfect self-restraint habitual to the speaker followed by an instant recovery. An extraordinary thing about them was the very slight change in the voice which they seemed to entail. It was like a mere breath of wind passing over the surface of perfectly still water.[5]

Even a hostile auditor, in a totally different setting, could fall victim to the spell of Newman's voice. Mr Justice Coleridge, the presiding judge at the Achilli libel trial in 1853, had to concede that all those present in his courtroom were transfixed at the moment when Newman rose to speak. 'What a sweet musical, almost unearthly voice it was, so unlike any else we had heard.'[6] The cumulative effect of these various ingredients – a message which rarely failed to evoke a response in the hearts of his hearers, the deceptively frail figure of the preacher, who seemed somehow to personify the feeling of awe that his words inspired, and that incomparable voice – gave to Newman, in Gladstone's estimation, an influence within the University unparalleled since the days when Peter Abelard lectured in Paris.[7]

Manning, powerful preacher as he was, did not have the advantage of an arena of such potential influence. A gifted incumbent of a university church, such as Charles Simeon in Cambridge and Newman in Oxford, was in a position to attract and to influence those of an impressionable age, one denied to a man whose ministry was in a rural parish. James Mozley, who heard them both, was so entranced by Newman that he found it difficult, in his own sermons, to refrain from imitating him. Manning – he thought, after hearing two of his University Sermons – was undoubtedly 'very deep, but not always in good taste, too nice and pointed in his style and his delivery',[8] an opinion not shared by W. J. E. Bennett, who delighted in Manning's 'exquisitely worded sermons', adding, 'truly he was then "great in the charm of a sweetened oratory"'.[9] Interestingly,

Newman again perhaps underrated his own very special gift, when he expressed the opinion to Maria Giberne that 'Manning *does* preach indefinitely better than I, say what you will'.[10] Richard Sibthorpe, who heard them both during their Catholic careers, seems to have agreed. He described Manning as 'the most profitable preacher I have ever heard in my whole life'.[11]

In 1879 the question was put to Gladstone, over the dinner table, 'Which of Newman's writings will be read in a hundred years?' His reply was: 'I think all his parochial sermons will be read.'[12] He elaborated a little further to R. H. Hutton in 1890. 'Is it not a fact', he asked, 'that these sermons are his largest gift to permanent, indestructible theology?'[13] This requires some consideration. In the first place, Newman actually very rarely embarked on technical theological questions in the course of his preaching. As he explained to Bishop Bagot in 1841, in justification of his conscious effort to steer clear of all controversy in the pulpit: 'In the general run of my Sermons I have much fainter or fewer traces than might have been expected of those characteristics of doctrine, with which my name is commonly associated ... My sermons have been far more practical than doctrinal.'[14] He occasionally touched upon the doctrine of the Trinity[15] and the Eucharist,[16] and there were echoes of his *Lectures on Justification* in at least three other sermons.[17] But the chief emphasis was placed on two related themes: 'concern for the authenticity of discipleship manifested in the moral life'[18] and the pervading sense that *omnia exeunt in mysterium*;[19] so that if one means by theology, the teaching of the abiding consciousness of living in the presence of God – *coram Deo* – then almost every page of Newman's sermons testifies to his own awareness of that privileged, yet awesome, relationship and his urgent wish that others should be enabled to perceive the same. The central core of his preaching is most clearly expressed in a sermon on 'The Stay of the Soul' in June 1839, where he cites biblical precedents to show

> that the soul of man is made for the contemplation of its Maker; and that nothing short of that high contemplation is its happiness; that, whatever it may possess besides, it is unsatisfied till it is vouchsafed God's presence, and lives in the light of it.[20]

In one of his Dublin lectures on 'University Preaching', Newman pointed out that the function of a preacher is not to supply intellectual edification but to minister to 'the spiritual good of his hearers'. Furthermore, 'what he feels himself, and feels deeply, he has to make others feel deeply'.[21] Herein, above all else, lay the secret of Newman's power as a preacher, and – indeed – Manning's also: their ability to convey to others their own intense consciousness of the reality of the spiritual world. In an Easter sermon, preached in 1839, Newman described the release of the soul from the body in words anticipatory of the exquisite verses of the opening of Part II of the *Dream of Gerontius*.

> We have had enough of weariness, and dreariness, and listlessness, and sorrow, and remorse. We have had enough of the troublesome world. We have had enough of its noise and din. Noise is its best music. But now there is stillness; and it is a stillness that speaks. We know how strange the feeling is of perfect silence after continued sound. Such is our blessedness now.[22]

Newman spoke of the haven for which the soul craves as if he had already found it himself. Exactly the same impression was gained by those who saw him, as a Catholic, celebrating Mass. It was as if 'he became transfigured at the altar'.[23] So too with the Catholic Manning. 'Many of us remember', Wilfrid Ward has written, 'passages in Cardinal Manning's discourses in which he appeared almost to *see* the City of God, and the Great White Throne, and the angel guards with flaming swords, and his audience listened as to one who saw what they did not see.'[24]

The second reflection about Gladstone's prediction must be this. Setting aside the enduring beauty of Newman's prose and the sublimity of his spiritual perception, there remains much in his sermons, as with the sermons of all nineteenth-century preachers, that gives them the flavour of a period piece; and Gladstone may be excused on this count in that it is difficult, if not impossible, in one's own day, to discern what will appear dated to a later generation. No congregation of the present day would have the stamina to cope with the length of many of them (his University Sermon in 1843 on 'The Purification of the Blessed Virgin' lasted one and a half hours).[25] There is much that would cause perplexity in their structure and format, quite apart from their content. As an Anglican Newman rarely, if ever, used the first person in his sermons. There is a complete absence of personal allusions by way of illustration, although his sermon notes, as a Catholic, suggest that he overcame his reticence in later years.[26] He very rarely, as an Anglican, used the name of the second person of the Trinity. Even more surprising, in the course of his parochial sermons all his quotations are scriptural, with the exception of a single reference to St Augustine, whom he does not actually quote.[27] In his Dublin lecture he defended his refusal to go beyond the Word of God by pointing out that 'it is not necessary for a preacher to quote the Holy Fathers, or to show erudition, or to construct an original argument.'[28] Manning differed here, but not to a great extent. In his four volumes of Anglican sermons, he quotes St Augustine four times,[29] with single quotations from St Irenaeus, Origen and Bishop Butler.[30]

The biblical quotations in Newman's sermons are legion. In an Epiphany sermon of 1840, he cites the Scriptures 64 times;[31] in a sermon of 1843 on 'The Shepherd of our Souls', there are 40 references,[32] and in the same year, one of the *Sermons on Subjects of the Day* contains 50 scriptural texts.[33] The Old Testament figures quite as conspicuously as the New. As Sheridan Gilley has pointed out, there is a very Hebraic element in Newman's Anglican sermons, a note which Matthew Arnold, whose ear was tuned to all things Greek, failed to discern.[34] It reveals itself in his emphasis on God the Lawgiver and God the Judge, which, in *The Grammar of Assent*, is 'the aspect under which Almighty God is presented to us by Nature ... One who is angry with us, and threatens evil.'[35] Newman is constantly invoking Old Testament characters as symbolic of types in the modern world. Balaam is the archetype of the man who 'did not give his heart to God'.[36] He appears in seven of the parochial sermons, four of the *Sermons on Subjects of the Day*, three of his (Catholic) *Discourses to Mixed Congregations*, with eight other references in his published writings or letters, a total of 22 references in all.[37]

The Angry God, the God who dispenses retributive justice – this is all of a piece with that aspect of Newman's sermons that excited most criticism in his own day, and which seems to those of a later generation most alien to their understanding of the nature of the Christian revelation: his preoccupation with the Law rather than the Gospel, and his constant elaborations of the theme of the Four Last Things – Death, Judgement, Heaven and Hell.

This needs to be put into context. The late twentieth century has become somewhat squeamish over all matters eschatological. Preachers tend to shun the issue, perhaps because they themselves hardly know what to say, or – if they do – they are reluctant to say it. The nineteenth century had no such reservations. A few bold spirits were able to reconcile a devout Christian faith with a rejection of the doctrine of eternal punishment: thinkers such as Coleridge, Erskine, F. D. Maurice and F. W. Robertson; and they were therefore prepared to challenge the orthodoxy of the time. Neither Newman nor Manning was of that number. Nor, it may be noted, was Gladstone. One of the reasons why he was so anxious that Newman's sermons should continue to be read by later generations was his alarm at the diminution of preaching on eternal punishment in the closing decades of the Victorian age. 'The danger of losing it ought at all costs to be averted,' he declared.[38]

If one believes in an infallible Bible, however, it is difficult to wriggle out of an unqualified acceptance of the certainty of future judgement and the reality of Hell-fire; and both Newman and Manning were fully convinced, almost from their earliest awareness of their Christian commitment, of the inevitablity of judgement, as well as the everlasting torments that awaited those whom God the Judge rejected. Both were profoundly influenced by the eschatological imagery of the Apocalypse; even to the extent, particularly with Newman, of interpreting that imagery with an uncompromising literalism in their picture of the Day of Judgement. Newman was almost obsessed, both as an Anglican and as a Catholic, with the notion that God actually had a Book in which all one's sins were recorded. In December 1829, he castigated those who fell short of their Christian duty by reminding them of a fearful encounter to come.

> What will you say, when heaven and hell are before you, and the books are opened, and therein you find the sum total of your youthful desires and dreams, your passionate wishes for things of this world, your low-minded, grovelling tastes, your secret contempt and aversion for serious subjects and persons, your efforts to attract the looks of sinners and to please those who displease God . . . ? Ah, I may seem to you to use harsh words; but be sure I do not use terms near so severe as you will use against yourselves in that day.[39]

His New Year message in 1832 was hardly more cheering: 'What a dreary prospect seems to be before us, when . . . the books will be opened.'[40] Again, in 1836, he warned his congregation of the dangers of a single sin left forgotten and unrepented. Punishment was inevitable, he said, at that 'fearful moment . . . when the books are opened'.[41] Even though in his later Catholic years his imagery becomes less painfully anthropomorphic – especially when he came to write the *Dream of Gerontius* – nevertheless that awful 'Book' continued to haunt him. In devotions dedicated to the boys of the Oratory School, there comes a meditation on the subject of 'Every Sin has its Punishment', in which Newman reflects that 'Thou art the all-seeing, all-knowing God. Thy eyes, O Lord, are in every place ... Thou hast a book: Thou enterest in it every day of my life.'[42]

Manning seems to have been rather more cautious in his references to the Day of Judgement. In one early sermon he used the image of God's 'Eternal Eye', before which 'on our knees' the full folly of worldly conceits would be exposed.[43] In a very beautiful and compassionate collection of meditations, written in his Catholic years, on *The Love of Jesus to Penitents*, he twice alludes to God's 'Book of Remembrance'.[44] He refers to Hell, but – wisely – refrains from trying to describe it. Christians who fall into sin after baptism, he once warned his congregation, are in a worse state than the heathen. 'For Christians know of life and immortality: to them Tophet and Gehenna are no parables, but well-known and horrible realities.'[45] He would frequently exhort penitents to keep a scrupulous record of their sins. They must never be thrust out of mind and therefore unrepented. That way lay declension and corruption. In a University Sermon at Oxford in November 1842, he observed 'how slight a cause is sufficient for the worst result. The injection of a solitary doubt has issued in settled infidelity; an impure tale has wrought itself out into the defilement of an unchaste life.'[46] Nevertheless, as Geoffrey Rowell has pointed out, stern as Manning could be on the need to strive for sanctification, there is in his sermons 'a lack of the almost frightening intensity which marks Newman's preaching'.[47]

Anthony Kenny, in a recent symposium, has observed with a delicate touch of understatement that 'Newman was not a comfortable man to hear'.[48] It was not his intention, as an Anglican, to offer the solace of comfortable words. His sermons, simple, direct and unadorned in their composition, were of a piece with his whole theology, which actually changed very little on his becoming a Catholic. The texts for the times in which he was preaching were taken from St Paul's Letter to the Philippians and from the first Epistle of St Peter – 'Work out your own salvation with fear and trembling' and 'Pass the time of your sojournment in fear'.[49] Faced with the text 'My yoke is easy and my burden is light', Newman invested it with a severity that the words hardly convey.

It is only 'grace makes it so', he wrote. 'In itself it is severe, and any form of doctrine which teaches otherwise forgets that Christ calls us to His yoke – and that yoke is a cross.'[50] To understand this fully requires appreciation of Newman's teaching on the role of conscience as 'the internal witness of both the existence and the law of God'.[51] For himself, as Michael Allsopp has pointed out, 'conscience was the creative principle of [his] belief in God, the basis of his awareness of a supreme governor and judge and the immediate origin of his prayer and worship'.[52] Therefore, as Newman explained in *The Grammar of Assent*, recognition of the existence of God comes initially through our conscience, which induces in us feelings of guilt. The 'large and deep' foundation of all religion 'is the sense of sin and guilt, and without that sense there is for man, as he is, no genuine religion'.[53] This essentially moralistic teaching is apparent in Newman's sermons from the first. A sermon preached in July 1831, and yet another in November 1836, proclaim the same message: 'a sense of guilt, indeed, every one, the best of us, must have'.[54]

Stephen Dessain is at pains to show that Newman's stern moralism has been sometimes misunderstood; but his examples are not wholly convincing. He points out that F. W. Faber, at least, thought Newman's sternness was less oppressive than Pusey's; and then he quotes two sermons to show that – to Newman – 'peace and joy are the keynotes of the Christian character' and that they reveal him to be 'a Christian humanist' making his own 'a joyful optimism which pervades the teaching of St Ambrose, St Athanasius and the Greek Fathers'.[55] It is true that Newman, on a rare occasion, preached on the theme that 'Gloom is no Christian temper; that repentance is not real, which has not love in it'. But the characteristic Newman sobriety has to be brought in to qualify what he has said. 'We must live in sunshine, even when in sorrow; we must live in God's presence, we must not shut ourselves up in our own hearts, even when we are reckoning up our past sins.'[56] And when he describes how 'we are Christ's, not by faith merely, or by works merely, but by love', the moralistic note immediately appears in the course of his elaboration. 'Love is the gentle, tranquil, satisfied acquiescence and adherence of the soul in the contemplation of God; not only a preference of God before all things, but a delight in Him because He is God, and because His commandments are good.'[57]

The problem for Newman, and also to some extent for Manning, was the coming to terms with the disturbing implications of the text 'Many are called, but few chosen'. Newman frequently preached on the theme, pointing out that election carried no guarantee of that sanctification which would fit us for heaven, because some of the elect will surely fall away. He explained this in an Epiphany sermon of 1834 in the course of an exposition of the predestination text in the eighth chapter of the Epistle to the Romans:

> It is not more inconsistent with the solemn announcement of the text ... that some once elected should fall away (as we know they do), than that an event should be spoken of in it as past and perfect, which is incomplete and future ... Hence it happens that the word 'elect' in Scripture has two senses, standing both for those who are called *in order* to salvation, and for those who at the last day shall be the *actually resulting fruit* of that holy call.[58]

In another sermon, he even suggests a sort of competitive element within the body of the elect. 'We fear to be too holy. Others put us to shame; all around us, others are doing what we will not. Others are entering deeper into the kingdom of heaven than we.'[59] The explanation of this somewhat unedifying race is Newman's preoccupation with the implications of another fear-provoking text: 'Without holiness no man shall see the Lord' (Hebrews 12:14). As he explained in one of the very earliest of his sermons to be published, preached in August 1826, 'heaven would be hell to an irreligious man'.[60] Therefore all our efforts in this life must be directed to striving for the attainment of holiness. Manning would certainly not have disagreed with this. He believed emphatically that there was within all of us the potential to aspire to the heights. 'The distinction ... between the visible Church and the invisible communion of saints', he wrote in *The Unity of the Church*, 'is no more than the distinction between *potentiality* and *actuality*.' All baptized Christians are 'saints *in posse*'.[61] But, of course, all men are sinners, too; and unfortunately – within the Anglican communion – no merit could be claimed for the good works that they performed. As Newman pointed out in his *Lectures on Justification*, the notion of merit is abhorrent because it amounts to a sort of undignified bargaining with God.[62]

This being so, the burden upon sinful man to aspire to a holiness that he could not actually earn was a very onerous one. Could one ever be sure? Manning, with his clearer understanding of the doctrine of penance and the efficacy of absolution, seems –

at least in the 1840s – to have been less perplexed than Newman on this uncomfortable question. As Archbishop Brilioth observed, 'the denial of any possibility of assurance is one of the corner-stones of Newman's practical teaching'.[63] Nor did he spare himself in drawing a lurid picture of what lay in store for those many unfortunates who failed the final test. 'Flames of fire and the lake of brimstone will be their meat and drink,' he wrote in a sermon entitled 'Present Blessings'; 'the heaven above them will be brass; their earth will be dust and ashes; the blood in their veins will be as molten lead. Fearful thought!'[64] Even more fearful, however, is the thought that if we can never count on God's mercy and forgiveness at the last, God may Himself prove to be a capricious Judge. The most frightening picture that Newman ever drew of the Judgement that awaits us all was in an early Catholic sermon, entitled 'Neglect of Divine Calls and Warnings', in which he describes the plight of seemingly honest but ineffective triers to live up to the demands of their faith, and how they scream with horror at what they discover to be their fate, a dreadful reminder – as Newman intended it to be – that God 'is not obliged to let off any; He has the power to condemn all'.[65]

Understandably, Newman had his critics, both as an Anglican and as a Catholic. One of the first to voice his disquiet was Samuel Wilberforce, after he had read a presentation copy of Newman's first volume of parochial sermons. He consulted his friend James Stephen, who was inclined to disapprove even more strongly. Samuel's main objection revealed his enduring Evangelical affinities, as befitted one who bore the Wilberforce name. Newman was effectively denying the free working of the Holy Spirit to bring sinners to repentance.[66] James Stephen agreed. It was to him a sorrow that a man of such manifest gifts 'should contrive to invest Christianity with an aspect so harsh and repulsive'. If the duty of a preacher lay in 'touching men's hearts and influencing their conduct ... Charles Simeon is worth a legion of Newmans'.[67] Barbara Wilberforce, Samuel's mother, who had done her best to follow her sons in their enthusiasm for Newman's stance at Oxford, confessed that she was defeated by the tone and content of his sermons, especially 'the want of comfort to the penitent and contrite'. A mutual friend had said to her, after reading the sermons, 'If I had no better hope than Mr Newman's views afford me I should be very wretched.'[68] It is interesting, too, that Manning felt precisely the same unease. He told his brother-in-law, Samuel, that he found this first volume of sermons

> the hardest book to criticise I ever met with . . . because . . . it exhibits
> religion most fully and pointedly as a system of *requisitions*, but seems
> to cramp the attractive, encouraging and cheering spirit of our 'better
> hope' . . . The omission of the agency of the Holy Ghost, as a person
> continually present, helping, teaching, strengthening, guiding, and
> enabling us to use God's appointed means of renewal, is especially
> unfortunate when the general tone of the Sermons is that of
> requisition.[69]

It has already been seen that there are several similarities
between the Anglican sermons of Newman and of Manning – the
same call to holiness, the stress upon the doctrine of election, the
emphasis on the need for repentance, and the dangers of religious complacency. But there are also significant differences.
Manning's stress is less on fear, and more on the love of God. In a
sermon of the late 1840s, he poses the question,

> On what, then, shall we stay ourselves in the day when the fear of
> death falls upon us? . . . First, upon the love of God, in giving His Son
> to die for us. 'God so loved the world' -- that is, so almightily, so
> divinely, with the infinite love of the eternal Godhead; – 'that He gave
> His only begotten Son' . . . 'God commendeth His love toward us, in
> that, while we were yet sinners, Christ died for us'. This is our first
> foundation: that God loves the world; that He looks upon the works of
> His hands with an eternal and steadfast love, with a tender yearning
> compassion. Whatever be doubtful, this is sure.[70]

Unlike Newman, he preached often on the themes of forgiveness
and assurance:

> If He have forgiven us so much, what is there that we shall not forgive
> our brother? if He have forgiven us so often, how can we ever refuse
> forgiveness? Seventy times seven, seven times in a day, what is this to
> those who have the forgiveness of God through the blood of Jesus
> Christ? . . . The great truth here revealed to us is, the love, clemency,
> forgiveness of God to sinners.[71]

These are not isolated sermons. In a sermon on 'The Gentleness
of Christ', he pointed to the tenderness of the Son as our surest
comfort. 'His tenderness is a thing so far above the thoughts even
of saints, that it is no wonder that sinners, fallen and soiled with
evil, should not be able to believe it.'[72] He returned to the theme
of assurance in a later sermon: the way may not always be smooth,
he said, but 'your way shall be sure'.[73]

Newman was unrepentant when taxed by his critics. He could cite biblical authority for everything he said. In a reply to a correspondent who complained about the severity of his earliest published sermon, on 'Secret Faults', he referred him to the first Epistle to the Corinthians. 'I hold to its awful views still,' he wrote, 'and wish it were more impressed upon my heart.'[74] In a sermon of November 1838, he justified his severity of tone by declaring 'it was scarcely too much to say that awe and fear are at the present day all but discarded from religion'.[75] He had put the point even more strongly in his replies to the complaints of Samuel Wilberforce and James Stephen. While he conceded that God 'has *many* mansions in His house ... I dare not *preach* so, lest I should be wise above that is written'.[76] He did not deny for one moment that his first volume of sermons induced fear and depression. 'It was meant to do so. We *require the "Law's* stern fires". We need a continual Ash Wednesday.'[77] He was also attempting to redress the balance against the facile assurance of the Evangelicals and the irreverent familiarity with which they spoke of holy things.

> The poorest and humblest ought to shrink from the irreverence necessarily involved in pulpit addresses, which speak of the adorable works and sufferings of Christ, with the familiarity and absence of awe with which we speak about our friends. Zaccheus did not intrude himself on our Lord – the woman that was a sinner silently bedewed His feet. Which of us is less refined than a 'tax-gatherer or a harlot'?[78]

In fairness to Newman, he was not alone in deploring the spiritual barrenness of his age. William Palmer shared his disquiet. 'Religion was no longer what it had been ... It had been encrusted by prosperity. Evangelicalism had lost the fervour of its first love.'[79]

The more difficult question to answer is why Newman's sermons attracted so many more admirers than critics, and why – in particular – the grim message appealed so greatly to the young? The character of the preacher goes some way to explain this. In his novel *Callista*, Newman described how effective as a Christian teacher was Caecilius: 'self-collected, serene, gentle, tender, unobtrusive, unstudied. It enabled him to say things severe and even stern, without startling, offending or repelling the hearer.'[80] This could almost be a portrait of Newman himself in the pulpit at St Mary's. His call to repentance was intensely compelling, and with it came occasional inspired glimpses of Christianity as it once had been, which in their own day had become pathetically misconceived, thereby failing to meet the needs of those who craved for something, they knew not what. Through Newman's words they found in their hearts an answer to their inchoate yearnings, words that spoke of far-off things, shrouded in mystery. Who could resist, for instance, the power of the contrast that Newman drew, in a sermon of 1831, between the easy relationship that the disciples enjoyed with Christ on earth and the whole changed order of things after His resurrection and ascension?

> When He had once ascended, henceforth for unstudied speech there were solemn rites; for familiar attendance there were mysterious ministerings; for questioning at will there was silent obedience; for sitting at table there was bowing and adoration; for eating and drinking there were fastings and watchings. He who had taken his Lord and rebuked Him, dared not speak to Him after His resurrection, when he saw and knew Him. He who had lain in His bosom at supper, fell at His feet as dead. Such was the vision of the glorified Saviour of man, returning to His redeemed in the power of the Spirit, with a Presence more pervading because more intimate, and more real because more hidden. And as the manner of His coming was new, so was His gift. It was peace, but a new peace, 'not as the world giveth', not the exultation of the young, light-hearted, and simple, easily created, easily lost; but a serious, sober, lasting comfort, full of reverence, deep in contemplation.[81]

Then again, Newman had the remarkable gift of speaking directly to the hearts and predicaments of those whom he was addressing, almost as if he knew them better than themselves. J. H. Walgrave has put it thus: Newman, in his sermons,

> lays bare every trace of egoism and pride, brings to light all the sophistries in which they shelter, unmasks the seeming virtues which disguise them ... This conjunction of high religious inspiration and acute psychological penetration gives a unique grandeur and beauty to these slight, completely unpretentious sermons. In the whole history of spirituality, they form one of the most striking documents of self-knowledge in the sight of God.[82]

But why the fear, and why the continual reminders of the horrors of eternal punishment? Nietzsche once observed, 'Distrust all in whom the impulse to punish is powerful'.[83] More recently Conor Cruise O'Brien, in an article in *The Times*, divided those who harped on this theme into two categories: those who did so out of 'vindictive joy' and those who did so out of fear.[84] Newman surely belongs to the latter category.

Thomas Arnold maintained that the secret of Newman's power in the pulpit was that he was preaching more to himself than to others, and this therefore gave to his words so total a sincerity that they could not but be compelling.[85] Newman was conscious of having received God's call; but he could not accept the comfort of final perseverance; and if it is true that the saintlier the man, the more conscious he is of his own inadequacies and secret faults, then Newman was likely to test himself against the highest, and perhaps impossible, standards. One of the reasons why he was reluctant to hear confessions – in this respect differing greatly from Manning – was his own doubts about the efficacy of absolution.[86] In his own mind, he echoed the apprehensions of his hero, Charles Reding, in his earlier novel, *Loss and Gain*. 'Reding . . . felt a difficulty in determining how and when the sins of a Christian are forgiven.'[87] Within the Anglican Church, Newman never found an answer to this question. It is not all that certain that he found an answer totally to satisfy himself in his early years as a Catholic. So, in his Anglican sermons, he shared his fear with others. Did not Callista, in the novel, say to Caecilius, when he was doing his best to convert her, 'Father, you are speaking to yourself'?[88]

V

The middle years of the 1830s were for Newman his time of plenty; for Manning, too, his prospects had never seemed brighter. Both, however, were to suffer grievous personal blows, which were to affect their lives more deeply than either of them perhaps realized at the time. On 28 February 1836 Hurrell Froude died, far away in the West Indies, at the age of thirty-three. Newman described the blow, which he had been long expecting, as 'the greatest loss I could have. I shall be truly widowed, yet I hope to bear it lightly.'[1] In the following year, on 24 July, Manning lost his beloved wife Caroline. This, too, was not unexpected. As early as February 1837, Manning had written to Newman to express his fears:

> I am sure I do not deceive myself in thinking that you will very sincerely enter into the trial which God is graciously pleased at this time to send me. I do not know whether you have heard, although it is most likely you have through H. Wilberforce or Wood that my wife

has been, and still is in a state of the most alarming danger . . . I try to leave all in God's hands – but it is very very difficult. I am sure you will both feel, and pray for me. If you can find time, I should very much like to hear from you.

I cannot say how much consolation the sympathy of Christian friendship and brotherhood gives me when I am tempted to feel myself alone, and the one who was in an earthly way all things to me seems to be bidden to an early rest.[2]

The letters that passed between the two men, whom the issues of later years were so sadly to divide, are the most moving of all their correspondence, and suggest a degree of sympathy and affection between them only to be exhibited again in one other phase of their lives, in the 1850s. Newman tried to assure his friend that God 'does not willingly afflict us, nor will put a single grain's weight more of suffering than it is meet and good for you to bear – and be sure too that with your suffering your support will grow.'[3] On 21 July, Manning reported that 'Suspense is no longer a trial. A few days will end all her sufferings . . . No man knows what it is to watch the desire of his eyes fading away – for such indeed is dying in this most gentle dispensation.'[4] Four days later, he sent the news of Caroline's passing. 'At last you will rejoice to hear that it has pleased God, with a tenderness of hand I could not have imagined, to fulfill this searching visitation. My beloved wife fell asleep, I believe in both senses of that blessed word, like a child yesterday evening at 10 m. to 5.'[5] She was only 25.

'Manning is calm and quiet,' Samuel Wilberforce wrote to his brother, Robert, after Caroline's funeral, at which Manning with exceptional self-control had delivered an exquisitely tender address. 'I trust [he] will not sink when this strain is over.'[6] The strain was, indeed, hardly bearable, but he was determined not to show it. Mrs Sargent took control of his household, and indeed lived with him, ministering to his every need as a mother to a son, until she was called away in 1841 to take charge of another stricken household, when Emily Wilberforce died. There were moments when she nearly broke down. A year after Caroline's death, Manning himself was taken ill with a painful obstruction, and Mrs Sargent slept on a sofa by his bedside. She described her feelings to Emily:

Henry bore his pain like a martyr, as you knew he would, but it was very severe . . . But my dearest Emily to find myself sitting up in that *room* – you can imagine but I cannot describe what I felt – and then he was obliged to take from his neck the chain that has long hung there this last year, and I saw her locket and the two dear rings he himself took from her fingers and I almost fancied she was there herself. As I was watching him sleeping I saw her lovely smile when she looked at me and said 'I am sure Mama you will do all you can to take care of Henry'. I felt fulfilling her wishes and was comforted.[7]

Manning just occasionally hinted to those closest to him how the tragic bereavement had affected him. He told Newman in October that 'one great thought is before me night and day, but I have long since been unable either to speak or write of it'. He added: 'I feel what passed between us then has given me a privilege in your friendship, which perhaps nothing else could.'[8] To his brother-in-law, Samuel, he confessed 'that I cannot trust myself to dwell upon the past except in direct acts of devotion – at these times, in church, but especially day by day at home – I both can, and do, fully and fixedly – and these are the most blessed moments of my present life. At all other times I feel the absolute need of full employment.'[9]

To secure this, he began to look further afield than the conscientious ministering to the needs of his tiny parish, and the responsibilities of Rural Dean (which he had been appointed in 1837). Challenges there were in abundance. One such was the controversy over the setting-up of the Ecclesiastical Commission on a permanent basis in 1836, with extensive powers to tackle the anomalies and abuses of the still lamentably unreformed Established Church. This was seen by the Tractarians as yet another, and more serious, encroachment by the State upon the independent authority of the Church, the more so because of the mixed composition (both clergy and laity) of the Commission itself. The obvious fact of the urgent need for reform, and the redistribution of endowments to eradicate gross inequalities and to redeploy the Church's finances in areas of pressing need, was almost forgotten in the fury over the totally unacceptable instrument which Parliament had devised to achieve so necessary an end.

Pusey entered the fray with a strongly-worded protest. Manning then, in 1838, published his *Principles of the Ecclesiastical Commission examined*, following the accepted form of addressing it as an open letter to a suitable dignitary, in this instance his diocesan, the Bishop of Chichester. In the context of the needs of the time, it was not his weightiest contribution. Geoffrey Best has likened it to Pusey's 'melancholy spectacle of a high-principled

clerical mind almost unhinged by excitement and morbidity'.[10]
Already Manning had renewed his friendship with Gladstone,
with whom – from 1837 – he regularly corresponded, sometimes
to offer each other mutual support, as, for instance, over the
contentious issue of increasing the government grant to the
Roman Catholic seminary at Maynooth; sometimes to amend or
qualify each other's expressions when they differed in detail, if
not on principle. On the Ecclesiastical Commission, Gladstone
thought Manning was pushing his objections too far. 'I do not
think I take quite so strong a view as you of the *de jure* disqualification of Parliament to counsel the Crown touching the Church in
matters primarily or partially relating to her temporalities,' he
wrote; '. . . I do not say that I shall like the Commission . . . but I
am not certain that . . . it may not be right and wise to endure it.'[11]

Over this same period Manning was seeing Newman frequently, and in December 1837 Newman was sufficiently impressed to recommend to his friend, Edward Churton, that the rising
young Rector of Lavington should be offered the vacant editorship of the main organ of Tractarian principles, the *British
Critic*.

> What think you . . . of Manning of Merton? [he wrote] . . . He is an
> exceedingly sound man – a clever man – with some time his own . . . I
> know him very well, and he agrees with me in views – but he is no
> Pupil of mine . . . He is, in no conceivable sense, of the Oxford school
> (to use a wrong word) – Pusey knows him now, being drawn to him by
> congeniality of opinions – but he is Pusey's only so far as Pusey's is
> Truth.[12]

Nothing further came of the proposal, and Newman actually took
over the editorship himself.

Manning's attentions, in any case, had turned to a sphere of
action that was to occupy his energies, at different times and in
changing circumstances, for the rest of his life, both as an
Anglican and as a Catholic: the challenge to the Church of taking
responsibility for national education, especially the education of
the poor. This drew him into active partnership with both
Gladstone and S. F. Wood. In May 1838, he delivered one of the
most powerful sermons in his life, denouncing secular education
and State control, and describing in almost visionary terms the
part that the Church ought to be playing, through its cathedrals,
training colleges and a network of diocesan boards and parochial
schools, whereby 'the first aim and groundwork of education'

should be confirmed 'by the formation of Christian habits, for God's service here and for salvation hereafter'.[13] S. F. Wood was so enthusiastic that he pressed Manning to have copies circulated throughout the country.

In June of the same year, Manning delivered his second Visitation Sermon in Chichester Cathedral, published under the title *The Rule of Faith*. The theme was one which he had been long preparing, going back to his correspondence with Wood two years before, and drawing on his researches on St Vincent of Lérins and his controversy with Wiseman on the Catholicity of the Church of England. It pleased the Evangelicals not at all, because of his rejection of the Protestant doctrine of *sola scriptura*, but it was equally dismissive of the Roman claims. 'The Roman Church, how much soever it may appeal in words to antiquity, does in practice actually oppose it. The infallibility of the *living* Church absorbs all proof into itself. Antiquity, as well as Scripture, is made to follow the interpretations of the present Church.'[14] What he was advocating was precisely Newman's current hypothesis, developed in his *Lectures on the Prophetical Office*, that the Anglican Church was the true and pure *via media*, because it had remained faithful to the Church of primitive times, whereas 'Romanism' and 'ultra-Protestantism' had been 'the two great departures from it'.[15]

Not surprisingly, Newman heartily approved, and wrote to Manning to tell him so, offering one or two minor criticisms of points of detail.[16] In the same letter he expressed concern about Manning's health. He was not the only one to do so. His Bishop, William Otter, warned him that he was taking on too much, despite recurring and severe attacks of asthma.[17] He was strongly advised to rest and to spend the winter months abroad. Somewhat reluctantly, Manning agreed; and hearing that Gladstone was intending to spend Christmas in Rome, he decided to join him. It was to be the first of twenty-two visits to the Eternal City.

Whether he knew it or not, Manning was now treading a road that would lead him shortly to substantial preferment. The road that Newman had been travelling had seemed straight enough, but was soon to degenerate into a series of hazards and pitfalls. For three years and more he had been developing his theory of Anglicanism as the *via media* between Romanist corruptions and popular Protestant heresy, ecclesiologically in his *Lectures on the Prophetical Office*, and theologically in his *Lectures on Justification*, both of them originally delivered at regular intervals in the Adam de Brome chapel at St Mary's. He had first explored this rationale of Anglicanism in two of the *Tracts for the Times* in 1834 (nos 38 and 41). That he was obliged to probe rather deeper arose from his somewhat reluctant agreement to take over from Benjamin Harrison a controversial correspondence initiated with a very persistent and perceptive French priest, Jean-Nicolas Jager, finding himself rather more stretched in defending his cause than he liked to admit. In the end, Newman went back to the drawing-board and tried to work out, in his series of lectures, the basis for a theory of Anglicanism which – he admitted – 'had never had existence except on paper';[18] or, as he put it in his article 'Home Thoughts Abroad', building up a theory on the principles of Archbishop Laud in the seventeenth century, 'a fine-drawn theory, which has never been owned by any body of churchmen'. The theory of the *via media* 'had slept in libraries'.[19]

As a theory it made a great deal of sense. The formularies of the English Church, especially the Prayer Book, revealed clearly the distance between Anglicanism and the popular Protestantism of the Continental reformers and their successors; equally certain was the Anglican Church's adherence to the 'rudimental' Apostles' creed, as opposed to corrupt deviations therefrom in the Creed of Pope Pius imposed by the Council of Trent, confirming that the Roman Church maintained that faith depends on the Church and 'we that the Church is built on the faith'.[20] So far, so good. Not so good, however, was the stumbling-block of the Thirty-nine Articles, which Jager had triumphantly pointed out were binding on all 'ministers', while Newman tried, not very convincingly, to play them down as merely 'instruments of teaching ... heads, as it were, of important chapters of revealed truth'.[21] He also had to concede that Anglicanism possessed no other corpus – or even consensus – of doctrine, and that to establish his own theory he was forced to indulge in eclecticism by quoting from the works of this Caroline divine or that.[22]

Almost as soon as he had enunciated his theory, brilliantly expounded as it was, Newman – as he admitted later to Henry Wilberforce – began to feel less confident about its tenability. 'It is difficult to say', he wrote in 1846, 'whether or not a flagging zeal involves an incipient doubt.'[23] Two seeds, however, had been sown in his mind through his writing of the lectures and his correspondence with Jager. The first was the implications of his distinction between Episcopal Tradition (the apostolic tradition transmitted by bishops) and the Prophetical Tradition, prophets being 'the interpreters of the revelation' who 'unfold and define its mysteries . . . illuminate its documents . . . harmonize its contents' and '. . . apply its promises'.[24] As both Günter Biemer and Louis Allen have pointed out, it is this prophetic tradition within the Church which supplies dynamism and assumes growth.[25] Growth, of course, suggests development; and Jager had sown another seed in Newman's mind, when he wrote: 'when you develop a truth, you do not change it, on the contrary, you give it more force, more lustre, greater scope.'[26] When this seed germinated nearly ten years later, Newman was to describe this form of development as 'preservation of type'.

If the *Lectures on the Prophetical Office* are mainly significant for the light they throw on Newman's personal development, the *Lectures on Justification* have an enduring place in contributions to the theology of grace. What Newman attempted might appear to be a rather wordy compromise between two unacceptable polar doctrines – that of the Protestant (and Pauline) justification by 'faith alone' (as it appears in Article XI of the Thirty-nine Articles), and the Catholic doctrine of good works, resting largely on the text of St James ('by works a man is justified, and not by faith alone'). If there is scriptural authority for both assertions, then – in a sense – both must be correct; and certainly there were dangerous implications in resting totally on the one or the other. The Pauline text could lead, at worst, to antinomianism (an indifference to morals, if righteousness has been imputed to a sinner in spite of his sinful self) and, at best, to a very ill-defined distinction between justification and the requirement of sanctification. The Catholic emphasis had led to corruptions plain to see – over-systematized devotional practices, indulgences, and the treasury of merit. In one sense, Newman's solution was a sort of Aristotelian mean, pruning the excesses of the one and supplying the defects of the other; but it was also much more profound than this. He saw that justification did not merely involve God's pardoning of a sinner; it bestowed on the justified (or 'imparted' to him) the indwelling Word. As summarized by Sheridan Gilley: 'God does not merely pronounce a sinner forgiven; he also *makes* him just, as he renews or regenerates him by his own divine indwelling. Man is thereby reborn into a new quality of life.'[27]

Newman's interpretation, therefore, provides for an element of growth lacking in the Protestant doctrine; it is objective rather than subjective; and it satisfactorily links the regenerating sacrament of Baptism with the sacrament of the Eucharist, sustaining the Christian in holiness and infusing his soul with the presence of Christ. As he himself put it: 'Whether we say we are justified by faith or by works or by sacraments, all these but mean this one doctrine, that we are justified by grace, given through sacraments, impetrated by faith, manifested in works.'[28] It would appear that Newman never abandoned this understanding of justification as 'adherent'. The doctrine of the divine indwelling appears again in one of the verses of the great hymn 'Praise to the Holiest in the height', in his *Dream of Gerontius*:

> And that a higher gift than grace
> Should flesh and blood refine,
> God's presence, and His very Self,
> And Essence all-divine.[29]

From February 1836, however, something had gone out of Newman's life. To be exact, Hurrell Froude had; and Newman was not to find any truly intimate friend to take his place until Henry Wilberforce's curate at Walmer, Ambrose St John, joined him in his retirement at Littlemore in 1843. He had friends and admirers in abundance, but those who had been closest to him and might have filled Froude's place in his heart had taken the dreaded step which destroyed any prospect or promise of intimacy. They had chosen to marry. One of the first had been George Ryder, who had been somewhat offended by finding among the letters congratulating him on his engagement to Sophia Sargent a 'grave remonstrance' from his former tutor.[30] But this was nothing in comparison with the displeasure visited upon Henry Wilberforce on his engagement to Sophia's sister, Mary. Henry had made things far worse by refraining from telling Newman himself for fear of his hostile reaction, so that the news reached him through a mutual friend. Newman was so hurt that he informed Henry that 'for three years from the date of the offence [Christmas 1833], I shall bind myself to a definite line of conduct as regards you',[31] provoking Henry in return to remonstrate on such lack of Christian charity and on what he saw to be a serious defect of character in the incapacity to forgive a personal slight or difference of opinion:

> I cannot help observing that here is one instance out of several of the
> practical evil which springs from your habit of refusing either to state

what the conduct you complain of is – or to hear any explanation of it
... I most deliberately say that it does not seem to me compatible with
our Blessed Lord's teaching to resolve to retain the memory of a
personal wrong and to mark that memory in this conduct for three years
no nor three days.[32]

Newman eventually relented, but the estrangement lasted until
the summer of 1835.

Why did Newman take this so much to heart? Did it go deeper
than a temperamental weakness, as Marvin O'Connell has expressed it, of suffering acute 'frustration consequent upon the
failure of people to be and to act as he wanted them to'?[33] Three
explanations may be offered. In the first place, Newman believed
deeply and sincerely that the perfect state of the priesthood was
'the glory of virginity'.[34] 'If there is one grace in which Christianity stands in especial contrast to the old religion,' he stated in an
Easter sermon on the subject of Judaism, 'it is that of purity.
Christ was born of a Virgin; He remained a virgin; His beloved
disciple was a virgin ... He said that there were those who for the
kingdom of heaven's sake would be even as He.'[35] When St Basil
and St Gregory determined 'to devote themselves to the service of
religion', he wrote in an essay in his *Historical Sketches*, 'they put all
idea of marriage out of their minds.'[36] Both William Robbins and,
more recently, David Nicholls have commented on a passage in
Newman's novel *Loss and Gain*, where Charles Reding's reaction at
seeing a young clergyman with a pretty girl on his arm, in a
bookshop in Bath, was one of nausea, 'as might beset a man on
hearing a call for pork-chops while he was sea-sick'.[37]

The repugnance arose partly from the feeling that respectabil-
ity and domesticity were alien to the vocation of Holy Orders,
Hurrell Froude having first drawn his attention to the 'moral
superiority of the single life' as universal in the Catholic
priesthood;[38] partly also because the thought of the lifelong
commitment horrified him. He told George Ryder in 1832 that 'it
is a fearful thing to tie yourself to one person for life',[39] a
sentiment echoed in *Callista*, when he opens a chapter with the
words, 'It is undeniably a solemn moment ... and requires a
strong heart, when any one deliberately surrenders himself, soul
and body, to the keeping of another while life shall last.'[40]

The second explanation is the inevitable loss of intimacy
between those who have been close friends. This is what so
distressed him about Henry Wilberforce's decision to marry. In a

letter, which he subsequently decided not to send, he wrote:

> You ask me to give my heart, when you give yours to another . . . but I
> cannot, as a prudent man, so forget what is due to my own comfort
> and independence as not to look to my own resources, making my own
> mind my wife, and anticipate and provide for the loss of friends which
> the fashion of the age makes inevitable. [41]

Newman's ideal, which he at one stage thought of trying to create
at Oriel, and actually did go some way to realize for a short while
at Littlemore and eventually at the Oratory at Birmingham, was
the medieval coenobium – a group of celibates, living together
and devoting their lives to study.[42] In this respect, as Newman saw
only too clearly, the Roman Church, with its celibate priesthood
and its monastic ideal, wore the marks of a true Church upon its
body in a way denied to the Anglican establishment with its 'smug
parsons and pony carriages for their wives and daughters'.[43]

The third explanation must surely lie in the temperamental
disposition of Newman himself. There seems to be little doubt
that he had a deep psychological aversion to unchastity; that
nature intended him to live a virgin life because the physical
aspect of marriage so repelled him. He could not bear to be
smothered. There is a passage in *Callista* when his heroine
expresses her distaste for countryside that seems to shut her in –
'luxuriant foliage, the tall, rank plants, the deep close lanes'.[44] He
seems, too, to have had a horror of being touched – even by his
own mother. 'I recollect about two years ago,' he wrote in June
1836, 'after I had fainted away, my Mother most kindly stooping
down to take up my feet and put them on the sofa. I started up – I
could not endure it. I saw she was hurt, yet I did not know how to
put things right.'[45] This must stand as perhaps the saddest
self-revelation that Newman ever vouchsafed; and it is all of a
piece with a propensity to express his deepest emotions for people
by the medium of letters, while reserving any physical expression
purely to inanimate objects. He kissed the newspaper which
contained the news of Frederic Rogers' success in the Oriel
Fellowship examination; he kissed the mantelpiece of his room in
Littlemore when he left it for ever.[46]

The problem, then, that Newman faced, after his personal loss
in 1836, was that he had no one to confide in as he had been able
to with Hurrell Froude. Even Keble had taken to himself a wife,
and had mildly rapped Newman's knuckles for his discourtesy in

not acknowledging her existence in one of his letters.[47] There was Pusey, of course; a man who, while now in Newman's circle, was yet also detached enough to have a circle of his own as well as a charisma all his own – 'a nameless something', as Isaac Williams put it, 'which was wanting even in Newman and, I might almost add, even in Keble.'[48]

It was in Newman's resolute defence of Pusey against the first serious charge of Romanism levelled against the Tractarians that the uneasy alliance against R. D. Hampden began to disintegrate. Pusey had come under attack from the Evangelicals over his tract on Baptism, the *Christian Observer* accusing him of 'irrational fanaticism' and 'intellectual drivelling under the abused name of faith', worthy of a Professor at Maynooth or the Vatican.[49] This, in turn, provoked an equally forthright reply by Newman in Tract 82, in which he rose to the challenge of defining the Tractarian position *vis-à-vis* the Articles and the Homilies in terms that foreshadowed his fuller treatment in Tract 90. More prominent Evangelicals, and therefore more dangerous, were also entering the field to warn against Popery – Archdeacon Spooner delivered a temperate and learned remonstrance to his clergy, and in Oxford C. P. Golightly announced his switch of allegiance, becoming in due course one of the bitterest adversaries of all.

All this might have been anticipated, notwithstanding Newman's conscious resolution during 1836 to balance the content and tone of the Tracts by writing explicitly on the subject of Roman Catholic abuses. His first offering appeared in Tract 71, 'On the Controversy with the Romanists', in which he discussed certain specific corruptions – transubstantiation (only very mildly), the denial of the cup to the laity, the necessity of the priest's intention to the validity of the sacrament, the Tridentine ruling on the necessity of confession, the doctrines of Purgatory and Invocation of Saints, the worship of images and the unwarranted anathemas that the Roman Church had delivered over the years.[50] But he was a bit too explicit in his admission of the defects of the Anglican Church, at least in the eyes of the 'Z's, and this was to lead to a more serious breach just at the moment when the Tractarians needed every ally they could secure.

Newman had already lost the support of Benjamin Harrison, Archdeacon of Maidstone, in the course of a correspondence of mounting asperity over a criticism by Harrison of one of Newman's letters to the Abbé Jager.[51] More unfortunate, however, was the way in which both Newman and Pusey undervalued the support and advice of Hugh James Rose. Newman's relationship with Rose, to whom he owed so much in the formulation of his understanding of the rationalistic origins of early Christian heresy,[52] seems to have been somewhat fickle. At one moment he could write to Keble to say that 'I never have regarded him in his opinions as one of ourselves', accusing him of inconsistency and liability to shift allegiance.[53] At the next, he could write a charming acknowledgement of his influence in his dedication to Rose of his fourth volume of parochial sermons. In May 1836, Rose felt that the time had come to warn Newman, in a long letter of scrupulous courtesy, against using extravagant language in his criticisms of the English Church, exhorting Pusey – at the same time – to 'keep where you are, and go no further'.[54] Newman's reply, on 23 May, was uncompromising, frankly admitting that 'I do *not* love the Church of England' as it currently was ('its very title is an offence . . . for it implies that it holds, not of the Church Catholic, but of the State'), adding ominously that 'My heart *is* with Rome, but *not* as Rome, but as, and so far as, she is the faithful retainer of what we have practically thrown aside.'[55]

Nevertheless, it was precisely these sentiments that were given to the world in the first two volumes of Hurrell Froude's *Remains*, edited by Newman and Keble and published in February 1838. It was a blunder of the first magnitude. It could hardly have appeared at a worse moment; and the editors compounded their error by including in the first volume so much potentially explosive material: Froude's journal, with its revelations of the austerities that he had imposed upon himself as penances for his sins and faults, which could not but appear to those who did not know him as morbid broodings over ludicrous peccadilloes, as well as letters which suggested a conspiratorial background to the writing of the Tracts, rendered the more suspect and outrageous by the tone of utter contempt for the Protestant reformers. Here was the proof that his enemies needed. More than that, it confirmed the worst fears of many of his friends. H. J. Rose lived just long enough to read the volumes (his long battle against ill-health coming to an end in December 1838). He wrote to Joshua Watson to say that the publication of the *Remains* was 'the most to be regretted of anything which I have seen from our Oxford friends'.[56]

Another wing of the High Church party, known as the 'Bisley

Group' (or, in Newman's phrase, 'the country people'), parted company with him on this same issue. This was a small but influential circle who regarded as their leader and exemplar Keble's brother, Thomas, the Vicar of Bisley, who had been a contributor to the Tracts. Thomas Keble was more belligerent than his more famous brother, a convinced Tractarian but an equally determined opponent of Romanist sympathies, and he counted among his disciples Isaac Williams, Sir George Prevost and W. J. Copeland. Both Tom Keble and Prevost made their sentiments plain to Newman by objecting to his plan to publish a translation of the Roman Breviary, and the rift was to widen still further with the appearance of the *Remains*. Prevost, in particular, took great exception to Newman's attempt to defend his position in controversy with Godfrey Faussett, the Lady Margaret Professor of Divinity, who in May 1838, from Newman's own pulpit in St Mary's, had preached a sermon in condemnation of the Romanizing tendency of both the *Remains* and the recent Tracts.[57]

Newman's published reply to Faussett's sermon was a brilliant piece of polemical writing, as dignified and measured in its tone (at least in part) as his private comments about Faussett were the very reverse. This was deliberate, in order to drive home the unacceptable nature of the aggressive and strident language of his opponent, who had described Froude's teaching as 'poison'. Then, asked Newman, 'What words do we reserve for heresy?'[58] He could not resist, however, holding up to derision Faussett's guarded and prosaic description of the Eucharist, in comparison with the reverent language of the Anglican divines of old:

> Alas! what a decrepiture has come on us since Hooker's day! 'How has the fine gold become dim!' How has the promise of spring played us false in the summer! How have the lean kine eaten up the fat kine, and the thin ears choked the full ones! What a spiritual famine, or rather what locusts and cankerworms are our portion! the olive tree can be content with its own fatness, and the fig-tree with its sweetness, and the vine reckons it much 'to cheer God and man'; but the thin and empty ears of Zurich and Geneva think it scorn unless they devour and make a clean end of the pleasant and fair pastures of Catholic doctrine, which are our heritage.[59]

This was not calculated to make a friend of Faussett, and he could prove to be a dangerous and powerful enemy. A more disconcerting rebuff was to come, when Bishop Bagot, whom Newman had expected to speak out in defence of the Tracts in his episcopal Charge that summer, felt it necessary to deliver a mild rebuke in the form of a warning against taking their admiration for antiquity too far. Newman's response, in deference to his firmly-held principle that 'a Bishop's lightest word ex Cathedra is heavy',[60] was to offer to stop publication of the Tracts at once. The kindly Bagot, shocked by the degree of censure that Newman had imposed upon what he had intended to be sympathetic advice, replied with suitably calming words.

But Newman was now thoroughly unsettled. He had no regrets over the publication of Froude's *Remains*. But the list of alienations was growing. Whereas in October 1837 he had rejoiced to Robert Wilberforce that 'we have the most gratifying news in every direction of the spreading of Church principles. Indeed I think nothing but a Star Chamber or Court of High Commission can (humanly speaking) hinder it,'[61] he had to admit some ten months later, in a letter to Pusey, that the situation had changed. Ignoring the number of warnings that he had failed to heed, he wrote: 'I have for several years been working against all sort of opposition, and with hardly a friendly voice.'[62] Towards the end of 1838 he was so discountenanced by the state of affairs that he put himself in Keble's hands. Perhaps it would be better if he put an end to the Tracts after all, he reflected. 'I will do whatever you suggest. I really do hope I have no wish but that of peace with all parties.'[63]

VI

By this time, Manning had left the country for Rome. Did he have any inkling of the change in Newman's fortunes? He would have known that his brother-in-law, Samuel, had been added to the list of those whom Newman no longer wished to count as supporters, as a result of his preaching in the University pulpit a sermon criticizing Pusey's tract on Baptism. Newman had, in consequence, refused to accept any article from Samuel's pen for the *British Critic*, because 'I am not confident enough in your general approval of the body of opinion which Pusey and myself hold'.[1] Manning, too, had been uneasy about the publication of the *Remains*, and some passages in *The Rule of Faith*, particularly in the appendix containing a number of references to Cranmer and Ridley in support of his arguments, suggest that he wished to

distance himself from the controversy;[2] not altogether success-
fully, it must be admitted, because the *Record* dismissed his
efforts by declaring that 'the Sermon was bad enough. The
Appendix was abominable!'[3]

Towards the end of his time in Rome, Manning wrote to
Newman a long letter, giving his reflections on Rome and his own
musings on the superior virtues of Anglicanism.

> I wish I could exactly define the sort of feeling everything I see here
> gives me. At present it is a sort of general and indistinct impression of
> a multitude of things good and bad, recalling our blessings, or
> contrasting all our defects ... What I have seen abroad makes me turn
> homeward with a feeling, I hope, of thankfulness for a state of society,
> which with great defects has also great excellences. I hardly think any
> country can endure comparison with England, in the hold which
> religion seems to have upon the hearts and consciences of the upper
> classes. When we think of the little amount of coercive discipline which
> retains them in the Church it seems their attachment is a voluntary
> surrender of affection to a system which by its excellence attracts the
> pure sympathies of the mind.
>
> When we think of the 150 years past, we must wonder that we have
> so much ... In learning we ought to be behind no body of men. This
> makes me very hopeful, especially when I think of the fine heads and
> hearts and the high tempered character of our middle and upper
> classes. We most certainly want an affirmative system of Religious
> teaching, which shall keep men steadfast by filling the mind with
> *positive* truth ... And now you will scold me for telling you nothing
> interesting. The fact is I am a lazy correspondent in the matter of
> descriptions, above all to a man who has seen more of Rome than I
> have – and somehow my thoughts always turn homeward so obstin-
> ately that I can hardly write of anything else. I hope to be able to get
> on to Sicily and see the country of which you once talked to me on
> Magdalen Bridge ... The things I most wish to say I do not like to
> write. There are silly people here who are doing neither to themselves
> nor to their countrymen any good. I am very much convinced that we
> must be more decidedly Anglican. I am growing a stiff Anglican –
> from a conviction that advantage is being taken largely of every
> expression of dissatisfaction; and conscious imperfection. I believe it
> has the effect of emboldening, and that it confirms the resolution to
> yield nothing, but to aim at a total extirpation ... Wo [*sic*] unto us if we
> be fainthearted.[4]

The next letter that Manning wrote to Newman, on his return
to England, was in September 1839, when he had just read an
article by Nicholas Wiseman in the *Dublin Review*, in which the

Anglican Church was represented as schismatic in precisely the same way as the Donatists of the fourth century, for offending against the Augustinian principle that lay at the root of the Papal claim to universal jurisdiction: *securus judicat orbis terrarum* (the judgement of the whole world is sure). It had not troubled Manning for an instant.

> We might well work off his Donatist parallel on him with Augustine's argument about the arrogance of appropriating the name Catholic. They seem to nose Cyril as a dog does a hedgehog. Half glad to find it, and three-quarters afraid of it ... I do want hugely to see you, as I have all sorts of things which I want to talk over ... Sometimes, here all alone, I get mopish and foreboding – but not often – for things seem full of promise ... I cannot think Romanism will long hold out.[5]

A month later, he returned to the same theme. Wiseman's argument in his article, to prove the invalidity of the Anglican succession, 'old as it is,' he wrote, '[is] very plausible, and therefore very misleading and mischievous. I can also conceive it to be made much more so by the way in which it is answered, that is, by treating the Roman Jurisdiction in England as anything but a usurpation ... But I am sending owls to Athens, so no more.'[6]

Newman had not been all that troubled by Wiseman's article at first. But he could not get it out of his mind; and by the time that the owls had come to Athens, unknown to Manning, Newman had taken a walk with Henry Wilberforce in the New Forest. In the course of that walk he had had some disturbing things to say.

CHAPTER 3

Roads to Rome

'Sober churchmen are in no danger from the Pope.'
Newman in an unpublished sermon, 29 June 1830

'I am reduced to the painful, saddening, sickening necessity of saying what I feel about Rome.' Manning to Pusey,
22nd Sunday after Trinity, 1843

I

NEWMAN'S FIRST essay in story-telling, *Loss and Gain*, published in 1848, must surely rank as one of the most static novels in
the whole of English literature. Spiced though it is with lively
caricature, it consists for the most part of a series of conversation-
pieces – round the tea-table, in a friend's room after dinner, in a
garden, on a railway-train, or in the course of walks and talks
innumerable; all of them searchingly ecclesiastical or theological,
as they chart the progress of the very serious-minded young hero,
Charles Reding, towards the same refuge that Newman himself
found in 1845 by submission to the Church of Rome. One cannot
but feel that the Oxford Movement itself partook of something of
the same character: heart-searchings and soul-searchings between
friends on the minutiae of doctrine or the nature and credentials
of this Church or that, of one party or the other, poured out on
paper but also endlessly wrangled over in the course of walks and
talks.
Dr Johnson once remarked that the ancient Greeks could argue
good-humouredly about religion because they did not believe in
it. But there were no unbelievers, at least officially, at Oxford; and
if *Loss and Gain* is anything to go by, the wrangling over religious

issues was singularly devoid of humour (if sometimes humorously described). The past is rarely recorded in the spoken word; and of these historical conversation-pieces, little but an occasional phrase or hint survives. Froude's perambulation of the Trinity College gardens with Isaac Williams concluded with the temperamentally unrousable Williams being exhorted, if not persuaded, to act out of character. Manning and Newman talked together about Sicily on Magdalen Bridge; and on a day in early October 1839, Henry Wilberforce and Newman took a stroll in the New Forest; and such was their talk together that a casual passer-by might well have paused to speculate over the sight of two clergymen in earnest converse, when one of them – the more well-built of the two and almost certainly the more garrulous – was suddenly rendered speechless, as his customary joviality was transformed into painful reflection.

Fortunately Henry Wilberforce, thirty years later, recorded what passed between them. Newman had been studying the role of St Leo in controversy with the Monophysites, while editing the works of Theodoret, Leo and Cyril for Pusey's *Library of the Fathers*; and he had also been considering the implications of Wiseman's *Dublin Review* article (on the Donatists) on which he and Manning had already exchanged views. Both these issues had raised disturbing doubts in Newman's mind, which he was still hopeful that he might allay after further study. But, he said to Henry, 'I cannot conceal from myself that, for the first time since I began the study of theology, a vista has been opened before me, to the end of which I do not see.' When Henry replied by saying that he hoped his companion would die rather than take the step that he was hinting at, Newman told him 'with deep earnestness, that he had thought, if ever the time should come when he was in serious danger, of asking his friends to pray that, if it was not indeed the will of God, he might be taken away before he did it.'[1]

It is almost inconceivable that Henry, so keen always to be the first with news, could have kept this to himself. Actually, Newman had already expressed his anxieties to Frederic Rogers, in two letters dated 15 and 22 September. Robert Wilberforce, he told Rogers, had drawn his attention to Wiseman's article. 'I must confess it has given me a stomach-ache ... At this moment we have sprung a leak, and the worst of it is that those sharp fellows, Ward, Stanley and Co, will not let one go to sleep upon it ... I have not said so much to any one.'[2] This letter contains one of the earliest references to the man who was soon to become the *enfant terrible* of Newman's closing years in the Anglican Church – William George Ward, the brilliant but persistently argumentative Fellow of Balliol, whose enthusiasms and allegiances, always unbounded at the time, had at this youthful period of his life exhibited a certain fickleness. For a while Ward had shared his friend A. P. Stanley's admiration for Thomas Arnold (until he met him, when he came to the rapid conclusion that they were not two of a kind); and it had been Stanley who persuaded Ward to attend one of Newman's lectures in the Adam de Brome chapel, which effected a transference of affection quite as rapid. 'This is the man for me,' Ward had declared.[3]

Bishop Bagot was the first to warn Newman of the dangers of ardent discipleship of this sort, in the course of his Charge in August 1838, when he acknowledged the good service rendered to the Church by the original Tract writers, adding – however – 'I have more fear of the Disciples than of the Teachers.'[4] Newman did not immediately take the point to heart. When he heard that Ward had emphatically declared his switch of allegiance to the Tractarians, he told John Bowden that he considered him 'a very important accession'.[5] Less circumspectly, in a letter to Keble, who had warned him about the evidence of his estrangement from the Bisley Group, he had declared that 'I do not write for them. Of course, as is natural, I write for those I do see, viz. the generation, lay or clerical, rising into active life, particularly at Oxford . . . I do not consider that for them I am going too fast . . . One cannot stop still.'[6]

To Rogers, however, Newman was admitting that it was the way of the younger devotees to press him to go faster still; and just at that moment, seriously disturbed by grave doubts, he wanted rather to consult his older and wiser friends than to give snap answers to questions from eager, impulsive spirits like W. G. Ward and his Balliol colleague, Frederick Oakeley, which they would have done better not to have raised. It would be too much to say that Newman, in 1839, lost his faith in the Anglican Church; but he lost his confidence in defending the Church on the basis of the *via media*. To argue such a position was, in effect, to put the Church of England on to the same level as schismatical sects of primitive times. As Newman himself expressed it, in a later editorial note to his *Lectures on the Prophetical Office*, 'to his confusion and distress, he found in early history a veritable *Via Media* in both the semi-Arian and the Monophysite parties, and they, as being heretical, broke his attachment to middle paths';[7] and in his twelfth lecture on the *Difficulties of Anglicans*, in 1850, he wrote:

> It was difficult to make out how the Eutychians or Monophysites were heretics, unless Protestants and Anglicans were heretics also; difficult to find arguments against the Tridentine Fathers which did not tell against the Fathers of Chalcedon; difficult to condemn the Popes of the sixteenth century, without condemning the Popes of the fifth. The drama of religion and the combat of truth and error were ever one and the same.[8]

Henry Wilberforce and Frederic Rogers were both badly shaken. Those who did not know Newman well – the critics of the *Record* and the *Christian Observer*, even Godfrey Faussett and Golightly – could accuse him of 'Popery', but his closest friends knew that the distinction in Newman's mind between 'Rome' and 'Romanism' was one genuinely and passionately felt. He was later to explain it succinctly in his justificatory letters, both to Bishop Bagot and to R. W. Jelf, in the course of the storm that broke out over Tract 90. 'If there ever was a system which required reformation, it is that of Rome at this day, or in other words (as I should call it) Romanism or Popery,' he wrote to Jelf.[9] 'I say that we can have no peace with that Church, however we may love its particular members,' he assured Bishop Bagot.[10] It is sometimes forgotten how deep was Newman's detestation of the Roman Church in the early days of the Oxford Movement, and how – of all its leading spirits – he must have seemed the least likely to fall victim to either argument or blandishment on behalf of the Roman claims. In an unpublished sermon, dated 29 June 1830, he had preached on the Petrine texts in Matthew. 'Now I do not suppose,' he declared, 'that any of us are likely to fall away to Popery. It is not in the way for churchmen to depart from their excellent forms and worship to the corruptions of the Romish Church . . . Sober churchmen are in no danger from the Pope.'[11]

He was strongly influenced by Protestant interpretations of prophecies relating to Antichrist, and from time to time suggested candidates for that fearsome role – the miracles of the wonders of modern science might be the work of his hand;[12] even poor Dr Hampden was cast as his 'forerunner';[13] but the chief candidate was the post-Tridentine Church, as opposed to the papacy of the Middle Ages; and survivals of that suspicion, despite the influence of Keble[14] and Froude, recur even as late as 1840, in his expression of horror at the alliance of the Catholic Church in Ireland with the infamous Daniel O'Connell.[15] On the other hand, his actual knowledge of modern Catholicism and of Roman Catholics was extremely limited, and occasional glimpses of the real thing sometimes gave him furiously to think. His visit to Rome, during the Mediterranean tour, had exhibited both the bad and the undeniably good (Manning had felt precisely the same). 'The unity of the Papists, their enthusiasm and zeal, their feelings towards their Bishops, *we want it all*,' he had written in 1834.[16] He loved the Breviary, and began to use it daily during the closing months of 1836 and thereafter.[17] In October 1837 he read for the first time Manzoni's novel *I Promessi Sposi*, and was overwhelmed by the spirit of Catholic sanctity. 'It quite transported me in parts,' he reported to Jemima.[18] 'That Capuchin in the "Promessi Sposi" has stuck in my heart like a dart,' he confessed to Rogers in September 1839. 'I have never got over him.'[19]

So the situation in 1839 was effectively this: the argument for Anglicanism, based on the *via media*, created more problems than it solved. But Rome, as it then was, seemed indelibly tainted with Romanism, and at the heart of the corruptions lay the unwarranted claims of the Papacy to universal jurisdiction. What he had now to do was to establish, to his own satisfaction, that the corruptions of Rome really were corruptions and to seek within the Anglican Church the evidence for its claim to Catholicity based primarily on its possession of those 'notes' or 'marks' of authority and, above all, sanctity, which the true Church must surely bear somewhere upon its body. For this he needed time and relative peace. But affairs in Oxford, as the year drew to its close, only increased his problems. Golightly, once his friend and very nearly his curate at Littlemore, was on the warpath, with his proposal to effect an embarrassing riposte to Froude's *Remains* by launching an appeal for the Martyrs' Memorial, commemorating Cranmer, Ridley and Latimer, its main object being to put Newman, Pusey and their party to a test of their allegiance. Newman duly obliged by having nothing to do with it. This was an irksome piece of provocation, but no more. More embarrassing was the insensitivity of one of his younger devotees, J. B. Morris,

Fellow of Exeter, who chose to preach two extravagant sermons on fasting and the Mass in the presence of the Vice-Chancellor, from the University pulpit, as a result of which he was summoned to explain himself before this affronted dignitary; all of which confirmed to Newman that sometimes one's friends could be more of a nuisance than one's enemies. 'The Heads of Houses are getting more and more uneasy,' he wrote to Jemima in November 1839. 'I should not wonder if the Bishop got uneasy, in which case I suppose I should resign the living.'[20]

During 1840 the atmosphere gradually became rather more peaceful, both within and without Oxford. In March that year, S. F. Wood reported to Newman that

> there is a great *lull* generally, not only in theological matters (as an instance of which I have not so much as heard *one* remark (friendly or adverse) in miscellaneous Society relative to the Second Part of the Remains), but also in Politics; both sides seem tired of discussing abstract points, and are turning to matters of business.[21]

Later that year Newman told Rogers that he was beginning to feel more comfortable about things than he had, and that Keble had pooh-poohed any suggestion that he should leave St Mary's. The time had come, however, to put the English Church to the test. 'We don't know yet what the English Church will bear of infused Catholic truth. We are, as it were, proving cannon.'[22] He had, indeed, already made a start by assessing reactions to a long article that he had published in the *British Critic* in January 1840, entitled 'The Catholicity of the Anglican Church'.

This was Newman at his best, confirming the impression that all his finest writings were the pieces that he produced under stress (arguably, it was the converse with Manning, who when writing under stress tended to lose a sense of proportion). Very character-istically, Newman put the case for the Roman Church fairly and emphatically, not for one moment denying that their claims to Catholicity were unanswerable, while the Anglican Church – as a breakaway communion – had the appearance of being in schism. That being so, Anglicans had to set out to prove that 'the few may be right and the many wrong', while Catholics had to convince their opponents that 'Revelation is progressive, and that Christ-ians now know more than the Fathers'.[23] In the arguments that follow, Newman rested largely upon the testimony of St Ignatius and St Cyprian that 'each bishop [is] an autocratic channel of grace, and ultimate centre of unity'[24] (a contention that Manning would develop more fully in his *Unity of the Church* in 1842). Then he turned to the 'Notes of the Church', arguing chiefly from two standpoints – the criterion of vitality and the evidence of holiness.

> For three centuries [the Church of England] has endured all vicissitudes of fortune. It has endured in trouble and prosperity, under seduction and under oppression. It has been practised upon by theorists, browbeaten by sophists, intimidated by princes, betrayed by false sons, laid waste by tyranny, corrupted by wealth, torn by schism, and persecuted by fanaticism . . . Yet what has been its career upon the whole? . . . Lutherans have tended to Rationalism; Calvinists became Socinians; but . . . as far as its formularies are concerned, it may be said all along to have grown towards a more perfect Catholicism than that with which it started at the time of its estrangement; every act, every crisis, which marks its course, has been upward.[25]

On the other side, what had the Church of Rome to show?

> Till we see in them as a Church more straightforwardness, truth, and openness, more of severe obedience to God's least commandments, more scrupulousness about means, less of a political, scheming, grasping spirit, less of intrigue, less that looks hollow and superficial, less accommodation to the tastes of the vulgar, less subserviency to the vices of the rich, less humouring of men's morbid and wayward imaginations, less indulgence of their low and carnal superstitions, less intimacy with the revolutionary spirit of the day, we will keep aloof from them as we do . . . 'By their fruits ye shall know them' . . . We see it attempting to gain converts among us, by unreal representations of its doctrines, plausible statements, bold assertions, appeals to the weaknesses of human nature, to our fancies, our fears, our frivolities, our false philosophies. We see its agents smiling and nodding and ducking to attract attention, as gipsies make up to truant boys, holding out tales for the nursery, and pretty pictures, and good gingerbread, and physic concealed in jam, and sugar-plums for good children. Who can but feel shame when the religion of Ximenes, Borromeo, and Pascal is so overlaid?[26]

This is rhetoric, of course; and much, if not all of it, Newman would later have to take back. But it was sincere enough at the time that it was written. It is interesting that the unlovely picture of 'gipsies and truant boys' seems to have been provoked by his anger at the efforts of a convert Catholic priest, the Hon. George Spencer, to launch a 'Prayer Union' for reconciliation between the two Churches, which seemed more likely to be a cover for a crusade to convert Anglicans to Rome. Newman refused an invitation to meet Spencer at a dinner arranged by William Palmer (of Magdalen College, as opposed to the 'Z' of the same name), taking a dislike to his 'smooth ways'.[27] The trouble with Roman Catholics who made friendly overtures was that 'the voice is Jacob's voice, but the hands are the hands of Esau.'[28] Manning had come to a similar conclusion, when approached by Charles Marriott, who had heard of Spencer's proposals:

> Mr Spencer forgets that we do pray for those in the 'Catholic Church' [he wrote to Newman on 15 January 1840] – that they do not pray for us, except once a year among all Calvinists, heretics etc. They owe us their prayers ... I do not indeed feel the desire to be harsh and suspicious, but I must say that the last year has taught me such a lesson of their smooth duplicity that I cannot trust them. Their smoothness in England is worse than their bitterness abroad. From the persons I have had to do with, on whom they have practiced [*sic*], I have learned how they use our words, and acts, so as to make me feel it a duty never to mix with them in anything. English Romanism is its most fraudulent aspect.[29]

Over this same period of tension, other masterpieces appeared from Newman's pen. Three of his fifteen University Sermons, on the relationship between faith and reason, preached in 1839 and 1840, constituted his boldest expression so far of a theory of the dual function of head and heart and the role of antecedent probability in the determination of certitude; a quest that would occupy his mind for years to come until his final exposition, much expanded but differing little in substance, in *An Essay in aid of a Grammar of Assent* in 1870. In 1841 he produced one of his most brilliant pieces of polemical rhetoric in his denunciation of Useful Knowledge, in a series of letters to *The Times* under the title 'The Tamworth Reading Room', making mockery of Lord Brougham and (his old unmerited target for derision) Robert Peel. Then, in March 1841, came another publication, which by general consent, including his own, was not a masterpiece at all: Tract 90 on the Thirty-nine Articles, the last of the *Tracts for the Times*, the work least worthy of his gifts and most notorious in terms of the controversy that it provoked.

The Thirty-nine Articles represented to the Tractarians the greatest stumbling-block in their assertion of Catholic principles because, at their face value at least, they seemed to anathematize one Catholic doctrine after another in order to state the orthodox

Protestant position. Newman had been embarrassed by this uncomfortable fact in his controversy with Jager; and in the *Lectures on Justification* he had given a hint of what was to come in his comparison between the 'shadowy and unreal' theology of the Article on justifying faith, compared with the language of the Homilies.[30] In Tract 90 Newman examined the most apparently anti-Catholic Articles, one by one, in order 'to show that, while our Prayer Book is acknowledged on all hands to be of Catholic origin, our Articles also, the offspring of an uncatholic age, are, through GOD's good providence, to say the least, not uncatholic, and may be subscribed by those who aim at being catholic in heart and doctrine.'[31]

Right from the start, he makes the questionable assumption that the aim of the framers of the Articles was to be inclusive rather than exclusive, even to the extent of maintaining that 'the Articles are evidently framed on the principle of leaving open large questions ... They state broadly extreme truths, and are silent about their adjustment ... their framers constructed them in such a way as best to comprehend those who did not go so far in Protestantism as themselves.'[32] He seemed to want, however, both to have his cake and to eat it, in that he tried to protect himself against those who refused this assumption by saying that 'it is a duty to take our reformed confessions in the most Catholic sense they will admit; we have no duty towards their framers.'[33] Furthermore, in the course of his analysis of the Articles under discussion, Newman strained interpretation and ambiguity to their very limit – by arguing, for example, that 'Romish' doctrine could not refer to the Tridentine decrees because the Articles were framed prior to their official promulgation;[34] nor could the condemnation of 'sacrifice of masses' actually refer to the Mass itself.[35]

Almost as soon as he had written it, Newman knew that he was in for trouble. On 9 March he wrote to his sister Harriet: 'I have got into what may prove a serious mess here. I have just published a Tract (90) which I did not feel likely to attract attention. I sent it to Keble before publishing it; he, too, made no remark upon it. But people are taking it up very warmly – thanks, I believe, entirely to Golightly.'[36] What, one wonders, did he expect? He had delivered himself into his enemies' hands. Events then followed thick and fast. Golightly secured as many copies of the Tract as possible and sent them off to every bishop in the land,

and he approached individual Heads of Houses and other senior members of the University, exhorting them to take action. First came a published protest from four senior tutors (of Brasenose, St John's, Wadham and Balliol), in which they demanded that the anonymous author of the Tract should give up his name (it was, of course, well known that the author was Newman). The Heads of Houses, acting somewhat precipitately in failing to allow Newman time to state his case, published an official resolution repudiating the Tract as defeating the object of the Articles and being 'inconsistent with the observance of the Statutes' enjoining their subscription,[37] although they stopped short of bringing the issue before Convocation. Newman apologized, without – however – retracting the contents of his publication; then he published an open letter to R. W. Jelf (an Oriel colleague) to explain that his main purpose in writing the Tract was to prevent secessions to Rome, because 'she alone, amid all the errors and evils of her practical system, has given free scope to the feelings of awe, mystery, tenderness, reverence, devotedness, and other feelings which may be especially called Catholic'.[38]

All eyes then turned on Bagot, Bishop of Oxford, to see what action he would take. Probably, left to himself, he would have preferred to do nothing. He had a genuine admiration for Newman and knew only too well how painfully sensitive he was to the slightest indication of displeasure from his bishop. On the other hand, neither his fellow-bishops nor the University authorities could envisage the possibility of Newman escaping some form of episcopal censure. In the end, Bagot acted with characteristic sensitivity by using Pusey as his go-between, expressing to him in a letter his own personal unease at Newman's arguments, at the same time enclosing a letter to be forwarded to Newman in which he suggested that it would be prudent to write nothing further on the subject of the Articles. Newman's response was to offer to do very much more, if the Bishop were to require it: to suppress the Tract, to suspend the series, even to resign from St Mary's. As doubtless he anticipated, Bagot – as he had done once before – intimated that Newman was reading much more into his censure than had ever been intended, and they agreed that the matter should be concluded by Newman publishing a letter in which he accepted the Bishop's wish that the Tracts should be discontinued, Bagot – for his part – accepting that there should be no further censure of Tract 90 itself. Sadly, Newman never seemed to appreciate just how sympathetic and tactful Bagot had been in handling a delicate situation. The time soon came when other bishops chose to have their say in their Charges to their clergy, and extremely forthright in their condemnation some of them were. Newman interpreted this as a breach of the 'understanding' with Bagot,[39] not appreciating that his bishop was in no position to prevent others from expressing their views. Indeed, if any undertaking were broken, Bagot might well have accused Newman himself (although it was not in his nature to do so) for sanctioning a subsequent reprint of the Tract that had caused so much offence.

'What I have written I have written' seems to have been Newman's defiant attitude to Tract 90 at the time, although years later (in 1857) he conceded that while he was not dissatisfied with 'its drift', there were 'in detail ... strained interpretations'.[40] Historical judgements have tended to be more brutal. Brilioth described the Tract as 'a very melancholy document. It shows how a really great man can become little in a false and ambiguous position.'[41] Gladstone said something similar to R. H. Hutton. 'Tract 90 opened a joint in Newman's armour. It showed that in his wonderful genius there was a distinct flaw – a strong sophistical element.'[42] Recently, Henry Chadwick has supplied perhaps the most judicious assessment of all. 'Tract 90', he wrote, 'was more Anglican than it was represented to be ... Newman's delight in exact logic made the argument sound clever, enjoyably so if you wanted to agree, evasively sophisticated if you did not.'[43] Sympathetic contemporaries differed in their opinions. William Palmer, very nobly, rushed to Newman's defence;[44] Joshua Watson, on the other hand, disowned it.[45] A. P. Perceval thought the appearance of the Tract was ill-timed, but approved its sentiments.[46] Manning was somewhat embarrassed about it, because he did not share Newman's contempt for the Reformers, but was prepared to vote against its censure in 1845. Pusey was in general sympathetic, but had qualms about the concluding section of the Tract in which Newman had represented the framers of the Articles as acting a double part.[47]

If it is true to say that during the Hampden crisis of 1836 everybody behaved rather badly, at least it must be conceded that – in the controversy over Tract 90 – all the major figures involved had a point, and a reasonably sound one too. Could the Heads of Houses have totally ignored the challenge? Richard Whately, who had a habit of making judicious observations from far off in Dublin, summed up the issue as follows:

> Tract 90 was elicited from Newman by the solicitations of a great body of his followers, who insisted on having, if they were not to join the Roman Church, some scheme of interpretation laid before them by which they could professedly adhere to the Articles. And they accordingly obtained one which would have taught them, if need were, to subscribe to the Koran.[48]

More to the point, he expressed the fear of many of the bishops (in a later letter to the Vice-Chancellor of Oxford) that if the Articles were to be accepted in the interpretation given by Newman, might not individual bishops reasonably have reservations about accepting an Oxford education (as it then was in terms of religious instruction) as qualifying a man for Holy Orders?[49] But Newman had a point too. The trouble arose, he observed in his letter to R. W. Jelf, from the fact that 'the Tract was addressed to one set of persons, and has been used and commented on by another'.[50] Of course, this was an explanation rather than an excuse, because given the climate of the times, it was inevitable that the Tract would be seized upon by the very people whom Newman was not intending to address.

Defiant as Newman was, he was severely shaken. The University had inflicted upon him a humiliation; perhaps no more than the humiliation that it had inflicted upon Hampden five years earlier, but that was no comfort to his injured feelings. Then the bishops had 'charged against him'.

> Charges are very serious matters [he explained to James Hope in October 1841] as virtually silencing portions of the truth in particular dioceses, and as showing that it is not impossible that our Church *may* lapse into heresy. I cannot deny that a great and anxious *experiment* is going on, whether our Church be or be not Catholic. The issue may not be in our day. But I must be plain in saying that, if it does issue in Protestantism, I shall think it my duty, if alive, to leave it.

He was not yet in despair. The crucial test might be 'the work of years'.[51] As it happened, another event occurred in a matter of months, which was to confirm his worst fears: a proposal, emanating from no less a person than Prince Albert, together with his adviser and friend, Baron Bunsen, that a new bishopric should be created, set up by England and Prussia jointly, its diocese being the Holy Land, and its seat the city of Jerusalem.

II

Newman's years of plenty had now come to an end. By contrast, Manning's were just about to begin. Active as he had been before the necessity of his rest-cure in Rome, on his return he threw himself into ecclesiastical affairs, both local and national, with a redoubled energy. As a member of the Corresponding Committee of the National Society, he rejoined his friends S. F. Wood and Thomas Acland in completing the establishment of the Theological College at Chichester and in securing Charles Marriott (whom he had met in Gladstone's party at Rome) as its first Principal. He published a more effective, because more positive, pamphlet against what he conceived to be the latest iniquity of the Ecclesiastical Commission, entitled 'The Preservation of Unendowed Canonries' ('a beautiful little letter', S. F. Wood exclaimed,[1] a somewhat improbable response to a seemingly arid treatise). Manning returned to the same theme in an article for the *British Critic*, with an impassioned defence of cathedrals as 'seminaries of theological learning'.[2] He was also proving himself to be by far the most active of the twenty-six newly-created rural deans, and acknowledged as such by the Dean of Chichester (Chandler). But the most surprising conquest of all was his gaining the close friendship of Julius Hare, Archdeacon of Lewes; for Hare was a man whom Newman would have had no hesitation in describing as a latitudinarian. Perhaps nothing better demonstrated Manning's ability as a conciliator than his affectionate letters to Hare, making light of any differences of churchmanship between them, exchanging views about books and theology, Manning assuring him, on one occasion, that 'though in opinion we may differ, we have a solid oneness in our desire for brotherly love among the clergy – and this a pledge of all things running clear at last'; then again, 'with a man who reads and reasons I can have no controversy; and you do both'.[3]

Those who met him or saw him at work, or heard him on a platform, had to concede that he seemed to be possessed of every gift necessary for substantial advancement. In Rome he had had a series of lively discussions with the renowned sceptic, James Sterling, once in Holy Orders, who reported his impressions of Manning to R. C. Trench.

> He is one of the most finished and compact specimens of his school of manhood and of theology that I have ever fallen in with, and it was

amusing to see how by faultless self-command, dialectic acuteness, coherent system, readiness of expression, and a perfect union of earnestness and gentleness, he always seemed to put in the wrong the gentlemen of the so-called Evangelical class, who muster strong here, and whom he frequently met with . . . I conceive him to be, in his own place and generation, one of the most practically efficient and energetic men I have ever known, and in a state of freer and more fluent life in the ecclesiastical polity he would rise high and do considerable things.[4]

Four years later, F. D. Maurice in a letter to Edward Strachey made a similar judgement.

Manning is one of the completest, perhaps the completest man I ever met with: there are doubtless deficiencies, which completeness itself implies, seeing that the incomplete is that which is ever seeking the infinite and eternal to fill up its hollows; and in him there is a logical rotundity which I should not wish for. But it is united with so much appreciation of everything good, such great refinement, tolerance and kindliness, that I know not where one would look, rather, for a wise and true bishop in these times.[5]

Appearance played its part, too. No wonder that George Richmond, who met him at Rome, wanted to undertake his portrait. 'He was in those days strikingly handsome,' he wrote, 'and as graceful as a stag in every movement and motion.'[6] His hair was beginning to recede, so that those who met him in 1840 found it difficult to believe that he was only 32. 'Venerable' was the word that came to mind in describing him.

And 'Venerable' he officially became just as the year was closing, the letter containing the offer to him to succeed Charles Webber as Archdeacon of Chichester reaching him on Christmas Eve. He had not expected it, having put aside such hopes when, on Bishop Otter's death in the summer of 1840, Lord John Russell appointed as his successor one of the fiercest of the anti-Tractarian Heads of Houses at Oxford, the Warden of New College, William Shuttleworth. No one was surprised, however, that Webber had at last chosen to resign. He had been too senile to discharge his duties for some years, and much of his work had actually been undertaken, unofficially, by the Rector of Lavington. But Webber did Manning one great service. He recognized his debt to him. 'Give Manning the office for he has done all the work,' he is reported to have said to Shuttleworth when he handed in his resignation.[7] It seems evident that both Dean

Chandler and Julius Hare expressed the same view to the new bishop.

Congratulations poured in by every post. First came a letter from his mother. 'You can better imagine my surprise and joy, my beloved child, than I can describe it,' she wrote.[8] Among the many others was a particularly touching one from Mary Wilberforce, Henry's wife. 'May it please God to bless you, you dear creature.'[9] Gladstone's letter was a little more staid in expression.

> Sure am I that you are one of the men to whom it is especially given to develop the solution of that great problem, how all our minor distractions are to be either abandoned, absorbed, or harmonised, through the might of the great principle of communion in the body of Christ; may you have the gifts of God in proportion to all the exigencies of your position.[10]

Newman's letter was briefer: 'My best congratulations to you. I hope it will turn out all that your own anxieties can wish, or the Church anticipate. I had had a report of it from Charles Marriott, but hardly knew, as he, whether to believe it.'[11]

It cannot be doubted that, in a winter of discontent for the Tractarians, Manning's appointment seemed to bring the promise of a better spring. He was the first of the contributors to the *Tracts for the Times* to receive recognition, and from the unlikeliest source. If the brighter spring did not come, this was for two reasons. In the first place, Tract 90 was published a month later; and secondly, Manning seemed to take an early opportunity to distance himself from its sentiments in his first archidiaconal Charge of July 1841. He began by extolling the virtues of the Reformation, describing it as 'this gracious act of God's providence towards His Church'. It was not the cause of the calamities of the sixteenth century, but the 'divinely prepared remedy . . . a gracious and searching work wrought by the purifying hand of God.'[12] Then he spoke of the virtues of the Church of England, with a harsh reference to the condition of those countries, especially Spain and France, who had been most successful in resisting the Reformation, and who were now 'the most destitute of Christianity'.[13] The Charge concluded with a strong affirmation of the destiny of the Anglican Church:

> It may be she shall build again the Tabernacle that is fallen down, and purify the Catholic world. Who can be familiar with her true character and not read the admonitions of her Divine Master? Who can see that

she is primitive and yet purified . . . and how, in all the inclinations of Western Christendom to one or other of the great religious extremes, she has been impelled forward in a middle path?[14]

There is more than a suggestion in Purcell's coverage of this period in Manning's life that his strident defence of Anglicanism and equally vehement denunciation of Romanism were studied for the particular purpose of advancing his career still further. Such a viewpoint would be better established if there were any evidence that Manning had actually changed his convictions. He had never subscribed to Froude's or to Newman's contempt for the Reformers; and if the words of his 1841 Charge jar unharmoniously with what Newman had written in Tract 90, then all this denotes is that Manning had not been as discountenanced as Newman had been by Wiseman's *Dublin Review* article (which his letters at the time confirm), and that he had not abandoned, as Newman had done, belief in the tenability of the *via media*. It is true that Manning found much in Roman Catholicism to admire; but there is no doubt at all of the sincerity of his condemnation of the aspects that he utterly rejected.

It has to be remembered, too, that Manning's position was very different from that of Newman. He had a definite responsibility to discharge towards the clergy of his archdeaconry. This would certainly call for restraint on his part in too militant a statement of extreme churchmanship, even if he were disposed to indulge in it. Nevertheless, on issues where his convictions were absolutely resolute – on matters of social injustice, or usurpations of the authority of the Church – he was prepared to speak out boldly, regardless of the consequences. One thing is very clear about Manning's character. He was never prepared to compromise his principles; he was never a 'trimmer'. That is not to say that he lacked ambition. He was well aware of his gifts and undoubtedly would have welcomed the opportunity, were it to come, to exercise them where they could most effectively serve the Church. But not at any price; and he was to give ample evidence of this in the future. Then again, his new position vastly increased the scope of his influence; and there were to his mind more pressing issues for the Church of England to face up to than trying to make the Thirty-nine Articles bear a meaning contrary to what their actual words appeared to say.

One was its role as a missionary Church, which he believed had been shamefully neglected. In all her vast colonial possessions, England in the early 1840s had only six colonial bishops; and it was on this subject that Manning, in April 1841, delivered one of the most influential speeches of his life, at Willis's Rooms in London. Fifty years later Gladstone recalled its effect:

> There was a remarkable speech made on that day, which sent a thrill of exaltation through the whole assembly at Willis's Rooms, delivered by a man of eminence, of known devotion to his work in his own sense, whose whole mind and whose whole heart was then given to the service of the Church of England. He was then known as Archdeacon Manning ... He pointed out upon how gigantic a scale we were then occupying the waste places of the earth ... and then he pointed to the scanty evidence which, up to that time, had been given of any care which had been taken by the Church of England for the propagation of the Gospel in these vast countries. He contrasted the meagreness and feebleness of our spiritual efforts with the wonderful, undying, untiring energies of the commercial powers ... He said the Church of England has now to make a choice between the temporal and the spiritual. She has to determine whether she will be the beast of burden, or whether she will be the evangelist of the world. That was a noble appeal – a noble challenge. The force of it was felt; it was taken up and duly answered.[15]

George Selwyn, first Bishop of New Zealand, always regarded Manning's speech (he was in his audience on that day) as the turning-point in his life. Years later, when he was Bishop of Lichfield and Manning had recently become Archbishop of Westminster, Selwyn wrote to him:

> There is no old friend of whom I have thought more frequently than of you, because the remembrance of your speech at the first establish-ment of the Colonial Bishoprics Fund has never faded from my mind. When I read an extract from it in a report of a speech delivered by Mr Gladstone, it seemed as fresh as if I had only heard it yesterday ... There is sorrow, no doubt, mingled with these remembrances; but I cherish them as spiritual sympathies which even now are not without their value, and which may be revived in greater perfection when ... these bonds shall have passed away in a better world.[16]

Manning never forgot, or ceased to love, George Selwyn. In a reference to this letter in his journal, he wrote, 'George Selwyn was a heroic Christian soul – a rebuke to most of us.'[17]

The most striking feature of Manning's career during the 1840s was the establishment in his mind of certain priorities and preoccupations which remained, to all intents and purposes, the same during his Catholic years, and pre-eminently when he rose to a position to declare these priorities as archiepiscopal policy. Education was one such; education under the auspices of the Church rather than the State, and especially the education of the poor, and the proper training of the priesthood. In his work in the National Society, he would be remembered for the role that he played in the setting-up of diocesan theological colleges, and for his acting as spokesman of what Kay-Shuttleworth described as 'the medieval party',[18] determined to resist the abandonment of denominational religious teaching if such was the price to be paid for grants from the State. At the same time, he showed both realism and moderation in toning down the demands of the intransigent element, led by G. A. Denison,[19] just as he was later prepared – against the views of the majority of the Roman Catholic hierarchy – to work with the government rather than against it over Forster's Education Act of 1870.

A significant theme of his Charges was his plea for recognition of the dignity of the working-man and the Church's obligation to the outcasts of society. There would come a time when, as Archbishop, he would cause a shock-wave through the respectable and propertied classes, in both his own Church and the Establishment, in his proclamation of the 'Dignity and Rights of Labour' in his address to the Mechanics' Institute at Leeds in 1874. His first enunciation of a similar concern was in a series of lectures given to the poorer elements of his own parish in Graffham Church in 1840.

> Time must be redeemed for the poor man [he said]. The world is too hard upon him and makes him pay too heavy a tale out of his short life ... Those who have lived as it is our blessing to do among the agricultural poor will know that with some rudeness of address and with faults not to be denied, they are still a noble-hearted race, whose sincerity, simplicity, and patience we should buy cheap at the cost of our refinements.[20]

He spoke more plainly in his Charge of 1845. 'The possessors of land are the natural guardians of the poor who live and die upon their soil,' he wrote. 'The laws of property are altogether second in the scale of God's providence, compared with these laws of local and personal obligation.' Again he showed his repugnance to commercial self-interest. 'There is a grace of life which is

more real than political economy, more living, active and beneficent than efficient management and statistical exactness.'[21]

In his Charge of 1842, he made a direct attack upon one of the
most closely-guarded privileges of the well-to-do – the system of
private pews in Church.

> Now I would have all such persons to consider whether it be
> wholesome and sound to train their devotional habits upon a support
> which is peculiar to the richer among us – whether, in reality, the true
> and living devotion be not rather that of the poor man, who, with no
> such refined and sickly helps to devotion, worships God in His house
> with open face.[22]

Another evil that he was forthright in denouncing, in his Charge
of 1846, was the horror of transportation to the penal colonies in
Australia. Most of his fellow-countrymen preferred not to think
about such things. Interestingly, the man who was most outspoken, through his own personal witness of the appalling atroci-
ties and degradations, was one whom Manning would come to
know so well and greatly to admire in his Catholic days – William
Bernard Ullathorne, Bishop of Birmingham.

Manning's major preoccupation in the field of theology, both as
an Anglican and as a Catholic, was the scandal of schism; and in
1842 he published his first significant theological treatise, dedicated to Gladstone, under the title *The Unity of the Church*. Perhaps
nothing that he wrote thereafter quite equalled it for scholarship
and breadth of vision. Not only did it establish him as a theologian
of consequence in the eyes of contemporaries such as Gladstone
and Robert Wilberforce, but it has since been acclaimed, by
George Tavard in his *The Quest for Catholicity*, as standing on its
own, in the writings of the time, for its penetration into the very
heart of the meaning of Catholicity. 'None of the Tractarians', he
wrote, 'approached the forcefulness of Manning's formulas and
the cosmic grandeur of his theology.'[23] In some ways it is very
characteristic of Manning's approach to a problem, its structure
being one favoured by him in all his subsequent writings – very
logical, proceeding from statements of supposedly unassailable
facts, thence to the history behind them, and the theological
implications, concluding with the arguments to substantiate his
interpretations.

His starting point is the statement, resting on patristic authority, that 'a belief in the Unity of the Church forms an article in

every Baptismal creed of every Church, both in the East and in the West'.[24] Following St Augustine (the authority most quoted), he acknowledges the distinction between the invisible and the visible Church, and the imperfect nature of the latter as a *civitas permixta*, having within it those far short of perfection, including evil men. From apostolic times, he argues, there was 'unity in plurality', it being 'plain that the divinely appointed ministry of the Church was the bond which knit together the members of Christ in one visible communion'.[25]

Unity, he maintains, is of two types – subjective (which is essentially moral, consisting of 'two great elements: subordination and charity')[26] and objective, which is organic, and relates to the faith, sacraments and organized polity of the Church. This distinction becomes somewhat opaque in his development of it, and he adds ugliness to opacity by making a distinction between 'oneliness' and 'oneness';[27] but at least he makes it quite clear that the essence of moral unity is 'the communion of the blessed Eucharist', and although in fact diversity has led in many cases to suspension of actual communion between members of different Churches, 'yet the sacrifice and sacrament of the blessed Eucharist being one and the same in all places, the very act of oblation and communion is actual unity with all branches of the Church. The Eucharist of the whole Catholic Church is one Eucharist. "We being many are one bread."'[28]

It was very obvious, of course, that the reality of things was far short of perfection. There is the fact of schism – and his treatment of schismatics and those outside the whole Catholic Church, who may yet not be denied a means of grace even if it has not been revealed, is very similar to what he would write later in at least two of his Catholic works.[29] Who was at fault within the Western world? Certainly not the original Reformers. Luther's case, he argues, was an entirely just one, as was his appeal to a general council. Leo X's unjust excommunication of Luther, before his case had been heard, clears him from the guilt of schism.[30] It was the 'after-acts' of the first Reformers which led their successors into 'rationalism, Socinianism, and infidelity'.[31] Indeed, a great deal of the blame falls on Rome because of the claim of the successors of St Peter to universal jurisdiction, in defiance of the fact that the commission to Peter was afterwards given to all the Apostles. 'They all were what Peter was.'[32] This was precisely Newman's contention, at that time, resting on the authority of St

Ignatius and St Cyprian. Manning, however, quotes Newman only once in the course of his work, with a reference to his *History of the Arians*.[33]

He concluded his argument with an attack on Rome for the damage that it had inflicted on the organic, or objective, unity of the Church by acts of usurpation, making claims that assemblies such as the Council of Florence and the Council of Trent were general councils when they were not, and − most of all − in claiming jurisdiction over the *Ecclesia Anglicana*, whose credentials for its independence from Rome went far back into the Middle Ages.[34]

The time would come when Manning would have to retract some of these contentions; and indeed he explicitly did so in his work, *The Temporal Mission of the Holy Ghost* in 1865.[35] The central theme, however, became more boldly proclaimed in his Catholic days, especially when he marshalled arguments to refute the 'branch theory' of the Catholic Church, so dear to Pusey's heart, which conceded equal claims to the title 'Catholic' to the Eastern and Anglican Churches as well as Rome.[36] What he wrote in 1842, nevertheless, was a faithful elaboration of his standpoint on the Reformation and the usurpations of the Papacy in his first Charge of 1841; and he was not to alter his views when he came to preach the November 5th sermon in Oxford in 1843.

He could attack Rome while looking longingly at some of its virtues, insights and practices, for the want or neglect of which the Church of England was undoubtedly impoverished. Her greatest deficiency seemed, to Manning, to lie in the sphere of moral or ascetical theology. Could the Church of England ever become a Church of the Saints without a proper penitential system and while it continued to neglect the means by which a Christian is led towards the goal of sanctity through spiritual direction and regular confession? As early as 1839 he had begun to undertake the role of confessor, and one of his first penitents so yearned for the solace of the Roman system that Manning sought advice from Newman. His reply expressed succinctly the dilemma facing all who were striving to inculcate a Catholic ethos into the Anglican Church.

> Our blanket is too small for our bed [Newman wrote] ... We are raising longings and tastes which we are not allowed to supply − and till our bishops and others give scope to the development of Catholic-ism externally and wisely, we *do* tend to make impatient minds seek it

where it has ever been, in Rome. I think that, whenever the time
comes that secession to Rome takes place, for which we must not be
unprepared, we must boldly say to the Protestant section of our
Church – '*You* are the cause of this; you must concede; you must
conciliate; you must meet the age; you must make the Church more
efficient, more suitable to the needs of the heart, more equal to the
external. Give us more services, more vestments and decorations in
worship; give us monasteries; give us the signs of an apostle, the
pledges that the Spouse of Christ is among us. Till then you will have
continual secessions to Rome.'[37]

The very word 'confession' was the reddest of rags to the
Protestant bull. It conjured up, in an English mind, the worst
excesses of continental priestcraft, the sinister exploitation of the
simple and the weak, especially of gullible women penitents, the
subtle casuistry of the Jesuits and the manipulative power that it
delivered into their hands. Even Gladstone felt that there was
something unmanly and offensive to the English character in such
practices. He wrote to Manning in 1847:

> The twofold system of compulsory confession for retrospect, and
> direction for prospect . . . do in practice so work as very frequently and
> extensively to take out of the hands of the individual Christian the
> chief care of, and therewith the chief responsibility for, his own
> conduct, and that *therefore* it is that in this country, notwithstanding
> our sins and miseries, the moral sense upon the whole is at this
> moment more generally clear and strong than in the lands where the
> Roman Church bears sway.[38]

Keble, whose views on sacramental confession were similar to
Manning's, was scrupulously careful to avoid the worst features of
'foreign Penitentiaries'. In a review of a book entitled *Parochial
Work*, by E. Munro, Vicar of Harrow Weald, he drew a picture of
idealized English village piety, difficult to read today without
either a wince or a smile:

> A few grains of old English common sense, or rather of Christian
> prudence and charity, applied to the realities of English life (a grace to
> be specially prayed for as well as cultivated), will effectually guard us
> from all these and the like absurdities, and will be rewarded, through
> God's blessing, with many a repetition of that sight, dear to angels (if
> one may say so without presumption) of a noble-hearted English
> peasant on his knees in humble confession, making an unreserved
> offering of himself, and never dreaming that what he is about is at all
> out of the common.[39]

Pusey, of all the Tractarians, was the most zealous in encouraging spiritual direction, not surprisingly in view of his teaching on the gravity of post-baptismal sin; and he was certainly thought to be guilty at times of lacking a few grains of old English common sense, especially by his new diocesan, Samuel Wilberforce, who succeeded Bagot as Bishop of Oxford in 1845. 'You seem to me to be habitually assuming the place and doing the work of a Roman confessor, and not that of an English clergyman', was the chief ground of his episcopal censure leading to Pusey's inhibition from officiating in the Oxford diocese in 1850.[40] This was a predictable clash because Manning and his brother-in-law had agreed to differ on this very issue as early as 1837.[41] By 1850, however, Newman's prophetic words had received disquieting evidence of their truth. Although he himself had never felt entirely easy about hearing confessions, stopping the practice altogether in his last months at Littlemore,[42] others – including Manning – were becoming more and more convinced that the penitential system and the recovery of an ascetical theology were going to prove, sooner or later, to be the crucial test of the Anglican Church's validity as a branch of the Church Catholic. The first to declare the sense of utter frustration at the inhibitions imposed by the Establishment was F. W. Faber, Rector of Elton, in 1844, when – in a letter to Newman – he protested that 'I could [do] all things in my parish if I were Roman, and had not my feet in the stocks of our system'.[43] A year later Henry Wilberforce, then Vicar of Walmer, discussed the parlous state of affairs with T. W. Allies, Vicar of Launton, when they attended together the consecration of St Saviour's Church at Leeds. Allies recorded the conversation in his journal:

> Henry Wilberforce had a long talk with me. He said: 'I am fairly vexed – done in my parish. I feel we can do nothing in the Church of England without confession, but how we are to get it I see not.' He expressed the highest opinion of J.H.N. 'I consider N. the greatest blessing God ever gave to any Church' . . . Considered Manning the best spiritual guide we have; superior to Pusey as having more judgment.[44]

Allies had come to the same conclusion in 1844;[45] and in December 1848, he called on Manning to pour out his own grievances and anxieties. Henry Wilberforce was also present.

> H.W. and I both agreed that we could find no theology in the Church of England – no one divine who held the whole Catholic faith. M. did

not attempt to disprove this. He said this morning that should anything be determined against confession, it would move him more than anything else, for it would be an actual impediment to holiness of life.[46]

All four men – Faber, Henry Wilberforce, Allies and Manning – eventually gave up the struggle and found, as Newman predicted, what they sought 'where it has ever been, in Rome'. And that was their great consolation. Even Newman, who in his early Catholic sermons never quite lost the forbidding note against presumptions of assurance, could preach on Penance in terms denied to him as an Anglican. 'Such is the power of the Sacrament of Penance', he wrote, 'that, be your load of guilt heavier, or be it lighter, it removes it, whatever it is. It is as easy to Him to wash out the many sins as the few.'[47] Nor did he lose any opportunity to point out to those who remained behind, in his lectures on the *Difficulties of Anglicans*, that Catholics were released from the terrible burden of post-baptismal sin. 'The Catholic knows just where he is and what he has to do.'[48] To Manning the theological transition was easier, because he had preached frequently on the theme as an Anglican. In his Catholic days, two of his most moving devotional books – *The Love of Jesus to Penitents* and *Sin, and its Consequences* – reveal something of his power as a spiritual director and of his depth as a moral theologian. Often enough he would hold out to the penitent the consolation to be found in the story of the Prodigal Son[49] and in what had been shown to them in the life of Mary Magdalene.[50]

So during the ten years of his archidiaconate, most of the major concerns of Manning's later career had been exhibited or articulated in at least an embryonic form. But in the early 1840s he could not have had an inkling that they would receive their fullest expression within the Roman Church. So preoccupied was he with his new responsibilities that even affairs at Oxford made only a slight impression upon him. Anti-Tractarian feelings within the University had again been stirred up by the contest for the Poetry Professorship, following the expiry of Keble's tenure. His obvious successor was Isaac Williams, but because he was tainted with Tractarian sympathies, a rival Evangelical candidate was put up by the opposition party, the Revd James Garbett, an amiable and inoffensive man and, as Marvin O'Connell has observed, 'an ideal candidate in an election which had nothing to do with qualifications for the post contested';[51] for Garbett had no claims to be a poet at all. It rapidly became a *cause célèbre*, in which Newman, somewhat reluctantly, found himslf acting as a sort of party manager on Williams' behalf, and with Gladstone doing his utmost to persuade both candidates to withdraw. In the end, Williams withdrew when it became obvious that his chances were hopeless, and the whole affair ended with bitter feelings and recriminations all round. Manning wanted nothing to do with it, although he had initially caused Pusey to remonstrate with him by saying that, if he voted, he would support Garbett, who was a friend and neighbour. He then decided to abstain.[52]

He was in two minds, also, over the affair of the Jerusalem Bishopric, partly because his friend and colleague, Julius Hare, had been involved in the planning of the project; but he eventually declared his opposition on the grounds of its doubtful legality, in trespassing upon the preserves of another branch of the Catholic Church.[53] Even Pusey, as well as High Churchmen such as W. F. Hook and William Palmer, rather welcomed at first what they conceived to be a defiant extension of the Anglican episcopate. But Newman saw precisely what was at stake and was horrified. For the Church of England to act in conjunction with the Prussian Lutherans was 'forming a special league which she has never done before with foreign Protestants', thereby putting her 'on a more Protestant footing than [she] has hitherto acknowledged'.[54] As he expressed it later in the *Apologia*, following the successive blows of the collapse of his confidence in the *via media* and the hostile episcopal Charges, repudiating the arguments of Tract 90:

> This was the third blow, which finally shattered my faith in the Anglican Church ... [It] might have the Apostolical succession, as had the Monophysites; but such acts as were in progress led me to the gravest suspicion, not that it would soon cease to be a Church, but that (since the 16th century), it had never been a Church all along.[55]

For Newman, this was the beginning of the end. On all sides the Catholic edifice that he had seemed to be building up was crumbling. His work on the writings of Athanasius against the Arians, during 1841, had confirmed his worst fears from the initial doubts caused by Wiseman's *Dublin Review* article. 'The ghost had come a second time ... I saw clearly, that in the history of Arianism, the pure Arians were the Protestants, the semi-Arians were the Anglicans, and that Rome now was what it was then.'[56] His friends were beginning to be persecuted. Keble's curate, Peter Young, was refused priest's Orders by Bishop Sumner of Winchester, because of his Tractarian views on the nature of the Eucharist; then Pusey himself, in April 1843, was delated to the Vice-Chancellor by Godfrey Faussett, for preaching the doctrine of the Real Presence in the Eucharist in Christ Church Cathedral, as a result of which, after an examination by a court of six Doctors of Divinity, he was suspended from preaching within the University for two years.

By this time Newman had retired to Littlemore – an outlying hamlet, part of the parish of St Mary's, where he had built, through subscriptions, a small church which had been conse-crated in September 1836. He had for some time regarded it as a haven of peace, a refuge from 'critics and carpers',[57] as he once explained to J. R. Bloxam, who was his curate there from 1837 to 1840. In the summer of 1840 he purchased some ten acres of adjoining land on which he erected a range of outbuildings, cloistered with private rooms and a library, to form a tiny college or study-centre, where like-minded young men in Orders could join him in a sort of nascent religious community. As early as 1840 he was contemplating a severance of Littlemore from St Mary's, with a view to resigning his primary charge. Then Littlemore would become a real retreat, his 'Torres Vedras', a place of withdrawal where his followers could recuperate for perhaps a further advance in due course. In April 1842 he took up residence there, soon to be joined by various celibate colleagues, some – like J. D. Dalgairns and William Lockhart – long-term residents whose allegiance to the Anglican Church was under a similar strain to Newman's own; others, like Mark Pattison and James Anthony Froude, came to stay for short periods of study in a devotional setting. Another troubled soul who joined Newman a year later was Ambrose St John. 'If quiet and retirement are able, as they very likely will be, to reconcile you to things as they are,' Newman wrote to him, in welcoming him to their community, 'you shall have your fill of them.'[58]

The peace and quiet that they craved for was not always granted them. Suspicions were aroused that these premises, given the character of their inmates, might be hives of Popery; and Newman was well aware of prying eyes and unwarranted clandes-tine intrusions by ill-wishers eager to find evidence to report back to the authorities. Bishop Bagot found himself obliged to enquire politely of Newman if there was truth in the contention that he had formed at Littlemore a species of Anglo-Catholic monastery. Newman's indignant rebuttal of the charge was understandable ('What have I done that I am to be called to account by the world for my private actions in a way in which no one else is called?'), but was not entirely truthful. He rejected such terms as 'monastery' or 'cells of dormitories', claiming injured bewilderment at such imputations.[59] He conveniently forgot that he had used precisely the term 'monastery' in letters both to James Hope[60] and to Bloxam, adding – to the latter – because of the sensitivity of the issue, '*This is a secret*'.[61]

In February 1843, however, as a prelude to taking the decisive step of resigning the living of St Mary's, he published, in a letter to the *Conservative Journal*, a 'Retractation' of all the harsh things he had previously written against the Church of Rome. There followed a long and agonizing correspondence with Keble, who strove to dissuade his friend from committing himself to 'withdrawing from your ministerial place', not least – as he shrewdly added – because of 'what I fear might come after'.[62] Newman's official letter of resignation was written to Bishop Bagot on 7 September. On 25 September he preached his last sermon as an Anglican at a communion service at Littlemore, Pusey acting as celebrant, and nearly breaking down under the strain, so emotional was the occasion. Newman's sermon bore the title 'The Parting of Friends', concluding with a peroration so powerful that none present could hold back their tears.

> O my brethren, O kind and affectionate hearts, O loving friends, should you know any one whose lot it has been, by writing or by word of mouth, in some degree to help you thus to act; if he has ever told you what you knew about yourselves, or what you did not know; has read to you your wants or feelings, and comforted you by the very reading; has made you feel that there was a higher life than this daily one, and a brighter world than that you see; or encouraged you, or sobered you, or opened a way to the inquiring; or soothed the perplexed; if what he has said or done has ever made you take interest in him, and feel well inclined towards him; remember such a man in time to come, though you hear him not, and pray for him, that in all things he may know God's will, and at all times he may be ready to fulfil it.[63]

Manning was not present to hear this moving valediction. He wrote, however, to Newman on 8 October:

I had intended to come to Littlemore yesterday to see you; but I was in so much pain from a cold in my face that I most unwillingly gave it up ... You have been constantly in my thoughts ... And yet my chief reason for wishing to see you would be for the sake of old kindliness; for I do not feel that I ought to volunteer any unsought expressions on your late resignation of St Mary's, for which ever since you talked to me 2 or 3 years ago I have been more or less prepared. Also I feel that one ought to know and understand far more of the interior of each other's minds to be able to form any view of what is right and reasonable in each one's position. I believe the amount of all I should endeavour to express is an affectionate regard and a real participation in all that distresses you. I suppose it is next to impossible that employments so distant and different as ours, if I may venture to compare them, should not introduce differences of views and feeling; and I have always a desire to understand yours more clearly, and to be understood by you in turn.[64]

For sensitivity and maturity of judgement, this is a remarkable letter. It provoked from Newman a reply hardly calculated to bring much cheer. 'I fear I must confess', he wrote, 'that in proportion as I think the English Church is showing herself intrinsically and radically alien from Catholic principles, so do I feel the difficulties in defending her claims to be a branch of the Catholic Church ... Men of Catholic views are too truly but a party in our Church.'[65] Manning wrote again on 23 October:

Surely you cannot feel that the Church of England regards you as a foreign ingredient. With whose writings has it so strongly and widely sympathized? For years, who has been more loved and revered? Individuals have opposed you always, and latterly, since no. 90, persons bearing office in the Church, – but what has the Church as such – or any great man of the Church expressed? ... Has not God prospered you in the last ten years in a measure which makes it – may I venture to say – impatience something like Jonah's to ask for more? ... Surely if one compares the English Church now with what it was ten years back it cannot be said truly that it is showing itself intrinsically alien from Catholic principles. That the Church has passed under a fearful influence for 150 years is sadly true; but surely the last ten years have dispelled much and brought the living church back again in a wonderful way ... Shall we not be too hasty? – patience and love one to another is what we want most.[66]

Newman then came out with his most forthright statement so far. 'I am deeply sorry for the pain I must give you,' he wrote. 'I must tell you then frankly ... I think the Church of Rome the

Catholic Church, and ours not a part of the Catholic Church, because not in communion with Rome.'[67] Manning passed this letter on to Gladstone, who wrote back in near despair. 'Alas! Alas! . . . My first thought is "I stagger to and fro, like a drunken man, and am at my wit's end".'[68]

A month later Manning had the unenviable task of preaching the November 5th sermon at Oxford. By tradition, of course, it was expected to be anti-Roman in tone; nor did Manning, at the time, feel inclined to depart from tradition, so convinced was he of the falsity of the claims that Newman had now conceded. But whatever he said was bound to incur displeasure. If he had hidden his true feelings, in deference to Newman, he would be shirking his responsibility, as well as sounding insincere; if he spoke his mind, he would be accused of disloyalty to his friend. He chose to speak out. He deplored the 'manifold secularity' which had spread itself within the Western Church, and how 'spiritual powers were turned to worldly ends'.[69] Through 'the mercy of God', however, 'the English Church and people' had been preserved 'from the secular domination of the Roman pontiff'.[70] It was the mission of 'our highly-favoured Church, amid much chastisement and rebuke of heavenly discipline', to become a principle of reconciliation between east and west, bringing 'unity and peace to mankind'.[71]

It was not, by any means, the finest sermon that Manning had ever preached. J. B. Mozley, who heard it, told his sister:

> I did not like either the matter or tone. He seemed really so carried away by fear of Romanism that he almost took under his patronage the Puritans, and the Whigs of 1688, because they had settled the matter against the Pope . . . I suppose he wants to disconnect himself regularly from the ultra party, and has taken this means.[72]

Whatever his motives were, Manning explained to Pusey that he felt that he had no choice in the matter. Newman's letters had so alarmed him that he was 'reduced to the painful, saddening, sickening necessity of saying what [he] felt about Rome'.[73]

How Newman responded to Manning's sermon has been the subject of some speculation. There is no doubt that, while in Oxford, Manning called at Littlemore to explain to Newman why he had used the strong language that he felt the occasion demanded. According to J. A. Froude, Newman refused to see him and told Froude to pass the message to Manning, who was so

upset that Froude accompanied him part of the way back to
Oxford, not realizing that the Archdeacon – in his confusion –
had left his hat behind, and was offending the custom of the day
by walking the streets bareheaded.[74] Newman himself, however,
assured R. W. Church that there was no truth in this. The reason
why Manning failed to see him was because he happened to be out
at the time.[75] In any case, the correspondence that passed
between them later that year does not suggest hurt feelings on
either side. Manning wrote to Newman on 21 December 1843,
sending him a copy of his Visitation Charge of that year:

> I do not wish you to think me other than I am . . . I felt . . . you might
> think my words the smooth words of one that would leave you for the
> world. I will use no professions of attachment to you, or of my own
> intentions and desires for myself. I had rather submit to any thoughts
> in your heart, or in others. You have a hard life and an empty home
> before you, and so have I, and I trust we shall walk together long
> enough to trust the singleness of each other's eye and to love each
> other as friends . . . My dear Newman, do not suspect me as an empty
> pretender if I say that the only thing that has kept me up in the last six
> years and more of trial, and the only thing I look for until death is to
> save the Church in which I was born again. Doubtful thoughts about it
> are dreadful – and seem to take all things from me.[76]

Newman's reply confirmed that he respected Manning's sincerity.

> It is no pleasure to me to differ from friends – no comfort to be
> estranged from them – no satisfaction or boast to have said things
> which I must unsay. Surely I will remain where I am as long as I can –
> And believe me, the circumstances of such men as yourself being
> contented to remain is the strongest argument in favour of my own
> remaining. It is my constant prayer, that if others are right I may be
> drawn back – that nothing may part us.[77]

III

A hard life and an empty home were what awaited both of them,
Manning had said to Newman. He was, of course, thinking of
Graffham Rectory without Caroline, and – since 1841 – without
Mary Sargent, who had left him to look after the stricken family
of Samuel Wilberforce, following Emily's death after giving birth
to their sixth child. Newman's home at Littlemore was not exactly
empty, however. He had the company of a few like-minded

friends. Not that they could afford him much comfort. William Lockhart had already deserted the community for the Roman Church, despite his pledge to Newman not to make a move for at least three years. Some of the others were clearly looking to Newman to follow his lead should he come to the same decision; and the last thing that he wanted as he entered his limbo period at Littlemore – the two years 'on his Anglican death-bed' – was to be pressed or harried by others.

The main pressure was coming from the younger extremists who had virtually taken over the *British Critic* under Tom Mozley's editorship – men like W. G. Ward and Frederick Oakeley, who – as Newman put it – 'arrived late into the Movement ... resolute minds ... who knew nothing about the *Via Media*, but had heard much about Rome ... These men cut into the original Movement at an angle, fell across its line of thought, and then set about turning that line in its own direction.'[1] They became more and more of an embarrassment to him. Oakeley contributed an article in the *British Critic* on Bishop Jewel, which Newman felt obliged to disown because of the violence of its language; and W. G. Ward, in the words of his son Wilfrid, had a mind which perceived 'a truth so keenly' with a disposition to adopt 'an opinion with such energy and force, as to exaggerate its true character'.[2] They would not let Newman be, and kept plying him with questions that he was neither ready nor disposed to answer. Ward, in particular, rigorous logician as he was, was continually putting forward arguments, in his *British Critic* articles, which – Newman complained – were forcing him 'beyond what I can fairly go'.[3] 'When I wanted to be in peace and stillness, I had to speak out,' he recalled in the *Apologia*, 'and I incurred the charge of weakness from some men, and of mysteriousness, shuffling and underhand dealing from the majority.'[4]

At last, in 1844, Ward came fully out into the open with his book, *The Ideal of a Christian Church*: a work so defiantly admiring of everything Roman, so contemptuously dismissive of everything Protestant and so unequivocal in its restatement of the arguments of Tract 90, that the authorities could not ignore it. Out came the knives again at Oxford. The Hebdomadal Board, having failed to gain a retractation from Ward, summoned Convocation, in February 1845, putting to the vote three resolutions: the condemnation of the offending passages in Ward's *Ideal*; the deprivation of the author's degrees (he was a Fellow of Balliol at the time);

and, finally, the imposition of a new test, requiring subscription to the Articles in the sense intended by their original framers. Not surprisingly, this last resolution met with howls of protest from the liberal element within the University. It was therefore withdrawn and replaced by a resolution condemning Tract 90. This did not appease the liberals either. They had defended Hampden in 1836, and they were not going to associate themselves with any further attempt to restrict freedom of interpretation, even though the 'victors of 1836' might have deserved to have been 'the victims of 1845', as A. P. Stanley so neatly put it, savouring the full irony of the occasion.[5] But nothing could save Ward, who indeed did nothing to save himself. He lost on both counts; as for the condemnation of Tract 90, the Proctors (one of whom was R. W. Church) intervened by employing their veto before it could be put to the vote.

It would be too much to say that Newman was indifferent to the outcome of these events. But he took no part in them, and viewed them all with a certain detachment. His mind was really set on other things. Manning, however, came up to vote, and wrote to Newman beforehand:

> By this morning's post I have heard of the proposed vote about Tract 90. And I lose not a day in writing to you to say that even if I had not been coming to Oxford to vote against the censure on Ward, every feeling of affection and gratitude to you would have brought me at all costs, and hindrances to vote against this attack. I owe to you more than to any one living, so far as I know, and the thought of a difference from you in anything, much more in vital things, has weighed on me I may say all day long since October year ago.[6]

He duly attended the Convocation. Afterwards, with Pusey, he met Ward, apparently for the first time, and was shocked by the levity displayed by the Fellow of Balliol who could now sport only an undergraduate's gown. He assumed his Archdeacon's demeanour and reproved him. 'The situation seems to me, Mr Ward, to be one of the utmost gravity.'[7]

Ward and Oakeley were received into the Roman Church later that year, Ward (rather to Newman's disgust) having decided to get married in the meantime. When would Newman move? – was the question on everyone's lips. The wonder was that he had continued his limbo existence for so long. Whatever his state of mind, there were – he had consistently maintained – good reasons for long and sustained thought. In September 1843 he had given some straight advice to F. W. Faber, who was in the same unsettled state. 'Ought not ... a certain term of probation to be given to oneself, before so awful a change as that I am alluding to? e.g., I have sometimes thought that, were I tempted to go to Rome, I should for three years pray, and get my friends to pray, that I might die rather than go, if going were wrong.'[8] He had to wrestle with the force of words that he had written, years before, in Tract 71:

> 'Let every man abide in the same calling wherein he was called' is St Paul's direction. We find ourselves under the Anglican regimen; let every one of us, cleric and layman, remain in it till our opponents have shown cause why we should change, till we have reason to suspect we are wrong. The *onus probandi* plainly lies with them.[9]

By 1839 he had begun to shift his ground. The Wiseman article had shown him some cause why he should change; and the moment that he decided 'to prove the cannon' of the Anglican Church, he had come to the thought, at least, that the *onus probandi* lay with the Church that had every appearance of being in schism. Nevertheless, six years elapsed before he took the decisive step. Understandably, many of Newman's friends and admirers who remained faithful to the Church of their baptism maintained that whatever Newman stated to the contrary in the *Apologia*, the real reason for his change of communion was that – as Pusey put it – 'our Church has not known how to employ him'.[10] R. W. Church blamed the short-sighted Heads of Houses, and the bishops at the time, who between them drove Newman out of the Church of England.[11] In more recent years, F. L. Cross applied to Newman the Nietzschean term 'ressentiment', meaning a deep sense of injury and grievance arising from his treatment by the Church which he had tried loyally to serve, so that his conversion to Rome was really a sort of psychological retaliation against those who had rejected him.[12]

It is true that once Newman had resigned from St Mary's, his occupation was gone, and that the ostensible reason for the resignation was that, after the censures by the episcopal bench, he did not see how he could 'with any sense of propriety, retain' the living.[13] Thereafter it is almost impossible to imagine that Newman could have remained indefinitely in the shallows and without any cure of souls. Nevertheless, of the three 'calls' which Newman believed that he received to convince him that the Anglican

Church was outside the Catholic pale, only one – the hostile Charges of the Bishops – was related to rejection of his writings and influence. The other two – his researches into early Christian heresies and schism, and the alliance with continental Protestantism in the Jerusalem Bishopric project – were, to his mind, proofs positive that his understanding of the Catholicity of the English Church had been nothing but a dream. He had determined to 'prove its cannon', and it had failed in the test.

Not that that was sufficient for him to join the Roman Church forthwith. As he explained in the *Apologia*, 'great acts take time'.[14] And when he dismissed so eloquently the force of logic in such decisions, he was echoing a passage written years before in *Loss and Gain*, when Charles Reding mused over the nature of Christianity: 'I wish I knew *what* Christianity was ... But it's a work of time; all the paper-arguments in the world are unequal to giving one a view in a moment';[15] and when Charles was approaching the moment of decision to become a Roman Catholic, he observed to his friend, Carlton, '*Seeing* it to be *like* the Apostolic Church, I *believe* it to be the *same*. Reason has gone first, faith is to follow.'[16] Certainly this confirms one of Newman's leading ideas. In decisions of this sort there has to be a union of heart and head. 'The whole man moves.'[17] What is more difficult to determine, and perhaps impossible for the subject himself, is whether the head actually precedes the heart. Newman seemed to think so in his own case. He had put the Church of England to an intellectual test, and it had failed to answer. It was not so easy to decide where his heart lay. As early as 1836 he had admitted to Rose that it lay with Rome as it once was, not with the Church of England as it now seemed to be. On the other hand, it would be a heart-breaking experience to part with like-minded friends and companions, just as it was a 'personal humiliation'[18] to have publicly to admit that he had misled a whole generation of disciples, and especially the younger ones, by inspiring them with an ideal and a cause in which he no longer believed.

Nevertheless, he could not abandon the Church of his baptism until he had proved the cannon of the Church of Rome and come to grips with what he had so long believed to be its corruptions and accretions since the purity of the apostolic and patristic ages. Until then, as he expressed it, 'though the Church of England is only Samaria, it is enough, until and unless God issues some clear indisputable command ... to leave it.'[19] But what did he really know about Rome, as it then was? Precious little. As he explained in a letter of November 1844: 'I have nothing to draw me elsewhere. I hardly ever was at a Roman service; even abroad I knew no Roman Catholics. I have no sympathy with them as a party. I am giving up everything.'[20] He put similar words in the mouth of Charles Reding in *Loss and Gain*. 'He had never seen a Catholic priest, to know him in his life.'[21] This was not strictly true of Newman. He had met Nicholas Wiseman in Rome, and Dr Maguire had been introduced to him at Oxford in 1835; but he had not been favourably impressed. He had only the sketchiest knowledge of Catholic theology. He had read Bellarmine to assist him with his *Lectures on Justification*, and some Bossuet for his *Lectures on the Prophetical Office*, but very little else.[22] Yet he felt in his heart that Rome possessed, with all her faults, the most precious quality of all: a sanctity far removed from anything that could be seen (except in a few isolated individuals) in the Church of England. It was the difference, as he put it in his *Lectures on Justification*, between the '"dreamy talk" of modern Protestantism and "holy fear's stern glow" in the Church Catholic.'[23]

He needed help to guide him, and he found it in Charles Russell, President of Maynooth, the Catholic seminary in Ireland, whom he had met in Oxford in 1841 (at least one Catholic priest with whom he felt a personal rapport). 'He had', Newman subsequently acknowledged, 'more to do with my conversion than any one else.'[24] In a most careful and courteous letter, refreshingly free from any obvious intention to proselytize, Russell corrected Newman's misconceptions, as stated in Tract 90, on the Roman doctrine of transubstantiation; he then gently took in hand his basic education in Catholic devotional theology, sending him sermons of St Alphonsus Liguori, the *Spiritual Exercises* of Ignatius Loyola, and even some cheap popular Italian tracts, to convince him that Protestant and English prejudices had vastly exaggerated what might seem to be the most unpalatable features of the Roman system – casuistry and superstition. Perhaps most important of all, he disabused Newman of the supposition that the Roman Church was forever intruding intermediaries between the individual and his Creator, through images, relics, and the intercessory role of the Saints and the Blessed Virgin.[25]

So, gradually, Newman was drawn to the exercise of rethinking his whole understanding of the extent to which Christian doctrine might legitimately have been developed from the original deposit.

There had already been hints that he was changing his mind from his earlier adhesion to the criteria of the Vincentian Canon. Even his early grasping of the truth of the aphorism of Thomas Scott that 'growth [is] the only evidence of life' predisposed him to finding 'the principle of dynamism congenial',[26] and in both Tract 85 (1838) and his essay on 'The Prospects of the Anglican Church' (1839), he had used the image of a seed as the principle of germination and growth. In his fifteenth Oxford University Sermon, however, preached in 1843, he prepared the way for his fuller exposition in the *Essay on Development of Christian Doctrine*. 'Even centuries might pass', he wrote, 'without the formal expression of a truth, which had been all along the secret life of millions of faithful souls.'[27]

When he embarked upon the *Essay on Development*, it certainly appears that he had already arrived at the conclusion that he set out to prove. No longer does the *onus probandi* lie with the Church of Rome. Since it is more probable than otherwise, he argues (taking a typical Newman stance), that the Christianity of modern times is 'in its substance the very religion which Christ and His Apostles taught in the first' century, then the obligation to prove otherwise must lie with those who are tempted to 'assert what is unnatural to expect'.[28] The method he employs is, understandably and perhaps unavoidably, historical; but he makes it plain from the start that all the advantages lie with him, not his opponents, by his occupying the historical ground. 'Whatever history teaches, whatever it omits, whatever it exaggerates or extenuates, whatever it says or unsays, at least the Christianity of history is not Protestantism. If ever there were a safe truth, it is this.'[29] One might reply that no historical truth is quite as safe as Newman implies, and the fact that he expresses his view so emphatically suggests that he might have had just a flicker of doubt himself. Nevertheless, all this – and indeed all that follows – is quintessentially Newman. 'All the main arteries of his thought, during the Anglican period,' J. H. Walgrave has written, 'converge on this book';[30] and it is because of this that it caused raised eyebrows and puzzled frowns when it was read by the Jesuits at Rome, and by Perrone in particular. It is essentially an Anglican rationale of the Roman position. As Stephen Prickett has described it, 'it was written in limbo, defending the claims of a Church he did not belong to with the weapons of the Church that had abandoned him'.[31]

Arguably, although by no means the first exposition of the idea of doctrinal development (Coleridge had his own views on this, and – within the Roman Church – Bossuet, Suarez and Möhler were the acknowledged authorities), the *Essay* constitutes Newman's most original and influential contribution to theology. From his personal point of view, it has the special significance that it convinced *him*; and in two major respects. In the first place, it helped him to clear the last hurdle which blocked his wholehearted acceptance of the Roman claims – the validity of the claim to Papal supremacy. There had to be 'infallible arbitration in religious disputes' in the past; therefore, so 'much more is it welcome at a time like the present,' he writes, 'when the human intellect is so busy, and thought so fertile, and opinion so manifold'.[32] He asserts its antecedent probability,[33] and then shows that history confirms it. He elaborated this later in the *Apologia*, and also in a footnote to the revised edition of the *Lectures on the Prophetical Office*. 'The highest authority speaks last', and it might be centuries before it finds itself compelled to speak.[34] This was not, however, the clinching factor in Newman's conversion, and here he differed significantly from Manning. As he explained in 1862,

> I certainly did not become a Catholic, as others have, on the ground 'ubi Petrus, ibi Ecclesia', but because, whereas the Church is to last to the end of the world, unless that large Communion which happens to be Roman be the Church, the Church has failed.[35]

The second conviction, arising from the writing of the *Essay*, was the crucial one – the principle of legitimate inheritance or continuity of ethos. It received its first expression in the *Essay*, as follows:

> On the whole, all parties will agree that, of all existing systems, the present communion of Rome is the nearest approximation in fact to the Church of the Fathers . . . Did St Athanasius or St Ambrose come suddenly to life, it cannot be doubted what communion he would (we will say) mistake for his own.[36]

When he was asked, in the early years of his Catholic career, by others to supply his reasons for joining the Church of Rome, it was always to this argument that he returned. 'The overbearingly convincing proof is this,' he wrote to A. J. Hanmer, trembling on the brink of Rome, 'that were St Athanasius and St Ambrose in London now, they would go to worship, not to St Paul's Cathedral, but to Warwick Street or Moor Fields. This my own reading of history has made to me an axiom, and it converted me, though I cannot of course communicate the force of it to another.'[37] This is precisely the sort of test that an Anglican would be disposed to apply. Newman was still assessing the Roman Church in terms of the features that it had in common with the patristic age; and this surely is what he meant when, in his *Letter to Pusey* (in reply to Pusey's *Eirenicon* of 1864), he declared that 'the Fathers made me a Catholic, and I am not going to kick down the ladder by which I ascended into the Church'.[38]

Again, it is a typical Newman argument. It is hypothetical and sounds, perhaps, more convincing than it actually is. It is impossible to prove or to disprove, because the saints in question could not be brought back to demonstrate the truth or falsity of it. Not that that necessarily reduces its force. The point is, that the argument was convincing to Newman, and he could only convince others who shared his views and antecedent disposition (as he was honest enough to admit to Hanmer). Newman was searching for a particular ethos; when he found it, there would the true Church be. 'Be my soul with the saints', he said in his lectures on the *Difficulties of Anglicans*, 'and shall I lift up my hand against them?'[39] It had ever been so; quite early on, he had shuddered at Anglicanism as the Church of the Establishment, in comparing it with the 'fresh vigorous power of what I was reading in the first centuries . . . I recognized the movement of my Spiritual Mother. "Incessu patuit Dea"'.[40]

The Church of Rome still bore these marks; and with that conviction, heart and head became as one. He now *knew* where the true Church was; were he to die as an Anglican, there could be no plea of 'invincible ignorance' for him. 'Our Church may be a place of grace and security to another, yet not to me', was the conclusion he came to in December 1844.[41] While writing the *Essay*, this conviction became stronger with every sentence that he wrote; so that he eventually brought it to an abrupt end. Why wait any longer?

It was natural enough, at that moment, that Newman's mind should return, consciously or unconsciously, to Thomas Scott's *The Force of Truth*. After all, what he had been engaged in writing was really an extended essay on 'Growth the only evidence of life'. In an eloquent passage of *The Force of Truth*, Scott had invited his readers to acknowledge that once one has seen the way forward, there can be no excuse for delay. It is never too early to mend one's ways. 'Time, how short! Eternity, how long!'[42] Newman echoed Scott's precise words, with one addition very much his own, in order to forestall those who might accuse him of forsaking the Church of England out of bitterness:

> And now, dear Reader, time is short, eternity is long. Put not from you what you have here found; regard it not a mere matter of present controversy; set not out to refute it . . . Seduce not yourself with the imagination that it comes of disappointment, or disgust, or restlessness, or wounded feeling, or undue sensibility, or other weakness. Wrap not yourself round in the associations of years past; nor determine that to be truth which you wish to be so, nor make an idol of cherished anticipations. Time is short, eternity is long.[43]

On 8 October 1845, a Passionist priest, Father Dominic Barberi, arrived at Littlemore, like Nicodemus, in the night. On the following day, after perhaps the longest confession that the priest had ever heard, Newman was received into the Roman Church, with two of his companions, Richard Stanton and Frederic Bowles. Two others, Dalgairns and Ambrose St John, had taken the same step at the end of the previous month. The long agony was over, to be replaced in time by a sense of inner peace; but first Newman had the distressing task of informing his family and his friends.

IV

One of the first of his friends to whom he wrote was Manning; a letter written actually while he was waiting for Father Dominic to arrive. It merely expressed the fact of what was to take place. 'I shall ask him to receive me into what I believe to be the One True Fold.'[1] Manning replied on 14 October:

> If I knew what words would express my heartfelt love to you, and keep my own conscience pure, I would use them. Believe me that I accept the letter you wrote me at such a moment, as a pledge of your affection. I shall keep it among many memorials of past days, and lasting sorrows. Only believe always that I love you. If we may never meet again in life at the same altar, may our intercession for each other, day by day, meet in the Court of Heaven. And, if it be possible for such as I am, may we all who are parted now be there at last united.[2]

Thereafter there was no communication between them for nearly six years, apart from a chance meeting in Rome towards the end of 1847, when Newman, recently ordained priest, was shortly about to return to England, and Manning was convalescing after serious illness. What passed between them, history does not record; perhaps only an exchange of greetings, because Newman was just boarding a *carozza* when Manning ran up to him, looking still so ill, Newman commented, that at first he failed to recognize him.[3]

Who was to step into the breach to rally the waverers and the dispirited among those who had looked to Newman as their guide? The obvious candidate might seem to be Pusey, faithful to his friend to the last, while solidly loyal to the English Church. So indeed was Keble, although not by nature a leader, and too cast down by the turn of events to do more than advise individuals, while admonishing himself for failing to impress upon Newman and those who had seceded that they had all along been too sanguine of success, forgetting that the penalty for declaring truths must always be a measure of suffering.[4] And there was Manning, who would not have been the first choice of Newman's most devoted followers, because the anti-Romanism of his November 5th sermon still rankled. But he had position in the Church, and a reputation for being 'safe'.

Pusey, during 1845, still had reservations about the extent of Manning's total loyalty to the Catholic cause, having been shocked by his acquiescence in the judgment of the Court of Arches prohibiting the erection of a stone altar in the Church of the Holy Sepulchre at Cambridge, thereby calling into question the doctrine of the eucharistic sacrifice.[5] Manning regarded the issue as a 'thing indifferent'; Pusey felt compelled to say that 'I dread your line being to keep things smooth'.[6] But Manning had slight reservations about Pusey, too, accusing him of being more charitable to Rome than to the Eastern Church, receiving the uncomfortable reply that 'I have now done with speaking against the Roman Church ... I do think any speaking against it, without explicit confession of our own sins, a great moral mistake.'[7]

Manning had no wish to be cast in the role of a party leader. 'Henceforth', he wrote in his journal in November 1845, 'I shall endeavour, by God's help, to act by myself, as I have done hitherto, without any alliances.'[8] But Pusey soon began to forfeit the goodwill of many sympathetic to at least a moderate Anglo-

Catholicism, largely because of his failure to restrain the excesses of the over-exuberant Catholic-inspired clergy at St Saviour's, Leeds, the church which had been built under his inspiration and by his munificence, to stand as a model of the Anglo-Catholic ministry and worship. He had himself to admit that he had become a 'suspected person', and that – as he confessed to Gladstone in February 1847 – 'all confidence in me is gone ... I am not a physician for these days; and my medicine is stronger than people would take, so I had best keep it to myself.'[9]

By contrast, Manning increasingly seemed to be the ideal physician. Soon after Newman's secession, he had written to Edward Coleridge, the Eton master who had become the close confidant of men like George Selwyn, T. W. Allies and James Hope, former pupils who shared his Tractarian sympathies; it was a letter that exuded total confidence. Newman's loss was 'a heavy sorrow', but there was a lesson to be learnt from it.

> To rely on individual minds has been a strong temptation to many of late, and one design of the Head of the Church may be to correct this dangerous inclination. We have perhaps all been too intellectual, too much related to persons, or to a school of opinions; too little to the Church and to the Person and Presence of our only true Master.

He then instanced the remarkable transformation that had taken place in the revivification of the Church of England during the last fifteen years. 'What may not be hoped for a body that has conceived such works of Faith?'[10]

Gladstone had no doubts that this was Manning's hour. The Church needed a competent theologian to write a reply to Newman's *Essay on Development*. Who better than the Archdeacon of Chichester? He pressed Manning to accept the challenge; and the result was the last thing that he could have conceived. Manning began work on a reply which never actually materialized. And for good reason. He became more and more impressed by the strength of Newman's arguments, and doubts within his own mind began disturbingly to grow. As he told Robert Wilberforce some years later, he began to see the inadequacies of his own earlier work, *The Rule of Faith*:

> In 1845, I read Newman's book on Development. It did not satisfy me; but it opened my eyes to one fact, namely that I had laid down only half the subject. I had found the *Rule*, but not the *Judge*. It was evident that to put Scripture and Antiquity into the hands of the individual is

as much private judgment as to put Scripture alone . . . The perpetuity of the Faith must have a higher basis than the individual or collective intellect of the Church.

It was at this point that Manning's serious study of Roman Catholic theologians really began; and it proved an eye-opener. 'The Universal Church of the first 700 years believed in divine, infallible guidance in its office.' Then again, 'What does Reason say, but that the *certitude* of revelation to succeeding ages demands a perpetual provision secure from error?'[11]

Although he did not arrive at these conclusions all at once, the seeds of unsettlement had been sown; and Manning's difficulty in the winter of 1845 was that he could not truly confide his incipient doubts to anyone. It was one thing to be one's own man; it was quite another to find oneself very vulnerably alone. During the middle years of the 1840s, something of a realignment of his relationships had perforce taken place. S. F. Wood, probably his closest friend, was dead; his brother-in-law, Samuel Wilberforce, with whom he had shared so much in their earlier years, had become Bishop of Oxford in October 1845, determined to be a peacemaker in that troubled diocese, and supremely confident that he would succeed. Manning could send him a mild rebuke for treading on the prerogatives of archdeacons (by commissioning rural deans to act under direct episcopal authority),[12] but he could not give even a hint of his own private anxieties. Another of his brothers-in-law, George Dudley Ryder, together with his wife Sophia, were known by Manning to be in extreme danger of following Newman, ever since the summer of 1845 when Ryder had put to Manning a question that could have no answer, save to intensify his own unease: 'What grounds are there for our feeling more certain about you than about Newman five years ago?'[13] The Ryders seceded to Rome in May 1846; two years later, Sophia died, the sixth of the seven Sargent children to predecease their mother. This, at least, was a sorrow that Manning could share with Samuel: 'Twelve years ago,' he wrote, 'I remember writing in a private book, "Of four brothers I am called to go first through this fire". You soon followed, and now a third. Only our dearest Henry tarries outside the furnace. God knows for how long.'[14]

It was with Henry and Mary Wilberforce that the family bonds became closer during these years, and most particularly with Mary, who became Manning's penitent in 1845. The letters that passed between them, preserved at Ushaw, were apparently never

seen by E. S. Purcell. What he would have made of them one can
only conjecture, but certainly they shed a light on a facet of
Manning's character which neither he nor Lytton Strachey, after
him, seemed able to perceive or to comprehend. For all his charm
and social graces, Manning could sometimes give the impression
of aloofness and austerity, especially in his later Catholic days. As
a priest writing for priests, he would insist that to be true to one's
calling required 'no unbalanced human attachments'.[15] That he
profoundly believed. On the other hand, ever since Caroline's
death he was enduringly aware of an aching void which he knew
could never be filled. On the few occasions when he gave way to
his need to unburden himself, his instinct seemed to lead him
more naturally to confide in a woman. Miss Stanley, the sister of
the Dean of Westminster, one of his Catholic converts, and
Florence Nightingale, whose soul he so earnestly hoped to cap-
ture, were both recipients of his confidences. But the letters to
Mary Wilberforce, Caroline's sister, were of a different order
altogether. He loved her deeply; probably something in her close
resemblance to Caroline stirred his heart, and she – in turn –
responded both to his need and to his affection. In this respect
Manning and Samuel Wilberforce, as widowers, were very much
alike. When Emily died, Samuel felt the need to find a soul-mate,
almost a surrogate wife by correspondence; and this came to be
Emily's closest friend, Louisa Noel. For Manning, it was Mary, the
last link with the never-to-be-forgotten days of carefree happiness
at Lavington.

So he wrote to her in October 1845, after the news of Newman's
secession:

> My dearest Mary, You do not know what I felt in reading your letter
> this morning. Neither do you know how I love you. Such words as
> yours are now almost more than I can understand: they seem to wake
> up something which I have dreamt and cannot remember. The other
> night I was full of sad thoughts of things past and to come: and the
> past and the future jarred harshly together, and I could not talk of
> what I felt most. But it was a heartfelt pleasure to see you, my most
> dear Sister. I trust you do love me for I feel that I should grow worse if
> people left off loving me as I desire they should.[16]

Such was the tone of all his letters to Mary. 'I cannot say to you
what is the happiness I feel in your affection' (in July 1847);[17]
'God is very good to me to give me love like yours',[18] and 'It would

be hard to say how I love you – how nobody else is to me what you are' (in 1848).[19]

As Henry and Mary moved closer to Rome, one has to believe that Manning would not be far behind them. Indeed, in a letter marked 'Most Private' to Henry, dated 2 October 1848, he wrote: 'I feel that in the end nothing will ever part us three. Either we shall all die where we are, or thro' much heart-breaking we shall all meet elsewhere.'[20] In Holy Week 1849, Manning wrote to Mary again to state his conviction that their destinies would be bound together. 'Surely if anything ever brought us to the Foot of the Cross it is confession, the altar, and the Sacrifice. I grow very sick, sad, and weary and but for my sins long to lie down that all these stirrings and contradictions may be over.'[21] Then a fearful cholera epidemic broke out among the Irish hop-pickers in Henry's parish, and Henry and Mary ministered to the sick with the Roman priest, who had to be brought over from Tunbridge Wells, and with two nuns from Hammersmith who stayed in their house. Their own lives were at serious risk. It was actually Mary who made the first move. She was received into the Roman Church on 22 June 1850, just after giving birth to a son. Henry followed in September. It would only be a matter of months before Manning joined them.

During this same period he had drawn closer to the one Wilberforce brother whom he had met but rarely before 1843 – Robert, now Vicar of Burton Agnes in Yorkshire and – since 1840 – Archdeacon of the East Riding. What drew them together was their common theological interest, which was taking them both to works of Roman Catholic theology, Robert having embarked upon a major undertaking in the writing of three scholarly treatises on the doctrines of the Incarnation (1848), Holy Baptism (1849) and the Eucharist (1853). He had never been a Tractarian, and had on the whole found himself in more sympathy with his brother Samuel's moderate High Churchmanship than with Henry's more extravagant Catholic tastes. At least there were two things on which he and Manning firmly agreed. They deplored the lack of systematic theology in the Anglican Church and they shared a deep distaste for any State interference in ecclesiastical concerns. Gradually, through correspondence, in the course of which there was a mutual picking of brains, they became more confiding about their own private views and anxieties, Robert being by nature more cautious than his friend and, because of his preoccupation with his researches, more inclined to apply such conclusions as they agreed upon to his theological studies rather than to his own personal predicament, and therefore always lagging a little behind. One of the first problems on which Manning chose to pick Robert's brains was, somewhat ironically in the light of future events, what tactics they should employ to deter penitents from joining the Roman Church.

> My dear Robert [he wrote on 30 June 1845], I have longed greatly to see you in quiet, and to have the help and benefit of your judgment on some of the heavy events which are hanging over us. The extent to which unsettlement has extended itself is a serious matter. At this moment (let this be kept to yourself) I am directly or indirectly in communication with not less than seven cases, I might make the number larger. And I deeply feel that, with my little reasoning and constant active work, it is impossible for me, even if I were by nature able, to deal with the merely intellectual questions which are coming upon us. I especially desire to join with you in this ... Whenever we have compared our thoughts I have felt that we feel the same points to be weak and strong.[22]

Manning's problem, towards the close of 1845, was an uncomfortable feeling that the stronger points on behalf of the Roman claims were considerably outnumbering the weak. His official position, however, his growing number of penitents seeking help and guidance, and the stronger bonds of friendship that he was now forging with those who looked upon him as the one man truly capable of rallying the Catholic and High Church party – all forced him to suppress the nagging doubts that were beginning to assail him. Gladstone was one such, with whom friendship had ripened into intimacy, a man so rock-solid in his loyalty to the English Church and in his dismissal of Roman pretensions that, on the few occasions when Manning ventured to express disquiet, Gladstone stopped his ears. Another new friend, belonging to Gladstone's circle, was James Hope, a distinguished lawyer, who had been closer to Newman than any of the others and, had Manning realized it at the time, was experiencing exactly the same doubts as himself.

A third, and more recent, friendship was – on the face of it – somewhat improbable: Henry Phillpotts, Bishop of Exeter, the doyen of the old High Church party, thirty years Manning's senior, a man of sternly inflexible views and forbidding demeanour. Manning and Phillpotts had begun to correspond together in 1842 over matters of mutual concern, chiefly arising from Manning's involvement in the National Society and his efforts to promote diocesan seminaries. Phillpotts prided himself in recognizing the up-and-coming; and he had no doubt at all about the young Archdeacon of Chichester. He valued his advice; accepted his criticisms meekly; wrote to him in terms of respect and affection. 'I longed for your letter,' he once admitted to Manning. '. . . *Pray* for me; *advise* me; *judge* me. Do not think I shall take it unkind. I need a monitor.'[23] Indeed, looking at Manning and his London friends, Phillpotts asserted that there were three men on whom the country had to place its hopes: 'Manning in the Church, Gladstone in the State, and Hope in the Law.' He added: 'No power on earth can keep Manning from the Bench.'[24]

No power on earth, except perhaps himself. In December 1845 his opportunity had come in the shape of the offer of the post of Sub-Almoner to the Archbishop of York, a position generally acknowledged to be a springboard to higher office in the Church, as it had proved to be for Samuel Wilberforce, the vacancy having been caused by his elevation to the Bishopric of Oxford. Had the offer been made two years earlier there would have been no doubt in Manning's mind, for he had had hopes, at the end of 1843, of securing a similar post of prestige in the Preachership of Lincoln's Inn. On this later occasion, however, while fully appreciating the significance of the appointment, he decided that he ought to decline, to the surprise and consternation of his friends, and with no little distress to himself. This decision has a dual significance. In the first place, it exposes the injustice of accusations against Manning that he was capable of placing personal ambition above the dictates of his conscience; and secondly, although he denied in a letter to Robert Wilberforce that his refusal was due to any unsettlement,[25] it marks the first clear indication that his doubts about the claims of Anglicanism were real ones. He wrote in his journal: 'Anything which complicated my thoughts and position may affect the *indifference* with which I wish to resolve my mind on the great issue. Visions of a future certainly would.'[26]

What would have been the effect upon the history of both the Anglican and Roman Churches, one might reasonably speculate, had he decided otherwise, and had not a change of government in 1846 seen Robert Peel replaced as Prime Minister by Lord John

Russell? It is not beyond the bounds of possibility at all that Peel would have nominated Manning as Bishop of Hereford in 1847. He was young, certainly – only 39; but Samuel Wilberforce had been only 40 when he became Bishop of Oxford, and Gladstone only 34 when he first achieved Cabinet status (under Peel). Lord John Russell, however, created a storm of protest by nominating R. D. Hampden.

Manning's initial unsettlement, then, seems to have dated from his first serious attempt to come to grips with Newman's *Essay on Development*. Then had come the defection of the Ryders; so that by the summer of 1846 he could write in his journal:

> I am conscious to myself of an extensively changed feeling towards the Church of Rome. It seems to me nearer to the truth, and the Church of England in greater peril. Our divisions seem to me to be fatal as a token, and as a disease. If division do not unchurch us it will waste us away. I am conscious of being less and less able to preach dogmatically. If I do so, I go beyond our formularies. Though not therefore Roman, I cease to be Anglican.[27]

He ventured to hint as much to Gladstone, only to be told, in reply, that the divisions in the Anglican Church were no worse than the conflicts within the Roman Church between the Jansenists and the anti-Jansensists.[28] Manning was not convinced. He tried to conceal his anxieties from others and to submerge himself, and his doubts, in active work.

In this respect Manning's situation was different from that of Newman, who as his doubts intensified went into effective limbo at Littlemore. This was never Manning's way. Besides, he had the important duties of his office to discharge. But the strain upon him was intense, and his health began to suffer. In February 1847 he fell seriously ill, with symptoms similar to the illness that had caused Caroline's death – a tubercular condition, first diagnosed as he began to cough up blood – and for the best part of three months he was confined to bed, the thought never far from his mind that he might not recover. *Timor mortis*: this had been the prelude to G. D. Ryder's decision to seek the safety for his soul that his heart told him could be found only in Rome; it was to play a similar role in the decision of Henry and Mary Wilberforce while they were tending the cholera victims in Kent in 1849. It had induced in Newman, on his sick-bed in Sicily, that state of anxiety for his soul that led him into harsh self-examination and spiritual questionings. So too with Manning, forced now to wrestle with his doubts and to try to recognize with scrupulous honesty his motives, temptations and failings. A man may sometimes be unduly hard on himself when he thinks that he is lying on his death-bed. Manning, for instance, suffered agonies of remorse when he had to concede that he had felt jealous of the success of his curate at Lavington, Charles Laprimaudaye, in attracting more Easter communicants than his Rector had been able to do. He prayed for forgiveness; he begged that he might be crucified with Christ. 'I had rather suffer any humiliation and disappointment than harbour the accursed shame of jealousy.'[29]

He could not resolve, however, what his ultimate destination should be, except to decide, on his recovery, that immediately he should make for the Continent for a long period of convalesence. Celebrating communion at Lavington, shortly before he left, had made him feel ashamed that he could even think of abandoning his flock. 'I never felt the power of love more,' he reflected.[30] But he had to satisfy his need to know more, at first hand, of Catholic worship and devotions, appreciating that they might cast the same spell upon him as they had upon the Ryders. He needed, however, to see for himself. Before leaving, he opened his heart to his own spiritual director, Charles Laprimaudaye, in a long statement of his inner turmoil, sent to him 'under the seal' of the confessional. It is clear from this that he needed to put to the test his earlier convictions on the unity of the Church and infallibility. That the Church must be one, and that 'the infallibility of the Church [is] a necessary condition of the presence of the third Person of the Blessed Trinity' was – to his mind – a certainty. What remained in doubt was the validity of the Papal claims, which he had attempted to refute in his earlier published work. And herein lay the agony:

> All bonds of birth, blood, memory, love, happiness, interest, every inducement which can sway and bias my will, bind me to my published belief. To doubt it is to call in question all that is dear to me. If I were to give it up I should feel that it would be like death; as if all my life had become extinct. Believe me then, that nothing short of a mass of evidence inspired and uninspired all going one way, ... could make me hesitate to shut my eyes, and take the Church of England on trust for ever as I have done with a loving heart in times past.[31]

He was under no illusions, however, over the possible outcome of the long spell abroad. On the eve of his departure from England

(6 July 1847), he wrote in his journal: 'Tomorrow by the will of God I go forth, it may be for a year, it may be for ever. I feel to be in His hands. I know not what is good for myself.'[32]

He was away for about ten months, visiting Belgium, Germany and France in the first instance. A moment of panic that his illness was about to recur took him back to England for a fortnight that autumn; but the symptoms disappeared, and he resumed his continental tour, arriving at last in Rome at the end of November. He visited churches and shrines, noting every detail meticulously in his journal; sought out theologians for discussions; and on 8 December 1847 had his first sight of Pius IX, passing through the Piazza di Spagna, and sank to his knees (Pio Nono claimed that he cherished that sight to the end of his days).[33] He was presented to the Pope on 9 April 1848 and had a private audience of him at Mount Carollo on 11 May, when Manning was somewhat disconcerted to find that he knew very much more about the Roman Church than Pius IX knew about Anglicanism. They discussed the charitable work of Elizabeth Fry, and the Pope expressed his surprise on learning that Anglicans were permitted to drink from the Cup during communion (unhygienic, he thought, as well as liturgically irregular).[34]

So Manning imbibed the atmosphere of Papal Rome just at the moment when Pio Nono's popularity as a liberal reformer and an Italian patriot was entering its twilight period. He was in Rome when, on 29 April 1848, the Pope issued his Allocution repudiating republican sympathies and refusing to lend his authority to war against Austria. Overnight his popularity evaporated; and the forces were then set in motion that would later that year lead to armed insurrection and the Pope's temporary exile in Gaeta.

Throughout this period, Manning was in constant touch with friends in England. He was well aware of the furore caused in November 1847 by Lord John Russell's nomination of Hampden as Bishop of Hereford, a devastating confirmation of his worst fears of the damage that could be inflicted upon the Catholic pretensions of the Anglican Church by the wayward operation of the Royal Supremacy, in this case by elevating to the episcopal bench a man of known heterodox views. 'Of all questions I can remember,' Manning wrote from Rome to Robert Wilberforce, 'it is the most decisive ... the most critical.'[35] Samuel Wilberforce, as Hampden's diocesan, had taken the initiative, and with twelve other bishops had sent a remonstrance to the Prime Minister.

Russell was unmoved, and Samuel was then prevailed upon to sign Letters of Request to initiate proceedings against Hampden in the Court of Arches. The result was fiasco. Not only did Samuel bring upon himself the humiliation of having his personal over-tures to Hampden, for the sake of peace, indignantly rebutted, but he was also forced to concede, after reading Hampden's Bampton Lectures for the first time, that he could find in them no prima facie case for adjudging them heretical. He was therefore compelled to drop the prosecution. He had succeeded in displeas-ing all parties, causing embarrassment to his friends and exposing himself to cruel mockery from those less well-disposed.

Manning was deeply upset. 'Of course I have been grieved beyond measure about our brother's share in the Hampden matter,' he wrote to Robert Wilberforce in February 1848;[36] but it was typical of his kindness to write to Samuel without a hint of rebuke.

> You will believe me that I had thought much of you ... Knowing how hard it is to determine with all evidence before one, and on the spot, I felt assured that I could form no real estimate of the case you had to decide. I can of course have no sufficient idea of such responsibilities as yours ... One thing I am sure of, that what you have done, you believe to be just, and right ... It is great joy to me, parted as we are by lands and seas, to know that howsoever we have thought differently we have always loved and trusted each other. I feel to need this at your hands so much that it is not more my duty than my interest to give you this pledge in the fullest, largest and most loving way I can.[37]

Ever after, Manning regarded this exhibition of the reality of the power of the Royal Supremacy to be the first of his three calls to abandon the Church of his baptism. At the time, however, and during the next two years, his views and sentiments were con-stantly wavering. His continental journey had resolved nothing, except to pull his heart, perhaps more than his head, in opposite directions. On his way back to England, he had stopped at Milan to visit the shrine of St Charles Borromeo. There took place, he recorded, 'what I have always felt like a call from St Charles ... I was thinking in prayer "if only I could know that St Charles who represents the Council of Trent was right and we wrong". The Deacon was singing the Gospel and the last words, *et erit unum ovile et unus pastor*, came upon me as if I had never heard them before.'[38] Yet how could one tear up roots so very precious, from which had sprung both domestic happiness and the first sense of

1. Henry Manning aged 12

2. The interior of St Mary the Virgin, Oxford

3. Manning's name carved on his Harrow desk

4. Newman in 1845, by Sir William Ross

5. Manning when Archdeacon of Chichester, by George Richmond

6. Renn Dickson Hampden
by H. W. Pickersgill

7. Cardinal Wiseman by
Henry Doyle

8. Newman with Ambrose St John in Rome, *c.*1846–7, by Maria Giberne

9. 'Great Cattle Show: the Roman Bull that <u>didn't</u> get the prize.' Wiseman caricatured in 1850 by the then bitterly anti-Catholic *Punch*

10. The original Birmingham Oratory in Alcester Street: 'a gloomy gin distillery of which we have taken a lease', in Newman's words

11. The Birmingham Oratory at Edgbaston, to which it moved in 1852

12. F. W. Faber, *c.* 1860

13. The English Catholic Bishops at St Edmund's, Ware, in 1873, Manning in the centre

14. W.G. Ward

15. Bishop Ullathorne

16. Archbishop Manning, ascribed to Orpen from a portrait in Archbishop
House

17. Newman in a shovel hat

18. Pope Pius IX, 'Pio Nono'

19. Cardinal Manning's last reception in 1891. Manning talks to the Duke of
Norfolk whilst Herbert Vaughan, Manning's successor, looks on

"RAISING THE (TRADE) WIND."

Cardinal Manning. "THERE, THAT'S RIGHT! BOTH BE REASONABLE, AND WORK TOGETHER. BLESS YOU, MY CHILDREN!"

20. Manning mediates in the Dock Strike of 1889, from *Punch*

the reality of the Christian revelation and his vocation to the priesthood? In 1849, he recalled to Mary Wilberforce his contrasting emotions at Nice and Rome:

> The hymn tunes at Nice brought back the Lavington tunes of 15 years ago, the hill-side and the Spring evenings, the dusk and the stillness, the Evening Lecture at Graffham and at Norwood, and the world of inner thoughts, hope, faith and happiness without a doubt or cloud ... Then as I came inside the gate of Rome on Advent Eve and said the 1st Collect I felt myself in Lavington Church with all the thoughts of Advent, and a Lavington Xmas, the dressings of Holly, and the Altar, the Charity and Xmas communion, alms and kindliness, bright hearths and loving faces, and the homely plain Xmas joy of the Church of England. Then I thought of the severe majesty and awful near reality of the Roman Church, with its claims and its denials.[39]

While he did not know for sure, he could not move and had to remain faithful to his charge. This was not speaking with a 'double voice' in the somewhat sinister sense that Purcell has implied. While he was Archdeacon of Chichester, it would have been manifest disloyalty to pass on his doubts in his public utterances and his Charges. To trusted friends, in the same predicament as himself, he understandably confided his anxieties. Just occasionally, in his later sermons, he sailed rather close to the wind in his affirmation of Roman sympathies. At least, so it seemed to T. W. Allies, who – in 1850 – felt constrained to point out to him that some of his remarks on infallibility could well have led to his being cited in the Court of Arches.[40] But, almost to the very end, his sense of loyalty prevailed. While he had accepted the preferments of the English Church, his duty was to defend her.

Sooner or later, however, an issue would arise which would truly put the Anglican Church and the Royal Supremacy to the test. It occurred when Henry Phillpotts refused to institute the Revd G. C. Gorham to the living of Bramford Speke, on the grounds that he held Calvinist views on the doctrine of baptismal regeneration. The issue came before the Court of Arches, which ruled in favour of Phillpotts. Gorham then appealed to the Judicial Committee of the Privy Council. On 8 March 1850, the judgment of the Court of Arches was reversed; and, on Phillpotts' persistent refusal to institute Gorham, the Archbishop of Canterbury (J. B. Sumner) instituted him to the living by his own *fiat* in August of that year. These are the bare facts of the case. The implications, however, were profound.

To some, the scandal of this *cause célèbre* was that the highest court of appeal in ecclesiastical causes had ruled that acceptance of the doctrine of baptismal regeneration was not required of an ordained member of the Church; and indeed, Manning felt the force of this. But it was not, for him, the major principle at stake. 'The violation of the doctrine of Baptism was of less gravity to me', he wrote, looking back on the whole affair years later, 'than the violation of the divine office of the Church by the supremacy of the Crown in council.'[41] Even before the Judicial Committee had ruled in Gorham's favour, Manning had written to Robert Wilberforce: 'I cannot for the life of me feel that it makes personally to me much difference which way it goes. The fact that such a case is to be decided by such a court is the one great symptom which seems far to outweigh the consideration which way they may decide it.'[42] Here was a secular tribunal presuming to make a judgment on a doctrinal matter. It made a mockery of the authority of the Church of England as an *Ecclesia Docens*. In a test case, the Royal Supremacy had exhibited the extent of its powers and thereby exposed the fundamental disqualification of the Anglican Church to be a part or branch of the Church Catholic.

All manner of protests were discussed – solemn declarations, an address to the Bishops to assert their authority, the convening of meetings throughout the country to denounce civil interference with the Church's spiritual office. Some protesters, like Keble and Pusey, advocated prudence and caution; others, like James Hope, threatened immediate secession to Rome unless the judgment were somehow overturned. Manning's response was to write what was to be his last publication within the Church of England, entitled *The Appellate Jurisdiction of the Crown in Matters Spiritual*, in which he attempted to define the only acceptable limits of the Royal Supremacy. On the Gorham Case, he had this to say in conclusion: 'Nothing that I have heard as yet shakes my painful but stedfast belief, that this sentence violates the Divine Office of the Church, both in its custody of doctrines and in its power of spiritual jurisdiction.'[43]

Manning's days as an Anglican were now numbered. What he was seeing was the same old story of protests dismissed or ignored. It had happened over Hampden twice; it would happen again over Gorham, and with more disastrous consequences. At last perceiving the danger, but hardly comprehending it, Samuel

Wilberforce and Gladstone struggled to persuade Manning that all was not lost. As they saw it, the position was this: granted that the Gorham Judgment was wrong, both in its sentence and in the polity that had caused such a sentence to be delivered, the duty of loyal Churchmen was to combine together to mend the defects of their Church, not to abandon it. Manning's response was to point out that not only had all such efforts in the past been of no avail, but that the defects themselves were too fundamental. To put it succinctly, Anglicanism was unchurched by the fact of the Royal Supremacy; the Roman Church was validated by the evidence it presented as the true *Ecclesia Docens*, with its confident and unchallengeable claim to infallibility. Although the Gorham Judgment was, strictly speaking, by his own definition, his second call to abandon the Anglican Church, it was actually the decisive one. As a writer in the *Spectator* in 1896 shrewdly observed, Newman and Manning left the Anglican Church for different reasons because they posed different questions:

> Newman asked himself in the main 'Where am I to go to find assurance as to the true law of dogmatic development?' Manning in the main, 'Where am I to go to find assurance that the episcopate stands high above the craft and meddling of Ministers and Kings?' . . . Each alike was looking for an authority that could, if not reasonably, at least plausibly, arrogate to itself a lineage derived from the Church which the Apostles had governed, and to which martyrs of centuries had belonged.[44]

Manning's third call was really the occasion of his secession. In November 1850, Pius IX proclaimed the restoration of the Roman Catholic hierarchy in England; and Nicholas Wiseman, now a Cardinal with the new title of Archbishop of Westminster, fanned the flames of national and Protestant feelings by publishing a Pastoral 'From out of the Flaminian gate' in Rome, which exulted in the advance of Catholicism in England, making somewhat rash predictions of triumphs to come. The initial response to this 'Papal Aggression', as Russell described it, was the incitement, official and unofficial, of public meetings of protest throughout the land. Manning, as Archdeacon of Chichester, was required to convene his clergy to register their own repudiation of the effrontery of Pius IX and Cardinal Wiseman. He did his duty. He summoned the meeting, delivered a short speech, and announced his intention to resign. 'It was ... the end of my work in the Church of England,' he recorded.[45] He said goodbye to Lavington on 3 December 1850 and moved to London to stay with his sister.

There were forceful exchanges with his elder brother, Frederick, and some emotional and bitter discussions with Gladstone. Although it was not their formal leave-taking, the inevitability of the severance of the bond between them was made plain by Manning when they worshipped together for the last time on Sunday, 30 March 1851, at a chapel in Buckingham Palace Road. Manning, according to his own account, rose from his knees before receiving communion, saying to the other: 'I can no longer take Communion in the Church of England.' Laying his hand on his friend's shoulder, he then said, 'Come'. 'It was the parting of the ways. Mr Gladstone remained; and I went my way.'[46] On Passion Sunday, 6 April, he and James Hope went together to the Jesuit church in Farm Street, and there they were received by Father Brownbill into the Roman Communion.

Of the friends that he left behind, some – like Phillpotts – were outraged; others – like Samuel Wilberforce and Gladstone – were stunned. Samuel revisited Lavington two months later and was overcome with grief. 'The glory of our beloved little Church is departed,' he lamented.[47] Pusey and Keble had, of course, seen it all before; and if their loyalty to the English Church had not been shattered by the passing over to Rome of, to them, an even greater pillar of the Church five and a half years earlier, they were not to be shaken by this fresh blow. All, however, recognized that the promise of a great career in the Anglican Church had been blighted. Manning himself had no illusions on this score. He wrote dejectedly to Robert Wilberforce, 'After this I shall sink to the bottom and disappear.'[48]

CHAPTER 4

Teething Pains

'We were but babes in Christ.' J. H. Newman to A. Phillipps de Lisle, 19 October 1845

'We are their inferiors.' Nicholas Wiseman on the Oxford converts

I

NEWMAN AND Manning had no expectations that they would be welcomed into the ranks of the Catholic Church in England with open arms. As early as 1841, Newman had written: 'a convert is undeniably in favour with no party; he is looked at with distrust, contempt, and aversion by all. His former friends think him a good riddance, and his new friends are cold and strange.'[1] Only the year before, A. W. Pugin, who met him at Oxford, had warned him that even if 'the ablest and best of our men were to go over, they would be received coldly'.[2] The reality, for both Newman and Manning, was not quite as dreary as had been predicted, largely through the determination of Nicholas Wiseman both to recognize their gifts and to make the transition as painless for them as possible. On the other hand, the influx of scores of Anglican converts during the 1840s and early 1850s was a phenomenon which aroused feelings of wariness and suspicion among the bulk of English Catholics; and this for a variety of reasons, understandable if not always quite fair.

Probably the least fair of their suspicions was a questioning of the sincerity of those who had chosen to join them. How genuine, they were inclined to wonder, was the faith of those who had been rejected by their own communion and who seemed to be seeking the refuge of the One True Fold out of mere expediency?[3] But even if they respected their integrity, they resented the impression many of the converts gave that they were God's gift to the Church of Rome, putting too high a valuation on the advantages they had enjoyed which had been perforce denied to those of true Catholic stock. There could be no Oxford for cradle-Catholics; and the converts were practically all of them graduates of the ancient universities (some of the Cambridge products, like Kenelm Digby, George Spencer and Ambrose Phillipps de Lisle, antedating the more notorious Oxford secessions of 1845). More than that: most of the Oxford men had been Fellows of Colleges and in Anglican Orders; and with such a background they might well be supposed to cherish expectations of acquiring a status within their new communion commensurate with their former dignities. Many of them were accustomed to being in the limelight; whereas, as Newman himself so eloquently put it in his sermon on 'The Second Spring' in 1852, those whom they joined were the successors of 'a *gens lucifuga*, a people who shunned the light of day, . . . cut off from the populous world around them, and dimly seen, as if through a mist or in twilight, as ghosts flitting to and fro, by the high Protestants, the lords of the earth.'[4]

The converts had themselves been lords of the earth; and what might therefore be expected of their demeanour as Catholics? At best, perhaps, a touch of condescension; at worst, an arrogance unbecoming in those who had acquired such knowledge as they had of Catholic doctrines and practices from book-learning or from travels abroad, without any actual experience of living the faith. Even Ullathorne, who as Bishop of Birmingham was so supportive to Newman and – in later years – never disloyal to Manning, found it difficult to conquer a lingering distrust of the Anglican converts. One of the reasons why he found the intrusively controversial stance of the *Rambler*, under the editorship of the Anglican convert J. M. Capes, so offensive was that 'those who are but as children amongst us, forgetting their pupilage, have undertaken to rebuke, censure and condemn the acts of those in authority in our Church.'[5] Ullathorne was a blunt Yorkshireman, who had started life as a cabin boy before becoming a monk at Downside, and just occasionally – when roused – the Yorkshire bluntness would get the better of him. In a gentle passage of arms with Manning, when Archbishop, he felt obliged to remind him of a simple fact of life. 'My dear sir,' he said, 'allow me to say that I taught the catechism with the mitre on my 'ed when you were a 'eretic.'[6]

It was not easily forgotten that the converts had once been heretics. It seemed at times (and this was a criticism that Newman had to face) that they had never entirely shaken off their disposition to exercise their private judgement against the authority of the Church. Furthermore, since so many of them had belonged originally to the Evangelical wing of the Anglican Church, they seemed to carry about their persons uncomfortable traces of methodistical enthusiasm. As David Mathew has observed, the old English Catholics 'had been brought up to a strict reticence in everything that related to religious practice. The only type of convert they accepted was the layman who adopted their own code ... They disliked a clergyman who might show himself excitable or emotional; not such were their own priests.'[7] Paradoxically, this very enthusiasm which seemed to old English Catholics alien to the temper or ethos of the faith in which they had been reared, was precisely the impetus which made so many of the converts espouse, with an extravagance equally unpalatable to their fellow-countrymen, the more overt and popular devotional practices which they had found so compelling in their observation of Catholic worship abroad in the course of their continental travels. This is hardly surprising. Driven from the Anglican Church by its neglect of usages and practices which they had yearned as priests to be able to employ in their ministry, in order to inculcate deeper devotion and a stronger spiritual discipline, many of the converts were only too ready to revel in the opportunity of gratifying these cravings to the utmost. Offer a feast to a starving man and he is not likely to be fastidious in his choice of food. And since by nature converts are inclined to be men in a hurry, the temptation to rush to extremes, and to lose a sense of proportion, will be very strong. Different temperaments would react in different ways. Newman, for instance, had never been attracted to continental Catholicism, and he had long since dissociated himself from all the attributes of 'enthusiasm' in the Evangelical sense. Even he, however, displayed during his first years as a Catholic, as he later admitted to Pusey, a more reverential attitude to 'foreign books of devotion' than was either prudent or useful.[8]

F. W. Faber, by contrast, had never been blessed with a sense of proportion. He was highly-strung by nature and was not of a disposition to do anything by halves. His posterity has not been very kind to him, on the whole, mainly because of the tastelessness and sentimentality of some of his effusions on the cult of the Virgin Mary and his predilection for Italianate devotions. The positive virtues of his religious ardour (he was – after all – the author of 'There's a wideness in God's mercy') have tended to be overlooked.[9] Such aggressive championship of all the facets of Roman Catholicism that Protestants found most repellent was equally little to the liking of the old English Catholics, nurtured as they had been on the sober and unpretentious piety of Bishop Richard Challoner's *Garden of the Soul*. Manning, too, was regarded with some suspicion on his arrival into their midst, but for different reasons. His was a temperament wholly unlike Faber's. Manning's battle had been against Erastianism first and foremost. The marks of the one true Church, for Manning, were its infallible voice under the guidance of the Holy Spirit, and a visible centre of authority in Rome. Both his loyalty and his mission were fixed and defined from the moment of his reception. If Faber was inclined to be more Italianate than the Italians, Manning's disposition, after the agonies he had endured as an Anglican in trying to defend the indefensible, was henceforth to be, if not more Roman than Rome, at least to become the unquestioning servant of a Pope whose experiences at the hands of those who had forced him into temporary exile had only strengthened him in his resolve never willingly to surrender one iota of his God-given authority, or one inch of his temporal domain.

Although Manning's devotion to the Ultramontane cause could not be discerned by his fellow Catholics at the moment of his reception, at least it soon became very clear that he stood high in the favours of Wiseman, recently elevated to the cardinalate on becoming the first Archbishop of Westminster; and Wiseman himself was regarded with some apprehension and distrust in certain quarters of the English Catholic community, not least because of his Roman background and loyalties.

From the beginning of the nineteenth century the number of Roman Catholics in England had been steadily growing, and with the increase came a gradual change in the nature of their composition, which in turn began to have a perceptible effect upon the power structure within the Church. It is difficult to supply precise statistics. From estimates based on the religious census of 1851, the number of Catholics in England and Wales appears to have been about 750,000,[10] an increase over the eighty years since 1770 of as much as tenfold.[11] Although still very much a minority of the whole population (about 18 million in 1850), the Roman community was becoming substantial enough to constitute a pressure group, and it was to continue to grow until, by 1903, it had reached the figure of 1.3 million. From the seventeenth century this community had been divided into districts administered by four vicars-apostolic (increased in 1840 to eight), bishops *in partibus infidelium* whose titles bore no relation to the districts that they governed. Since England was deemed by Rome to lie within the missionary field (since the Reformation), the actual government of the Church was vested in the Congregation of Propaganda at Rome; and so it remained until 1908.

During the eighteenth century (until about the year 1770), the control of the Church exercised by the vicars-apostolic was little more than nominal. The real power was still in the hands of the laity, particularly the great aristocratic landowners like the Cliffords, the Petres and successive Earls of Shrewsbury at Alton Towers. With occasional exceptions, they had guarded the traditional faith staunchly and unobtrusively through the troubled times and had refused to concede that there could be any conflict of conscience between their Catholicism and their loyalty to the Crown. They had status and prestige; and, perhaps most important of all, they had the wherewithal to dispense patronage. The same was true, in a lesser degree, of a not inconsiderable squirearchy beneath them, who regularly supplied one at least of their family to the priesthood, and on whose wealth the meagre finances of the Church largely depended.

As John Bossy has shown, however, the years between 1770 and 1850 saw the gradual eclipse of lay control.[12] In spite of the fact that the abolition of the penal laws had been largely the work of the urban Catholic laity, in a somewhat improbable alliance with Dissenters, 'the decline of seigneurial Catholicism had become effectively irreversible'.[13] There were various reasons for this: the clergy had become less dependent upon the financial resources of the wealthy Catholic families; there had been an exodus of rural Catholics to the rapidly-expanding urban centres; and there was a growing determination among the vicars-apostolic, and notably John Milner, Vicar-Apostolic of the Midland District from 1803 to 1826, to reassert their authority.

Milner was exceptional among his colleagues in his dislike of
what he regarded as too independent (or 'Gallican') a spirit in
English Catholicism. Even after the abolition of the penal laws,
the majority of priests preferred to keep Rome and the Papacy at
a respectful distance; and sensitivity to the 'No Popery' prejudices
of their fellow-countrymen inclined them to an attitude of decent
obscurity. In their dress they endeavoured to pass themselves off
as parsons rather than priests, eschewing the Roman collar,
wearing an ordinary black frock coat with high black stock, and
sometimes trousers rather than knee-breeches. They referred to
the Mass as 'prayers', and expected to be addressed as 'Mr' rather
than 'Father' (except perhaps by the poorer classes). The sermons, too, could be singularly lacking in evangelizing zeal. W. G.
Ward discovered a superb specimen of the old school who
regularly treated his humble congregation to readings from the
old court sermons of Bourdaloue. On one occasion – in Ward's
hearing – he rounded upon his little group of working men with
the sonorous exhortation: 'Hear this, you young voluptuary!
Hear this, you butterfly of fashion! Hear this, you that love to
haunt the antechambers of the great!'[14]

The Continent, however, had a very different tale to tell. The
aftermath of the French Revolution and the downfall of Napoleon had seen a powerful conservative reaction and a resurgent
Catholic militancy, centering on the person and authority of the
Pope. Sooner or later its impact would be felt in England; and
even at the time of the Revolution itself, when priests in their
thousands fled from France to take refuge across the Channel, the
insularity of English Catholics received its first taste of things to
come. Many of the *émigrés* returned in 1801, but not all; and
thereafter such continental devotions as the Benediction of the
Blessed Sacrament and the cult of the Sacred Heart of Jesus
gradually began to find a place, not without some resistance, in
English worship. More significant still was the return of the exiled
religious orders – the Benedictines, the Carmelites, many orders
of women, even the much-despised Jesuits – who, during the
period of the penal laws, had settled at Douai, St Omer and other
continental centres. They brought back with them both fresh
vitality and new tensions. It is difficult to conceive how a Catholic
revival could have been effected in England without the influence
of Downside, Ampleforth and Stonyhurst. The episcopate,
however, saw these establishments as a mixed blessing. The

Regular clergy, and the Society of Jesus most of all, prided themselves on their independence of episcopal authority, a privilege which the hierarchy viewed with mounting resentment. The formidable and scholarly old English Catholic, John Lingard, accused the Jesuits of importing un-English practices. 'Many of them must be mad', he said, 'in the strange ways they pursue.'[15]

But stranger ways still were soon to be seen with the arrival of representatives of the truly missionary orders and congregations – the Passionists, Redemptorists and Rosminians. They shocked many of the English Catholic clergy by wearing their habits quite openly; and a Passionist in public could draw a crowd on the instant to watch with incredulity the sight of a man walking the streets in sandals and a habit bearing the distinctive badge of a heart surmounted by the symbol of the cross. Some scrabbled at the ground to find mud to sling; but others listened with increasing fascination, not least because of his quaint attempts to master the English tongue.

The returning exiles, and visitors such as these, might serve to break down English insularity, but they did not account for the extraordinary increase of the Catholic population, except through the success of their missions to effect conversions. The major cause of both the numerical increase and the change in the composition of the Catholic population was the immigration on an unprecedented scale of the Irish. It had started in the 1790s, mainly because there was, or seemed to be, opportunity for employment denied to them in their home country, and especially in the 1830s with the vastly-increased need for navvies and labourers in the construction of the railways. But in the 1840s those who poured into London, Bristol, Liverpool and Glasgow, boatload after boatload, came in desperation – victims of famine. Between 1841 and 1851, 400,000 Irish emigrated to England; over 100,000 of them were living in London in appalling conditions.

They needed help and some sort of refuge, first of all; they needed churches to worship in and priests to minister to them. All these requirements were to strain the already straitened manpower and finances of the Roman Church to breaking point. This was not the only reason, however, why their presence was not exactly welcomed by their co-religionists. Most came as paupers, and many lived and died as paupers. Through no fault of their own, they were dirty and disreputable. They had bugs. It seemed to the respectable Catholic population that somehow the tone of their community was being debased. Some individuals responded nobly to the challenge; but the major responsibility fell upon the Church, which meant, in the first instance, upon the two men who successively occupied the top position in the hierarchy – Wiseman and Manning. Rome was not able to help them; and many of the clergy and the laity did not want to acknowledge that the problem existed. In terms of the changing composition of English Catholicism, the huge influx of Irish brought about a sociological phenomenon without a parallel in the structure of modern English society. Effectively the Catholic Church in England became a two-class society: a prosperous upper class and a massive urban labouring class, with a relatively exiguous representation within the middle class between them.[16]

The fate of many of the Anglican converts was, perforce, to find such employment as they could within this small middle-class stratum of Catholic society. If they had been in Anglican Orders and were married with a family, their situation could be grievous, as men like Henry Wilberforce and T. W. Allies were to discover. Their Orders debarred them from careers in the law or politics; their marital status disqualified them from the Roman priesthood. So they were forced to fall back on teaching (in the very limited number of Catholic schools prepared to employ laymen), lecturing or journalism. As a result, they faced a constant struggle to maintain even a modest standard of living. The old Catholics who were so lukewarm in their welcoming of the converts seemed to give hardly a thought to the sacrifices that they had been compelled to make. Newman and Manning were in a better position, the one being a celibate and the other a widower. Their sacrifice had been of a different kind, but no less agonizing in terms of the positions of power and influence that they had had to surrender and the recriminations that they had had to face in doing so. One Catholic writer, looking back over the anguished spiritual wrestlings that Newman and Manning had experienced before their reception, felt obliged to invite any cradle-Catholic with a disposition to underrate them to 'turn his eyes inward upon his soul, and ask himself if *he* had ever had . . . to take the trouble of finding a reason for the faith that is in him.'[17] He might then find cause to think again.

From such an implied rebuke, Nicholas Wiseman must be totally exempt; a fact which did not endear him to some of the old

English Catholics. In no sense could he be counted as one of their number. He was actually born in Spain, although of Irish descent. From the age of eight until he was sixteen, he had been educated at Ushaw, displaying exceptional brilliance. Rome then became his base for 22 years, first as a student at the newly-founded English College and eventually, as he acquired a European reputation as an Orientalist of the first rank, rising to the position of Rector in 1828. In 1840 he was consecrated bishop and dispatched to England as coadjutor to Bishop Walsh, Vicar-Apostolic of the Central District, also becoming President of St Mary's College, Oscott, near Birmingham, which served as both a seminary and a school for boys. Some of his colleagues eyed him with suspicion even then, supposing that – after 22 years at the heart of the Eternal City – he could not but be infected with the spirit of the new Ultramontanism. When, in 1850, the long-awaited moment came for the restoration of the Roman Catholic hierarchy in England, and Wiseman was nominated by the Pope as the first Archbishop of Westminster, with the dignity of a Cardinal, English Catholics were divided in their reactions. Ullathorne, for instance, now styled Bishop of Birmingham, had taken the lead on behalf of the vicars-apostolic in the negotiations leading up to the restoration. He regarded his work as 'the most important and most eventful of the labours of his episcopal life'.[18]

But he did not speak for all. Bishop Brown (whose See became Newport and Menevia) was so nervous at the prospect that he threatened to resign.[19] There was some doubt, too, which re-mained a niggling point of conflict thereafter, whether the appointment of a Cardinal Archbishop entailed some loss of episcopal autonomy. Newman had his initial doubts. 'It gives me the stomach-ache,' he wrote to Faber, fearing political reprisals and picturing in his mind the forlorn spectacle of Wiseman and Ullathorne as convicts together *en route* for Tasmania.[20] Some of the Catholic aristocracy were hotly opposed to the measure. Wiseman's indiscreet Pastoral 'From the Flaminian Gate' had made it quite clear that the Church in England was now restored to a position of direct papal jurisdiction, and therefore the days of its backwater existence were over for good and all. They feared, too, the backlash of 'No Popery' agitation, as Lord John Russell prepared to counter the so-called 'Papal Aggression' with hostile legislation. In fact, a ludicrous situation arose. The expected legislative reprisal, in the form of the Ecclesiastical Titles Bill of

1851, imposing a heavy financial penalty on any Catholic dignitary who assumed a territorial title, was actually supported by the senior Roman Catholic in the House of Lords, the Duke of Norfolk, while his heir, in the House of Commons, voted against the measure. The ultimate result might have been predicted. Not only did the law prove to be a dead-letter from the moment of its enactment, but – as Owen Chadwick has observed – 'Persecution may help a Church, always helps it if the persecution is trivial and ineffectual'.[21] The divisions and differences among English Catholics came temporarily to be forgotten as they closed ranks against the storm of 'No Popery' insults, riots and vandalism to which for a while they were subjected.

Wiseman acted sensibly and coolly through it all, after the initial error of his inflammatory Pastoral; and his resolve to transform a persecuted people into a proper Church never weakened; nor his confidence in the role that the converts should play in such a work. 'Let us have an influx of new blood,' he had written of the Tractarians at Oxford.

> Let even a few such men, with the high clerical feeling which I believe them to possess, enter fully into the spirit of the Catholic religion, and we shall be speedily reformed and England quickly converted. I am ready to acknowledge that in all things, except in the happiness of possessing the truth ... we are their inferiors.[22]

He never changed his mind. In this passage may be seen so much of Wiseman's strength, and perhaps also his weakness. He was a visionary and a Romantic; he could inspire and he could charm; he liked to see the best in people and never the worst; he had the highest expectations, which were sometimes little more than dreams; and his delight in making grandiose plans was rarely matched by the administrative ability to carry them through. Because he wished to be friends with all men, he was inclined to make promises in good faith before realizing that they could not be fulfilled. Nevertheless, despite these weaknesses, some the defects of his own virtues, at least one revered Catholic scholar of the present century, in presuming to pose the impossible question – who of the four great figures of the Catholic revival in England (Newman, Manning, Wiseman and Ullathorne) deserves the palm? – answered thus: 'The impression finally and clearly graven on my mind is that taken all in all, Wiseman stands out as the greatest.' Setting aside the closing years of his archiepiscopate when his powers were failing, Abbot Butler based this judgement on Wiseman at his best, up to the year 1855. With this one qualification he reiterated his conviction: 'As a complete man, he surpassed them all.'[23]

II

If Wiseman did nothing else to warrant this claim, he perceived the qualities of the two most distinguished of the converts. He found for both Newman and Manning exactly the right work for them to do. Who knows what might have happened to Newman had Wiseman not taken him under his wing in the closing months of 1845? – or to Manning, had somebody other than Wiseman been Archbishop at the time of his reception? To both he showed kindness and trust. Realizing that Newman and those who had been received with him desperately needed to maintain their companionship, he made available to them the premises of Old Oscott, rechristened by Newman 'Maryvale', so that it might seem to them 'to be Littlemore continued'.[1] When Newman sought help over his future vocation within the Church, it was Wiseman who pointed him in the direction of St Philip Neri, the sixteenth-century founder of the Oratorians,[2] discerning rightly not only that the function of theological study and pastoral work within a community without Regular vows was best suited to his gifts and temperament, but also that the character of the founder would immediately attract him; as indeed it did. 'This great Saint reminds me in so many ways of Keble', Newman wrote, as he learnt more about Philip Neri's life and work, 'that I can fancy what Keble would have been, if God's will had been he should have been born in another place and age.'[3] There is little doubt that when Newman and Ambrose St John left for Rome to study for the priesthood, Wiseman had already done his best to ensure that their seniority would be respected and that at the College of Propaganda they should be treated – in Newman's own words – 'as if we are princes' (adding, 'much to our distress').[4]

With Manning, Wiseman was even more anxious to acknowledge both the dignity of his former position and the depth of his study of Catholic theology. A place was found for him in the most prestigious of the seminaries at Rome, the Accademia Ecclesiastica, regarded generally as the nursery for future cardinals. So confident was Wiseman of Manning's readiness for service that he resolved to ordain him to the priesthood before he left for Rome. On Trinity Sunday, 14 June 1851, barely ten weeks after his reception, Manning's ordination was conducted by Wiseman himself. 'I look upon you', he said, 'as one of the first fruits of the restoration of the hierarchy by our Holy Father Pius IX. Go forth, my son, and bring your brethren and fellow-countrymen by thousands and tens of thousands into the one true fold of Christ.'[5]

No amount of kindness, however, could render the pain of separation less sharp or remove the sense that as grown men they were in reality no more than children in this strange new world. Father Dominic had told Newman that he could expect no more. 'We were but babes in Christ, and that is the beginning and end of it.'[6] During his first weeks as a Catholic, while still at Littlemore, Newman and the others were obliged to walk two or three miles to the little Catholic chapel of St Clement's to attend Mass, celebrated by the same priest whom years before he had visited, not without embarrassment, as supposedly one of his parishioners. After receiving minor Orders, Newman felt painfully self-conscious at being seen in public in strange attire. 'Fancy *me*, who have never been in costume, wearing a straight cut collar to my coat, and having a long skirt to it,' he confided to Dalgairns. 'I know I look like a fool.'[7] The sense of being sent to school again, at Maryvale, seemed at times a deliberate humiliation, although perhaps more so in recollection than at the time. The thought of having to study at Rome filled Newman with apprehension. 'At my time of life and with my stationary habits it is a very great trial,' he wrote.[8] When he arrived there, in October 1846, the reality proved worse than his fears.

It was not that he ever doubted the fateful decision taken a year before. There were compensations that atoned for any amount of humiliation: the consolation of the Mass ('How can any one even fancy that the Mass is in the English Church?'),[9] the reserved sacrament in all the churches, making one feel that one had 'come from clouds and darkness into light'.[10] But he disliked Rome intensely and never found cause to change his mind. He had no good opinion of the Italians – their cruelty to animals, their dishonest ways, their doctors who were for ever bleeding their patients,[11] their language, which he found impossible to master,[12] and, above all, their dirty habits. In this respect they resembled the Irish. 'If you don't like the Irish,' he advised Mary Holmes (also a convert), 'much less will you like the Italians. You like cleanliness and Gothic. The Italian Church have [*sic*] neither the one nor the other.'[13]

Nothing seemed to go right for him in Rome. The Jesuits were bewildered by the arguments in his *Essay on Development*, and – for his part – equally bewildering was the prevalent Thomist scholasticism of the Roman theologians.[14] His first experience of preaching a sermon in Rome, an invitation reluctantly accepted to give an extempore address at the funeral of a niece of Lady Shrewsbury, was not a success ('I did not like it at all,' Newman confessed).[15] After his ordination to the priesthood in May 1847, he had the misfortune to lose his voice when celebrating his first Mass; and his first of two audiences of Pio Nono started off badly, too. As he bent down to kiss the papal foot he misjudged his obeisance and banged his head against the Pope's knee. His only consolation was that Maria Giberne had committed an even greater gaffe. She clutched the Pope's foot in both hands and practically toppled him over.[16] Newman was glad to see the back of Rome.

Manning felt much more at home there; partly because he was fluent in the language, and partly because he was wholly familiar with Roman ways. It seems almost that he was more in his natural element there, at least at first, than in the perplexing backwater of insular English Catholicism, so utterly different from the active life, at the very centre of ecclesiastical politics, in the Anglican Church. 'When I came from the broad stream of the English commonwealth', he wrote, 'into the narrow community of the English Catholics, I felt as if I had got into St James's Palace in 1687. It was as stately as the House of Lords and as unlike the English commonwealth as my father's mulberry velvet court dress was to his common-day blue coat and brass buttons.'[17] But the relief of being free from paralysing doubts was intense. Unlike Newman who, in his first years as a Catholic, seemed diffident and uncertain about his future, Manning's disposition was to plunge into active work at once. Before he left for Rome in the autumn of 1851 he was already working for the conversion of others, targeting his own family first of all and scoring an immediate success with his brother Charles and his wife. This zeal, as if to make up for so many wasted years, was to earn him the reputation of being 'a forward piece' (the phrase originated from William Hogarth, Bishop of Hexham);[18] but Newman, at least, appreciated that a greater convert of earlier times had behaved in precisely the same way. Writing of St Augustine, he once observed: 'he had "counted the cost", and he acted like a man whose slowness to begin a course was a pledge of zeal when he had once begun it.'[19]

At the same time, Manning was well aware that he had still much to learn. If it had been his own decision he would have preferred to delay his ordination for at least a year, spending the time in study.[20] As it was, he found himself a priest before he had even been instructed on how to say Mass, and had to enlist the help of Faber to teach him.[21] A protracted spell in Rome was the obvious answer, and Newman conceded the wisdom of such a course, even though he had invited Manning to join him at Dublin as Vice-Rector of the new Irish University – an invitation promptly and wisely declined. He observed to Manning that 'it would be well for you to go to Rome, for if the Cardinal's life dropped you would not be known'.[22]

So to Rome he went, in the company of his brother Charles and Aubrey de Vere (received into the Church by Manning *en route* at Avignon) and a third companion, a convert of longer standing who would play an increasingly significant role in the lives of both the future Cardinals: the Hon. George Talbot, considerably their junior in years, but of seemingly impeccable credentials, being of noble birth and educated at Eton and Balliol. He was journeying to Rome, having just been appointed by Wiseman to act as his personal representative there. Here was a strange twist of fortune. In March 1847 Talbot had approached Newman in Rome with a request to accompany him to England and to join him and the others of the original Littlemore group in the formation of the Oratory at Birmingham. Newman turned him down. 'The peculiarity of the Rule', he told Talbot, 'makes us very anxious not to implicate in a trial which may be a failure, anyone beside ourselves. We have lived together and are prepared to run the risk.'[23]

It is difficult to imagine these two men working together in harmony in view of the later discord between them. Perhaps Talbot took this as the first of other snubs that he was to hold to Newman's account. As it was, a friendship with Manning was cemented, in the course of their journey, both men being ardent admirers of Wiseman, as they always remained. Both were equally devoted to the person of Pius IX, Talbot becoming a papal chamberlain soon after his arrival in Rome, and Manning, whose charm, devotion and abilities had impressed Pio Nono deeply at their first meeting, rapidly establishing so close a rapport with the Pope that – as he observed to Robert Wilberforce in 1854 – he was granted the rare privilege of free access to him at any time he wished.[24]

Life at the Accademia Ecclesiastica could be very trying for him at times. 'I found myself at forty-two among youths; and a stranger among foreigners.'[25] The lectures proved unrewarding, so that he soon abandoned them, choosing to study privately and in discussion with the Jesuits at the Collegio Romano. Despite the rapidity of his ordination, he actually served a long apprenticeship, remaining at the Accademia until the spring of 1854; but he returned regularly to England during the summer months. In the first of these breaks from study he delivered a course of four lectures at St George's Church, Southwark, entitled *The Grounds of Faith*, which constituted his first public repudiation of the errors of Anglicanism, in a similar spirit to Newman's more celebrated, and certainly more effective, series of lectures on the *Difficulties of Anglicans*, delivered two years before. Their interest lies in the declaration of certain propositions from which Manning never deviated during the rest of his life, the germ of which had already appeared in his Anglican writings where they had been expressed more in the spirit of hope than of certainty. The root of all schism is private judgement. 'All knowledge must be definite ... The guarantee of certainty is the infallible Church guided by the Holy Spirit.'[26] With an echo of Newman's *Essay on Development*, he asserted that 'If Christianity is historical, Catholicism is Christianity';[27] and concluded with his first published condemnation of the 'branch theory', so dear to the heart of Pusey and others. 'It is ... a pleasant illusion in many pious minds ... if we would have this illusion dispelled, it must not be by rough handling or derision, but by the simple demonstration of its impossibility.'[28]

Less cutting, less subtle, less wounding to his former friends than Newman's lectures, they were no less assured. On his return to Rome at the end of the summer of 1852, Manning had another set of travelling companions – Herbert Vaughan, a young man of 20, studying for the priesthood, Robert Whitty, who had been an Oratorian for a brief period, and William Lockhart, now a Rosminian. Vaughan, high-born of old Catholic stock and edu-

cated at Stonyhurst, found Manning a less than congenial companion:

> I was a raw and restless youth [he recalled] ... and no doubt very
> trying to the grave and solemn convert parson, as I then called him,
> who gently, and, I fear, unsuccessfully, sought to keep me in order. So
> at Lyons I said to Father Whitty, 'I can stand this old parson no longer;
> let us go straight on and leave him to follow as long after as he likes.'

Leave him they did, joking about the older man's excessive
fussiness in trying to prevent his silk hat being crushed by the
other occupants of a crowded carriage.[29] Within weeks, however,
their opinion of each other changed. Vaughan became Manning's
regular server at six o'clock Mass, and gradually 'the old parson'
came to command in the young priest, half his age, 'his highest
and intimate reverence'; Manning, in return, thereafter treating
Vaughan almost as if he were his own son.[30]

During the period that Manning was studying at Rome, returning to England at intervals, Newman saw little of him. The
establishment of the Oratory on English soil had proved to be not
the easiest of tasks. As Newman once observed to Richard Stanton
with masterly understatement, 'men do not easily learn to live
together'.[31] Certainly not a group of ex-Oxford and Cambridge
dons who had been Anglican clergymen and were in the process
of learning what was entailed in close community life. Littlemore
had been one thing; but the observance of the Oratory Rule was
quite another. Even at Maryvale, where they had first for-
gathered, there had been grumblings about Newman's over-
sensitiveness as a sort of unofficial superior.[32] On 1 January 1848,
however, the Oratory began its life in Birmingham with Newman
appointed as Superior by papal brief, and he was at once beset
with problems from all sides.

F. W. Faber was the source of most of them. On his conversion,
he had taken a mixed bag of converts with him from his former
parish at Elton, some of them mere country boys who fancied that
a semi-monastic life as lay brothers would be an interesting new
experience. At Cotton Hall, near Cheadle, Faber had founded his
own little community, called St Wilfrid's; but his real wish was to
amalgamate with Newman, bringing all his little band with him.
In February 1848 Newman agreed to admit the Wilfridians as
probationer-Oratorians, and it proved a recipe for disaster. For a
while they all moved to St Wilfrid's while negotiations were

conducted to obtain new premises in Birmingham, at 40 Alcester Street. Then, for a while, the community divided into two, with Faber remaining at St Wilfrid's as Master of the Novices. But the marriage between the two groups was never a happy one. There were acute financial problems; the lay brothers frequently flouted the Rule; there were constant carpings and bickerings, Faber accusing Newman of being indecisive as Superior, and others protesting that he indulged in favouritism, especially with Ambrose St John, prompting Newman to cite biblical precedents for 'particular friendships' in his defence.[33] Eventually the only possible solution was agreed upon – that St Wilfrid's should be abandoned (not without legal difficulties) and the Oratory should split into two independent communities, with Faber and seven other Oratorians moving to London to premises in King William Street, Faber becoming Superior of the London house, which was duly released from any dependence upon the original foundation at Birmingham.

This was by no means the end of the troubles. Faber wanted to run when Newman preferred to walk; to court publicity while Newman tended to shun it. To his credit, however, Newman was supportive of Faber in the first controversy in which he found himself involved, with the unhappy consequence that he was forced to cross swords with his new bishop, Ullathorne, almost on their first encounter. Faber had since 1847 been publishing a series of 'Lives of the Saints', translated from foreign sources, which exuded exactly the sort of extravagant and credulous piety which English Catholics found distasteful and Protestants merely ridiculous. To have chosen a Dominican life of St Rose, Flower of the Andes, to launch the series was provocative, to say the least; unfortunately, too, he was not over-scrupulous in his proof-reading and had let through a misprint implying prayers to an image of the Blessed Virgin. It provoked a blistering review from *Dolman's Magazine*, and Ullathorne thought it prudent to advise suspension of the series 'as not adapted to the state of the country'.[34] Newman. in taking Faber's part, earned a gentle remonstrance from his bishop for over-sensitiveness, with a delicate reminder that past experience might have inclined him to lack of deference to episcopal authority.[35] Behind this difference of opinion, however, also lurked misunderstanding about the degree in which the Oratory was exempt from the bishop's jurisdiction. The matter was eventually resolved as mistrust gave way to mutual affection and respect, confirming what Newman suspected when he observed to J. M. Capes that 'the way to be good friends with [Ullathorne] is to begin with a boxing bout'.[36]

All in all, this was not a happy phase of Newman's life. None of his writings had received universal approval. His *Essay on Development* had provoked accusations of heresy from an American journalist, a convert from Unitarianism, called Orestes Brownson. He had displeased Wiseman over the tone of harsh severity in his *Discourses to Mixed Congregations*;[37] his lectures on the *Difficulties of Anglicans* had admittedly gained for him a papal doctorate, but many of his former friends had been hurt by the tone of mockery and mischievous hyperbole, although William Froude assured him that those who had been closest to him had been understanding and forgiving.[38] The ominous phrase, 'we have no friend at Rome', began to appear in his letters (a suspicion arising from the hostility of Thomas Grant, who as Rector of the English College had opposed the award of the DD degree to Newman and in 1851 returned to England as Bishop of Southwark).[39]

In April 1851, however, came the first hint of what seemed to be an enticing prospect – a letter from the Archbishop of Armagh, Paul Cullen, seeking his advice over the establishment of a Catholic university in Ireland. In July this led to the official invitation to him to become its first Rector. Here, at last, was a challenge truly suited to his gifts, or so it seemed, despite his aversion to the Irish ('I believe you can hardly ever depend on an Irishman,' he had said to Ambrose St John in July 1848).[40] Suddenly he was flooded with work and engagements. Cullen wanted him to deliver a series of lectures on 'The Scope and Nature of University Education'; and the storm over 'Papal Aggression' supplied him with the opportunity to display his satirical gifts in a series of lectures at the Corn Exchange in Birmingham on *The Present Position of Catholics in England*, in order to expose the absurdity and injustice of English prejudices against Roman Catholics. He himself regarded it as the best book he had written, and also the one that had given him the most enjoyment.[41] The temporary ray of sunshine, however, was soon obscured by a dark cloud when he heard that his exposé of the calumnies of a renegade priest, Dr Achilli – in his fifth lecture of the series – was to be made the subject of an action for libel.

He had a moment of panic, too, when rumours reached him that, with the creation of the new sees consequent upon the restoration of the hierarchy, Wiseman had put forward his name for consideration as the new Bishop of Nottingham. He wrote at once to Talbot to beg him to use his influence to scotch such a proceeding from the start. It would be ruinous for the Oratory, and '*my writings would be at an end*, were I a Bishop ... You cannot think how strongly I feel this. Surely my opinion on the subject is of weight.'[42]

The point was taken. At the first Synod of the new episcopate, however, at Oscott in July 1852, Newman was present in a position of prominence, and with him also was Manning. Nothing more surely displayed Wiseman's pride in his converts than the honour he paid these two men in inviting them to preach sermons on this historic occasion. Manning preached first (on 11 July), on a text which could well stand as the motif of his later archiepiscopate – 'I have compassion on the multitude'. He, as Newman after him, saluted the work of the old Catholics. 'You are the offspring and the heirs of a perseverance which flows from no source lower than the power and compassion of the Son of God,' he said. Having dwelt on the spread of indifference among the ranks of 'those who smote you,' he concluded with an expression of hope: 'If we be faithful now as you of old, what a future is before us!'[43] It was one of his finest sermons and would perhaps have been the high point of the Synod but for an even more powerful address given two days later – Newman's 'The Second Spring'. The rhetoric was unashamed, as he indulged in what John Bossy has described as 'tendentious ecclesiastical propaganda' in echoing Wiseman's own confident prediction that a miraculous rebirth was about to take place in the fortunes of English Catholics.[44] His peroration, however, brought tears to the eyes of his congregation.

> Arise, Mary, and go forth in thy strength into the north country, which once was thine own, and take possession of a land which knows thee not. Arise, Mother of God, and with thy thrilling voice, speak to those who labour with child, and are in pain, till the babe of grace leaps within them! Shine on us, dear lady, with thy bright countenance, like the sun in his strength, *O stella matutina*, O harbinger of peace, till our year is one perpetual May ... O Mary, my hope, O Mother undefiled, fulfil to us the promise of this Spring.[45]

Both the words and the sentiment seem nearer to Faber's utterances than to the restrained prose of the former Vicar of St Mary's. The occasion, however, was an intensely emotional one, and Newman himself was under great strain with the Achilli libel action gnawing at his mind; but he had gauged the mood of his congregation exactly. They were so overcome, and the preacher himself so overwhelmed by his reception, that Manning had to lead him away, taking him back to his room. They had both more than fulfilled the expectations of Wiseman, who had risked criticism by paying two converts such honour. Later, when the sermon was published within a collection entitled *Sermons on Various Occasions*, in 1857, Newman dedicated the volume to Manning, dating his inscription on the day of the opening of the new church and mission of the Oblates of St Charles Borromeo, at Bayswater, the congregation that Manning had recently founded. He expressed the hope that his book of sermons would be accepted 'as my act of devotion to the great St Charles, St Philip's friend, and your Patron, and as some sort of memorial of the friendship which there has been between us for nearly thirty years'.

Friends those two great sixteenth-century saints had been, but they did not always find it easy to work together, and sadly they had their quarrels.[46] The coming years would see a similar parting of the ways between the two converts who had found in Philip and Charles their respective patrons; like them they would experience the embitterment of misunderstanding and conflict.

III

But not quite yet. In Manning's acknowledgement of Newman's dedicatory tribute, he had declared that: 'Old memories are sweet beyond words, and I do not readily form new friendships. The old is better. And ours, if not always close, has never had a jar, much less a breach even for a day.'[1] Whether he valued them less highly than Newman's, the fact remains that new friendships had been forged; and by the middle years of the 1850s, the beginnings of a split into opposing factions could be discerned. As a generalization it is true to say that as Manning's stock seemed to be rising steadily higher within the quarters of the Church from which honours and promotion were most likely to flow, so Newman's reputation within those same quarters appeared to be falling. Conversely, as Manning's rising fortunes provoked opposition and resentment among those many English Catholics who mistrusted his motives and regarded him as a 'forward piece', so proportionately Newman's standing in their eyes was to rise. In consequence, such tensions and disagreements as were soon to see them arraigned in opposition came to be exacerbated by their friends and allies, who did not always serve their respective champions well. In such a way differences can be heightened into conflicts.

Paradoxically, the Achilli affair played a part in preparing the way, though no one could have foreseen it at the time. Achilli was undoubtedly a villain – an ex-Dominican who had been expelled from his Order and brought before the Inquisition for flagrant immorality. He sought his revenge by delivering lurid, defamatory lectures on the evils of the Roman Church, greedily digested by Protestant audiences at the height of the 'No Popery' agitations. Newman castigated him, supplying chapter and verse for his enormities in his fifth lecture on *The Present Position of Catholics*, feeling confident that, since Wiseman had been the first to expose him, having written evidence of Achilli's offences, he could safely defend himself against an action for libel. He was duly taken to court; but the Cardinal let him down badly – not deliberately, but through negligence, because he had mislaid the necessary papers. When they were found, it was too late. Although witnesses had been brought over from the Continent to testify against Achilli, and Catholics rallied round to produce funds that more than covered Newman's expenses and costs, judgment went against him, partly because his legal advisers slipped up in their handling of the case. It had been an agonizing time for Newman, exposed as he was to some gratuitous comments on his moral deterioration from the presiding judge, Mr Justice Coleridge. His sentence, however, was – in the circumstances – almost derisory (a fine of £100), so that the general reaction was that he had virtually been acquitted.

The consequences were to prove significant. In the first place, Newman came to regard Wiseman's seeming indifference to his plight as the beginning of strained relations between them. As he observed to Henry Wilberforce in 1857, 'The Cardinal has a thousand good points, but you must never *trust* him. My first severe lesson on the point was the Achilli affair.'[2] Secondly, the fact that Newman had been prepared to suffer humiliation on behalf of the Catholic cause was counted much to his credit by the traditional English Catholics. It established Newman in their eyes.

'Suffering, especially public suffering,' David Mathew observed, 'formed a link between Newman and the men who did not forget the proscribed centuries. This was a bond that Manning always lacked.'[3]

But there were other reasons why Manning aroused feelings of unease. He was thought to be stiff and remote. This was actually something of a mask, a sort of self-consciously imposed new persona, which he once explained to Aubrey de Vere as the chastening effect, during his journey to Rome in 1851, of the theft of his bag containing all Caroline's precious letters. Henceforth he would 'sever all bonds to earth'.[4] The inflexibility of purpose (he had always had that) could be off-putting, too. Robert Coffin eventually took him to task on this unfortunate image, as well as for his over-zealous quest for converts, and was quite surprised by Manning's meek acceptance of the criticism. Manning said to him: 'Now you must promise me one thing ... For the glory of God, you will always speak out to me thus the truth.'[5]

He kept a tally of his converts in a locked book. By 1865 they numbered 346,[6] and because among them there figured titled personages such as Lady Herbert, the Duchess of Argyll and the Duchess of Buccleuch, names which would have aroused more public interest than those of a humbler class, he was described disparagingly as 'the Apostle to the Genteels'. Many of these conquests were gained during his summer breaks in England, lodging with the Jesuits at Farm Street. He also brought into the Roman Church, in 1854, one other Anglican dignitary of equal rank to himself, his dear friend of his latter years in the Church of England, Robert Wilberforce, Archdeacon of the East Riding – to the anguish of his brother, the Bishop of Oxford, now the only surviving Wilberforce of his generation to remain faithful to the Church of his baptism. Gladstone described Robert's defection as the loss to Anglicanism of the man who 'stands at the head of our living divines'.[7]

Manning was also accused of trying over-hard to impress those in authority and in a position to reward him. It would certainly be idle to deny that power attracted him. If he had any doubts on the measure of his sacrifice, on becoming a Catholic, he was soon disabused when told in 1854, by a member of the Cabinet, that had he remained an Anglican he would have secured the Bishopric of Salisbury, to which Walter Hamilton had just been appointed. 'What an escape my poor soul did have,' was Manning's response.[8] Ought he to expect recognition in the Roman Church? He mused on this in his journal, that same year:

> I am conscious of a desire to be in such a position (1) as I had in time past, (2) as my present circumstances imply by the act of others, (3) as my friends think me fit for, (4) as I feel my own faculties tend to. But, God being my helper, I will not seek it by the lifting of a finger or the speaking of a word.[9]

Newman was equally honest in his self-analysis, although he came to a very different conclusion. He knew that his particular qualities did not suit him for a position of power. Shortly after his arrival in Rome in 1846, he opened his heart to Henry Wilberforce.

> I am always egotistical to you, but I believe to no one else. So . . . I will add what (as far as I know) I have never told to any one, – that, before now, my prayers have been so earnest that I never might have dignity or station, that, as they have been heard as regards the English Church, I think they will be heard now also.[10]

What Newman yearned for was not power, but influence; and they are very different things.

In this respect, both men knew themselves, and were totally sincere. Manning was to achieve power, and very quickly. But he achieved nothing that he did not earn, and nothing that he earned came to him through importunity or scheming. His early years in Rome, protracted rather against his will by the wishes of the Pope, supply evidence of this. A papal doctorate was bestowed on him at the conclusion of his studies. Talbot was sufficiently impressed, as early as September 1854, to make the tentative suggestion that he should be appointed as auxiliary bishop to Wiseman, and Pius IX tempted him to remain in his permanent service by the offer of the position of Papal Chamberlain, carrying with it prelatial rank.

Manning, however, was anxious to return to England. He was presented with an immediate challenge on the outbreak of the Crimean War in 1854. He had long been a friend of Florence Nightingale, who he had hoped might, under his influence, become a Catholic. If he was not to succeed with her, at least he saw how he might supply her with nurses, by offering her the services of nuns from convents in London, and then – after a minor tiff, because she had not been consulted – from Ireland. It needed all his diplomatic skill to obtain from the hierarchy permission for the nuns to work under a Protestant command, and also to negotiate with his contacts in the government freedom for Catholic chaplains attached to the army in the Crimea from subordination to the Protestant Chaplain-General.

Wiseman also wanted Manning to return. Of all the converts, he was the one who shared Wiseman's deep concern for the plight of the London poor. All Wiseman's efforts to persuade others to take on this responsibility had failed. In 1852 he had expressed his frustration to Faber. The Jesuits had pleaded 'dearth of subjects'; Faber and the London Oratory had objected on the grounds that such work would be an infringement of their Rule; the Redemptorists had given the same reply; and yet all conceded that the task was beyond the resources of the limited parochial clergy.[11] What Wiseman contemplated was a new congregation which would act as 'an Oratory with external action', and Manning – in full sympathy – while in Rome began to draw up a Rule, using as his model the sixteenth-century congregation of Oblates founded by St Charles Borromeo in Milan. A centre had to be found; and eventually a partially-built church in Bayswater (abandoned through lack of funds) was procured and completed, the new congregation beginning its active life in 1857. Manning's hopes that the nucleus of the Oblates would have included both Robert Wilberforce and Charles Laprimaudaye, his former curate, were dashed by their untimely deaths. A group of seven priests, including Manning as Superior, was, however, to grow to twenty within three years; and not even Wiseman, at his most sanguine, could have envisaged so rapid a fulfilment of his vision as within the same space of time he saw the number of weekly communicants grow from a hundred to a thousand. By 1865, when Manning had perforce to change his residence, Bayswater was transformed into a Catholic stronghold, with three new churches built and four convents established, as well as eight schools, a choir school and a reformatory.[12]

All this was achieved within a period of eight years which happened to coincide with the most bitter internecine battle within the Westminster diocese, provoked by Pius IX's decision early in 1857 personally to nominate Manning as Provost of the Westminster Chapter, in succession to Robert Whitty who had resigned in order to join the Society of Jesus. Manning himself was so amazed that he wrote to Wiseman to enquire if there had been some mistake, because all parties – including the Cardinal himself – had expected the vacancy to be filled by Wiseman's Vicar-General, Dr Maguire.[13] The old clergy were simply stunned by the news, and many of the Chapter were outraged. But the most implacable opponents of the neophyte, as they still regarded him, were the three men who regarded themselves, as of right, to be the Cardinal's inner council – Mgr Searle, Wiseman's private secretary, Dr Maguire and George Errington, Archbishop of Trebizond, who in 1855 had been appointed Wiseman's coadjutor, with right of succession to the See.

Errington, of course, was immeasurably the most powerful, not only because of the dignity of his office, but also because of his high standing among the traditional Catholic clergy. He also happened to be an expert canon lawyer. Wiseman's choice of Errington as his coadjutor was perhaps the greatest blunder of his life. They had worked well together in Rome, when Errington had been Vice-Rector of the English College. Wiseman's mistake was to suppose that the earlier relationship was any sort of guarantee of a harmonious partnership in the totally different situation at Westminster. In temperament they were complete opposites. Errington was an 'old Catholic to the marrow'[14] (perhaps Wiseman misguidedly supposed that this would be a healthy counterbalance to his own Ultramontanism); he loved rules and was a stickler for discipline. He even dictated to Wiseman the conditions under which he was prepared to move from the diocese of Plymouth to serve him as coadjutor. He also disliked converts, and distrusted them. There would be no favours to the Mannings of this world, if it was left to him. Before he became Provost Manning had had early testimony to this, when he had consulted Errington in Rome about the status of the Oblates and not only received a stony reception, but also precipitated a report from Errington to Propaganda that Manning was manoeuvring to remove the Oblates from episcopal control.[15]

Within six months of his appointment Errington had quarrelled with Wiseman, following a visitation to the seminary at St Edmund's when he took great exception to the appointment of a convert layman (W. G. Ward) as Professor of Dogmatic Theology. He proceeded to impose such strictures on Ward that his only option was to resign, but not before reporting his grievances to Wiseman, who promptly overruled the action of his coadjutor, thereby infringing one of Errington's conditions of appointment.

Wiseman did not help matters by shirking a confrontation with his touchy colleague, choosing to break the news to him from the platform of a railway station, blurting out his contrary ruling through the carriage window as Errington's train pulled out of the station.[16] Errington was so incensed that he contacted Talbot in Rome, suggesting that the only course open to him was resignation and offering to take over the vacant diocese of Clifton, if only as a temporary measure. Talbot then committed blunder number two in this unfortunate saga. Given a golden opportunity to restore peace at Westminster, he was foolish enough to write to Wiseman exhorting him to heal the differences with his coadjutor in order to avoid 'the great scandal' that might result from 'a rupture between the two men', notwithstanding the fact that he had previously warned Wiseman that Errington would prove a source of endless trouble because of his rooted antipathy to converts.[17]

He was soon to regret the missed opportunity. Errington next directed an attack upon Manning and the Oblates. After a minute scrutiny of the original Milanese Rule, his eager eye alighted upon a discrepancy in Manning's version, suggestive of an evasion of canonical episcopal control. Wiseman was reluctant to act, but Manning accepted the correction with good grace. Not satisfied, Errington then questioned the right of the Oblates to take possession of the church of St Mary of the Angels in Bayswater, on his interpretation of the original trust deeds. Wiseman refused to take the matter further. This was the background to a battle royal against the Oblates, aimed at their apparent take-over of the seminary at St Edmund's – three Oblates, including Herbert Vaughan as Vice-President, having been appointed to the teaching staff. It was fought out within the Westminster Chapter, led by Maguire and Searle and orchestrated by Errington, whose chief opposition to the presence of the Oblates was his aversion to the introduction of Italianate usages, alien to the English tradition. Manning was requested to submit the Rule of the Oblates for scrutiny by the Chapter. He refused, and Wiseman supported him. When he offered to compromise by allowing an informal discussion of the Rule, the Chapter outvoted him. With the Rule in their possession, they declared the meeting to be an official capitular session and requested the Provost to leave the room. On his refusal to do so, the Chapter then withdrew under protest.

It was in effect a mutiny against the Provost and also against

Wiseman, who annulled the Chapter's proceedings. The matter, therefore, had to pass to Rome. Errington drafted the appeal on behalf of the Chapter, and Wiseman was put in the intolerable position of having (as he expressed it himself) 'my coadjutor . . . acting as solicitor against me in a law suit'.[18] As all parties moved Romeward, it soon became clear that there were three separate, if related, issues to be resolved. The particular issue between Manning and the Westminster Chapter soon broadened into a general issue of dispute between Wiseman and the hierarchy over episcopal control of theological colleges, which became a point of heated contention at the synod held at Oscott in the summer of 1859; the most articulate of Wiseman's opponents were Errington and Bishop Grant of Southwark, Errington insisting on his right to speak as an independent bishop and not as Wiseman's coadjutor. In the event, he actually opposed the Cardinal on every issue. As a result, a third matter had soon inevitably to be resolved at Rome, and that was the complete breakdown of relations between the Archbishop of Westminster and his coadjutor.

Manning had his own corner to fight in connection with the Oblates, and went to Rome in March 1860 to put his case. Although in the end he did not win it, and accordingly withdrew the Oblates from St Edmund's, Wiseman had written a highly significant letter to Cardinal Barnabò, the Cardinal Prefect of Propaganda, on his behalf. He instanced the excellent work of the Oblates, made no secret of the fact that behind all the attacks upon Manning lay 'the hostility of the Archbishop of Trebizond' and saluted the much-abused Provost in words that would be long remembered in Rome: 'I do not hesitate to say that in all England there is not another priest who in double the time has done what Dr Manning has for the advantage of the Catholic Church.'[19]

Manning kept clear of the Errington issue. This was Wiseman's battle, although he could not but be interested in the outcome. If Errington remained in post and eventually succeeded Wiseman, Manning's position would become practically untenable, and that of the Oblates too. He might well have done what he could to strengthen Wiseman's resolve, knowing how much the Cardinal hated unpleasantness.[20] But he was scrupulous in keeping clear of any involvement, more so than Herbert Vaughan, who was not slow in expressing his own views.[21] That the conclusion of the unhappy saga became so bitter was most probably due to another piece of ineptitude on Talbot's part. He wrote to Searle in 1859 to express his opinion that Errington was 'radically anti-Roman and retrograde in his policy'.[22] Searle lost no time in communicating this information to Errington.

This induced Errington to refuse to take an easy way out of a situation that even he must have seen was impossible. His loyalty to Rome had been called in question. If he were to resign, this might be taken as confirmation of Talbot's allegation. He treated with dismissive contempt the offer (proceeding from Barnabò but communicated to him by Talbot) of the Archbishopric of Trinidad, and when he was given an audience of Pius IX, who begged him to reconsider this decision, he refused. In fact he went further. By producing a pocket-book to take down precisely what the Pope was saying to him, he so angered Pio Nono as to forfeit all sympathy.[23] The matter was passed to a commission of three cardinals, who ruled that Errington should be 'liberated from the office of coadjutor and deprived of his right of succession'.[24] On Errington's continued refusal to resign, the sentence of deprivation was formally proclaimed by the Pope. Whatever might occur thereafter, Pio Nono would not look with any kindness on the reappearance of Errington's name when, in 1865, the time came to decide on Wiseman's successor. Wiseman himself, understandably, refused even to consider the nomination of another coadjutor in his lifetime, and so the matter was left wide open. Since he had already suffered one heart attack, and his health was clearly failing, speculation soon began to mount.

IV

In December 1855 Newman had made one of his rare visits to Rome. His purpose was to obtain a ruling from Propaganda concerning a disputed interpretation of the Oratorian Rule; and this was not the only feature in common with Manning's battle on behalf of the Oblates. If at the root of Manning's conflict lay the personal animus between him and Archbishop Errington, so – in Newman's issue – a personality clash was involved. It was the culmination of the rivalry between the Birmingham and the London Oratories, effectively between the persons of Newman and Faber.

By comparison with Manning's dramatic clash, this may seem to be rather small beer. It had all started with an application to

Propaganda from the London house (now in new premises at Brompton) to suspend an article of the Rule in order to allow them, with Wiseman's strong backing, to hear the confession of nuns. It would have been courteous to consult Newman first, but they were not legally bound to do so, being independent of the Birmingham house (now also in new premises, at Edgbaston). With Newman, displeasure turned to anger when he heard from Ullathorne – incorrectly, as it turned out – that Propaganda, in permitting the relaxation of the Rule, had applied the dispensation to Birmingham as well. Newman protested in the strongest terms to Faber, and demanded that the London house should at once petition Propaganda to recognize that the two Oratories were completely separate and that 'what one does is not the act of the other'.[1] He also wrote in somewhat intemperate terms to Wiseman, who was so puzzled by Newman's objections that he showed the letter to Faber, and then offended Newman further by neglecting to reply.[2] Faber chose that moment to fall ill, and left the task of communicating the London house's refusal to approach Propaganda a second time to Richard Stanton, in his capacity as Secretary of the Congregation.

Temperatures rose on all sides. Newman saw Faber's hand behind it all. 'He has acted but according to his nature,' he confided to Ambrose St John.[3] When the Rescript from Propaganda actually arrived, it became clear that Ullathorne had been misinformed and that the dispensation applied only to London; and at that point it might be supposed that the whole affair would have blown over, being seen to be merely a storm in a teacup. Not so. Newman believed that an important principle was at stake, and wanted a definite ruling that the petition of one Oratory should not be binding upon another, and that consultation should always take place (between the branches of the Oratory) whenever an application to Propaganda was contemplated.[4] Faber then went on to the attack. He suspected that Newman was being egged on in his opposition to the Brompton Oratory by Ambrose St John, and complained to Wiseman that Newman seemed determined 'that no reconciliation shall take place. Deeply as he has wronged us it seems as if he were becoming actually hostile to us.'[5]

There seems little doubt that Wiseman's sympathies were with Faber; nor did he feel more warmly disposed towards Newman when he heard that he had left for Rome without prior discussion to appeal for a ruling from Propaganda. It would have been better for Newman if he had let the matter drop. He received no support from the Provost of the Roman Oratory, who challenged his interpretation of the Oratorian Rule.[6] He found Barnabò almost incomprehensible (he 'speaks in his throat and very quick, quite unlike an ordinary Roman'); the Pope seemed to be under the impression that Newman had really come over to assert his claim to be head of both Oratories, and at his audience appeared disconcertingly anxious to change the subject. He 'mumbled things like "we must think about it"', Newman reported, admitting that he found the Pope's Italian difficult to follow.[7] All in all, Newman came away with no higher opinion of the way things were conducted at Rome than he had had in 1847. There seems, he wrote, 'a prima facie prejudice against any one who comes to Rome to oppose, or protest, or interfere, or explain, or the like . . . I think they wish their subjects at a distance, especially in missionary countries, to use a large discretion.'[8]

There the matter closed; and so did any real reconciliation with either Faber or the London house. As Newman observed to one of his community at Birmingham in July 1856, Faber 'is too clever not to understand perfectly well that he can never replace himself in my confidence, do what he will'.[9] These are strong words from a priest writing of another priest. Faber had behaved badly, but Newman had been precipitate in jumping to conclusions. Wiseman decided to try to act as peacemaker (to mollify the 'noble wounded spirit', as he described Newman to Faber),[10] but actually made matters worse. From the kindness of his heart, he proposed to dedicate to Newman and Faber jointly a panegyric that he had composed to St Philip Neri, and was greatly offended by Newman's cold response to this gesture. 'I hope you will not think I presume upon your kindness', Newman wrote to Wiseman on 1 June 1856, 'if I accept it with a *condition*. The condition is, that, if I am not to stand by myself in the Dedication, you will be kind enough to include the Birmingham Fathers in it.'[11] This was tactless; Wiseman showed the letter to Faber, interpreting it as an insolent rebuff,[12] and let the dedication stand. Newman had little doubt that all this fuelled Faber's love of gossip; but he was himself totally unrepentant.[13]

His relations with Wiseman had already been further strained by the non-fulfilment of the Cardinal's promise in 1854 to obtain for Newman the honour of a bishopric *in partibus*, in order to give him status with the hierarchy in Ireland in his capacity as Rector of the new university. The promise was typical of Wiseman's generosity; equally typical was his unwisdom in informing Newman that the Pope had approved his proposal before receiving any official ratification.[14] That nothing eventuated was because Archbishop Cullen intervened to express his disapproval.[15] In the long run this proved a blessing for Newman because, had the honour been conferred, he would have found it difficult to resign from the Rectorship in November 1858. But at the time it hurt, especially as he was receiving congratulations (including a warm letter from Manning)[16] and even gifts – including two mitres from the London Oratory[17] – from delighted well-wishers. Wiseman was not to blame for the failure to redeem his promise, but he erred in never giving Newman any explanation, probably because of his reluctance to face personal unpleasantness.[18]

At the time of his breach with Faber, Newman was already enduring countless frustrations in his attempt to set up the Irish university on a secure footing. When he first submitted his resignation as Rector in April 1857 (to take effect, as he hoped, in the following November), he knew in reality that he could achieve no more. In any case, his divided allegiance between his responsibilities at Birmingham and at Dublin were imposing a severe strain upon his health. There had been an ambiguity of purpose from the start. Newman believed, from the text of the Rescript from Rome of 9 October 1847, condemning mixed education in Ireland, that what the Pope intended was the foundation of a Catholic university on the model of Louvain – a university of imperial character to serve all Catholics who spoke the English tongue.[19] This was never how the Irish hierarchy viewed their obligation. The committee set up at the Synod of Thurles in 1849, under the presidency of Cullen, defined their brief as the provision of 'a superior university for the youth of Ireland'.[20] From this initial ambiguity, all the tensions and frustrations of the seven years of Newman's Rectorship really sprang.

It was not entirely a failure, even if it may have seemed so at the time to the disillusioned Newman. Something enduring grew from its tentative beginnings, although the later University College as the Catholic part of the so-called Royal University of Ireland bore little resemblance to Newman's original vision. When the time came for him to abandon his charge, he had set up a medical school which continued to flourish; he had built a University Church, which left him with a financial liability which the bishops were maddeningly dilatory in relieving; he had created a personal loyalty to himself from a university staff who were downcast at seeing him go;[21] and he had made a life-long friend of David Moriarty, Bishop of Kerry, the man whom Newman would have liked to see as his successor as Rector.

But if the venture was not a complete failure, it was far from being a success. To some extent Newman himself has to take the blame. He suffered under the great personal disability of knowing practically nothing about the Irish. He had never set foot in the country before September 1851; and although he admitted his ignorance and perplexity,[22] he never made any great effort to get to grips with the complex political issues of that troubled land. It would, however, be too severe to accuse him of having no real interest in the Irish – his support for the study of Irish culture and his encouragment to a great Irish scholar like Eugene O'Curry[23] give the lie to this. On the other hand, in his heart of hearts his real interest lay in building up a Catholic university which English students would patronize. 'I had no call simply to labour for Irish Catholics,' he admitted some years later.[24] Although his Oxford background was always likely to influence his thinking on both the structure and the prospects of the university, the vision he originally cherished, that Oxford might be 'imported into Ireland, not in its members only, but in its principles, methods, ways and arguments',[25] was utterly unrealistic. He was accused of appointing too many Englishmen to university posts and of favouritism to the highly-born. Neither charge was quite fair. Unless he could secure scholars of acknowledged prestige and attract some of the abler products of the best Catholic schools (which effectively meant looking to England), the university would never acquire a respected name. More to the point were the criticisms of his capacity for the tasks that a Rector must inevitably undertake. As Fergal McGrath has observed:

> He had certain subtle but definite limitations as an administrator. His frequent personal avowals that he had not the gift of governing cannot be attributed solely to humility, for he was just as frank in acknowledging the qualities which made him suitable for his position ... Further ... there would appear at times to have been an over-insistence on the importance of his own views, and an over-sensitiveness to the opposition of others.[26]

On the other hand, the conditions under which he had to labour made the fulfilment of his ambitions practically impossible.

For the larger part of each year he was non-resident; and since the Irish hierarchy, and Cullen in particular (who had become Archbishop of Dublin in 1852), were determined to maintain ultimate control of the university, this entailed endless correspondence with a busy man who had the irritating habit of failing to answer letters. Wiseman was bad enough, but Cullen was intolerable. Both had learnt the Roman trick – Newman ruefully observed – of regarding delay as the best way of settling problems.[27] This meant that important appointments, like that of Vice-Rector, could not be settled or confirmed; and financial dealings could not be concluded. A further problem was that Cullen never really understood the nature of a university. Abbot Butler's father, who was Professor of Mathematics at Dublin during Newman's period as Rector, was wont to maintain that Cullen and the Irish bishops never really grasped that the university was anything more than 'a glorified seminary for the laity'.[28]

The other thorn in Newman's side was John MacHale, Archbishop of Tuam, who initially had supported Newman's appointment, and on their first meeting at Maynooth in 1854 had shaken his hand with such cordiality that he nearly bruised his nose.[29] Thereafter he became steadily more critical and grudging in support. His diocese had been the hardest hit by the famines of the 1840s and he nourished a hatred for the English. The known opposition of this formidable prelate – 'the Lion of the fold of Judah', as he had been christened by Daniel O'Connell – was one of the reasons why Catholics in England suspected that their presence would not be welcome in Dublin.[30]

Newman felt bitter about the lack of support for his venture. The Catholic schools in England failed to send him students; the government would not grant the university a charter; and Rome itself proved a broken reed, having originally called the university into existence. 'I was a poor innocent as regards the actual state of things in Ireland when I went there,' Newman wrote in 1870, '. . . I relied on the word of the Pope, but from the event I am led to think it not rash to say that I knew as much about Ireland as he did.'[31]

Very much more a failure than a success; but when one attempts to make a final assessment of Newman's seven-year struggle to achieve a great work for which he was temperamentally unsuited, and against impossible odds, a phrase of A. L.

Smith, writing of the impetuous idealism of the medieval *respublica Christiana*, comes to mind: 'there are some failures which are greater than success'.[32] If the celebrated lectures that he delivered, under the title *The Idea of a University*, were actually no practical blueprint for what could be achieved in Ireland, or even what Ireland needed, they have a timeless nobility. They speak of things past rather than things to come. As G. M. Young once observed: 'If ever the Dark Ages return, and two books only come through, then, if those books are Aristotle's *Ethics* and Newman's *Idea of a University*, they will be enough to show a reviving world what civilization meant.'[33] Even when his rectorial days were practically over, Newman was determined to support *Atlantis*, the University periodical he had founded, with a series of thoughtful contributions from his pen. He made, too, a noble proclamation of priorities in his work with John Hungerford Pollen, the architect of his University Church; and posterity has shown that his name has ever since been remembered in Dublin with great affection and respect.

He was profoundly relieved to be free of it all. A new challenge was offered to him in August 1857 by Cardinal Wiseman – a commission, agreed by the bishops, to undertake 'an accurate, idiomatic, and well-annotated translation of the Bible'.[34] Newman set to work with his plans, eager to make a start. In the following year, however, he was informed that a similar translation was already in progress in America, under the aegis of the hierarchy there, and a proposal was then made that Newman might wish to co-operate with the Archbishop of Baltimore, who had already produced a draft of the New Testament. He turned to Wiseman for advice, and effectively received none. Discouraged by the impression that Wiseman was 'washing his hands of the whole affair',[35] Newman realized that without official backing he had really no alternative but to let the matter drop.

It probably never even occurred to Wiseman that Newman had come to feel increasingly estranged from him. But the score was mounting up: the mislaying of the Achilli papers, the unfulfilled promise of the bishopric, the snub (as Newman understood it) of the joint dedication in Wiseman's panegyric; and now the unfeeling loss of interest in the translation of the Scriptures. In 1859 and 1860, however, new issues came to the fore which threatened to sour their relations still further; of more serious consequence, too, because they concerned matters of ecclesiastical policy over which it might prove perilously inexpedient to adopt an independent or contrary stance. Furthermore, Wiseman's line was certain to be Manning's line, too, in view of the closeness of their intimacy during the Cardinal's declining years. To offend the one would be to offend the other. The first such issue centred on the organ of Liberal Catholic opinion, the *Rambler*.

V

Newman had taken a mild and detached interest in the *Rambler* under the editorship of J. M. Capes from its establishment in 1848, even for two years (1850–2) agreeing to advise Capes on the propriety of any articles touching on theological matters. He had not, however, contributed any articles himself. He was vaguely sympathetic to its aims, but no more. In so far as the Liberal Catholic movement stood for the encouragement of Catholic laymen to write about matters of cultural and intellectual interest on the same terms and in the same spirit as their Anglican counterparts, Newman approved. It could only be good for Catholics to be seen to be making their own contribution to the intellectual life of the country. But when it came to laymen expressing views on theology and dogma he was, on the whole, at one with the hierarchy. Within an essentially dogmatic Church, ecclesiastical authority must always have the right to intervene in matters of theological speculation, and say 'thus far shalt thou go and no further'. All his life long Newman had distrusted liberalism and had firmly upheld the dogmatic principle; and while he recognized that the contributors to the *Rambler* had no kinship with the detested latitudinarians, against whom he had fought so resolutely at Oxford, he was uneasy and wary when confronted with a mind like Sir John Acton's. Acton had been the devoted pupil of the great German scholar Ignaz von Döllinger; and such was his mind that if his own scholarship came into collision with the authority of the Church, he never had any hesitation in asserting his independent right to expose error, however exalted its source.

During the middle years of the 1850s, the *Rambler* began to provoke mounting irritation among the hierarchy by its aggressive criticism of the evasive attitude of Catholics to contemporary historical and scientific research. Newman was worried about the

tone of its articles and warned Capes of troubles ahead. Manning
went so far as to advise Wiseman to handle the matter 'after the
manner of the Holy Office'.¹ Worse was to come when, in
February 1858, Capes was succeeded as editor by Richard Simpson, with Acton as his assistant. Simpson was the first to cause
offence, with an article contesting Wiseman's published assertion
that John Lingard had been made a cardinal *in petto* by Leo XII
(claiming that the honour had been conferred on Lamennais).
Acton followed, causing even greater offence by describing St
Augustine as 'the father of Jansenism', and then compounded it
by enlisting Döllinger's learned support. Wiseman had had
enough, and delated Döllinger's article to Rome.

Acton, despite his dismissive opinion of Newman as a 'foolish
old man' earlier that summer,² now sought his advice. He called at
the Oratory on 30 December 1858, and told him about the
impending denunciation of Döllinger. Newman's first reaction
was to sympathize with a victim of ecclesiastical tyranny, even
suggesting that Faber and the London Oratory were probably
behind the attack. Acton wrote to Simpson: 'The venerable Noggs
. . . was quite miserable when I told him the news and moaned for
a long time, rocking himself backwards and forwards over the
fire, like an old woman with the toothache.'³ But the next day
Newman wrote to him, having collected his thoughts, and told
him straight that 'I certainly have long thought that the Rambler
was in a false position'. He recalled that, at its inception, it was
intended to be a literary periodical. 'I think it was a mistake to
treat of Theology proper at all; and a double mistake to treat it in
a Magazine fashion. And a third mistake, for laymen to do so.'⁴

To his great dismay, however, the hierarchy, in the person of
Ullathorne, acting on behalf of Wiseman, then turned to him to
ask for very much more than advice. They enlisted Newman's
reluctant help to persuade Simpson to resign, in consequence of
an article in the issue of January 1859 in which the Catholic
bishops had been taken to task for their failure to co-operate with
the Duke of Newcastle's Royal Commission on Education. Newman had no wish to appear as Wiseman's lackey. He assured
Simpson 'that the principal person who has unfairly used you,
and whose wishes I have been executing in my negociation with
you, has been personally unkind to me, by word and by deed'.⁵
Even less did he welcome the eventual outcome – the request that
he should take over the editorship himself; and he agreed to do so

only because no other name was acceptable to Wiseman. He was in trouble from the start, and perhaps inevitably so. Whatever line he took, he was likely to offend either Acton and the Liberal Catholics by being too tame, or the hierarchy by being too bold. In seeking a mean between the two parties, he was practically certain to offend both.

In his very first issue (May 1859) he ventured to make a claim on behalf of the lay element in the Church, asserting the right of the faithful to be consulted when a dogmatic definition was being prepared, citing the recent instance of the doctrine of the Immaculate Conception. This created a storm. Wiseman protested; the President of Ushaw was up in arms; and even Ullathorne took him to task ('He said something like, "who are the laity?"', Newman recorded. 'I answered that the Church would look foolish without them – *not* those words.')[6] It had turned out as he feared. He expressed the essence of his dilemma to Manning, comparing his plight to that of Brunel's steamship the *Great Eastern*, which at her launching stuck fast on the slipway in the Thames for three months: 'I too was striving to steer an unmanageable vessel through the shallows and narrows of the Thames.'[7]

Newman then made a great mistake. Having agreed with Ullathorne that his best course was to resign as editor after the next issue (in July), he decided to include in that number an essay in justification of his earlier remarks – anonymous, but no one could have doubts as to the authorship. Fourteen years earlier, in the *Essay on Development*, he had quoted the words, 'There is a time for every purpose under the heavens; a time to keep silence and a time to speak'.[8] In his *Idea of a University*, he had suggested that one of the attributes of a truly educated man was that 'He knows when to speak and when to be silent'.[9] Unfortunately, Newman's own judgement on the timing for speaking out was by no means faultless. As Christopher Hollis once observed of the Tract writers at Oxford, they seemed to be constantly 'surprised that people were surprised at what they had to say'.[10] Newman had learnt nothing from his experience of Tract 90. His final contribution to the *Rambler*, in John Coulson's judgement, was

an act of political suicide from which his career within the Church was never fully to recover; at one stroke he, whose reputation as the one honest broker between the extremes of English Catholic opinion had hitherto stood untarnished, gained the Pope's personal displeasure, the reputation at Rome of being the most dangerous man in England, and a formal accusation of heresy preferred against him by the Bishop of Newport.[11]

In his ninth lecture on *The Present Position of Catholics*, Newman had written that 'In all times the laity have been the measure of the Catholic spirit'.[12] If the eyebrows of the hierarchy had not been raised then, they would be now, as Newman proceeded to develop this contention. The passages that prompted Bishop Brown's delation of the article to Rome were, above all, the argument that, during the greater part of the fourth century,

> Fidelity to the Nicene dogma was maintained ... 1. not by the unswerving firmness of the Holy See, Councils, or Bishops, but 2. by the 'consensus fidelium' ... There was a temporary suspense of the functions of the 'Ecclesia docens'. The body of Bishops failed in their confession of the faith.[13]

Hence, Newman concluded:

> I think certainly that the *Ecclesia docens* is more happy when she has such enthusiastic partisans about her ... than when she cuts off the faithful from the study of her divine doctrines and the sympathy of her divine contemplations, and requires from them a *fides implicita* in her word, which in the educated classes will terminate in indifference, and in the poorer in superstition.[14]

Brave words, indeed; perhaps prophetic, too; but in the climate of opinion of the time, impolitic in the extreme. Newman did not help himself by occasional mischievous asides and sophistries, especially when he mused about the different meanings of the word 'consult'. 'We cannot remodel our mother-tongue.'[15] 'I suppose a person may *consult* his glass, and in that way may know things about himself which he can learn in no other way.'[16] Newman's friends and long-standing admirers would smile as they recognized the inimitable touch; but this was not the language that Jesuits would employ in discussing a theological proposition. What was actually dispatched to Rome by Bishop Brown, moreover, was not the text of Newman's article, but Brown's own translation into Latin of the passages which he deemed to be heretical; and the Latin rendering certainly imposed a more heretical implication than the carefully-nuanced English wording of the original article.[17]

Both Wiseman and Ullathorne happened to be in Rome when

news of the delation broke. Ullathorne at once called on Wiseman to make a vigorous defence of the Oratorian, instancing the occasions when Newman had felt resentment over Wiseman's failure to support him. This reduced the Cardinal to tears. 'Tell Newman I will do anything I can for him,' he assured Ullathorne,[18] who – on his return to England – pressed Newman to write to Wiseman at once. The letter was duly written on 14 January 1860. He began by questioning the propriety of taking steps to condemn an anonymous article before the author had been requested to release his identity (he had reacted in exactly the same way when the Heads of Houses took umbrage at Tract 90). He then stated his readiness to 'explain the animus and argument' which lay behind any dogmatic proposition which had allegedly been infringed, provided that the precise passages which had caused offence were communicated to him. He could not resist a touch of special pleading in conclusion:

> I marvel, but I do not complain, that, after many years of patient and self-denying labour in the cause of Catholicism, the one appropriate acknowledgement in my old age should be considered to consist in taking advantage against me of what is at worst a slip of the pen in an anonymous un-theological paper. But I suppose it is a law of the world, that those who toil much and say little, are little thought of.[19]

Old age is, perhaps, a subjective concept; he was still under 60. But he was not well at the time, and desperately wanted to avoid having to make a personal appearance in Rome. One might also question the accuracy of his contention that his Catholic career had been marked by reticence. His sense of bitterness, however, was sincere enough. In a private memorandum, written on the same day as his letter, he gave vent to his frustration:

> All through life things happen to me which do not happen to others – I am the scapegoat. It was the Cardinal who got off in the Achilli matter, while I suffered, as now Döllinger gets off, not I . . . On looking back to my life I found myself . . . as Sisyphus, rolling my load up the hill for ten years and never cresting it, but falling back.[20]

Newman's letter was certainly passed by Wiseman to Propaganda, because its reception was officially minuted on 30 January, and the Secretary (Archbishop Bedini) dispatched to Wiseman, on the same day, the schedule of offending passages, as requested.[21] Curiously, Cardinal Barnabò subsequently denied any knowledge of Newman's letter, and declared himself 'quite thunderstruck', seven years later, when told of its contents.[22] At this point the whole affair becomes shrouded in mystery. Newman never received from Wiseman the schedule of complaints on which he had offered to comment. The only further communication on the matter came from Manning, who had arrived in Rome some time later (in March 1860). In a letter to Newman, dated 29 April, asking 'if I could be of use to you in this place', he appended a postscript: 'The Cardinal desires his kind regards to you, and tells me to say that he has thought it better to wait till his return, when he hopes to bring the matter of your letter to a termination which will be acceptable to you.'[23]

What happened? The only satisfactory answer appears to be that Wiseman, in poor health and with his mind wholly occupied with the Errington crisis, forgot to do any more about it. There is no evidence of sinister intent. A subsequent viciously irresponsible accusation by Edmund Ffoulkes (already in dispute with Manning over other matters), that Manning had deliberately intercepted and suppressed Newman's letter to Wiseman, was a piece of pure invention, and accepted as such by Newman himself.[24] Wiseman was surely at fault. On the other hand, it could be argued that Newman himself, or Manning (so close to Wiseman at this time), or – most of all – Ullathorne, who had heard from Barnabò in 1861 that Propaganda was still waiting on Newman's reply,[25] should have reminded the ailing Cardinal that the initiative lay in his hands. As a result of the oversight, Newman's reputation at Rome undoubtedly suffered; and he remained under a cloud until the matter was eventually sorted out in the course of discussions between Barnabò and Ambrose St John at Rome in 1867.

Newman's involvement with the *Rambler* did not, at least at this stage, involve any serious breach with Manning. It is true that Manning could not have subscribed to Newman's view on the *consensus fidelium*. In his later work, *The Temporal Mission of the Holy Ghost*, published in 1865, he made an emphatic declaration that the *ecclesia docens* can never be subordinate to the *ecclesia discens*;[26] and in September 1859 he had, after discussion with Wiseman and Ullathorne, endeavoured to persuade Newman to remove suspicions of his heterodoxy by writing something on the office of the Church.[27] He did not agree, however, that Newman should be persuaded to abandon the *Rambler*. The consequences could be serious, he pointed out to Talbot. The Church had to be mindful of the needs of

> our ablest and most active laymen. There is a tone in matters of education, government, politics, and theology, which is free up to the boundary of legitimate freedom, if not beyond it, and they are men who deserve a good and fair treatment. Moreover, they cannot be put down or checked like boys. I am seriously afraid that we shall have a kind of De Lamennais School among some who, like him, were intellectual champions of the Church, and nothing will produce this so surely as snubbing. They could be easily directed by any one whom they thought fair or friendly, especially if, in the way Dr N[ewman] has done, he grapples with their intellectual difficulties.[28]

No serious breach in their relations yet; but on another issue, much closer to Manning's interests, the signs of tension were beginning to show. This was the vexed question of the Temporal Power of the Pope. The story of the papal struggle for the retention of its time-honoured patrimony, against the threat of Garibaldi from the south and the steadily expanding power of Piedmont in the north, belongs properly to the history of the Risorgimento in Italy. Pius IX had already experienced a period of exile in Gaeta from December 1848 to June 1850, and when he returned to Rome on the fall of Mazzini's republic through the armed intervention of the French, his conviction that his spiritual and temporal powers were inseparable was henceforth unshakeable. During his exile he had issued the Allocution *Quibus quantisque*, declaring the sanctity of the Temporal Power, and it was therefore the duty of all Catholics to be unwavering in their support. That he seemed to need more than just their prayers was evident by 1860, when Garibaldi launched his campaign against the Sicilian kingdoms and Cavour, in Piedmont, secured the annexation of Umbria, the Marches and the Romagna as the result of the withdrawal of Austrian troops following the Peace of Villafranca, assisted by the convenient wish of the revolutionaries in those areas for Piedmontese intervention. The Temporal Power was now reduced by the loss of its central states to the immediate area around Rome itself, preserved from Piedmontese annexation only by the presence of a French garrison in the city.

Pio Nono remained resolute; he neither accepted what he had lost nor contemplated the slightest concession over what remained. As he pointed out to Napoleon III, the rights which he held in trust were not dynastic rights; they were 'rather the rights

of all Catholics . . . I cannot concede what is not Mine.'[29] Nor
would he consent ever again to leave the city of Rome, however
desperate his plight, he assured Odo Russell, England's unaccredited agent in Rome. He would 'prefer the death of a
martyr to the repetition of the blunder he committed in going
to Gaeta in 1849'.[30]

Manning could sympathize with this, but by no means all his
fellow English Catholics, and certainly not the majority of his
countrymen, felt the same. To them, the Papal States were an
anachronism, an affront against the nationalist and democratic
spirit; popular sympathy for Garibaldi inclined them to accept,
with questionable justice, Gladstone's dismissive description of the
papal theocracy as a government which puts 'the gospel itself to
shame'.[31] Since many English Catholics were anxious to demonstrate their loyalty to the crown, and also tended to equate support of the Temporal Power with Ultramontanist sentiments,
the issue gradually became – as Derek Holmes has noted – the
point 'on which English Catholics finally divided'.[32]

It divided Newman and Manning, but not diametrically, at least
at first. In January 1860, Newman was prepared to concede that a
Declaration of Catholic Laymen in support of the Pope's be-
leaguered position was reasonable enough in its wording for him
to have signed, had he been a layman.[33] But, as he explained in
the same month to one of his penitents, it was not an issue over
which one should be unduly disturbed. 'No one can touch [the
Pope's] real power: and, that being the case, we are sure that, if his
temporal power is curtailed, there is some providential purpose in
it.'[34] On the whole he maintained this moderate stance, refusing
to be drawn into any categorical condemnation of those who
opposed the preservation of the Temporal Power. When, in 1866,
a special day of prayer was proclaimed for Pio Nono in his plight,
Newman's sermon ('The Pope and the Revolution', which he
added to a later edition of his *Sermons on Various Occasions*)
offended the Ultramontanes by its inclusion of uncalled-for
reservations. Newman conceded that the threat to the last threads
of the Pope's temporal dominion was

> a real and very trying difficulty. While his subjects are for him, no one
> can have a word to say against his temporal rule; but who can force a
> Sovereign on a people which deliberately rejects him? You may
> attempt it for a while, but at length the people, if they persist, will get
> their way.[35]

To Manning this seemed unacceptably lukewarm. In Rome, the suspicion gained currency (quite unjustly) that Newman, at heart, was 'a Garibaldian'.[36] If Manning did not actually subscribe to this, at least he could not rid his mind of the belief that somehow his own domestic troubles with Errington and the old Catholics had brought to the surface a national spirit among the opponents of Ultramontanism in England which was not all that dissimilar to the machinations of the Italian liberals on behalf of a 'national' Italian Church.[37] In 1860 he delivered three lectures at Bayswater with the specific intention of disabusing his fellow-countrymen of their ignorant prejudices against the Temporal Power; in the following year he gave two further series of lectures on the same theme, dedicating the second, somewhat improbably, to Newman, to whom he owed 'a debt of gratitude for intellectual help and light, greater than to any one man of our time'.[38] In 1866 he published his own sermon for the day of special prayers for Pius IX, in which he stated emphatically that 'the Temporal Power of the Popes is as manifestly and as fully ordained of God as the power of Queen Victoria'.[39]

Manning's expressed debt to Newman might seem, on the face of it, slightly mischievous. His actual sources for his lectures were de Maistre's great treatise *Du Pape* (1819), for which he was indebted to W. G. Ward, and a study by J. F. Maguire.[40] But, as E. R. Norman has pointed out, Manning based his justification for the gradual emergence of the Pope's Temporal Power on the central argument of Newman's *Essay on Development*. Dismissing, as he was bound to do, the Donation of Constantine as 'fabulous',[41] he argued that the possession of temporal dominion 'was inherent in the divine mission of the Church from the beginning, and emerged as historical and cultural developments influenced the conditions in which religious truth unfolded itself'.[42]

And this for good reasons. It was not only the pragmatic argument that the Pope could never operate freely if he ever became the subject of another sovereign, greatly as that influenced Manning, who had fled from one Erastian Church and could never face the prospect of the Vicar of Christ suffering the humiliation of becoming a sort of Archbishop of Canterbury.[43] The divine mission had a purpose, the function of 'elevating, directing and sanctifying', the Papacy standing above all governments as the supreme moral force of Christendom.[44] More significant still, Manning was giving expression for the first time to his deeply-held convictions on the nature of the power-base of the Roman Church. If it is absurd to suppose that Newman had doubts about the Temporal Power because of liberal leanings, it is equally wrong to suppose that Manning's views were coloured by conservatism.

Quite the reverse. To Manning, the power-base of Rome lay, first, in its dogmatic authority, independent of secular power or pressure; and, second, in its popular roots, its recognition that its primary obligation was not to the princes of this world, but to the peoples. The spectre that haunted Manning in the 1860s and thereafter was the phenomenon that he was wont to describe as 'Caesarism', the only effective antithesis to which was Ultramontanism. He had seen Caesarism at work in the Piedmont of Cavour and Ricasoli – the viciously anti-clerical legislation, disguised under the hypocritical slogan of 'a free Church in a free State',[45] which in actual fact amounted to the suppression of the religious Orders, the confiscation of Church property, and state control of education. He was to meet it again, and fight against it no less resolutely, in Bismarck and his persecution of the Church in the *Kulturkampf*.

So strongly did he feel this that his earliest utterances on the Temporal Power assumed an apocalyptic tone, and most conspicuously in his lectures on *The Present Crisis of the Holy See*, when in his final lecture he drew a fearful picture of a third great persecution unleashing itself upon an unsuspecting Church. The first had come from the Jews, the second from the pagans; and the third – identified with nationalism – could well result in the reign of Antichrist in Rome itself.[46] It was thought that he had gone too far, and some unfriendly critics gleefully awaited censure from Rome; Pius IX, however, expressed his pleasure in the lectures, and no action was taken.[47]

So to Manning, the issue of the Temporal Power was crucial; to Newman, it was a thing indifferent; and since Manning came to regard loyalty to its safeguarding as a test of the soundness of a Catholic's devotion to Rome, friction between them was bound, sooner or later, to arise. Unfortunately, their relations over this issue were not helped by a misunderstanding. The *Rambler* was in trouble again. In November 1861 Simpson, writing anonymously, launched an attack on the exaggerated apocalyptic tone of Manning's lectures, claiming that he was confusing a matter of ecclesiastical politics with an article of faith. It was the beginning of the end of the *Rambler*, as the Ultramontanes closed ranks against its repeated failures to respond to censure. It ceased publication in May 1862, only to reappear again later that year under its new title, *The Home and Foreign Review*. Manning, however, had been deeply offended by the article – not so much by its contents, because criticism never worried him unduly, but by his totally erroneous supposition that the author was Newman.[48] Why the misunderstanding should have rankled for so long is something of a puzzle. A year later, Manning applauded Newman's stance in supporting Ullathorne's forthright denunciation of *The Home and Foreign Review*. Having seen what Newman had written in support of his bishop, Manning wrote to Ullathorne to say that he had read the letter 'with great thankfulness; not that I doubted what he would say, but I feared that he would not say it. He has a sort of sensitiveness about standing by friends even when in the wrong which is very honourable to his generosity.'[49]

The reason why Manning jumped to the conclusion that Newman had attacked his views probably went back to an incident of July 1861. Wiseman had decided to form a sort of forum for the discussion of intellectual questions of the day, to be called 'The Academy of the Catholic Religion'. Obviously, Newman was invited to be a member. On hearing, however, that Wiseman was minded to devote his Inaugural address to the Academy to the subject of the Temporal Power (and no one doubted what his Ultramontane line would be), Newman took offence. In a curt letter to Manning, he wrote:

> You will not, I know, fancy that I am capable of writing any thing in the shape of a threat, but . . . should His Eminence put out any matter, bearing on the . . . question [of the Temporal Power], in *his Inaugural Address on the 29th*, I certainly will not remain a member of the Academia.[50]

Manning did his best to persuade Newman to change his mind; and in actual fact he never did resign. But, thereafter, in Manning's mind there lurked an uneasiness about Newman's loyalty. At least, that was his judgement in later years, when he tried to explain why a friendship that he had so much valued seemed to be coming to an end. 'From that day', Manning wrote, 'a divergence began between us.'[51]

VI

During the 1860s, Manning's preoccupation with the issue of the Temporal Power seemed to his critics to border on the fanatical. When Rome actually fell to Victor Emmanuel in 1870 and the settlement of the Pope's independent position was finally resolved by the granting to him of what Gladstone was to describe as 'a mathematical point (which hath position but not parts) of actual sovereignty',[1] Manning came gradually to soften his views and eventually to accept a *fait accompli*. While his condemnation of Caesarism never weakened, his sense of political realism prevailed, and in his later years he made every effort to persuade Leo XIII, Pio Nono's successor, to work out some sort of accommodation with the Italian government.[2] On this issue, however, Newman had exhibited a more temperate and judicious assessment throughout.

Manning may have diverged from him over the Temporal Power, but Newman's divergence from Manning really centred on an issue much dearer to his heart, and much nearer home. In 1854 the Oxford University Act passed through Parliament (the Cambridge Act followed shortly afterwards), and among its provisions was the removal of the ban upon Nonconformists attending the University and proceeding to a first degree. Catholics could now take advantage of an Oxford education. But would the Church permit it? More personally, as far as Newman was concerned, when the possibility occurred in 1864 for him to purchase land in Oxford for an Oratory mission or even to build a church there – would the authorities look kindly upon his presence on his old stamping ground, bearing in mind the inevitable implications on the wider issue? On this, Newman and Manning were to have very different views, as will be seen. A foretaste of what was to come, however, occurred in the summer of 1863.

For some four years, Newman had been much bothered with the problems of the Oratory School, which had opened in May 1859 in the face of doubts from his bishop, opposition from Faber (questioning its validity within the Rule), and reservations from the Catholic gentry about its location in Birmingham. By 1862 the original nucleus of seven boys had increased to seventy. Nevertheless, a combination of financial worries and internal domestic conflicts (involving the resignation of its headmaster,

Nicholas Darnell, with half the staff, arising from a passage of arms with the matron, Mrs Wootten) meant that Newman had to rely upon as many gestures of goodwill as he could secure if the school was to be rescued from its precarious position. In July 1863, Manning contributed an article to the *Dublin Review* on 'The Wants and Work of the Catholic Church in England', in which he assessed the pros and cons of Catholics being allowed to proceed to Oxford and Cambridge.[3] He conceded that since the Catholic body could now boast a number of colleges (which he listed by name) educating boys to a sufficient standard to cope with university demands, such a destination might seem desirable 'as an arch demands its keystone'. Newman would not have disputed that. What hurt him profoundly was that the Oratory had not been included as one of the named colleges, while other recent foundations, such as Beaumont and Mount St Mary's, had figured in Manning's list. Newman regarded this as a slight at the time, and never changed his mind.[4] 'The omission had all the appearance of being calculated,' Edward Kelly has written; probably because Manning harboured suspicions that the Oratory was preparing boys for Oxford in spite of the official disapproval of the hierarchy.[5]

Newman was in no mood for feeling charitable in the early years of the 1860s. He felt at his lowest ebb. It all poured out to Manning, who visited him in August 1862 to invite him to join the staff of the *Dublin Review*. He was 'very kind as always,' Newman reported to Ambrose St John. But in his depressed state, Newman admitted to Manning that whereas he had in print described the Catholic Church as 'the land of Canaan', he had come to the conclusion that 'looking at it in a temporal earthly point of view, it was just the contrary. I had found very little but desert and desolateness ever since I had been in it – that I had nothing pleasant to look back on – that all my human affections were with those whom I had left.' Years later, Newman annotated this letter with the words, 'This was one of the last times that Manning wormed things out of me. Our Bishop put me on my guard.'[6]

One can understand his bitterness, if not so easily his grumpy rejection of Manning's sincere endeavours to console him. He was not expressing his regret at joining the Roman community. 'Protestantism is the dreariest of all possible religions – the thought of the Anglican service makes me shiver,' he had written to the *Globe* in June that year, in reply to a malicious suggestion that he was about to return to the Anglican fold.[7] But he felt a sense of failure and a burning resentment at the questioning of his orthodoxy at Rome. He gave full vent to his feelings in his journal:

> I am nobody. I have no friends at Rome. I have laboured in England, to be misrepresented, backbitten and scarred. I have laboured in Ireland, with a door ever shut in my face . . . 'Not understood' – that is the point . . . O, my God, I seem to have wasted these years that I have been a Catholic. What I wrote as a Protestant has had far greater power, force, meaning, success than my Catholic works – and this troubles me a great deal . . . I am passé, in decay, I am untrustworthy; I am strange, odd. I have my own ways and cannot get on with others . . . I must say, that the converts have behaved to me much worse than Old Catholics, when they might have had a little gratitude, to say the least.[8]

These passages were written intermittently, over periods of deep depression. Those who knew Newman at the time, when he put a brave face on his miseries, might well have expressed surprise had they known these private thoughts; but they were not so private as to deter him from writing them down and preserving them for posterity. One might feel more sympathy for the unashamed note of self-pity had he made some acknowledgement that the troubles he faced were, at least in part, of his own making; had he given even a hint of appreciation that his opponents were as sincere and as loyal to the Church they served as he himself was; and had he, perhaps, paused to consider whether or not it is part of a Christian's duty, if not to forget injuries, at least to forgive those whom he blamed for them. Newman never seemed to be able to master this flaw in his character – an over-sensitivity to opposition (which both his mother[9] and John Keble[10] had warned him against years before), and an incapacity to forgive. The same limitation may be seen in his theology, especially exemplified in his sermons, where – whenever he came to speak or write of the divine qualities of mercy and forgiveness – he always seemed to falter and to draw back, almost as if he had a secret fear that God might turn out to be even less disposed to forgive than himself.

Even his admirers tended to shrink from Newman's displeasure. He could become 'amazingly black', according to James Mozley;[11] 'flinty' was the word used by Rogers; 'ponderous and icy', by Mark Pattison.[12] A serious difference of opinion, if persisted in, was liable to induce coldness and withdrawal of trust.

J. D. Dalgairns (Father Bernard of the Oratory) felt the frost as soon as he suggested that the work of the London Oratory seemed better suited to his particular gifts than what Birmingham had to offer. He described Newman's response in a letter to Père Ravignon in Paris: 'a coldness such as none but he can shew'.[13]

Faber would have understood this. Admittedly, Newman had never really liked him; indeed, there were elements in his character that must have been profoundly irritating to a man of Newman's fastidious tastes. But Wiseman had a high regard for Faber's work in London; and W. G. Ward, who would have had no truck with a fool, chose him as his spiritual director. Be that as it may, he had offended Newman deeply during the conflict between the Oratories, and Newman had declared that he would never be forgiven. Nor was he, even when he sought reconciliation and asked for forgiveness as serious illness gradually incapacitated him, from 1861 until his death from Bright's disease in 1863, after a period of great suffering. When Faber wrote to him (through an amanuensis, having lost the power to write himself) in June 1862 to tell him of his state, Newman's response, in a letter to Ambrose St John, was almost to gloat:

> Fr Faber writes to say that he is threatened with paralysis 'from *responsibility*' i.e., he has now some portions of the anxieties which I, which we, have had so many years. It was good fun sailing with the stream, speaking against the Brummagem Oratory, and criticizing me as slow. It was good fun playing against us in 1855, 1856. But now anxious times are coming on *him*.[14]

Then, when Dalgairns wrote to him to ask him to come to Faber before it was too late, fearing that he would not last out the year, Newman's response was, 'how many times has Fr Faber been a-dying?'[15] In the end, he relented and called at the Brompton Oratory. Faber's account differs totally from Newman's. 'No woman could have been tenderer than he was', Faber reflected.[16] Newman's memory of their last meeting has a slightly cynical ring to it. Faber had done practically all the talking. 'He said he had loved me the best of anyone in the world.' He had then made excuses for the trials that had separated the two Oratories, underplaying his own role.

> My own view of Faber, poor fellow, is not much changed by the above. It is quite certain that he has from time to time spoken against me . . . But all through, poor fellow . . . he was, as it were arguing with himself

that he had not been so unkind to me; rather than boldly saying he had ever been a hearty friend. How different e.g. would have Ambrose had to speak, if he were at the last! . . . He would know he was always loyal and true to me. Dear Faber has not been so, and feels it.[17]

This does not read well. There is not a word about Faber's sufferings; the whole account is preoccupied with whether Faber's loving words about Newman himself rang true in comparison with what a genuine lover of Newman might have said.

When Faber died, his eulogy was actually given by Manning, on the day after his funeral; not, as might have been more fitting, by the man who established the Oratory in England. One wonders, and hopes, that a day came when Newman felt some remorse. The only indication that he did was when, as he himself was near to death, he asked for a hymn to be played for him on a harmonium which was put in the passage by his door. He did not choose 'Lead, kindly light', as the Fathers of the Oratory expected, but Faber's hymn 'Eternal Years'.[18] This was not exactly forgiveness, but it was the nearest that Newman ever came to paying Faber a compliment.

CHAPTER 5

A Case of Dr Fell

'I do not like thee Dr Fell, The reason why, I cannot tell.'
Seventeenth-century jingle

'Is it not a case of Dr Fell?' Newman on Manning, 1866

I

By the spring of 1864 the 'divergence' between Newman and
Manning had widened into a plainly discernible rift. The polarity
within the Catholic body that W. G. Ward was wont to describe as
'the right side' and 'the wrong side' was beginning to take definite
shape. At its root lay the long-standing animus of the Old
Catholics against the Ultramontanism of both Wiseman, now
visibly failing in health, and his loyal lieutenant, Manning, who
had become so closely associated with the conflicts that soured the
Cardinal's declining years that it was not altogether clear, to those
who distrusted and feared him, who was the mouthpiece of
whom. This showed how little they understood Wiseman. On the
issues that divided English Catholics in the early 1860s, Wiseman
and Manning may have been largely of one mind, but imputations
that the Cardinal allowed himself to be influenced, let alone ruled,
by Manning were the inventions of jealous troublemakers. Only
once did Manning attempt to make his opinions prevail over
Wiseman's; and that was when he entreated him to appoint
Ullathorne as his coadjutor. He not only failed, but provoked
such anger in Wiseman that their good relations underwent a
temporary strain.[1] 'It was still the Cardinal's own hand that
guided his affairs, for all that the grasp was weak,' Brian Fother-

gill has written[2] – an opinion confirmed by Wiseman's most recent biographer. 'He saw himself as a lonely warrior almost to the end.'[3]

No one could describe Newman as a jealous troublemaker; nevertheless, on at least one issue – the shipwreck of his Oxford plans – he suspected that Wiseman was speaking with Manning's voice. Not that Manning ever made any secret of his views, even invoking Newman's support for them,[4] since at an earlier stage the two men had stood shoulder to shoulder in opposing Catholics attending Oxford and Cambridge. In November 1858 Newman had written to G. A. Denison, declaring his opposition in unqualified terms.

> As things are, a residence in Oxford will be found to weaken their faith in Catholicism. In consequence, if many Catholics went there, a movement is sure to take place for obtaining Catholic halls or colleges. There are parties who are aiming at this, I am sure, though I do not sympathize with them from my dislike of mixed education.[5]

Even in August 1863 he was still expressing reservations, fearing the influence of 'Protestant' tutors and lecturers on susceptible Catholic youth.[6]

What caused him to change his mind was the opportunity to purchase a five-acre site behind St Giles, where the old Oxford workhouse had stood; and Ullathorne, in August 1864, proposed that a Catholic mission, run by the Oratory, should be established there. This was at least an implicit acknowledgement that Catholics were already attending Oxford, and would continue to do so, and that there was therefore a field for the Oratorians to minister to their needs, to protect them from Protestant proselytizing and to help them withstand what Newman described as 'so terrible a billow of laxity and scepticism in faith',[7] which had seemed to sweep over the University in the aftermath of the Oxford Movement. On the whole the wealthy Catholic laity were excited at the prospect, and for good reason; but the hierarchy was profoundly uneasy, and there was likely to be even stronger opposition from Propaganda, in view of the Pope's condemnation of the principle of mixed education. Pusey was greatly alarmed, too. He wrote to Newman to warn him that 'Germanism' was 'the real enemy' in Oxford, and that the presence of a Catholic mission, especially if Newman himself were to be personally involved, would weaken the Anglican position in fighting against the rationalist influence.

The anti-Romanism controversy would gain a new lease of life and 'ultra Protestant spirits [be] awakened', and 'any weakening of the so-called High Church would be very fatal'.[8] Newman assured him that his plan was to build a Catholic church on the land he had acquired, and that he himself, once the Oxford Oratory was established, would remain in Birmingham.

Money had to be raised; and Ullathorne took fright at Newman's circular with its reference to caring for Catholic youth at Oxford, feeling it prudent to hold matters until the bishops had considered the question at a meeting in December. The venture turned sour at that moment. A series of questions was drawn up by Wiseman and dispatched to a sample of university converts (although not to Newman himself); they appeared, from their wording, to be so loaded against mixed education that they amounted – as Newman interpreted them – to a threat of condemnation should the recipient answer in any other way than an emphatic rejection.[9] The result was a foregone conclusion. The bishops duly pronounced against the establishment of a Catholic hall at Oxford and expressed their disapproval of any encouragement to expose Catholics to mixed education. Propaganda confirmed the judgement of the bishops in January 1865. Newman gave up the whole project in disgust, sold the land that he had bought, and then gave vent to his understandable frustration at the thwarting of his plans.

His wrath was directed against Manning and W. G. Ward most of all, accusing them of trying to exercise a 'dull tyranny' over the Church in England.[10] This was rather strong, bearing in mind that they were only expressing his own views of a year before; but – deep down – Newman suspected that a personal animus lay behind their opposition. 'There are those', he wrote, 'who cannot endure the thought that I should have the *forming* of the young Catholic mind at Oxford. This is the one point of battle. It is I, or not I.'[11] There may have been some truth in this; but the suspicion that Manning had succeeded in imposing his will on Wiseman[12] has no evidence to support it except the gossip of the disaffected Edmund Ffoulkes, who had been agitating for a Catholic hall, and was also in bad odour over his activities in connection with the Association for promoting union between the Roman and Anglican Churches.[13] There is no doubt that Manning was hostile. His own wish was to promote discussions on the founding of a Catholic university in England, or even to establish an English university in Rome. Newman dismissed this last idea as 'mad'.[14] The contention of Abbot Butler that Wiseman's series of questions was actually drawn up by the joint efforts of Manning, Ward and Bishop Grant of Southwark[15] is not supported by evidence. The 'interrogatory' survives in Wiseman's own hand; and the role of Grant was purely to act as the co-ordinator of the replies.[16] It is, however, certain that Manning made his views known to Propaganda, through his close relations with Talbot and Barnabò, in a strongly-worded letter to Mgr Capelti at Rome.[17] In doing so he was only relaying the opinion of the majority of the hierarchy, and many of the Oxford converts too. As Sheridan Gilley has observed, 'Newman was not simply opposed to a "small active clique", but to the defensive Catholic mentality of his day.'[18]

Newman's efforts to secure a Catholic base in Oxford ensured him the support and sympathy of the more prosperous Catholic laity. During 1864, however, a year of frustration was to a large extent relieved by a fortuitous circumstance – intended to cause him even more discomfiture, but which he was able to turn to his own advantage by raising his stock still higher within the Catholic body as a whole. In an article in *Macmillan's Magazine*, Charles Kingsley launched a personal attack on Newman in which he accused him, in particular, and the whole Catholic Church in general, of teaching that 'truth, for its own sake, is no virtue'. On 31 January 1864, following an exchange of letters with the publisher and Kingsley himself, Newman published all the correspondence that had passed between them, together with some additional biting comments of his own, in a pamphlet entitled 'Mr Kingsley and Dr Newman', and so forthright a riposte seemed, at least for a while, effectively to throw the insult back into the teeth of his assailant.

The immediate expression of Catholic support for Newman came in the form of an Address from a large number of priests in the Westminster diocese, congratulating him on making 'one further claim ... to the gratitude and veneration of Catholics', trusting that the reception of the pamphlet would be 'the omen of new successes which you are destined to achieve in the vindication of the teaching and principles of the Church'.[19] Significantly, Newman noted the absence of Manning's name, together with the names of some other Oblates, from among the signatories; and, possibly because the instigator of the Address was none other than Dr Maguire, the ringleader of the mutinous Westminster

Chapter, Newman interpreted the gesture as a

> movement against Manning more immediately than any one else ...
> For three or four months past the Westminster clergy have been in a
> state of extreme anxiety, lest Manning should be made coadjutor to
> the Cardinal. And, tho' it is not obvious how a Letter to me could have
> any bearing on this dreaded measure, yet I think there is a connection
> between the two.[20]

But this was only the beginning. In March 1864 Kingsley
returned to the attack in a more detailed and more vituperative
pamphlet entitled 'What then does Dr Newman mean?' On 10
April Newman began his lengthy reply, published in seven weekly
instalments, completed at the beginning of June and with an
Appendix which followed a fortnight later. It was written in
extreme haste, and was no less powerful for that; friends rallied
round to supply him with helpful letters (Manning was one of
them).[21] Kingsley's charges of dishonesty, credulity and sophistry
provoked Newman into writing what turned out to be a personal
history of his changing religious opinions from his first Evangelical conversion to his decision to find salvation within the Roman
Church. This was given to the world in his most celebrated book,
the *Apologia pro vita sua*.

Unwittingly, Kingsley had delivered himself into his opponent's
hands. This was partly because of the crudity and extravagance of
the language which he employed in his attempt to appeal to the
basest Protestant prejudices of his readers. He thereby made it
easier for Newman to demonstrate the extent to which Kingsley
had tried to poison the wells against him by insinuating that his
subtle sophistries were so much part of his nature that nothing he
could say in reply could be taken as truthful or sincere. Kingsley
had gone too far, enabling Newman to appeal to the English sense
of fair play. But in other ways he had passed the advantage to his
adversary. He gave Newman the heaven-sent opportunity to set
the record straight for the benefit of other parties than just his
assailant's. 'I have always looked forward to the possibility of that
opening being presented to me,' Newman wrote to Edward
Badeley in March 1864;[22] and to J. D. Coleridge, in October of
that year, he admitted: 'I had, for some years, had a sort of tacit
understanding with myself, that, if ever I was publicly and
formally confronted with those charges which from time to time
... had drifted to my door, I would accept the challenge.'[23]

Martin Svaglic even suggests that Newman deliberately provoked Kingsley, in order 'to tell the story he had so long wanted to tell'.[24] He could now scotch for ever the notion that he might one day return to the Anglican fold; he could also dispel idle rumours among his co-religionists that he was really only half a Catholic. Finally, he could be seen to do a great service to his Church by exposing the absurdity of the popular prejudices against it, so that the book would stand as an apology, not only for himself, but for the whole Roman Catholic faith.

Every page, every phrase, identifies the author. Newman liked to write about himself. His style was best suited to the *livre de circonstance*: a direct challenge in reply to which rhetorical devices, if handled by a master, could be so devastatingly effective. Granted this, he could hardly fail; and the result was the most immediately, and perhaps most enduringly, successful book he ever wrote. This does not mean, however, that it was necessarily his best production. While achieving his objective in silencing Kingsley once and for all, the *Apologia* – if assessed by the accepted canons of exculpation from specific charges – hardly deserved the triumph that it scored. What Newman succeeded in doing was to pay Kingsley back in his own coin so effectively that his opponent knew that any reply that he contemplated would be fruitless, for the simple reason that Newman, by the supreme demonstration of his rhetorical arts, had stolen the sympathies of his audience. He quite deliberately ignored Kingsley's specific charges against him until he had created in his readers' minds so intimate a personal rapport – through the poignantly-drawn picture of his spiritual wrestlings, interspersed with warmly charitable acknowledgements to former Anglican friends (and opponents) who had walked part of the way with him – that by the time several hundred pages of seductive prose had been absorbed, the impression left on the mind would be that if Kingsley could so misjudge the man, he must also have misunderstood his teaching. Newman knew precisely what he was doing. As Walter Houghton has observed, his tactical approach was entirely in accordance with what he had written earlier, in his essay on 'The Tamworth Reading Room', about the process of conviction. 'Persons influence us, voices melt us, looks subdue us.'[25] This is why the *Apologia* is 'a record of such influences far more than a record of advancing logic'.[26] Newman's voice certainly melted his readers – an expression of loving anguish, with all the charm of his delicately and sensitively cadenced prose, which made Kingsley's voice sound raucous and brazen; if the one lulled a reader's critical faculties, perhaps unconsciously, the other just jarred in his ear.

Edwin Abbott was the first to draw attention to the inaccuracies in the *Apologia*;[27] and since then most Newman scholars have conceded that – masterpiece as it is – it is far from flawless. Newman himself excused its limitations on the grounds that it was written 'extempore'.[28] The emotional strain that he underwent in the staggering achievement of completing a book of this length in under ten weeks may condone the occasional over-dramatization, lapses of memory and some of the contradictions. Those who had read his letter to Wiseman on the occasion of his delation, when he made a plea on behalf of those 'who toil much and say little',[29] might well wonder if this could be the same man who, in the *Apologia*, appealed for sympathy for one 'whose natural impulse it has ever been to speak out; who has ever spoken too much rather than too little; who would have saved himself many a scrape, if he had been wise enough to hold his tongue'.[30] He described himself as a 'Protestant' when he preached his final University Sermon in 1843 (Kingsley having taken exception to the passage that a lie can sometimes be 'the nearest approach to truth'), but stated that an article in the *British Critic* in 1839 contained 'the last words that I spoke as an Anglican to Anglicans'.[31] The most serious criticism is that Newman does not actually supply satisfactory answers to some of Kingsley's accusations. The Appendix (where – at last – he attempted to do so) sees a complete change of tone – a mixture of mocking condescension and petulant jocularity – suggesting that Newman was aware that he was being evasive, especially in his defence of his credulity over some of the more dubious ecclesiastical miracles. One contemporary Anglican critic, F. J. A. Hort, dismissed the Appendix as unworthy of Newman's gifts, describing it as 'an utterly detestable style of repartee'.[32] As far as most of Newman's readers were concerned, however, this hardly seemed to matter. The victory had been won in the substantial body of the book.

Manning never liked the *Apologia*. He thought that Newman was on very dangerous ground in rejecting any logical proof for the existence of God,[33] and that he was too charitable in his comments about the Church of England, thereby encouraging Anglicans to remain where they were.[34] His disciple, Herbert

Vaughan, read the book 'with a mixture of pain and pleasure. The egotism may be disgusting, but it is venial. There are views put forward which I abhor.'[35] Both Manning and Ward winced, as they were doubtless intended to do, at the disparaging comments about 'a violent ultra party, which exalts opinions into dogmas, and has it principally at heart to destroy every school of thought but its own',[36] recognizing that this was Newman's sole acknowledgement to themselves. They were aware, however, that they constituted very much the minority among English Catholics. Henceforth Newman's influence would be immeasurably stronger than it had been at any previous point in his Catholic career. This was not a prospect that they accepted with equanimity.

So the events of 1864 all served to widen still further the sense of estrangement between Newman and Manning. On the face of it, however, their divergence was never one of such diametric opposition that the gulf between them could not be bridged. Newman, for instance, cheerfully described himself as 'ultramontane' in a letter to Henry Wilberforce in 1855;[37] he never doubted the infallibility of the Pope as a doctrine of the Church (its proof, he was wont to say, 'is as good as that of the Divinity of Christ . . . the same in *kind*').[38] If he had reservations on the Temporal Power, as has been seen, he was not actively opposed to its maintenance, believing only that its loss would not affect the Pope's spiritual supremacy. What gave to the issues that divided them a belligerent tone was Newman's temperamental inclination to view conflicts in intensely personal terms. Manning always seemed more concerned about the principles involved in an issue, Newman more aware of, or sensitive to, the people behind the principles. If the process of conviction, to him, was the experience of 'persons influence us, voices melt us', or – to put it in an even more characteristic Newman phrase – 'heart speaking to heart', then the converse was likely to be as true. Allegiance could not easily be given to someone whose heart could not communicate with one's own. Loyalty, discipleship, harmonious and friendly relations, all depended on mutual trust. It had ever been so with Newman. Even as an Anglican, his distrust of an opponent's influence always gave the impression of being that little bit stronger than the actual *casus belli*. He disliked latitudinarianism; but he abhorred latitudinarians. So with Faber. The actual issue which destroyed their relationship was a comparatively trivial one; what Newman found unforgivable was the falsity of a friend.

In his mind he divided his Catholic career into two separate phases, each coinciding with conflicts exacerbated by untrustworthy opponents. Faber and Wiseman filled this bill in the first phase; in the second, the so-called 'three tailors of Tooley Street' (who had presumed to style themselves 'We, the people of England')[39] – Manning, Talbot and Ward. Of these three Ward, who was actually more aggressive in his differences from Newman, was reckoned as a truer adversary than the other two, worthy of respect and even some affection because 'he is thoroughly honest and above board'.[40] In one of his University discourses Newman had written, 'I prefer to live in an age when the fight is in the day, not in the twilight; and think it a gain to be speared by a foe, rather than to be stabbed by a friend.'[41]

Ward fought with a spear; but Newman had a nasty suspicion that Talbot and Manning fought with knives. To change the metaphor, they were pullers of strings behind the scene. This was one of the reasons why Newman felt so uneasy about Rome, the haven of string-pullers.[42] Both Talbot and Cardinal Barnabò could be very kind to your face, while harbouring an 'underhand hostility'.[43] Only this can explain what appears, on the face of it, an almost unpardonable snub to Talbot who, in July 1864, had, after talking with the Pope, invited Newman to Rome to preach, thinking that his willingness to accept would help his image with the ecclesiastical authorities. Probably Talbot meant well, but the invitation was couched in such condescending terms (which included an unnecessary allusion to the better-educated congregation to be found in Rome as opposed to Birmingham) that Newman replied with calculated rudeness in a curt letter of two sentences, concluding, 'Birmingham people have souls; and I have neither taste nor talent for the sort of work, which you cut out for me.'[44] This had been Talbot's gauche attempt at reconciliation. It was intended as an olive-branch. Newman certainly did not help himself by so ruthlessly snubbing a Papal Chamberlain; but he was not prepared to make even a gesture of courtesy to a man whom he could not trust. What he forfeited by his action, of course, was any right to expect any favours from Talbot thereafter.

If Ward, by contrast, was an honest fighter, he nevertheless shared with the other two the perilous attitude of ascribing a sort of infallibility to their own opinions. To act so was to defy the sound maxim *in necessariis unitas, in dubiis libertas, in omnibus charitas*. By turning their own opinions into dogmas they were 'narrowing the terms of Catholicity'.[45] The consequence was that, in the atmosphere of siege mentality that was gripping Rome in the 1860s, the workings of the Holy Spirit were being, as it were, anticipated before their time. The pressure of external events seemed to be working towards an unhealthy urgency to define as dogmas propositions that might indeed be true, but which required the calm passage of time before they could be properly assimilated, so that any ultimate definition would be seen to be the expression of the *consensus fidelium*. This explains why Newman, although Ultramontane in sympathy, was essentially an inopportunist. The whole theme of his *Essay on Development* had been a demonstration of the gradual emergence of dogmatic definitions; it might take centuries for what had been implicitly received to become explicitly defined. The Holy Spirit cannot be hustled. Newman's maxim in this, as in almost all his responses to the crises of his day, was 'Give it time'.

'Great acts take time', Newman had written of his own conversion, in a famous passage in the *Apologia*.[46] 'Time is necessary for the full comprehension and perfection of great ideas,' he explained in his *Essay on Development*.[47] Why did Callista delay for so long, even in her prison, before becoming a Christian? 'Why? – because it takes time.'[48] One should never be frightened by 'certain reasonings which seem contrary to faith', he wrote in his introduction to a paper on biblical inspiration in 1861. 'We should take time calmly to consider how the matter stands ... Cultivate the Xtian virtue of patience',[49] a sentiment repeated in the *Grammar of Assent*: 'I should be patient. I should look for better days.'[50] He wrote to Pusey, in September 1865, to explain why he was loath to reply to controversial notices of things he had written. Why? 'Time would decide for me.' He quoted (not quite accurately) some lines of a poem by Crabbe:

> Leaving the case to Time, who solves all doubt,
> By bringing Truth, his glorious daughter, out.[51]

Years later, in 1877, he wrote to John Morley, declining to reply to a challenge on his theory of belief. 'I shall cheerfully leave it to Time to do what Time has so often done in the last 40 or 50 years. Time has been my best friend and champion: and to the future I lovingly commit myself with much resignation to its award.'[52]

This was one of Newman's profoundest insights. If Manning

did not subscribe to it, there were also very good reasons why, in his own particular sphere of operations, he neither could nor should, as will become clear later. By the end of 1864, however, it began to seem as if the two men could not happily subscribe to anything in common. The press did not fail to notice it, and poured their own dose of vinegar into Manning's wounds. On 5 November 1864 the *Daily News* commented, with a clear reference to the Oxford issue, that

> the best features, moral and intellectual, of Roman Catholicism have their fitting representative in Dr Newman; and it is a matter for hearty congratulations that it should have fallen to him to form the minds of the Roman Catholic youth of England, rather than to any member of that school which finds a leader in Dr Manning, and an organ in the Dublin Review.[53]

Soon, however, the Church in England was bound to have a new leader, because Cardinal Wiseman was nearing the end of his days. In February 1865, when the end was very near, Newman told Pusey that 'there is a great idea that Manning will succeed him'. He put the 'dreaded measure' out of his mind. That 'I can't believe.'[54]

II

Newman saw Wiseman for the last time on 4 November 1864. The meeting was not one of his own choosing, nor did it leave pleasant memories. He had made one of his rare visits to London, and the Oxford issue was still very much an open question. Meeting J. L. Patterson (also an Oxford convert, who became, in later years, Manning's auxiliary bishop at Westminster) practically outside York House, Newman was prevailed upon by Patterson to accompany him to pay his respects to the Cardinal, in the hope that such a courtesy visit would serve to restore good relations on both sides. As it turned out, the timing was unfortunate. Wiseman had just started his lunch and was put out at being disturbed. He was also far from well. It was the wrong moment for Newman to broach the subject of his Oxford plans, and Wiseman gave him no encouragement, complaining about the effect of London fog on his eyes, and then terminating the interview in a matter of minutes. On returning to the dining-room he lapsed into 'sulky silence'. Patterson was very upset. When, thirty years later, he was told by William Neville, on apparently good authority, that Wiseman had written to Rome to complain that Newman had been insolent, he was even more perplexed at a report that exhibited both men as acting entirely out of character.[1] There seems little doubt about Wiseman's coolness, and the probable explanation is that this desperately sick man, who had barely three months to live, had been deeply hurt by Newman's comments in the *Apologia* about his early years at Oscott and Rome, suggestive of lack of sympathy from the hierarchy and from Wiseman in particular.[2]

Whatever the explanation, it was a sad parting; and when Wiseman died on 15 February 1865, Newman's assessment of their relationship, in a letter to Charles Russell, was equally cool. He conceded that the Cardinal had accomplished a great work, but 'personally, I have not much to thank him for, since I was a Catholic. He always meant kindly, but his impulses, kind as they were, were evanescent, and he was naturally influenced by those who got around him and occupied his ear.' He owned that he was relieved that he had not received an invitation to the funeral. 'It would have been painful to refuse.'[3] It was Manning's responsibility, by contrast, to take centre stage on that occasion, and to deliver the panegyric at the Requiem Mass on 23 February, thereby fulfilling the late Cardinal's express wish.

> If the command of authority had not bid me speak today, I should not have ventured on this task. It would be a hard task to anyone. It is a harder task to me than to most. It is beyond the power of any of us to speak as we ought of the great Pastor and Prince of the Church who lies here in the midst of us. It is altogether beyond mine. I have, moreover, a farther hindrance – the private sorrow for the loss of the truest of friends, the last in this kind I can ever have in life.

Inevitably he had to speak of Wiseman's most cherished aims, which some were inclined to dismiss as the vain expectations of a 'dreamer of dreams':

> The conversion of England! Do men think that we expect the twenty million of Englishmen to lie down Protestant at night, and to wake up Catholics in the morning? ... He was a believer like one who for a hundred and twenty years built the ark; and a hoper like him who all alone entered imperial Rome, a simple fisherman, but the Vicar of the Son of God. Such were his expectations; and when he closed his eyes upon England, he had already seen the work he had begun, expand-

ing everywhere, and the traditions of three hundred years everywhere dissolving before it. Time is not with the Church of God. Converging lines may stretch beyond our sight, and overpass the horizon; but they must intersect at last. So with the work of grace upon the country of our birth and of our love; its desolations are not for ever.[4]

That Wiseman had chosen the convert Provost of Westminster to deliver his funeral oration might have signified to some of those present in that distinguished congregation that the dying Cardinal, at the last, had known over whose shoulders the mantle of Elijah should now rest. Did the thought ever occur to Manning himself? Of course it did, only to be rejected as an impossibility. Talbot told him as much. In his reply, Manning admitted that certain people 'out of kind but inconsiderate talk' had mentioned his name as a possible successor, but 'if I say that I have never for a moment believed the thing to be probable, reasonable or imaginable I should speak the strictest truth'.[5] This is not to say that he did not cherish the hope that the unimaginable might happen. Perhaps because he was so conscious of the temptations of ambition, he was wont to preach with such vehemence against worldliness, branding the seeking of power by illegitimate and unworthy means as the most loathsome of sins, and ultimately carrying with it a self-inflicted penalty. 'One last step,' he declaimed in one of his Anglican sermons, 'the last act which secures the desires of a life, is often one that henceforward makes life not worth the living.' Success may be the prize – 'but at what a cost!'[6]

It is true that a man may say one thing and do another; he may preach an ideal and then fail signally to live up to it. There is no evidence, however, that Manning was either hypocritical or guilty of self-delusion. Others may have worked on his behalf, but he never deliberately 'ingratiated himself with the Pope', as Newman rather sourly suggested to Pusey three years later.[7] During the ten agonizing weeks after Wiseman's death, Manning expressed his apprehensions about the impending appointment quite openly, however, to Talbot in Rome. He had every cause to fear the animus of the Westminster Chapter, whose responsibility it was to make three nominations (the *terna*) to Propaganda, suspecting that they would not resist the temptation to exact their revenge. 'They *may* put Dr Errington into the *terna*', he wrote to Talbot on 24 February, 'but I do not expect it: because it would be too direct an opposition to the Holy See.' Another nomination that he feared was that of Dr Clifford, Bishop of Clifton, which he thought would be even more disastrous to the Ultramontanist cause. He even thought that the Chapter might be truly perverse and offer Newman's name, 'for Oakeley and Dr Maguire have been literally playing the fool about him in this Kingsley affair'.[8] In the end, he came out most decidedly in support of Ullathorne, and quite disinterestedly so because he was clearly the strongest candidate. His second choice was Cornthwaite, Bishop of Beverley, and a safe Ultramontane.[9]

An independent observer, Odo Russell, who was following events closely and reporting back to the British government, was coming to similar conclusions, if not sharing Manning's views. 'Dr Ullathorne appears to have the largest number of adherents amongst his countrymen,' he told his uncle at the Foreign Office. He discounted Clifford as too young for the post. Then, he added,

> Italian and foreign ecclesiastics in general look upon Dr Manning as Cardinal Wiseman's successor, but I hear on good authority that neither the Vatican nor the Propaganda nor the Chapter are either inclined or likely to promote a convert at present. Cardinal Wiseman will not be replaced by a Cardinal, and the next English Cardinal nominated by the Pope is to reside in Rome.[10]

Ironically, the Westminster Chapter, in confirming Manning's fears, succeeded in obtaining the one result that they had hoped to avert. The three names submitted to Propaganda on 14 March were those of Errington, Grant (Bishop of Southwark) and Clifford; and since both Grant and Clifford made it quite clear that they wished to defer any claims on their own behalf to the manifestly superior claims of the man who had been Wiseman's coadjutor, Propaganda were in effect presented with the name of only one candidate, who – as a result of the Pope's sentence of deprivation – could not conceivably be accepted. Pius IX felt the action of the Westminster Chapter as a personal insult, and resolved to take the matter into his own hands. He ordered that special masses should be offered up for the guidance of the Holy Spirit; and in the meantime several interested parties set to work to insinuate guidance of their own. Propaganda overwhelmingly supported Ullathorne; the British government pressed the claims of Clifford; Talbot and Robert Coffin (in Rome at that convenient moment), by supporting Manning, subsequently claimed that they had exercised the decisive influence.[11] What actually passed through the Pope's mind, none will ever know. He was clearly aware of the dangers of splitting the Church in England into two irreconciliable factions if he were to take the step that would both rebuke the rebellious Chapter and satisfy the inclinations of his own heart. What he vouchsafed to Manning himself, on the occasion of his first audience after his elevation, was that he prayed for guidance and was conscious of a voice persistently directing him with the command 'Put him there! Put him there!'[12] On 30 April 1865 he took the plunge, defying the advice of Propaganda, the British government, the majority of the English bishops and (with a certain satisfaction) the Westminster Chapter. Henry Edward Manning was named as Wiseman's successor to the archiepiscopal see of Westminster.

The first hint that the tide had turned in his favour came to Manning from a member of the Chapter, Canon Hearn, five days before the Pope announced his decision;[13] but he refused to believe that the unimaginable had come to pass until he received the official confirmation from Rome on 8 May. He went at once to kneel before the Blessed Sacrament in the church of St Mary of the Angels; and there his nephew William Anderdon, also an Oblate, found him deep in prayer, his customary reserve for a moment overlaid with emotion. He had been crying.[14] As he reviewed the course of events that had brought him, within fourteen years of his conversion, to the head of the English hierarchy, his political sense told him that 'the Chapter of Westminster did it'.[15] But the Holy Spirit works in strange ways. Nothing would ever shake his conviction that despite his faults, which he enumerated with an almost masochistic severity during the week's retreat with the Passionists at Highgate on the eve of his consecration, 'Our Lord had called me by name and touched me with His hand'. His mind went back to his first conversion at the age of nineteen.

> It has impressed itself vividly upon me that God has predestinated me to Eternal Life, but that the way is by conformity to His Son … His image is the *Volto Sagro* which hangs over my bed at St Mary's, the Sacred countenance wounded and darkened by sorrow and suffering.

All through his life the calls had come – to abandon politics, 'to serve Him at the cost of all things as a Catholic', to the priesthood, to become an Oblate, and now 'He has … called me to the greatest Cross of my life and to the greatest separation from the world.'[16]

Talbot had warned him to expect a storm, once the appointment became public, but Manning was able to report back that 'none has come: on the contrary'.[17] The back-biting and the in-fighting subsided on the instant, and Manning was overwhelmed by the generosity of those who had been his opponents – the hierarchy, the Chapter (including Maguire and Searle), the religious Orders (excepting perhaps the Jesuits at Farm Street, from whom some individual letters came, but nothing from the Superior). Ullathorne was one of the first to write.

> I was descending on the station platform at Coventry yesterday morning when Mr Hanson came up and put the newspaper in my hand. When I read the announcement I broke into a little laugh, and suddenly found a sort of lightening and expansion of the breast, which proved to me that I had been for some days under an unconscious pressure of care. I never yet congratulated a bishop or an archbishop on his nomination. I do not do so now, I only congratulate the archdiocese.

He signed it 'your faithful and obedient suffragan'.[18] Even Errington, although he did not write personally to Manning, assured the Vicar-General of the Westminster Chapter that 'the decision of Rome being to us the manifestation of the will of God, we have the best grounds to trust that the welfare of the see has been most effectually provided for'.[19] Without any expression of resentment, he retired from the fray to work as a priest on the Isle of Man.

When Newman heard the news, he sent his first observations to his penitent, Emily Bowles, who had expressed delight at the Pope's vigorous action, not least because of the discomfiture of the Jesuits ('If you only saw the Farm Street faces!')[20]

> As to the new Archbishop [Newman wrote], the appointment at least has the effect of making Protestants see, to their surprise, that Rome is not distrustful of converts, as such. On the other hand it must be a great trial to the old Priesthood – to have a neophyte set over them all. Some will bear it very well – I think our Bishop will . . . [Manning] has a great power of winning men, when he chooses – witness the fact of his appointment – but whether he will care to win inferiors, or whether his talent extends to the case of inferiors as well as superiors, I do not know. One man has one talent, another another. I have generally got on well with juniors – but not with superiors.[21]

The remark in parenthetical dashes was a little ungracious, but the self-analysis was accurate enough. He was more expansive to Robert Ornsby.

> Manning's rise is marvellous – in fourteen years a Protestant Archdeacon is made Catholic Archbishop of Westminster, with the whole body of old Catholics, Bishops and all, under him. At the moment he is very unpopular – but, I suppose, there will be a re-action . . . Success is the goddess of an Englishman . . . Then, as to Catholics, a man in authority has such great opportunities of recovering his ground, if he chooses to employ them.[22]

Rather more ominous, however, was Newman's remark to T. W. Allies, four days later. 'If you write to inspire me with confidence in the Archbishop, laterem laves [i.e., you labour in vain].'[23]

To this extent Newman judged correctly. Manning was far too skilled a statesman not to take advantage of the surge of goodwill that greeted his appointment. He offered olive-branches all round. His kindness to Maguire and Searle was such that both soon felt ashamed of their previous efforts to malign him.[24] He consulted Ullathorne over whether he should offer Errington the hospitality of his house in the event of his visiting London (rather too premature, Ullathorne thought).[25] Three years later, he proposed Errington's name as Vicar-Apostolic of the Western District of Scotland, with the responsibility of restoring the Roman hierarchy there. Errington was clearly touched by Manning's offer, but decided to decline, largely on the advice of Clifford, Bishop of Clifton.[26] The man whom he most wanted to honour, however, was Newman. Somehow that rift must be healed. His plan was to procure for him a bishopric *in partibus*. On 30 May, from his retreat at Highgate, he wrote to Newman about his impending consecration:

> In calling to mind the old, and dear Friends who would pray for me at this moment your name arose among the first; I can not refrain from writing to you to ask you to give me the happiness and consolation of your being with me on the 8th of June next at Moorfields. No one will better know than you how much I need your prayers.[27]

Ullathorne had previously warned Manning to be careful about endeavouring to load Newman with honours. It would be misconstrued as an attempt to 'soothe him with ornaments, or something of that sort'.[28] Newman's reply to Manning's invitation suggests that he had no wish to be soothed. He consented to attend the consecration, 'as your friend, not as a Father of the Birmingham

Oratory', on two conditions: that he should not be expected to stay for the official luncheon afterwards, and – more to the point – that the efforts to make him a bishop should be immediately dropped.

> I . . . entreat you not to entertain it. If such an honour were offered to me, I should persistently decline it, very persistently; and I do not wish to pain the Holy Father, who has always been so kind to me, if such pain can be avoided. Your allowing me then to come to your consecration I shall take as a pledge, that you will have nothing to do with any such attempt.[29]

During his week's retreat at Highgate Manning subjected himself to intense self-examination. At the same time, he was formulating his programme for the future, in terms of both his priorities and his own personal conduct towards his clergy, studying Challoner's *Memoir of Missionary Priests* as his guide.[30] He would eschew all luxury.

> Everybody in high place stands in a room full of mirrors and sees himself multiplied without end by a servile reflection. My desire is to live the most retired life I can consistently with the government of the Diocese . . . As to mixing in the world, my wish would be to decline all dining out . . . I wish never to be seen except at work, or on occasions of legitimate recreation, such as the Royal Academy.

He renewed his special devotion to the Third Person of the Trinity, making the resolution to continue 'to make every day an act of reparation to the Holy Ghost'. Called to his position by the workings of the Holy Spirit, he interpreted such a vocation as a sanctification of his long-felt desire 'to hold inviolate the doctrines and laws of the Church without compromise . . . When I entered a system, which, being Divine, is definite and uncompromising, I threw myself with my whole soul and strength into its mind, will, and action. So it must be to the end. Less definite, positive, uncompromising, aggressive, I can never be. God forbid ! But I will try to do it *charitate formatus*.' His special mission must be to London.

> When I look down upon London from this garden and know that there are before me nearly three millions of men of whom only 200,000 are nominally in the Faith; that hundreds and thousands are living and dying without baptism, in all sins of the flesh and spirit, in all that Nineveh and the Cities of the Plain and Imperial Rome ever committed: that it is the capital of the most anti-Christian power of the nominally Christian world and the head of its anti-Christian spirit . . . I

confess I feel that we are walking on the waters, and that nothing but the word and the presence of Jesus makes this great calm . . . They will be my Chalice more than ever. To labour and suffer for souls who will not be redeemed. To go down into the fire and into the water to save souls, and to be wounded by them – all this I look for.

At the end of the retreat he recognized the extent to which the strife and struggles of the last few years had taken their toll.

I see it in my face . . . I desire to spend my last days in this spirit. I especially desire to be thus to the priests, who have sadness and cares enough of their own, and ought to find in me a Filius Consolationis . . . Walking on the terrace and looking down upon London in this broad sunlight has been very moving to me. The Son of God would have wept over it. What beautiful souls are in it, made in the likeness of God, with all the capacities of eternal life, but outcast, disinherited, darkened, stained, poisoned, distorted, disfigured, twice dead.[31]

At his consecration on 8 June at the Pro-Cathedral at Moorfields, conducted by Ullathorne, and assisted by Bishops Clifford and Grant, others saw the marks of suffering on his face. Sibthorpe described the new Archbishop memorably: 'He looked like Lazarus coming out of the tomb in cope and mitre, a richly vested corpse, but very dignified and placid.'[32] Newman was there. When he knelt to kiss Manning's hand, the Archbishop 'hastened to raise him up and embrace him'. Newman felt embarrassed. He wrote to Canon Walker: 'I suppose the Archbishop has got into the foreign way and does it naturally – but, with you, I feel awkward . . . I always feel ashamed, like a John Bull, who does not know manners.'[33] He did not attend the official luncheon afterwards, but returned to the house of an old friend with whom he had been staying – Frederic Rogers. R. W. Church was there – their first meeting for twenty years. Church recalled the occasion in a letter to J. B. Mozley:

He was very little changed in look or general manner or way of talking, except that he seemed almost stronger in body. He was in good spirits, very hearty, and talked very freely about all sorts of things; reminding us every now and then that he was across the border, but without embarrassment and without any attempt to flaunt anything in our faces. It was a much more easy meeting than I could have supposed possible. We seemed to fall into the old ways of talking.

He talked about Manning, and about his own position, and his differences of views about education. He thought Manning had certainly plans, but no one knew what they were; it was clear, however, that Newman did not much expect them to be what he would lay most stress upon. He spoke of the difficulty of getting interest or money for anything but immediate objects: the poor, or the training of priests; while literature, and higher education, and the education of the laity, no one cared much about or thought worth efforts.[34]

These were shrewd guesses on Newman's part. Even before his consecration, Manning had shocked a distinguished audience, assembled in Willis's Rooms to discuss how to raise funds for the building of a cathedral as a memorial to Wiseman, by pointing out that, while he saluted that objective, the plight of the London poor must come first. 'Could I leave 20,000 children without education, and drain my friends and my flock to pile up stones and brick?'[35] Newman was correct, too, in his surmise that Manning would press for a united effort, throughout the dioceses, to achieve effective training for the priesthood. Those outcast souls of London, and especially his Irish flock, desperately needed devoted priests to minister to their needs.

So the omens were not good. The honeymoon period, if indeed there ever was one as far as Newman was concerned in his dealings with the new Archbishop, was doomed to be short-lived. During the first two years of Manning's archiepiscopate the relationship between them, sadly, touched rock bottom.

III

Manning wished otherwise, of course. He realized that his task would be immeasurably easier if only Newman would stand beside him and lend the force of his influence and the power of his pen in support of what was now to be official policy. Just for a moment it seemed that he might do so, in the course of a controversial exchange with Pusey which, if it promised well in its beginnings, ended by deepening the sense of estrangement. It all began with a provocative statement by Pusey in a pamphlet against the exoneration, by the Judicial Committee of the Privy Council, of two of the contributors to the allegedly heterodox publication, *Essays and Reviews*, in 1864. Pusey wrote that he had the authority of 'a very earnest body of Roman Catholics' that they acknowledged and rejoiced in 'all the workings of God the Holy Ghost in the Church of England', and that they were saddened by 'what weakens her' as 'the great bulwark against infidelity in this land'. But – Pusey added – there were also other Roman Catholics, whose reaction to the embarrassment of the Anglican Church was 'an ecstasy of triumph at this victory of Satan'.[1] Since Newman, in the *Apologia*, had himself described the Church of England as 'a serviceable breakwater against errors more fundamental than its own',[2] it was thought (not quite correctly) that Pusey was contrasting Newman's sympathy to the Church of his baptism with Manning's hostility.

Later that year Manning replied, in a pamphlet entitled *The Workings of the Holy Spirit in the Church of England*. While he was prepared to concede that 'no Catholic ever denies the workings of the Spirit of God or the operations of grace' within the Anglican Church, and that the English people were freed from the guilt of heresy and schism because they could not be held culpable for acts committed by their predecessors of centuries past,[3] he repudiated its claim to be a part of the Catholic Church. They had no greater claim than members of dissenting Churches.[4] He concluded: 'I am unable to consider the Church of England to be ... the great bulwark against infidelity in this land.'[5] Pusey replied at length in an 'Eirenicon', in which he unsuccessfully attempted to enlist Newman's support. This was not only a reply to Manning's specific objections, but also a vindication of the claim to Catholicity by citing in great detail those parts of the Roman system which were repugnant to Anglicans, especially the 'vast system as to the Blessed Virgin' and popular teaching about purgatory and indulgences which had never been defined *de fide* by the Council of Trent.[6] Equally unpalatable and injurious to the prospects of unity were the exaggerated claims to papal infallibility by extreme Ultramontanes such as Manning and Ward.

While Manning set to work upon a treatise on the Blessed Virgin, pressure was also placed on Newman to write his own riposte. With great reluctance he eventually agreed. He was walking a tight-rope, and knew that he was. All the skills of the master craftsman had to be brought into play. His *Letter to Pusey*, judged as apologetic, exhibited his powers to perfection; more so, in some ways, than the *Apologia* itself. It was pithier, less subjective, and the rhetoric less strained because, by imposing his own limits on the specific charges that he chose to answer (steering clear of infallibility and concentrating on Mariolatry), he could base himself on surer ground. Up to a point, this meant occupying common ground with Manning. Neither was sympathetic to the efforts of Ambrose Phillipps de Lisle and his Association for the Promotion of the Unity of Christendom (founded in 1857), which had earned the censure of the Holy Office in September 1864. It was impracticable, and also served as an encouragement to Catholically-minded Anglicans to remain where they were.[7] In 1866 Manning issued a Pastoral Letter, explaining in detail the Papal condemnation, declaring that 'we are ready to purchase the reunion of our separated brethren at any cost less than the sacrifice of a jot or a tittle of the supernatural order of unity and faith' because 'we cannot barter, or give that which is not our own'.[8] He concluded: 'To hold out hope of impossible events is deception and cruelty. A true love of souls dictates another course.'[9] Newman said as much to Ambrose Phillipps de Lisle in the same year, defending Manning's words. 'He seems to be stern, when really he is but faithful to his trust.' Furthermore, the ideals of the Association would require for their realization a miracle such as the Thames changing its course. 'It would be to turn a panther into a hind.'[10]

On this issue Newman and Manning spoke with the same voice, but it would have been beyond Manning's power to display the mastery of courteous polemic that Newman employed in questioning the appropriateness of Pusey's description of his fierce indictment of Romanism as an 'eirenicon'. 'We at least have not professed to composing an Irenicon, when we are treating you as foes. There was one of old times who wreathed his sword in myrtle; excuse me – you discharge your olive-branch as if from a catapult.'[11] Newman set out to exhibit the extent of Anglican misconceptions about the Church's teaching on the Virgin Mary. In doing so, however, he admitted his own very English distaste for certain foreign devotions, distancing himself from the extravagances of some of his fellow-converts, and of Faber in particular. Of the authorities that Pusey had cited, 'Not one of them is an Englishman' with the exception of Faber 'who, great as are his merits, cannot ... be considered a representative of English Catholic devotion ... I suppose we owe it to the national good sense, that English Catholics have been protected from the extravagances which are elsewhere to be found.'[12] He confessed never to have encountered some of the extraordinary sources that Pusey had quoted. 'I never knew of them till I read your book, nor, as I think, do the vast majority of English Catholics know them. They seem to me like a bad dream.'[13]

This was just the sort of remark that would cause consternation at Rome. Nor would they much care for his statement that 'a people's religion is ever a corrupt religion, in spite of the provisions of Holy Church'.[14] It was hardly tactful, in his rejection of the extravagances of Faber and Ward, to include – by implication – a third party, of higher dignity. 'The only two English writers you quote in evidence', he wrote, 'are both of them converts, younger in age than myself. I put aside the Archbishop, of course, because of his office.'[15] This last remark infuriated Talbot, who wrote at once to Manning.

> I have read Newman's letter to Pusey. The patristic argument is admirable and unanswerable, but there is nothing new in it. The introduction and some other passages are detestable. His sarcastic remarks about you have given pain to many ... They are most uncatholic and unchristian ... Stand firm, do not yield a bit in the line you have taken ... Every Englishman is naturally anti-Roman. To be Roman is to an Englishman an effort. Dr Newman is more English than the English. His spirit must be crushed.[16]

Manning, licking his wounds, was inclined to agree, in private. He replied to Talbot on 25 February 1866:

> What you write about Dr Newman is true. Whether he knows it or not, he has become the centre of those who hold low views about the Holy See, are anti-Roman, cold and silent, to say no more, about the Temporal Power, national, English, critical of Catholic devotions, and always on the lower side. I see no danger of a Cisalpine Club rising again, but I see much danger of an English Catholicism, of which Newman is the highest type. It is the old Anglican, patristic, literary, Oxford tone transplanted into the Church. It takes the line of deprecating exaggerations, foreign devotions, Ultramontanism, anti-national sympathies. In one word, it is worldly Catholicism, and it will have the worldly on its side, and will deceive many. Now Ward and Faber may exaggerate, but they are a thousand times nearer to the mind and spirit of the Holy See than those who oppose them.[17]

This is an uncomfortable letter to read, but it expresses precisely the difference of stance between the two men. The one word that jars is 'worldly'. If Manning meant by that 'unspiritual', he could hardly have been wider of the mark. But this was not his meaning. On the many occasions on which he used this word, the meaning consistently attached to it is a readiness to tone down the doctrine of the Church for pragmatic reasons, a disposition to compromise or to dilute what the Church actually teaches in order to render it more serviceable in its ministering to the world. In an article in the *Dublin Review* in July 1863, Manning described 'worldly Catholicism' as 'tame, diluted, timid'.[18] In his explanation of the Vatican decrees to Gladstone in 1875, he pointed out that 'every motive of worldly policy would have tempted the Council to compromise'.[19] Similarly, when he expressed his fears to Talbot that Bishop Clifford might be chosen as Wiseman's successor, the reason he gave was that 'we should be overrun with worldly Catholics' as a result of his half-hearted Ultramontanism.[20]

Manning never doubted Newman's spirituality; what he disliked was his disposition to pander to the English anti-Roman spirit. This did not, however, deter him from making reconciliatory gestures. He refused to show offence over Newman's riposte to Pusey. In fact, he wrote to thank him for 'doing, so much more fully, that, which I was going to attempt'.[21] A month later, in March 1866, hearing the news of John Keble's death, he wrote again:

> I feel as if it had put me back half my life to the days when we used to look to him and his Christian Year as the service of our happiest thoughts. Nobody can understand this as you, and I write to you almost instinctively . . . Memory is very sweet, but the hope before us is sweeter.[22]

Ward also wrote to Newman, to tell him that there were parts of his reply to Pusey that he thoroughly liked, and 'some parts not at all', but – all in all – he adjudged the book 'among the very ablest things you have ever done'.[23] This did not stop him, however, as editor of the *Dublin Review*, writing a critique of the book, censuring Newman for his slur on foreign Catholics and for displaying 'anti-Catholic statements'. Manning was uneasy when he read Ward's draft, and asked Ullathorne to read it, assuring him that Ward would consent to withdraw the article if Ullathorne thought it prudent to do so. Unfortunately this only intensified the minsunderstanding, because Newman (when he heard about it) immediately put the worst construction on Manning's action, supposing that Ullathorne had been approached in order to add his episcopal authority to a censure upon him.[24] In view of the fact that Manning persuaded Ward both to tone down and to prune his article for the *Dublin*, this seems hardly likely.

But a bigger issue still was now brewing. Ullathorne decided to reopen the question of the establishment of an Oratory mission in

Oxford. Knowing that Newman had purchased some land in the city (opposite Christ Church) against some future undefined eventuality, he approached him, in vague terms, in August 1865, followed by a more definite invitation in March 1866, to see if he was still interested in taking responsibility for the project. Newman was understandably cautious, remembering his previous unhappy experience, and somewhat equivocal about his own role. 'Oxford never can be to me what it was,' he confided to Pusey, who was again a little jumpy about the effect of Newman's return. 'It will be like the dead visiting the dead.'[25] On 8 June, after Ullathorne had given him some reassurance about the financial liability, he decided to accept the challenge. Within a month he began to have doubts. Propaganda queried the repercussions on the 'mixed education' issue, and asked Ullathorne and Manning for their views. Manning did not send his official reply to Propaganda until the following April, but he wrote privately to Talbot, as soon as he heard of Newman's plans, that 'I am certain it will bring back the University question, and encourage the Catholics to send their sons to Oxford . . . I think Propaganda can hardly know the effect of Dr Newman's going to Oxford. The English national spirit is spreading among Catholics, and we shall have dangers.'[26]

Misunderstandings and misadventures followed thick and fast. Sadly, the good-natured and warm-hearted Ullathorne seems to have been responsible for most of them. The first occurred over a visit to England during July 1866 by Cardinal Reisach, a member of Propaganda, known to have a high regard for Manning. He came as the guest of Robert Coffin, who took him the rounds of places of interest, like Oscott and Oxford, and arranged for him to meet mutual friends, like W. G. Ward, with whom he stayed for three days. When Newman came to hear of the visit, as late as October, he was deeply hurt, assuming that Reisach had been officially commissioned to report on the Oxford scheme and that ill-wishers had deliberately contrived that he should not meet the man most deeply involved. Many of Newman's biographers have shared this assumption;[27] but, as Professor McClelland has convincingly shown, Reisach's visit was a purely private one. By his own account, in the Oscott archives, he had come over 'to study the English character', and had been particularly intrigued by the game of cricket, expressing 'almost unbounded surprise at the readiness with which all obeyed the decision of the umpires', from which he concluded that 'Englishmen must naturally be subservient to authority'.[28] Furthermore, it is now clear that Manning had expressly asked Ullathorne to ensure that Newman was invited over to Oscott while Reisach was there.[29] As it happened, Newman was not in Birmingham at the time. Ullathorne put the matter out of his mind, and failed to tell Newman either about the visit or about Manning's instructions.

Ullathorne caused a further upset by the reply that he sent to Cardinal Barnabò, in August 1866, in answer to Propaganda's query over the Oxford issue. Newman was holidaying in Switzerland at the time, sketching out some ideas for his *Grammar of Assent*, and the copy was sent on to him.

> It cannot be denied [Ullathorne had written] that in some degree and indirectly and beyond what is intended, if a church be built at Oxford, it will be an attraction for Catholics to the city and the University. And Fr Newman's name, as it will be an attraction in drawing funds for building the church, will also exercise an indirect attraction for those parents who are disposed to send their sons to the University. But Fr Newman does not intend to change his residence from Birmingham, but ... to make visits there from time to time.[30]

This was precisely what Newman did *not* want Ullathorne to say, and he pressed him to send off another letter in order to allay fears over mixed education. His presence in Oxford was to provide pastoral care for such Catholic undergraduates as were already there, and to work for the conversion of graduates.[31] Ullathorne disagreed; a second letter to Barnabò would only serve to rouse suspicions of over-anxiety. It was therefore with some relief, and not a little surprise, that Newman heard on Christmas Day that Propaganda had raised no objection to the scheme. 'Our Bishop has just triumphed over them,' he exclaimed in delight. What he did not know, because Ullathorne did not tell him, was that the permission from Propaganda contained a secret instruction: when the time was right, Ullathorne was requested to convey to Newman '*blande suaviterque*' (with blandness and suavity) that the permission was granted on the condition that Newman should not reside in Oxford.[32]

This was not an unreasonable solution to the problem. Up to a point, it should have satisfied all parties. There could be no objection to an Oratory mission at Oxford, which was Ullathorne's prime concern; there seemed to be every objection – from

Manning, the hierarchy, and the Pope above all – to any incentive for Catholic families to send their sons to a Protestant university; and Newman's presence there, on Ullathorne's admission, would have been just such an incentive. That complications followed may be partly explained by the fact that none of the major figures can be excused from displaying a touch of disingenuousness. Ullathorne shirked a confrontation with Newman and failed to tell him about the secret instruction, partly because he wanted the undoubted attraction of Newman's name in the circular sent out to collect the necessary funds for the building of the church. When the facts of the matter were leaked to the press, however, and the *Weekly Register*, in its 'Roman Letter' of 6 April 1867, proceeded to tell all, Ullathorne was obliged to explain his conduct to Newman; which he did, by letter of the same date, excusing himself rather feebly on the ground that the inhibiting clause was 'a private instruction to myself, given upon a contingency which in reality was not contemplated'.[33]

Newman, for his part, having previously assured W. J. Copeland that he dreaded the prospect of returning to Oxford because he was so happy at Birmingham,[34] even going so far as to tell Pusey that he would only go there 'under the imperative call of duty',[35] changed tack on the instant. On discovering that it was now the imperative call of duty *not* to go to Oxford, he refused to contemplate an Oratory mission at Oxford at all. 'If I am missioner at Oxford, I claim to be there, as much or as little as I please,' he wrote to Ullathorne in a letter which the other Fathers of the Oratory persuaded him to delay dispatching.[36] He resented – with some excuse – the implied slur in the inhibiting clause, now made public. Manning, too, was somewhat disingenuous. His letter to Propaganda was written subsequent to the insertion of the secret instruction, and he showed a copy to Ullathorne in order to counter accusations that he had been the promoter of the inhibition on Newman. All the letter said was that he had no objection to Newman going to Oxford 'if [he] did not bring Catholic youths there'.[37] This was all very well. But Herbert Vaughan had been in Rome, prompted – allegedly – by W. G. Ward[38] to resist the Oxford project, and he had done his utmost to convince all parties, including the Pope himself, that Newman's presence in Oxford would inevitably attract Catholic youths. Manning was aware of this, because Vaughan sent him a report on his audience of the Pope, on 10 April 1867.[39] Although this, too, was subsequent to Propaganda's decision, it is difficult to accept Manning's assurance that he was unaware that others were expressing his own views in the ears of some very important people.

Before Newman learnt from Ullathorne the contents of the secret instruction, a further source of grievance had arisen which prompted him to dispatch Ambrose St John and Henry Bittleston to Rome to clear his name of other allegations. In March 1867 he had received a letter from Cardinal Barnabò informing him that the Pope had been so distressed at hearing of 'the recent unhappy perversion of a number of Catholic youths' at Oxford that he had directed Manning to summon a meeting of the English bishops to discuss the whole Oxford question and to report back to Propaganda. Furthermore – and this was what hurt most of all – 'I am obliged to beg in the Lord your Paternity to abstain altogether from any activity or deed which may have the appearance of directly or indirectly favouring the entry of Catholic youths into the said University.'[40] Newman interpreted this as a direct charge against the Oratory School, it being supposed that some of the boys had been specially coached for Oxford entry. His reply to Barnabò was uncompromisingly blunt. He stated the facts of the case to demonstrate that the Pope had been wrongly informed, put in a plea on his own behalf, were he to be on the spot in Oxford 'to forearm' youths against any 'dangers with the weapons of faith and virtue', and concluded by expressing 'my surprise . . . that after my twenty years of most faithful service, your Eminence reposes so little confidence in me in the matter'.[41]

This might have been acceptable in its tone if written by the Vicar of St Mary's to the kindly Bishop Bagot, but it was wanting in the customary deference that the Cardinal-Prefect of Propaganda expected from a priest. Ullathorne had warned Newman, in his early days, about adopting a high-handed tone when writing to bishops, and his relations with Wiseman had undoubtedly suffered from his failure to learn this lesson. Barnabò was greatly offended, and was ill-advised enough to express his feelings to Vaughan, who duly passed them on to Manning. The trouble with Newman, Barnabò said, was that he had suffered from too much adulation, English Catholics tending to regard him as 'a new revelation vouchsafed to them, a prophet and more than a Prophet'. He declared that whenever Newman conversed with him he felt 'a heavy weight . . . upon his stomach'.[42]

At least the mission of St John and Bittleston did something to clear the air. The misunderstanding over the failure to respond to Propaganda's list of questions arising from Bishop Brown's delation was finally and satisfactorily explained; the allegations against the Oratory School were corrected; and the two Oratorians were conveniently at hand when news of the 'secret instruction' was made public, so that that issue could at least be ventilated. Barnabò assured St John that 'the Holy See would never sanction mixed education', and that was why the Pope would never permit 'so important a man as Newman to go to Oxford ... It was the Pope himself who had insisted on this special condition'.[43] It was all very bland, perhaps too '*blande suaviterque*', especially when Barnabò, after reciting all the instances which had led to Newman's poor reputation in Rome, described him as 'a saint' (and, after all, 'saints were persecuted'). 'I know both men, Manning and Newman. I know Manning best, but I love Newman.'[44] They had several conversations with Talbot, who kept switching from sententious criticisms to expressions of hearty cordiality, and two not very satisfactory audiences of the Pope. At their final audience on 18 May, after a wait of two and a half hours, Pio Nono listened with detached politeness to all their explanations and then assured them that prayers would be offered up for Newman's obedience to the Holy See, which was not exactly what the two Oratorians had come to Rome to secure. Talbot told them afterwards that the Pope had found the audience 'a bore'. Their impression, overall, was that 'the Italians think us all: Manning, Talbot, you, Ward etc. are a lot of queer, quarrelsome Inglesi'.[45]

Could they have been less quarrelsome? It was not for want of trying on Manning's part. Early in January 1867 he had visited Ullathorne to ask that a meeting should be arranged with Newman so that they could talk through the whole of the Oxford question together and clear the air. Ullathorne assured Newman that Manning's intentions were entirely friendly. Newman's reply was that 'I cannot trust the Archbishop. It seems to me he never wishes to see a man except for his own ends.'[46] This was an error on Newman's part – an error of courtesy, at the least – and it was surely wrong to judge Manning's intentions before he had even heard them. Manning did not give up. He next suggested to Newman, in March, that he should attend the meeting of the bishops (requested by Propaganda to discuss the Oxford issue) so that his own views should receive a fair hearing. Newman again turned down the invitation, making the excuse that the matter was now being taken up by the deputation of the two Oratorians at Rome.[47] The result of this failure to thrash out difficulties and misunderstandings was precisely what Manning had predicted and tried so hard to avert: an unhealthy division within the Church. The Catholic laity, not unreasonably, were only too eager to have the opportunity to send their sons to Oxford. The thwarting of Newman's plans could easily be represented as a form of persecution. In consequence, when the secret instruction was a secret no longer, a Lay Memorial, adopted at a meeting of the Stafford Club on 9 April 1867, was sent to Newman, and widely publicized, not least because of the large number of distinguished signatories who expressed deep pain 'at some anonymous attacks which have been made upon you ... We feel that every blow that touches you inflicts a wound upon the Catholic Church in this country'.[48]

Manning had to swallow this bitter pill. Talbot, on the other hand, gave vent to his rage in one of the most intemperate letters ever penned:

> I look upon the Address ... as the most offensive production that has appeared in England since the times of Dr Milner ... an insult offered to the Holy See ... What is the province of the laity? To hunt, to shoot, to entertain? These matters they understand, but to meddle with ecclesiastical matters they have no right at all ... Dr Newman is the most dangerous man in England, and you will see that he will make use of the laity against your Grace ... Dr Ullathorne has been the cause of the whole mischief. If he had only obeyed the letter of Propaganda and communicated to Dr Newman the inhibition placed to his going to Oxford, he could not have sent forth a Circular saying that the whole Oxford project had the approbation of the Holy See.[49]

Still Manning refused to be shaken from his conciliatory policy. 'The greatest prudence and circumspection is necessary,' he told Talbot. 'A word or act of mine towards Dr Newman might divide the bishops and throw some on his side ... A conflict between him and me would be as great a scandal to the Church in England, and as great a victory to the Anglicans as could be.'[50] How deeply Newman felt that Manning had been responsible for the collapse of the Oxford project, which was finally abandoned in August 1867, Manning may not have known at the time. Even before he had been told of the outcome of the issue, Newman had expressed his inmost feelings about the new Archbishop to his penitent, Charlotte Wood. 'Is it not a case of Dr Fell?' he wrote. '... I think he is of a nature to be determined to *crush* or to *melt* every person who stands in his way ... I must either go with him or be annihilated.'[51]

In this, the greatest of all issues that divided them, each man had a case, and – on the face of it – Newman's was the stronger. The universities were now open to Catholics; why, then, should they continue to be required by authority to suffer the disability and disadvantage of not attending them? If they would be exposed to the freedom of intellectual debate in, admittedly, the prevailing atmosphere of scepticism and infidelity at Oxford at that time, would they really be any more at risk from contact with non-Catholic attitudes there 'than Woolwich, than the army, than London?' 'I think you cannot keep young men under glass cases,' Newman argued.[52] And if, in spite of the bishops, Catholic families were prepared to send their sons there, ought not the Church to ensure that they had pastoral support and guidance near at hand? What Manning and others were exhibiting was another form of the siege mentality that was gripping Rome in the 1860s; only this was a ghetto mentality, an unhealthy over-protectiveness, which was actually putting Catholics at a disadvantage by preventing them from playing a full part in the public, intellectual and professional life of the country.

This seems unanswerable. But Manning's case should not go by default. In the first place, he was in duty bound to fulfil the explicit instructions of the Holy See, and the majority of the hierarchy did not need his persuasion to convince them of their duty as it was then defined. Then again, he could see no reason, in a country where the number of Catholics was steadily growing, why England should not follow the example of the United States and of continental countries in establishing its own Catholic university. This had been Newman's ideal, too, in the 1850s. He had abandoned it, but Manning had not; and he saw very clearly that once the official discouragement of Catholics attending the traditional universities was lifted, there would be no hope of realizing his own – and, as he believed, infinitely superior – ideal. In due course he made a serious, if ultimately unsuccessful, attempt to turn this ideal into reality. In addition to this, there was his own personal unease at the influence that Newman, being Newman, would actually exercise in Oxford. He would tend to create Catholics after his own image; and it was not an image that Manning much liked.

The price that Manning had to pay was to see his hopes of uniting the Catholic body behind him dashed by the bitterness of the Oxford issue. Others besides himself saw the danger of his estrangement from Newman. In July 1867, Frederick Oakeley decided to try to act as an intermediary, approaching Newman himself with assurances of Manning's sincerity in striving for reconciliation. Newman's reply was not hopeful. The essence of the problem, he said, was 'the difficulty I have in implicitly confiding in him'. The only positive step that Manning might take would be to repudiate his opposition to Newman running the Oxford mission. He was sure Manning would claim that he had never actively opposed him, but the fact was that 'York Place' has 'been a centre from which a powerful antagonism has been carried on against me'.[53]

Oakeley passed all this on to Manning, and in due course the Archbishop sent him a full statement of all the issues that had divided them over the years. He expressed bewilderment over the accusations against his entourage at York Place. He had consulted Herbert Vaughan, who assured him that 'all he had said or done had been not only without my direction but without my knowledge. It may be said that I did not restrain them. I could not restrain what I did not know.'[54] The correspondence continued for some time. Its main interest, apart from the growing impression of its ultimate futility, lies in the confirmation that Manning was inflexible when it came to principles and that Newman was equally inflexible in his judgement of people. Manning would not give way over the principle of mixed education;[55] Newman, for his part, would not give way over his conviction that Manning was 'difficult to understand' and that 'your words, your bearing, and your implications, ought, though they have not served, to prepare me for your acts'.[56]

By September the interchange of letters became decidedly cooler, Newman implying that Manning was too ready to listen to 'the endemic gossip of London',[57] with Manning replying that 'I am as little open to gossip as you are'.[58] The effective termination came when Newman wrote curtly on 2 September, 'I propose to say seven Masses for your intention amid the difficulties and anxieties of your ecclesiastical duties', to which Manning rejoined that he would, in return, say a monthly Mass for Newman's intentions. 'I have more confidence in this than in any thing else to bring about what we desire.'[59]

Two years later, Manning dispatched one more little olive-branch. He was about to leave England for a momentous gathering in Rome that winter. 'As return is always uncertain', he wrote, 'and may, at best, be distant, I leave with you the assurance that the friendship of so many years, though of late unhappily clouded, is still dear to me.' Newman replied in exactly the same vein as before. 'I can only repeat what I said when you last heard from me. I do not know whether I am on my head or my heels, when I have active relations with you. In spite of my friendly feelings, this is the judgment of my intellect.'[60]

Manning was leaving for Rome to attend the General Council. Sorrowful as he was at Newman's cold reply, he now had other things on his mind.

IV

In one of the most florid passages of his massive biography of Manning, E. S. Purcell speculated on how ephemeral Manning's reputation would have been, in the eyes of posterity, had he become Archbishop of Canterbury rather than Archbishop of Westminster. For all his gifts, he could never have exercised at the head of the Anglican hierarchy an influence of European dimensions.[1] His meteoric rise to the succession at Westminster, coming at such a time of crisis in the fortunes of the Roman Church, opened up for a man designed by nature to exult in the exercise of his capacities for ecclesiastical statesmanship a unique opportunity to make an enduring contribution to the history of Western Christendom. One had to go back three hundred years, to the days of the Counter-Reformation, for the last General Council, held at Trent; and nearly a hundred more years would pass before anything like what happened in 1870 was to be seen again.

That Pius IX would somehow create the opportunity to gather the Church together in council was always a likelihood. On three occasions in the 1860s he had summoned large numbers of ecclesiastics to Rome – in 1862, for the canonization of twenty-six missionaries martyred in Japan in 1597; in the summer of 1867 to commemorate the eighteenth centenary of the martyrdom of

Saints Peter and Paul; and yet again, in April 1869, to celebrate his own sacerdotal jubilee, the fiftieth anniversary of his ordination. It was entirely in character that Pio Nono timed these great demonstrations to coincide with moments when his secular fortunes were at their lowest ebb, almost as if to proclaim the solidarity of the Roman communion to those who sought to wrest from him the last vestiges of his Temporal Power.[2] So the greatest assembly of all, the General Council which formally opened on the Feast of the Immaculate Conception (8 December 1869), seemed the ultimate act of defiance to his enemies, because Rome was practically in a state of siege.

These were not empty parades of strength. It is sometimes forgotten that, notwithstanding the dangers confronting the Church from both political and intellectual forces, the Catholic Church, during the nineteenth century, had been growing steadily more powerful, both within and outside Europe; and the prestige of the Papacy had reached a height unparalleled in modern times. Territorially the bounds of the Church had been expanding through vigorous missionary enterprise (from France, in the main), the ubiquity of the Irish emigrants and the creation of new hierarchies, so that the Church of Western Christendom was firmly entrenching itself in the New World, Africa and the antipodes. In Europe itself, the conservative reaction consequent upon the fall of Napoleon had gathered strength as the century progressed. The cult of the Blessed Virgin, so unpalatable to English religious susceptibilities, had ministered to a surge of popular religious fervour, especially in France, rising to a climax with the Papal definition of the dogma of the Immaculate Conception in 1854, so dramatically confirmed in the minds of the faithful by the miraculous events at Lourdes four years later; and where the Marian devotions spread, so also did Ultramontane sympathies.

The central figure of this Catholic revival (almost a form of revivalism) was Pio Nono, whose change of heart from his early liberalism had done nothing to diminish his warmth of personality and irresistible charm. Around him there developed a personality cult unique in the history of the Holy See. The longevity of his pontificate, which eventually exceeded the Petrine years, undoubtedly helped; modern technology, too, because his speeches circulated world-wide and his picture could be displayed in every Catholic household.[3] His dominance over the bishops was partly the result of his long reign – he had, after all, personally appointed a good many of them – and by the time of his death, in 1878, he had witnessed an almost complete replacement of the episcopate.[4] He was lavish with the honours bestowed on faithful servants; and perhaps no Pope since Gregory VII was more conscious of the advantages of using his personal and diplomatic representatives – his legates and nuncios – to exercise direct papal control in individual dioceses, when he saw the need. In consequence, since an unwaveringly Ultramontane heart beat in the breast of the Pope himself, Ultramontanism became unquestionably the most powerful force within the Catholic Church in the decades leading up to the summoning of the first Vatican Council.

Tensions there were in plenty. The issues that divided Catholics in England were reflected even more sharply in the internecine conflicts on the continent. If the triumph of Ultramontanism had led to a weakening of the traditional independence of the French Church, Liberal Catholicism, weakened for a while by Gregory XVI's condemnation of Lamennais in his encyclical *Mirari vos* of 1832, still had powerful adherents. The most notable was Lamennais' former disciple, Montalembert, who had the support of one of the most influential of the French hierarchy, Dupanloup, Bishop of Orléans; and just as the liberal sympathies of the *Rambler* school in England provoked an extreme Ultramontane reaction from W. G. Ward and the *Dublin Review*, so – in France – an even more extreme form of what is sometimes called the New Ultramontanism was represented by the brilliant and implacable polemicist, Louis Veuillot, through the columns of *L'Univers*.

There were primarily two issues at stake in the conflict between the Ultramontanes and the Liberal Catholics in the early 1860s, one political and the other cultural and intellectual. The political issue concerned the relationship between Church and State, and Montalembert proved to be the most forthright spokesman for the Liberal Catholic ideal, at a congress at Malines in the summer of 1863 when he made an impassioned appeal for the disestablishment of the Church, the principles of religious toleration and freedom of the Press, and the union of Catholicism and liberty. He did not help his cause with the Papacy by adopting as his watchwords the hated formula of Cavour, 'a free Church in a free State' ; or by concluding the first of two much-publicized addresses by invoking 'the principles and the liberties proclaimed in '89'.[5] In the same year, in September, at a congress in Munich, the intellectual issue came to the fore. In an equally militant address, Ignaz von Döllinger attacked the inadequacies of Catholic scholarship and its failure to respect the independence of scholars, especially in the fields of historical and scientific research. By the Church's insistence on censorship, Catholicism was being impeded in withstanding the spread of unbelief.

Neither of these positions could the Pope accept. In spite of the efforts of Dupanloup, Montalembert was censured, courteously but firmly; and, in a letter addressed to the Archbishop of Munich (the so-called Munich Brief), Pius IX reasserted the right and duty of ecclesiastical authority to censure any teaching which conflicted with the dogmatic definitions of the Church or the rulings of the Index. In the following year, the encyclical *Quanta cura* was published, to which was appended the notorious document entitled 'The Syllabus of Errors'. *Quanta cura* on its own, despite its condemnatory tone, would perhaps have caused no more of a stir than *Mirari vos* thirty years earlier. The Syllabus was a different matter, however. It was a list of 80 propositions, constituting all the 'chief errors and false doctrines of our most unhappy age' (compiled, it appears, by Cardinal Antonelli)[6] which the Pope had found cause to condemn during the course of his pontificate: a technical document, requiring knowledge of the source and context of each condemnation, issued as a sort of *vade mecum* of errors (not heresies) to assist the episcopate.[7] Like Tract 90 before it, it was a document addressed to one set of people which was read by another. Pio Nono himself admitted that it was 'raw meat, needing to be cooked and seasoned'.[8] But the press had a field day, especially in their derision of the 80th proposition, in which 'progress, liberalism and modern civilization' appeared as the climactic error of the day, thereby giving the impression that the Holy See had plunged back into the Middle Ages. Dupanloup published an explanation designed to remove its sting, but it smacked too much of subtlety and sophistry to convince popular opinion, although Pio Nono accorded it somewhat subdued approval.

Newman, too, was quick to point out that the condemnations referred to specific errors, and should not be interpreted in the abstract.[9] He could not resist observing that 'there is little in [the Syllabus] which, when I was young, the Tory party did not hold, and which I did not hold myself'.[10] He was less happy about the papal reproof of Montalembert and the Munich Brief. Nevertheless, he had anticipated the Pope's objections in one of his University lectures (on 'Christianity and Physical Science'), in which he stated categorically that historical research, when touching upon matters of faith, must be 'subordinate to the magisterial sovereignty of the Theological Tradition and the voice of the Church'.[11] This was a sentiment echoed by Manning on several occasions, and most notably in his statement that 'the triumph of dogma over history . . . really means this: the Church defines its doctrines in spite of you, because it knows its history better than you.'[12] All this sounds very alarmist, but it should be remembered that German biblical criticism, the new critical school of historians, and the researches of Darwin, had caused church-men of all denominations to hold up their hands in horror; and the attitude of the Papacy was little different from the reaction of those who cried 'heresy!' against the contributors to *Essays and Reviews*. Newman, it may be noted, was less shaken than most, mainly because of his conviction that if a scientific discovery appeared to contradict a truth of revelation, all this actually exposed was a limitation in our understanding. In May 1868, he vouchsafed to a worried correspondent that 'Mr Darwin's theory *need* not be atheistical, be it true or not: it may simply be suggesting a larger idea of Divine prescience and skill.'[13]

Manning welcomed the Syllabus. Every exhibition of the su-preme power of the Papacy caused him to rejoice. He did not hesitate to point out in his Pastoral Letter of 1867 that the Syllabus had the authority of an infallible utterance, a line immediately endorsed by W. G. Ward and the *Dublin Review*.[14] In this way the Syllabus, and the ensuing debate about the force of its authority, brought to the forefront the question of the expediency or otherwise of a conciliar definition of the scope or limits of papal infallibility. Pius IX had already demonstrated his own confidence in his divine credentials when he pronounced the dogma of the Immaculate Conception on his sole authority, following consulta-tions with theologians and the episcopate, but without reference to a General Council. Even that seemingly unequivocal claim, however, could be interpreted in two ways, Manning declaring that the Pope's act was 'infallible or nothing',[15] while Ullathorne was anxious to point out that the definition was actually a signal example of the testimony and the will of the whole Church.[16] Therefore, as soon as Pio Nono announced in 1867 that he intended to summon a General Council, it became a virtual certainty that there would be strong pressure to include the infallibility question in the agenda.

Newman, who never personally doubted papal infallibility, but derived it from his prior belief in the infallibility of the Church, was nearer to Ullathorne than to Manning. He tossed the idea about in a series of notes during 1866, expressing his unease about narrowing the seat of infallibility to the Pope alone, without reference to bishops and theologians.[17] If infallibility were to be defined, the role of the Church should be determined first. 'There is very little *theoretical* difference between the *opinions* of the maintainers of the infallibility of the Pope and its deniers. They both hold that he is centre of unity, teacher of the faithful, possessed of universal jurisdiction. They both hold that, when his decision is generally accepted, it binds. The question merely turns on this, *whether* that acceptance is necessary as a *condition* of his decision being accepted as infallible.'[18] He disliked Manning's presumption, in his Pastoral Letter of 1867, that his own extreme views were unassailable, even before a Council had been summoned.[19]

Manning's pen seemed never for a moment idle on the subject during the 1860s. In his *Temporal Mission of the Holy Ghost*, his language became positively rhapsodic. 'Once infallible, always infallible; a truncated infallibility is impossible.'[20]

> The endowments of the body are the prerogatives of its head, who is the centre of the Divine tradition, and the focus of its supernatural illumination ... The accumulation of all the evidence, human and divine, and of all the lights, natural and supernatural, by which the revelation of God is known and declared ... resides by a special endowment in the visible head of the Church on earth.[21]

He devoted three Pastorals to the subject, two before the Council and one just after its conclusion. The apocalyptic note returns again and again, the belief that a time of suffering is to come, but that the Church will triumph in the end.[22] The portents of the coming cataclysm were the rising forces of Caesarism and secularism. That sight of London from Highgate Hill during his retreat – that maelstrom of lost souls, crushed by poverty, forced into crime and sin through deprivation – haunted him for years to come. In 1871 he admitted to Gladstone:

> Of this I am sure as of the motion of the earth. My belief is that faith is

gone from society as such; morals are going; and politics will end in the paralysis of the governing power. The end of this must be anarchy or despotism . . . I have been a fearless Radical all my life; and am not afraid of popular legislation, but legislation without principles is in strict sense anarchy . . . My belief is that Society without Christianity is the Commune . . . What hope can you give me?[23]

Now, we have heard this language before, or something very like it. This was Newman in the early 1830s, raising the cry of 'the Church in danger'. It is a curious role reversal. Newman's answer then, as he viewed with alarm the impending demise of the English confessional State, was Manning's answer in the late 1860s, when he witnessed with equal dismay the same phenomenon in a European dimension. The trumpet, therefore, must not sound an uncertain note. The Church must be seen to stand firm, to be uncompromising for the truth's sake. As Manning put it to Ward: 'Half Truth is our danger.'[24] There were differences of detail; differences, too, in their source of inspiration. Newman looked to the Church of antiquity for his model. Manning looked to the the golden age of the medieval papacy, from Gregory VII ('the greatest ruler the world ever saw')[25] to Boniface VIII. Where Newman would quote the Fathers *in extenso*, Manning would point to the text of the great papal bulls of Innocent III and Boniface VIII, *Novet Ille* and *Unam Sanctam*.[26]

In the events that followed, Newman and Manning found themselves in conflict yet again. Manning was uncompromising, from the moment he took a vow with the Bishop of Ratisbon, when they were together in Rome in 1867, that they would not rest until papal infallibility was defined.[27] Newman was nervous lest the extremists should so effectively carry the day that the eventual definition would divide rather than unite the Church.[28] He had little sympathy with the out-and-out opponents of the Council itself – such as Döllinger, writing under the pseudonym 'Janus' in the Augsburg *Allgemeine Zeitung*,[29] and Acton, sending out vehemently hostile bulletins from Rome under the name of 'Quirinus'. He was even less happy with the extravagant assertions of the extreme publicists on the other side, most notably the Jesuit-controlled *Civiltà Cattolica*. He feared, too, the influence of those whom he described as 'second-rate people' who clustered round the Pope and 'who are not subjects of the supernatural guidance which is his prerogative'.[30] He came more and more to feel that to define so grave a dogma in an atmosphere of haste and emergency was misguided. An issue as important as this should be 'a work of years'.[31] This, at root, was the standpoint of the Inopportunists.

He had his chance of attending the Council as one of the theologian–consultants. The Pope invited him; also Bishop Dupanloup. Then Bishop Brown of Newport, whose opinion of Newman's orthodoxy had been transformed by his reading of *The Dream of Gerontius*, asked him to serve as his personal theologian. Newman refused all three invitations, pleading ill-health. There was also a deeper reason. 'I have never got on intimately with ecclesiastical superiors,' he confessed. 'It arises from shyness, and a sort of nervous continual recollection that I am bound to obey them, which keeps me from being easy with them ... I never could make my presence *felt*.'[32] Manning was rather relieved.[33] He was going to have trouble enough with his own bishops, because only two of them, Cornthwaite (Bishop of Beverley) and Grant of Southwark, shared his uncompromising views.[34] Ullathorne occupied a moderate position, determined if possible to associate the episcopate with any definition of infallibility, if the occasion arose. Clifford was the leading spirit among the opponents of a definition,[35] and Goss, Bishop of Liverpool, was the most outspoken of Manning's critics. 'The Archbishop's position is a thing to be ashamed of,' he declared when he saw Manning at work in Rome. If he had his way, 'the Bishops who went to Rome as princes of the household ... will return like satraps'.[36]

Pius IX, when he came to review the whole proceedings, observed shrewdly that 'a council always passes through three phases. First there is that of the devil; then comes that of men; finally that of God.'[37] Since Manning came to be described by unfriendly critics as the *diabolus concilii* ('the most glorious of titles', was Manning's rejoinder),[38] it may be reasonably assumed that he played a conspicuous part in the first phase of the Council's activities. He did; and he was in his element. Since he virtually appointed himself as Chief Whip of the Infallibilist party, he made himself highly vulnerable to accusations of intrigue. Ferdinand Gregorovius, for instance, who relished gossip and delighted in painting unflattering verbal vignettes, was in Rome at the time and found a perfect field for his gifts. He had already summed up Cardinal Antonelli as having 'a jaw that is thousands of years old, and belongs to the creatures of the mud who devoured, devoured, devoured'.[39] On meeting Manning at a reception given by Baron Arnim, the Prussian minister in Rome, he wrote:

> Clearly observed the fanatic: a little grey man, looking as if encompassed by cobwebs. A certain Count Hahn kissed with mystic reverence the hand which he extended in the manner of an elderly courtesan, accustomed to such acts of homage.[40]

Manning had served his apprenticeship in the highest political circles as an Anglican; and he always felt at home in Rome. Even on his outward journey he was making diplomatic contacts as he passed through France, discussing the possible outcome of the Council with both Guizot and Thiers. He never lost an opportunity to impress his views on a potential waverer, quite scaring Canon Moufang, the theologian accompanying Bishop Ketteler of Mayence, by his apocalyptic vision of an impending cataclysm. It 'made my hair stand on end', Moufang admitted.[41] He soon recognized that interested parties were forming into lobbies; so he set to work to form his own lobby of forty Infallibilist bishops. At a series of private meetings, the last and most decisive being at the Villa Caserta on 23 December 1869, a sufficiently unanimous strategy was agreed upon to make it a virtual certainty that the issue of infallibility would be included in the Council's agenda.

Manning had already been nominated by the Pope as one of the 26 members of the congregation *de postulatis*, empowered to sift through individual petitions for inclusion of matters to be discussed by the Council. His chief concern, however, was to secure election to the crucially important deputation *de fide*, in whose hands the drafting of any resolution on infallibility, if it were to be discussed, would lie. Each country represented at the Council was allowed to put forward a nominee, elected by their number by secret ballot; and to Manning's audible dismay (he sniffed very loudly when the count was taken), the English bishops chose Grant in preference to their Archbishop.[42] Grant's nomination was taken no further, however. When the list of the 24 members of the deputation *de fide* was voted in *en bloc* by the Council, only one Englishman's name (quite properly) was on it – and that was Manning's; the candidate, as he maintained, of the Italian bishops. More to the point, every member of the deputation bar one (the Primate of Hungary – and that was an error, because he was believed to be a stronger Ultramontane than in fact he was)[43] – belonged to the Infallibilist party.

Ullathorne suspected some jiggery-pokery;[44] and Abbot Butler, whose history of the Vatican Council was based primarily on Ullathorne's letters, had little doubt that he was right. 'After going through the proceedings of the entire Council,' Butler wrote, 'I have to say that this appears to me as the one serious blot on its doings.'[45] Where he may have been mistaken, however, was in his claim that Pio Nono himself had expressed the wish that the deputation should be truly representative of all views, even suggesting that Dupanloup, as a known Inopportunist, should be included. The source of this is a letter written by Acton to Döllinger, and both men were guilty of spreading misinformation.[46] F. J. Cwiekowski, the historian who has most recently studied the records, both official and unofficial, of the Council's proceedings, does not exonerate Manning from a degree of intrigue. It appears that at one of the meetings of the forty Infallibilists (their lobby being described as the 'Manningites', as opposed to Dupanloup's rival lobby, the 'Orléanists'), there was indeed a resolution that no one should be elected to the deputation who was opposed to the definition. In this context, Manning was alleged to have said that 'heretics come to a Council to be heard and condemned, not to take part in formulating doctrine'. Cwiekowski adds:

> The blame for this manoeuvre has generally been placed at Manning's door, though the letters from Marmillod, the Auxiliary of Geneva, to Archbishop Dechamps ... suggest that Cardinal de Angelis' [who became President of the Council on the death of Cardinal Reisach] role was perhaps as important as that of Manning in the work of the Villa Caserta committee. If the responsibility for the tactic was not exclusively Manning's, it does fall upon him and the inner circle of 'zelanti' of which he was so enthusiastic a member.[47]

Doubtless he believed that so important an end justified somewhat questionable means. Acton, on the other hand, maintained that tactics of this sort only served to make the contest more bitter; and that, if wiser counsels had prevailed, 'the infallibility would have gone through relatively easily'.[48]

Acton undoubtedly had an axe to grind, and his particular hope was that he could stir up liberal feelings in England to such a pitch of hostility that Gladstone, in concert with other European powers, would intervene by applying sufficient political pressure either to enable the opposition to prevail or, if necessary, to 'torpedo' the whole proceedings.[49] *The Times* correspondent, Tom Mozley (Newman's brother-in-law), happily played his part in circulating any rumours that smacked of scandal or intrigue; and rumours tended to multiply because the formal proceedings within the Council were conducted under vows of secrecy. Ullathorne, without actually breaking these vows, supplied Newman with his own impressions of how matters were developing. In spite of the machinations of the ultra party, he was confident that 'everything will find its level', quoting Pio Nono's personal assurance that 'you will find the Holy Ghost inside the Council, not outside of it'.[50] Newman replied on 28 January 1870, still greatly disturbed by the rumours he had heard.

> When has a definition de fide been a luxury of devotion and not a strong painful necessity? Why should an aggressive insolent faction be allowed to 'make the heart of the just to mourn, whom the Lord hath not made sorrowful'? Why can't we be let alone, when we have pursued peace, and thought no evil?

It was a long letter and a private one, and Newman raised another question towards the end: ought he to make his views public?[51]

Unfortunately, public they became. Ullathorne was indiscreet enough to show Newman's letter to Clifford, who promptly copied it. Errington, too, made a copy on reading it. A further copy fell into the hands of Archbishop Connolly of Halifax (Nova Scotia);[52] and inevitably, in a very short time, the press received a copy as well. Suddenly Newman found that the *Standard* was gleefully informing its readers that the Superior of the Birmingham Oratory had described the Archbishop of Westminster and his fellow-conspirators as an 'aggressive insolent faction'. Ullathorne had made a serious blunder, which Newman then compounded by denying publicly that he had used the words ascribed to him, although not retracting their sentiments.[53] He was now in worse trouble, because the text of the letter could be verified, and he was forced to write again to acknowledge his error, offering as an explanation that his own copy was so rough that he had failed to spot the offending words when he first checked the draft.[54] He tried to shrug it all off. 'I have had too many knocks to care for this,' he wrote somewhat ruefully to Ullathorne.[55]

Manning's services to the cause so dear to his heart were, however, by no means over. He was in a particularly powerful

position to nullify Acton's efforts to obtain government intervention, which was by no means an idle threat. Prince Hohenlohe,
President of the Bavarian Ministry, had made a formal presentation to Gladstone in which he invited England to take the initiative
in bringing together the European powers for united action.[56]
Manning took advantage of the friendship of Odo Russell, which
he had already gained on a previous visit to Rome early in 1869.
They had enjoyed a walk and talk together 'on the Pincio', when
Manning had told him of the depth of his affection and respect
for Gladstone. That he had made a conquest of Russell is clear
from the letter that speedily followed from Russell to his uncle at
the Foreign Office:

> If you have time to cultivate Dr Manning when he returns to London
> ... I feel sure you will like him and find him useful. Austere and
> ascetic as he appears at first sight he can be a most agreeable
> companion and as cheerful as a Roman Monsignore. He is thoroughly
> straightforward, knows what he wants and speaks to the point, and his
> influence on the Pope and his Government as regards the Roman
> Church in England is as real as it is remarkable. None of his Brother
> Bishops have any, so that he is all powerful at the Vatican and at the
> Propaganda, which has not made him over popular with his clergy in
> England.[57]

This friendship paid great dividends. Odo Russell himself was
not above playing a slightly double game (there seemed to be
something in the atmosphere of Rome that compelled all parties
to do so). While he was constantly assuring the Foreign Office that
he was watching over Acton's interests, he was at the same time
regularly supplying Manning with useful information about the
tactics and intrigues of the opposition party.[58] Russell's most
important service, however, was to convince the Foreign Office
that intervention would be fruitless. 'I do not believe the governments of Europe can be persuaded to interfere in unison at
Rome,' he wrote to the Earl of Clarendon in February 1870.
'Single and separate interference would be worse than useless.'[59]
At least he was quite open over his conviction that a definition of
infallibility was inevitable, which Clarendon conceded in a letter
of 30 May. 'The moral of the whole tale', he wrote, 'is that you
have been right from the beginning and have steadily maintained
against all comers that the Pope would have his own way.'[60]
Gladstone had to be satisfied with muttering threats to Manning

that the government would be likely to take its revenge by anti-Roman legislation in England.[61]

Events were moving to a climax. On 25 May 1870 Manning rose to deliver his speech to the General Council. It lasted one hour and fifty minutes. 'Before I got up I was nervous,' he admitted, 'but once up perfectly calm. I saw dear Cardinal de Angelis look in despair at the Cardinals next to him, as if he thought I should never end. But the bishops never moved till I had done.'[62] He began by pointing out that 'Papal Infallibility *is* Catholic doctrine of divine faith, and all are already obliged to hold it . . . It is not an open theological opinion, but a doctrine contained in the divine revelation . . . Does any one of us present here doubt the doctrine? I have not heard any such word.' Perhaps the strongest point that he made was his assessment of the effect of a definition upon Protestant opinion in England. He took the opposite line to Newman, and indeed to some of the American bishops, who thought that it would actually deter potential converts,[63] elaborating on his favourite theme that people, in their hearts, yearn for an authority that will speak with a confident voice. They respect it; and what sickens so many Protestants is the 'confusion and chaos of the innumerable sects, and the lack of any tribunal able to teach with authority'.[64] It was a powerful argument; not one to appeal to liberal intellectuals, of course; but that was never the constituency that Manning felt either responsible to or much sympathy for. In Butler's words, the speech was 'one of the triumphs of Manning's life'.[65] He had used the practised debater's skill of turning an apparent weakness into a strength, and won the day.

Just in time. External pressures were mounting in the early summer of 1870. The very day that Bismarck dispatched the Ems telegram to Napoleon III (13 July), the General Congregation voted on the constitution *Pastor Aeternus*. Napoleon declared war on Prussia two days later. The French garrison withdrew from Rome, which now lay hopelessly vulnerable to the advance of Victor Emmanuel's army from Piedmont. If the infallibility decree had not been brought forward in the agenda, taking precedence over debates on the nature of the authority of the Church, it would never have been promulgated. As it was, hurried last-minute deputations had taken place to find a satisfactory formula to express the relationship of episcopal authority to that of the Holy See, Manning playing a significant part to the very end.

Perhaps Pio Nono was not all that mistaken when he said that the last phase of the Council would be 'that of God'. The final formula defined the infallibility as residing in 'the Roman Pontiff, when he speaks *ex cathedra*, that is, when in discharge of the office of Pastor and Doctor of all Christians, he defines a doctrine regarding faith and morals to be held by the universal Church', such definitions being 'irreformable of themselves, and not from the consent of the Church'.[66] There had been 88 *non-placets* at the General Congregation on 13 July, and most of those who had so voted followed Dupanloup in absenting themselves from the formal Public Session on 18 July, when the final vote registered 533 *placets* to 2 *non-placets* (who withdrew their opposition after the vote). Nature played its part to add drama to the occasion, a violent thunderstorm coinciding with the precise moment that the Pope rose to say the words *'definimus et apostolica auctoritate confirmamus'*, the darkness so intense that a huge taper was brought to him to enable him to read his text. The assembly duly dispersed. Within two months the city was reeling with thunderous explosions yet again, as the Piedmontese cannon bombarded the city gates. It was the signal that Papal Rome had gone for ever; and Pio Nono, with his spiritual sovereignty triumphantly confirmed, was fated to end his days as 'the prisoner in the Vatican'.

V

Pio Nono may have been prodigal in his distribution of honours in the years leading up to the Vatican Council, but he was cautious thereafter, anxious to avoid accusations of favouring those who had worked so loyally on his behalf during the months of in-fighting. Manning, to whom he owed so much, had to wait five years before he received his Cardinal's hat, in March 1875. Their friendship remained intimate to the end, and for the last five weeks of the Pope's life (he died on 7 February 1878), Manning was constantly at his bedside, 'conversing ... only on such thoughts and things as were consoling and cheerful'.[1] The Pope's good humour never deserted him. One day, towards the end, a nun visited him to beg him to autograph her cherished photograph of him. It was a very bad one. He scrawled across the bottom of the photograph 'the words of Our Lord, as He walked upon the waves: "Fear not, it is I"'.[2]

Although Manning was wont to say, in his old age, that the eight happiest years of his life were the early days at St Mary of the Angels, working as a mission priest,[3] the eight most exhilarating months of his life were undoubtedly those spent at Rome between the end of November 1869 and July 1870. Wilfrid Ward recalled visiting the Cardinal in May 1891 to ask him about his memories of the Council. His eyes lit up, as he lived again the sense of triumph when the dearly loved Pio Nono received his 'crown of glory'. As Wilfrid rose to leave, the Cardinal said: 'Come again. It makes me young again to go over these battles of bygone days.'[4]

Perhaps memory had allowed him to believe that it was more of a triumph than it actually was. The principle had been won: infallibility had been defined. But when it came down to the details of the definition, the outcome was less than Manning had really hoped for. No longer could he, or anyone else, talk about *Quanta cura* and the Syllabus as having infallible authority. So circumscribed were the conditions governing an *ex cathedra* infallible pronouncement that Manning was not to see in his lifetime either Pius IX or his successor Leo XIII exercise his divinely confirmed right. That being so, the Infallibilist party had surely rendered the Church a great service by insisting that the time was right for an accepted article of the faith to be the subject of conciliar definition. It put an end, once and for all, to the excesses of Louis Veuillot and W. G. Ward; and if it did not exactly bring peace to an embattled Church, at least it stifled for all time the unedifying faction fights among Catholics which had promoted the polemics and divisions of the 1860s. There were a few sad losses to the Church. Döllinger was one, because he refused to be reconciled. Lord Acton was nearly another, but in the end he declined to follow his old master. Pass a very few years, and prelates of all parties would be standing side by side against the very foe that Manning had predicted would be the shape of Antichrist in their time – Caesarism, as exemplified by Bismarck's persecution of the Catholic Church in the *Kulturkampf*.

Gladstone was in no mood to be conciliatory, however. His relations with Manning were never to be quite the same again. When Manning returned from Rome, he suggested a meeting with Gladstone at the beginning of August. Gladstone agreed, but added in his letter: 'Forgive me if I suggest that perhaps we had better not talk of what has been going on at Rome. Our opinions on the matter are strong on both sides, and are wide as the poles asunder: I am not vain enough to think I can act upon you, and for you to act upon me would tear up the very roots of my being.'[5] Convinced that the infallibility decree had created such a threat of divided allegiance within the State, Gladstone eventually put pen to paper in 1874 in his fierce 'political expostulation' against the Vatican Decrees, accusing the Papacy and the 'myrmidons of the Apostolic chamber'[6] of substituting 'for the proud boast of *semper eadem* a policy of violence and change in faith; when she has refurbished and paraded anew, every rusty tool she was fondly thought to have disused'.[7]

Manning replied at length in the following year, his major objective being to disabuse Gladstone of the notion that the Pope might at any time and at his own whim compel his Catholic subjects to withdraw their allegiance to civil government. 'There is no authority upon earth which can depose a just sovereign or release such subjects from their obedience,' Manning retorted.[8] He allowed that the Pope must regard a Protestant establishment as a 'second best', but 'Pius IX ... tolerates what he cannot cure'. There was therefore nothing to fear from Catholic subjects, who 'will never lend so much as a finger or a vote to overturn by political action the Christianity which still lingers in our public life'.[9] Mgr Thomas Capel, whom Manning had just appointed as Rector of the Catholic University College of Kensington, also joined the fray, using as his major source the exposition of the decree *Pastor Aeternus*, compiled by Joseph Fessler, who had been secretary-general of the Council, and was in the best possible position to explain its technicalities, and to illustrate how, in fact, exceptionally rarely, in the history of the Church, papal infallibility had been exercised.[10]

Sooner or later Newman was bound to be drawn into the controversy. He showed customary reluctance at first, but when at last he agreed to answer Gladstone's charges, in the form of an open letter to the Duke of Norfolk, he produced another masterpiece of careful and courteous apologetic. He made it quite clear that his own acceptance of the decree was unconditional; he dismissed all suggestions of chicanery in the conduct of the Council's business:

> It was an extraordinary gathering, and its possibility, its purpose, and its issue, were alike marvellous ... Only a Pontiff so unfortunate, so revered, so largely loved, so popular even with Protestants, with such a prestige of long sovereignty ... only such a man could have harmon-

ized and guided to the conclusion which he pointed out, an assembly so variously composed.

There followed a slightly ambivalent passage. 'For myself, I did not call it inopportune, for times and seasons are known to God alone, and persecution may be as opportune, though not so pleasant as peace; nor, in accepting as a dogma what I had ever held as a truth, could I be doing violence to any theological view or conclusion of my own.'[11]

It is worth noting that he also perceived a link between the Tractarian horror of Erastianism and the Roman Church's opposition to Caesarism. This 'deadly antagonism' was what had attracted Tractarians to Rome in the first place.[12] As Capel had done, he expounded the arguments of Fessler, who had succeeded in 'reducing what was said to be so monstrous to its true dimension'.[13] Very characteristically, he elevated specific counterarguments into the sphere of general philosophical discussion, most conspicuously in his concept of the sovereignty of Conscience as 'the aboriginal Vicar of Christ, a prophet in its informations, a monarch in its peremptoriness, a priest in its blessings and anathemas',[14] culminating in his personal declaration that in an admittedly impossible situation where he might have to choose between obeying the dictates of conscience or the commands of the Pope, conscience would have to come first, quoting various authorities to affirm that 'He who acts against his conscience loses his soul'.[15] He also returned to the relationship between history and dogma, on which he and Manning held identical views. While not wishing to be disrespectful to the historians whom Gladstone had cited to support his views, Newman observed that 'they seem to me to expect from History more than History can furnish, and to have too little confidence in the Divine promise and Providence as guiding and determining those enunciations'.[16]

Gladstone was not satisfied with Newman's reply, although he welcomed its 'genial and gentle manner'.[17] The vast majority of Catholics applauded it. Some modern critics have tended to admire its rhetoric, while expressing doubts about the validity of Newman's arguments and the unreality of some of his examples.[18] Manning could not have failed to perceive the few not very well disguised brickbats aimed at himself; especially the reference to 'those among us ... who for years past have conducted themselves as if no responsibility attached to wild words and overbearing deeds'.[19] W. G. Ward was dismissive. He took the *Letter to the Duke of Norfolk* as a good instance of his firmly-held belief that men do not change after the age of 45. 'Newman has not changed. He is but a badly tinkered Catholic now.'[20] There were passages in the book that caused offence at Rome. The minimizing tone was still apparent, and Newman's gratuitous comment on 'the Rock of St Peter', which 'on its summit enjoys a pure and serene atmosphere' while 'there is a great deal of Roman *malaria* at the foot of it',[21] was hardly calculated to please. Propaganda approached Manning to express the view that Newman should be required to make certain corrections.

On 9 February 1875, Manning replied to Cardinal Franchi:

> I warmly implore your Eminence to take no public steps as regards Father Newman's pamphlet, for the following reasons: the heart of Father Newman is as straight and Catholic as it ever was. His pamphlet has a most powerful influence over the non-Catholics of this country ... The aforesaid Father has never, up to the present, so openly defended the prerogatives and infallible authority of the Roman Pontiff, though he has always believed and preached this truth.

He agreed that sometimes Newman deviated from accepted modes of expression in writing of dogmatic subjects. Nevertheless, 'I see a grave danger if there should be a shade of public censure ... Under the circumstances, I warmly implore you to leave what is well alone. It is not only the petition of a true friendship and old, but the counsel of prudence.'[22]

This must stand as one of the most generous letters that ever one adversary in what had been a bitter contest could have written about another. In all his correspondence with Newman over the period of their estrangement, Manning had persistently refused to answer coldness with coldness; he had turned a deaf ear to the fulminations of Talbot and the belligerence of W. G. Ward. On this occasion, in a letter that Newman could never have known about, he took the most positive step in his power to restore Newman's reputation at Rome. Reading this letter, one can well understand what Gladstone, so often at variance with Manning, meant when he wrote to him about one of their many differences: 'You need not assure me as to your motives, as one-twentieth of the time I have known you would have sufficed to show how incapable you were of any spiteful act.'[23]

CHAPTER 6

―――――――――――――――――――――――

Indoor and Outdoor Lives

'I have been indoors all my life.' Newman to Ullathorne, 18 August 1887

'To be in the world, and yet dead to it, is the highest reach of faith.' Manning, in a sermon as Archdeacon of Chichester

I

WHEN ROBERT ORNSBY, Professor of Classics at the Irish University at Dublin, heard the news of Manning's appointment as Wiseman's successor, he wrote to Newman to share his thoughts. 'It is not in human nature to forget the comparative obscurity in which a greater name seems to be left all these years. But greatness is of many kinds, and I suppose it is after all uncommon to see the position of a leader of thought united with equally lofty official work.'[1] Newman could never have undertaken the load of responsibility that fell on Manning's shoulders: not for him the care of all the churches. He had made that abundantly clear from his earliest days as a Catholic. Just occasionally, as he grew older, he would ponder over the contrast between his own relatively sheltered life and those compelled to cope daily with the cares and pressures of high office. He observed to Ullathorne, when both men were nearing the end of their days: 'I have been indoors all my life, whilst you have battled for the Church in the world.'[2] So reflecting, he had expressed the essential difference between his own Catholic career and that of Manning.

The distinction is not quite as neat as this. Newman had battled for the Church in the world during his seven unhappy years as Rector of the Irish University. He had his own daily cares in the running of his community and the supervision of some highly volatile elements, especially in the early days. The fortunes and misfortunes of the Oratory School were never far from his mind; and the steady flow of factory-girls and bug-ridden Irish to the confessionals, first in Alcester Street and then in Hagley Road, ensured that his life was not quite as insulated from the realities of an urban ministry as he sometimes appeared to claim. Manning, for his part, swamped as he was with pastoral, administrative and political concerns, had an indoor life as well, which caused Newman on occasions to marvel. 'I cannot understand how the Archbishop manages to put through so much work,' he wrote to T. W. Allies in January 1866. 'I see besides the work on the Blessed Virgin, he is publishing on the reunion of Christendom.'[3] Not that he held any high opinion of Manning's writings. He never even read his *England and Christendom*;[4] and in 1875 he was markedly less appreciative of Manning's reply to Gladstone on the Vatican Decrees than Manning had been of his own. 'For some years', he wrote to a like-minded friend, 'I have wondered how a high ecclesiastic and a theologian could write some sentences which Cardinal Manning has written. The science necessary for a theologian and responsibility weighing upon an ecclesiastical ruler, one should have thought, would have precluded indulgence in rhetoric.'[5] Manning probably wrote too much; and the bulk of what he wrote, especially after his elevation to Westminster, was polemical or hortatory, supporting or explaining items of archiepiscopal policy.

The fact remains, however, that Manning's disposition inclined him, as his office required him, to exercise power in the service of the Church. What mattered to Newman, as has been seen earlier, was influence; and the most eloquent testimony to his success came from Manning himself, generous to the last, when he paid tribute to his brother Cardinal at his Requiem Mass on 20 August 1890. 'No living man has so changed the religious thought of England ... The history of our land will hereafter record the name of John Henry Newman among the greatest of our people, as a confessor for the faith, a great teacher of men, a preacher of justice, of piety, and of compassion.'[6]

Newman's own assessment of his influence was rather more

modest. 'I am a controversialist, not a theologian,' he once assured
W. G. Ward.[7] He slightly qualified this a year later, in a letter to
Pusey. 'I am not a deep theologian,' he said.[8] He was more explicit
to Maria Giberne, in explaining why he would have been out of
his depth at the Vatican Council:

> Really and truly I am *not* a theologian. A theologian is one who has
> mastered theology – who can say how many opinions there are on any
> point, what authors have taken which, and what is the best – who can
> discriminate exactly between proposition and proposition, argument
> and argument ... who can trace the history of doctrines in successive
> centuries ... This is to be a theologian, this and a hundred things
> besides. And this I am not, and never shall be.[9]

One must always be slightly distrustful of Newman's disclaimers.
He had a high respect for the role of theologians, as will be seen,
but at least his own self-analysis – if open to question – was
entirely sincere. He had no taste for metaphysics[10] and derived no
satisfaction from reading theological treatises. 'I gain more from
the life of our Lord in the Gospels than from a treatise *de Deo*,' he
wrote in his introduction to a study of the life of St John
Chrysostom.[11] To someone as sensitive as Newman to the reality
of religious experience, and who nourished so deep a conviction
of his personal relationship with God, theology seemed a dead, an
almost unreal, science. He excepted the writings of the early
Church Fathers, because their words took one back into the ethos
of the age of the saints and martyrs; but theological writing
thereafter smacked too much of the schoolroom. The 'very
perfection' of the science seemed to him to cause 'theologians to
be somewhat wanting in tenderness to concrete humanity'.[12] He
had the same reservations about philosophy. His turn of mind,
Terence Kenny has written, was 'logical, ethical and practical'.[13]
Gladstone would have agreed with this. 'I think Newman is not,
and never was, a philosopher – a philosopher, I mean, in the
sense of Butler,' he wrote. 'He has not the balance of mind, and
his aspects of truth are partial; he is not well settled on a centre of
gravity, his plumb-line is not true.'[14]

Gladstone's reasons may be open to dispute, but Newman
himself would not have questioned his conclusion. He often
philosophized, and sometimes profoundly, but he was as loath to
be considered a philosopher as he was a theologian. It has become
almost a commonplace of Newman criticism to reject J. A.

Froude's astonishing statement that Newman 'had read omnivorously, and studied modern thought in all its forms'.[15] He had never read Descartes;[16] he confessed to an ignorance of Kant,[17] while being at least familiar with his epistemological vocabulary.[18] Undoubtedly his memory was at fault when he declared so emphatically in 1884 that 'he had never read a word of Coleridge',[19] because he quotes from *Aids to Reflection* in his *Grammar of Assent*,[20] and acknowledged, in 1835, that – through the good offices of T. D. Acland – a first reading of Coleridge's works (probably *Biographia Literaria*) caused him to express surprise at 'how much I thought mine, is to be found there'.[21] Something appears to have deterred him from a deeper study of the Sage of Highgate, however. Perhaps he was altogether too Protestant for Newman's taste, perhaps too inclined to heterodoxy.[22] At any rate, it was his 'liberty of speculation' that prompted Newman to deliver a somewhat gratuitous judgement upon him in a famous passage in an essay of 1839, on 'Prospects of the Anglican Church'.[23]

Newman acknowledged few masters. Although he was captivated by the Alexandrian Platonists, his formal teacher from the ancient world was Aristotle. This led to an interesting fusion of forms of thinking derived from the two traditional opposing schools of ancient thought. Some of Newman's deepest insights have distinctly Platonic roots – the notion, for instance, that in the process of development 'old principles reappear under new forms', and that an idea 'changes with them in order to remain the same. In a higher world it is otherwise, but here below to live is to change, and to be perfect is to have changed often.'[24] On the other hand, Newman's method of exposition and argument is unmistakably Aristotelian. He extolled the inductive method in Discourse V of his *Idea of a University*:

> While the world lasts, will Aristotle's doctrine on these matters last, for he is the oracle of nature and of truth. While we are men, we cannot help, to a great extent, being Aristotelians, for the great Master does but analyze the thoughts, feelings, views, and opinions of human kind. He has told us the meaning of our words and ideas, before we were born. In many subject-matters, to think correctly, is to think like Aristotle; and we are his disciples whether we will or no, though we may not know it.[25]

Of thinkers of relatively modern times, Butler was the prime influence upon him; then, perhaps, David Hume. He was at least sufficiently familiar with Hume's writings to attempt to refute his dismissal of the miraculous.[26] For all his misgivings about this 'acute, though most low-minded of speculators',[27] Newman belonged, while retaining his own brand of idiosyncratic discipleship, more to the empiricist tradition associated with Locke, Berkeley and Hume, than to any other school of British philosophy.[28] But whether he was writing on theological or on philosophical subjects (and he never really distinguished between the two), he was always happiest when charting his own route unguided. He admitted that, in the writing of the *Grammar of Assent*, he deliberately refrained from reading other authorities.[29] It is therefore not surprising that, in this work, the thinker whom he most often quotes is himself.

Newman maintained that he was 'not well read in Medieval History'.[30] Again, this is a disclaimer to be taken with a pinch of salt. He was not a medievalist in the sense that Manning was, but – as will be seen – he looked back with longing to the great days of the medieval universities. He was also better read in St Augustine than he was prepared to admit.[31] One of the major themes of Augustine's *City of God* – on the sinful origin of States – had taken a deep hold on his mind. In one of his *Sermons on Subjects of the Day*, he echoes Augustine's famous passage, 'Set justice aside, and what are kingdoms but great bands of brigands?'[32] In a later sermon, an even more forthright denunciation of the unrighteous State occurs:

> Earthly kingdoms are founded, not in justice, but in injustice. They are created by the sword, by robbery, perjury, craft and fraud. There never was a kingdom, except Christ's, which was not conceived and born, nurtured and educated, in sin.[33]

No authority is quoted, but the sentiment (and some of the wording) is identical to Gregory VII's denunciation of the Emperor Henry IV in 1080, which is an elaboration of a passage from Augustine's *De Doctrina Christiana*.[34] Newman would probably be familiar with the text from reading his friend J. W. Bowden's study of Hildebrand. At least two commentators on Augustine's political thought – J. N. Figgis and Christopher Dawson – have seen a link between Augustine's grim judgement on the fallen nature of political communities and Newman's deeply-felt reservations about the argument from Design when, in the *Apologia*, he described his perception of a God-forsaken world, with 'the human race ... implicated in some terrible aboriginal calamity ... Out of joint with the purposes of its Creator'.[35]

Manning would not have quarrelled with this. His own theology was steeped in St Augustine, and he showed greater familiarity than Newman with the whole range of his writings, quoting him more frequently than any other source. His *Unity of the Church* at times reads like a commentary on the *City of God*;[36] his favourite theme of the perpetual mission of the Holy Ghost is supported by passages from Augustine's sermons;[37] he defends papal infallibility by quoting Augustine's writings against the Donatists.[38] There is nothing surprising in this. Although Manning was thoroughly well-versed in patristic writings, his leaning was towards medieval writers and the theologians of the Counter-Reformation. His favourite saint was the fifteenth-century mystic St Catherine of Genoa.[39] The language of the Roman schools was music to his ears, but not so to Newman's. On one of the rare occasions when Newman quoted St Thomas Aquinas, he ascribed to him a passage from St Alphonsus Liguori.[40] Perhaps this was why he was perfectly content to accord to Manning the title of 'theologian' which he denied to himself.[41]

And yet, Newman was a thinker of deep perception and a writer of genius. Manning, for all his gifts, was neither. If Newman was serious in asserting that he was 'not a theologian, nor a philosopher, nor a historian, nor a preacher, nor a poet, at least not in the front rank',[42] what was he? Granted that his chosen designations of 'controversialist' and 'rhetorician' are undeniable, it is equally unchallengeable that he was always thinking or writing about religion. All his conclusions ministered to the advancement of the spiritual perception of religious truths. He himself preferred the adjective 'religious' to 'theological'. 'Theology', he wrote in the *Grammar of Assent*, 'always is notional ... Religion, as being personal, should be real.'[43]

Not a poet? The medium that came most easily to him was actually the poetic, he once observed to R. H. Hutton;[44] but he abandoned the writing of verse in the mid-1830s, returning to it only once again in his life, when he wrote *The Dream of Gerontius* in the early summer of 1865. Perhaps he thought that the very facility of versification was too much of an indulgence, or – as Isaac Williams unkindly suggested – perhaps he was so put out by a hostile review of the *Lyra Apostolica* by Samuel Wilberforce in the *British Critic* that he lost his taste for such employment thereafter.[45] Except for 'The Pillar of the Cloud', which became a much-loved hymn, it is doubtful whether any of his early poems would have survived today but for the fame of their author, and the light that they throw upon his state of mind at a crucial period of his life. They are of a similar genre to Keble's 'hymns' in *The Christian Year*, and – as poetry – neither better nor worse. But the religious poetry of the early nineteenth century, with its stilted diction and its somewhat recondite ecclesiastical imagery, does not improve with age.

The Dream of Gerontius, however, being a work of Newman's mature years, and written in circumstances that Wordsworth would have recognized as one of those 'spots of time' which follow upon strain, exhilaration and anxiety, was of a different order altogether. Newman had consulted his doctor over some disturbing symptoms of paralysis, which had forced him to think about death and the hereafter. He had emerged triumphant but exhausted from his conflict with Kingsley. He wrote *The Dream* rapidly, under some irresistible compulsion. 'The whole work', Roger Sharrock has written, 'is an extraordinary feat. Colourless, pure, austere, it exhibits more daring in its metrical and sound effects than most of Newman's verse.'[46] Quite apart from the matchless achievement of finding words to express the inexpressible and to convey with such sensitivity the concept of timelessness and spacelessness, the poem reveals a softening of the customary severity with which Newman had hitherto treated the subject of the Four Last Things. His conviction of the reality of eternal punishment never weakened, but the prevailing note of Gerontius' ordeal is merciful and loving; and Gerontius himself is no saint. He is 'Everyman as believer'.[47] 'A man like us', at least in Elgar's understanding, so for his part he avoided 'church tunes and rubbish', preferring to give him a setting of 'good, healthy, full-blooded, romantic, remembered worldliness'.[48] Purgatory is depicted by Newman as a place of purification rather than of punishment. Gerontius is enfolded in the 'loving arms' of the Angel and borne 'o'er the penal waters'.[49] As Geoffrey Rowell has observed, Newman had moved closer to Manning, who derived the purifying as opposed to punitive image of Purgatory from St Catherine of Genoa, and further away from the fire image so distastefully congenial to Faber.[50] *The Dream*, solitary excursion as it was for the Catholic Newman to express his religious thought in poetic form, is a flawless masterpiece. If he had written nothing else, it earns him a place in the history of literature.

Not a historian? It was Charles Lloyd who directed Newman to the study of history. He sent him to Mosheim's *De Rebus Christianis ante Constantinum*, and thence to the sources of early church history: the works of Eusebius, Socrates, Sozonam and Theodoret.[51] He sensed an apt pupil, and the consequences proved him right. The Fathers may have turned Newman into a Catholic; but, more immediately, they turned him into a historian. He learnt then, and never forgot thereafter, that theology and ecclesiastical history should never be divorced.

> It is difficult justly to estimate the injury done to our whole view of Gospel truth by our ignorance of ecclesiastical history [he wrote in an article in 1841]. Every department of theology acts upon the rest, and if one is neglected the others suffer. Our view of doctrine affects our view of history, and our view of history our view of doctrine.[52]

Almost all the gifts necessary to the accomplished historian, Newman possessed: the determination to go back, wherever possible, to the original sources; an instinctive response to the *genius loci* of historical sites; the gift of empathy, of entering into the feelings and minds of those whom he studied so that they became figures of flesh and blood to him – so much so that, as Henri Bremond observed, this became almost a process of self-identification. He 'has himself in view whenever he represents to us the heroes of his choice ... He describes himself in them, because he finds in them either what he is, what he wants to be, or what he is on the point of becoming'.[53]

Bremond was inclined to take his observations just that little bit too far, but there is some truth in this. As with most men, Newman suffered from the defects of his own virtues, and empathy sometimes resulted in loss of detachment. He had an intensely powerful imagination, carrying him away into the realms of rhetorical hyperbole, especially when describing the darker corners of human history. His lectures on the history of the Turks, admittedly not his most thoroughly-researched piece of work ('trash' was his subsequent description of them),[54] made no attempt to conceal his extreme contempt for their 'foulness of life, ... the unutterable deeds which brand the people ... as the most flagitious, the most detestable of nations'.[55] When Newman had the opportunity to describe the grisly and the macabre, he seemed to seize it with relish. In his one historical novel, *Callista*, he gave his imagination free rein: the evocations of the hideousness of corruption and pestilence following the plague of locusts, the ghastly description of the crucifixion of a live baby by Gurta the sorceress, and the lurid details of the instruments of torture exhibited to the unfortunate Callista before her trial[56] – all convey a horror that haunts the mind.

In the company of the best historians, Newman had the gift of inspired provocative generalization. 'England surely is the paradise of little men, and the purgatory of great ones.'[57] 'Many a man will live and die upon a dogma; no man will be a martyr for a conclusion.'[58] 'The catastrophe of a State is according to its antecedents; and its destiny according to its nature.'[59] Sometimes he flirted with danger in elevating such statements into general historical laws, most conspicuously in his *History of the Turks*: 'Empires are sudden manifestations of power which are as short-lived as they are sudden.'[60] But he qualified his most sweeping statements with the reflection that 'I am but attempting to set down general rules, to which there may be exceptions, explicable or not'.[61]

Two limitations are exhibited in his historical writings. In the first place, because of a tendency to see the present reflected in the past, he was forever searching for analogies, and thereby used the facts of history highly selectively.[62] Second, he firmly believed that the role of history must be subordinate to dogma. For Newman it was always better to believe too much than too little. Miracles should not be rejected 'where there is a fair chance of their being true'.[63] In Tract 45, written in 1834, he argued that men should abide by 'the principle of being content with a little light, when we cannot obtain sunshine. If it is probably pleasing to the Church, let us maintain it.'[64] So, in the *Essay on Development*: 'to be just able to doubt is no warrant for disbelief.'[65] Twenty years later, in the *Grammar of Assent*, he reiterated the conviction: 'Of the two, I would rather have to maintain that we ought to begin with believing everything that is offered to our acceptance, than that it is our duty to doubt of everything.'[66] It was therefore 'safest to hold the stricter side'.[67] Not surprisingly, he deplored the damage to Christian belief that a liberal historian like H. H. Milman could inflict by touching 'the human element without handling also the divine . . . What will be our Christianity? . . . We shall all be unbelievers before we at all suspect where we are.'[68]

This is important in assessing two of Newman's major works: the *Essay on Development* and the *Idea of a University*. The *Essay* was not, at least in Newman's own estimation, a theological work. It was essentially an 'appeal to history', because Christianity was a historical fact.[69] Nevertheless, his historical method was open to question, in that he assumed the truth of what he was going to prove before he set out to prove it. C. F. Harrold has commented: 'Newman always approaches history with his mind made up and solidly established on principles which, for him, throw light on everything and are indeed truer and more real than historical facts.'[70] While the *Idea of a University* was not, of course, a series of historical lectures, nevertheless Newman's inspiration for his blueprint was rooted in the past. Here again, Newman's mind seemed to have been made up before he had given any serious consideration to the needs of the youth of Ireland. Even more curious, when he knew that the Pope's wish was to model the Irish university on Louvain, it never appeared to occur to him to cross over to Belgium to visit the great Catholic university, or even to ask for a copy of its constitution.[71] What purpose could this have served, Newman seems to have thought, if he knew already what he wanted?

What he wanted was in part a throw-back; in part a stopping of the clock at exactly the time he was writing. This is not to say that his vision, so exquisitely drawn, and his ideas, so elegantly presented, were valueless. No one would dispute that many of his insights have a timeless quality. But, at root, the picture that he displayed was based on three leading ideals. The first was something that Oxford had once stood for, in its structure and in its ethos, which should never be lost; and it is this Oxford basis that most critics of the *Idea* have fastened upon, mainly on the ground that what Newman was upholding as an ideal was really an anachronism at the time he was delivering his lectures. Manning, for instance, when Archdeacon of Chichester, had expressed grave reservations about the narrowness and parochialism of the Oxford curriculum, years before Newman put pen to paper.[72] Probably because he lived an outdoor life, in contrast to Newman's more sheltered existence at Birmingham, Manning perceived the fatal consequences to England's national prosperity if educationists failed to take note of the response of Germany and other continental countries to the challenges of modern times. 'Though our great productive supremacy has in time past been attained without systematic instruction,' he wrote, many years later, 'we can hardly hope to retain it in competition with foreign countries which are more systematically instructing their youth in the principles and practices of arts and manufacture. It is of absolute necessity that we should keep pace with them in this also.'[73]

The second ideal was Newman's noble proclamation of the Coleridgean concept of knowledge as a circle – that all the separate disciplines interlock and interrelate, and that therefore there is always something higher and beyond any particular field of study, 'a sort of science distinct from them all, and in some sense a science of sciences'.[74] The world has indeed had to pay a heavy price for the inevitable proliferation of new branches of research and the intensification of specialization. It needs reminding of this timeless truth, even though the age of the polymath has passed. Newman's third ideal follows on from the second. Within this circle of knowledge, theology has a role. No one could seriously quarrel with the syllogism that Newman advanced to prove this at the beginning of his second discourse.[75] What is more questionable is the predominance that he gave to theology. This was not just to appease Archbishop Cullen and the Irish hierarchy, nor part of the operation of transplanting Oxford on Dublin soil.

Newman here was calling history to witness; he was looking back 700 years to the great days of the medieval universities, as he made very clear in Discourse V of the original edition of his Dublin lectures, in a passage frequently quoted but rarely given in full. He was pointing an accusatory finger at London University for its separation of 'religion and secular knowledge', thereby treating a university as if it were

> a sort of bazaar, or pantechnicon, in which wares of all kinds are heaped together for sale in stalls independent of each other ... The majestic vision of the Middle Age, which grew steadily to perfection in the course of centuries, the University of Paris, or Bologna, or Oxford, has almost gone out in night. A philosophical comprehensiveness, an orderly expansiveness, an elastic constructiveness, men have lost them, and cannot make out why. This is why: because they have lost the idea of unity; because they cut off the head of a living thing, and think it is perfect, all but the head.[76]

This medieval ideal became almost an obsession with Newman. Following upon this lecture came a whole series of articles from his pen on the history of the rise of the great universities, which form the contents of the third volume of his *Historical Sketches*. What especially fascinated him was the role of the 'schola' of theologians, and the freedom of speculation they enjoyed at the University of Paris, for instance, at its height, in sad contrast to religious thinkers of his own day, forced to work under 'the Persian lash' of Propaganda. Lying behind his concept of the unity of disciplines, with theology as the centre of the circle, was a sort of nostalgia for a golden age, described most fully in a letter to one of his original professors at Dublin in 1863. 'Why is it that the Medieval Schools were so vigorous? because they were allowed free and fair play ... Truth is wrought out by many minds, working together freely.'[77] Fourteen years later he was to develop this idea more fully in his highly significant preface to the revised edition of his *Via Media*. It is a revealing example of how Newman's study of history proved to be the basis of so much of his religious thought, and how much his religious thought coloured his interpretation of history.

II

Not a theologian nor a philosopher? Some words of Professor J. M. Cameron are relevant here.

> Newman had the least compartmentalized of minds. We are as likely to find a remark on epistemology or on the relations between reason and feeling in one of the *Tracts for the Times* or in one of the *Parochial Sermons* as in a work such as the *University Sermons* which is mainly concerned with the philosophy of religion. It is as though he felt his intellectual problems like a passion, so that they forced their way to the surface no matter what the ostensible topic of discourse.[1]

Newman's preoccupation with the problem of religious certitude dated back to his first reading of Butler and subsequent discussions with his Oriel colleagues, Froude, Robert Wilberforce and Blanco White.[2] Apart from his *University Sermons*, most of his publications, whether books or articles, were written in response to a specific challenge. They were *livres de circonstance*. The *Grammar of Assent*, written during the late 1860s, appears to have been the sole exception, although the spur to its composition came from a private challenge in the course of a long correspondence with the distinguished naval architect William Froude, a younger brother of Hurrell, dating from January 1860. At any rate, Newman saw the opportunity to elaborate what he conceived to be his major contribution to the philosophy of religion. As early as 1853 he had declared that 'if I have brought out one truth in any thing I have written, I consider it to be the *importance of antecedent probability* in conviction. It is how you convert factory girls as well as philosophers.'[3]

The *Grammar of Assent* sets out to show how this can be. Apart from adopting a new epistemological vocabulary, which presents difficulties in the initial stages of the book, Newman had anticipated most of his arguments and conclusions in his University Sermons at Oxford. The one clear exception is the term 'the illative sense', which Newman employed to describe the faculty of 'right judgment in ratiocination':[4] the means by which a person is enabled by some sort of 'unconscious dialectic'[5] to grasp a truth by no obvious logical process, though not necessarily in defiance of reason. It is indisputable that, according to one's natural make-up and experience, this person or that appears to be endowed with a 'genius', for want of a better expression, which enables a Napoleon to assess the tactical situation on a battlefield without being able to explain it, or a peasant to forecast the weather with accuracy without knowing either why or how.

Furthermore, it is equally indisputable that all the logic in the world will not convince another person if he is not disposed to be convinced. That being so, if people actually accept or reject evidence according to the state of their hearts,[6] the determining factor must be the antecedent assumptions of the believer or unbeliever, or his 'elementary convictions of the mind', as J. B. Mozley put it in his review of Newman's book.[7] Only this can satisfactorily explain why one man may utterly reject a proof which seems logically unassailable, while another will be prepared to live and die for a belief that seems logically absurd. The reception of argument depends in fact on 'the fundamental mode of looking at things which exists in the mind of the reasoner'.[8] Butler's teaching on probability clearly influenced Newman's reasoning here; also the Aristotelian concept of 'phronesis', the word which Aristotle employed to describe the quality which enables us to make right judgements in matters of conduct, which is now translated by Newman into the sphere of epistemology.[9]

He was bravely tackling a genuine difficulty. The faith of a factory girl who cannot account for it must be as valid, or certain, as that of a scholarly theologian. Nevertheless, Newman's arguments laid him open to the charge of subjectivism. 'Conclusions' are arrived at, he wrote, 'not *ex opere operato*, by a scientific necessity independent of ourselves, – but by the action of our own minds, by our own individual perception of the truth in question, under a sense of duty to those conclusions and with an intellectual conscientiousness.'[10] This would suggest that there are no objective truths and that logically 'we should be constrained to give up absolutes altogether'.[11] On the other hand, Newman waged a lifelong war against private judgement in matters of doctrine and revelation. In the *Idea of a University*, he wrote that the error of Protestantism was to suppose that 'religion was based, not on argument, but on taste and sentiment, that nothing was objective, every thing subjective, in doctrine'.[12] His answer to the charge that he was being equally subjective was to point to the role of Conscience. Conscience is – to Newman – 'the safeguard against self-will'.[13] This presupposes, however, that conscience will prove to be a guarantee of orthodoxy, because 'it is the same God which each knows' and because conformity to conscience will reveal that all roads lead to Rome.[14] As H. L. Weatherby puts it: 'In Newman's view, once a person so directed encounters the Catholic Church, he cannot resist recognizing there is an echo of the same voice whose echo he has heard also in his own heart.' He discovers that 'the proof of the pudding is in the eating'.[15]

How far would Manning have subscribed to this? His own writings suggest that he followed Newman at least part of the way. In an essay on 'Ultramontanism and Christianity' he employed Butler's arguments on the weight that should be attached to the accumulation of probabilities, and also acknowledged that all his arguments for the credibility of Ultramontanism would cut no ice with those who refused to accept his original assumptions.[16] He was also at one with Newman in declaring that truth could never contradict itself and, consequently, 'every assertion contrary to the revealed verity of faith is necessarily and absolutely false'.[17] Where he felt most unease was when Newman exposed himself to the charge of scepticism by depreciating the power of reason to establish the certainty of the existence of God, of Christianity and the truth of the Catholic faith. He could never accept Newman's admission that 'reason could not reach complete certitude' and that therefore, as one recent commentator has put it, 'the actual act of assent is a leap across a logical gulf' which could only be bridged by a personal act of will.[18] Manning never wrote on the subject of epistemology. In his own work of straight apologetic – his *Religio Viatoris* – the arguments are simply and starkly marshalled in strict logical sequence to prove by reason and the moral sense the four crucial verities – the existence of God, the fact of revelation, the historical certainty that Christianity was what had been revealed, and the inevitability of recognizing that 'historical Christianity is the Catholic Faith'.[19]

Stephen Dessain has written: 'It seems to be generally agreed that the two most strikingly original contributions made by Newman to Christian thought are his theory of certainty based on the illative sense and his theory of the development of doctrine.'[20] It is interesting to reflect that while the Jesuits at Rome thought very little of Newman's *Essay on Development*, Manning strongly approved of it. Cardinal Gasquet assured Joseph Bacchus of the Birmingham Oratory that he recalled Manning speaking of the *Essay* 'in terms of the highest praise and agreement'. He considered it 'Newman's greatest and most important work'.[21] How innovative it actually was is a matter of dispute. Ian Ker has put it on a par with Darwin, describing it as 'the theological counterpart of the *Origin of Species* which it predates by over a decade'.[22] It may have struck new ground in English Catholic theology, but an organic concept of the Church was nothing new to the theologians of Tübingen. The comparison with Darwin, too, is somewhat facile, because development is only very loosely a synonym of evolution. While evolution can certainly mean development, the converse is not necessarily true. The time process by which truths, long implicit, become explicit has only the most tenuous relationship to Darwin's researches; and – in any case – most commentators have agreed that Newman never believed in progress.[23] A more temperate assessment of Newman's *Essay* has recently been offered by Professor David Brown: 'For Newman,' he writes, 'change is a divinely-given means of bringing the Church to a fuller understanding of the truth, as well as enabling it to adapt to changed circumstances.' The most permanent significance of his work lies 'in the seriousness with which he requires the Church to face the question of history'.[24]

In his later years Newman came to grips with another pertinent question of his times with a calmness of detachment unusual among contemporary churchmen: the issue of Biblical inspiration. Never once did his reverential respect for the authority of the Scriptures weaken, but as the years passed the somewhat naïve literalism of his early Anglican days[25] matured into a more judicious appraisal of the conclusions of sincere and devout critical study. He was never able to accept the role of myth, or indeed the force of it, in the Old Testament (in 1859 he even contemplated writing a treatise to refute such interpretations);[26] but in 1861 his thoughts on the wider issue had developed sufficiently for him to write:

> I consider that I satisfy all that the Church requires of me, if I believe that the Holy Ghost moved the sacred writers to write the books of both Testaments ... and preserved their writings from error ... in faith and morals ... but I consider a Catholic at liberty to hold if he will that their inerrancy does not extend beyond that subject matter.[27]

In any event, he argued that Catholics need never be discountenanced by such works as *Essays and Reviews*, for the simple reason that 'plenary inspiration of Scripture is peculiarly a Protestant question; not a Catholic. We indeed devoutly receive the whole Bible as the Word of God, but we receive it on the authority of the Church, and the Church has defined very little as to the aspects under which it comes from God, and the limits of its inspiration.'[28]

He was therefore privately less than happy at the Vatican Council's decree on the authority of Scripture which went beyond the Tridentine definition by declaring that 'the entire books [of the Bible], with all their parts, are divinely inspired'.[29] He therefore attempted, a little tortuously, to mitigate the seemingly unequivocal strictness of the decree by observing that 'till the Infallible Authority formally interprets a passage of Scripture, there is nothing heretical in advocating a contrary interpretation, provided of course there is nothing in the act intrinsically inconsistent with the faith, or the *pietas fidei*'.[30]

Newman was not easily persuaded to abandon a position that he had reached from his own individual study; and perhaps, in the long run, the most significant re-statement of one of his most cherished views on the *magisterium* of the Church came in his elaboration of the function of the prophetical office of the Church in his preface to the revised 1877 edition of the *Via Media*. To the last he boldly distanced himself from the siege mentality of late nineteenth-century Rome:

It is so ordered on high that in our day Holy Church should present just that aspect to my countrymen which is most consonant with their ingrained prejudices against her, most unpromising for their conversion.[31]

The Church, he argued, mirrors the functions of Christ in the three-fold offices of Prophet, Priest and King. She therefore has a regal office (the Pope and the Curia); a priestly office in her devotional and spiritual life, exercised by priesthood and laity; and a prophetical office, which is the prerogative of the theological schools (the *Schola Theologorum*); and it is primarily the prophetical office's function to regulate the whole, restoring and correcting 'such extravagances as have been committed, through human infirmity, in the exercise of the regal and sacerdotal powers'.[32] Newman's final word – for this preface was effectively his last publication of major significance – was both a warning and a prophecy. The warning was to remind his generation that religion is never 'in greater danger than when, in consequence of national or international troubles, the Schools of theology have been broken up and ceased to be'. The prophecy was that, in the course of time, the seeming excesses of the present would find their proper level. Theology would, in time, prove itself to be what it has ever been – 'the fundamental and regulating principle of the whole Church system'.[33] The passage of time preserves balance, because 'veracity, like other virtues, lies in a mean'.[34] So spoke most truly the disciple of Aristotle. But Newman would always be Newman right to the end. No Persian lash for him. He would not be silent when he had something important to proclaim.

There is not only a 'time to keep silence', but 'a time to speak' . . . In some states of society, such as our own, it is the worst charity . . . not to speak out, not to suffer to be spoken out, all that there is to say.[35]

III

In 1879, T. W. Allies suggested to Newman, shortly after he had been elevated to the Cardinalate, that it would be appropriate to send the Pope, Leo XIII, a gift of his complete published works. Newman begged to differ. 'I have no confidence that what I have written is worth much', he replied.[1] Far back in 1836 he had told his friend Hurrell Froude that 'you and Keble are the philosophers and I the rhetorician'.[2] He never really changed his mind. First and foremost he was an apologist; by nature and by circumstance, a 'controversialist'.[3] Henry Tristram has put that claim in its proper perspective. All Newman's writings 'fall into place', he wrote, 'as parts of a magnificent *Summa Apologetica*. Whatever lack of system there may be, is more than counter-balanced by the fact that they are informed by a spirit more precious than system, and that spirit the quintessence of their author's personality.'[4]

'Personality' is the key word. Style is the man. While Newman had a total command of the whole range of the rhetorical arts, all the sophisticated technique in the world cannot succeed in creat-ing the quality of enchantment whereby a writer conveys in his prose the sense of warmth, sincerity and charm – those most seductive of attributes – which casts the spell of his personality upon a reader, who responds almost unconsciously to the call of heart speaking to heart. This was Newman's supreme gift. The most elusive quality of Newman's prose was its tone: a combina-tion, as John Holloway has described it, of 'ingratiating modesty' with a sure confidence which compels the sympathy of the reader by the constant biographical touches.[5] A competent writer, however, can hardly fail to reveal his personality in his style. Newman explained this in one of his University lectures:

> We might as well say that one man's shadow is another's as that the style of a really gifted mind can belong to any but himself. It follows him about *as* a shadow. His thought and feeling are personal, and so his language is personal. Thought and speech are inseparable from each other.[6]

This is amply illustrated in the contrast between the writings of Newman and Manning. As their personalities differed, so did their style. Newman was a talented violinist, Manning was prac-tically tone-deaf. Newman's prose, at its best, seems to breathe (R. W. Church observed) 'a curious delicate music',[7] while Man-ning's writings lack a sensitivity to cadence in their sentence structure and to euphony in his choice of words. This is not to say that Manning was not an effective communicator. He was infin-itely more effective than Newman on a public platform, partly because of his complete confidence, born of his Oxford Union days, in extempore delivery. Newman, in such a situation, was out of his depth. On one occasion, at St Edmund's, when obliged to make an impromptu speech of thanks in acknowledgement of an address of support during the Achilli libel action, he began: 'There once was a king . . .', and could say no more. He covered his face with his hands and left the room.[8] The skill of the polished debater was often exhibited by Manning in his writings on controversial matters, especially his ability to marshal arguments lucidly and cogently. In his *Dublin Review* article of July 1863 on 'The Work and Wants of the Catholic Church in England', the pros and cons of Catholics being allowed to attend Oxford and Cambridge are analysed with scrupulous fairness, and the reader is left in no doubt as to the grounds of Manning's own conclusions, even if he should disagree with them.[9] He employed the same technique in discussing the case for and against the opportunism of defining Papal Infallibility at the Vatican Council, realizing that advocacy is always more effective when the case for the opposite point of view has been fairly and fully stated.[10] The style is the portrayal of a man at the heart of affairs – business-like, clear-headed, judicious.

Of course he knew a trick or two, as Newman did; as all accomplished rhetoricians do. G. W. E. Russell rightly observed that Manning's 'pointed and lucid style gave to his printed performances a semblance of cogency which they did not really possess'.[11] When faced with a weak case, he was inclined to trumpet his riposte or to resort to 'stately periods and . . . polished sarcasm', as R. W. Church described Manning's reply to Pusey's pamphlet on *Essays and Reviews*.[12] Newman, when he felt vulnerable, would adopt a taunting tone, most evident in his lectures on *The Difficulties of Anglicans*, thrusting the image of the 'mere beggar-woman' as opposed to 'the State's pattern man' down the throats of his critics, and drawing clever but questionable comparisons. 'Not till the State is blamed for not making saints, may it fairly be laid to the fault of the Church that she cannot invent a steam-engine or construct a tariff.'[13] He would sometimes resort to the oldest trick in the book – by seeming to make his weakest points his strongest, exemplified in the very first of the *Tracts for the Times*. Not all his clerical readers would accept the possession of the Apostolic Succession with quite the confidence in Newman's statement that 'of course, we shall come to the Apostles at last. We know we do, as a plain historical fact.'[14] F. D. Maurice took him to task, in his review of the *Essay on Development*, for bypassing an uncomfortable issue in his statement that 'Lutheranism, as is well known, has by this time become simple heresy or infidelity'. 'This fact is not well known', was Maurice's blunt comment.[15]

If Newman does not exactly concede that two wrongs make a right, he employs the device of the *tu quoque* argument times without number, and most frequently in the *Apologia*. If Catholics have to submit to the Church's rulings in keeping silence on certain matters bearing on religion, have not 'Protestant Churchmen . . . before now obeyed the royal command to abstain from certain theological questions?'[16] If St Alphonsus taught that in certain circumstances it was permissible to tell a lie, did not Jeremy Taylor, Milton, Paley and Johnson distinctly say the same thing?[17] If John Henry Newman can be accused of 'sapping the very foundations of historic truth', what about Grote and Thirlwall?[18] Although Newman protested, in the *Grammar of Assent*, that 'I do not want to be converted by a smart syllogism',[19] this did not deter him from employing the device when he thought it might score a point. 'To follow truth can never be a subject for regret', he wrote in Tract 85. 'Free enquiry does lead a man to regret the days of his childlike faith; therefore it is not following truth.'[20] William Robbins points out that Newman's cruel syllogism directed against his brother Francis ('St Paul bids us avoid those who cause division; you cause division; therefore I must avoid you') is 'a rhetorical flourish . . . open to the *tu quoque* retort'.[21]

One prerequisite of the accomplished rhetorician is the ability to adapt one's style and language to the audience that one is addressing, and also to modulate the tone in accordance with the theme. Both Newman and Manning were sensitively aware of this. Newman suffered agonies of apprehension over his Dublin lectures, not so much because he was uncertain about what he wanted to say, as because he was unsure how most effectively to address an audience of total strangers. Wilfrid Ward believed that the only occasion when Newman failed to produce a work capable of stirring his readers was in his *History of the Arians*, for the simple reason that he had no clear idea, in the writing of it, of the audience he was aiming at.[22] Thereafter, he never missed his mark. When preaching to an Anglican congregation, he assumed exactly the right tone of *gravitas* and chose a diction of extreme simplicity; when he became a Catholic he adapted quickly to the more florid style that his hearers expected. When appealing to a popular audience to hold to merited derision the prejudices of the uninformed, he employed his satirical gifts to devastating effect, most notably in his *Lectures on the Present Position of Catholics*. When replying to Pusey, or to Gladstone, the tone is courteous, measured and restrained.

Manning, too, learnt this lesson very quickly. Some of his most effective writing – always reverent and simple, without any affectation of eloquence – can be seen in his devotional works, such as *The Eternal Priesthood, Sin and its Consequences*, and *The Love of Jesus to Penitents*. When called upon to address an audience of manufacturers at the Mechanics' Institute at Leeds, he did not talk down to them, but was careful to intersperse what must have seemed a very radical message with plenty of homely allusions. He made it quite clear that he was entirely familiar with the various skills required in the processes of cloth-making, for instance.[23] But when his social conscience was afire and he wanted to rouse, he could rise to the heights of eloquence. When he made his great plea to society to show compassion for the 'worthless' among them, he put aside all restraint:

> If, then, the worthless are what they are because the society of today has wrecked them, what is society doing, or willing to do, to redeem and save the worthless? None are so bad that there is not still a hope ... Human sympathy, kind care, personal service, patient goodwill, are policies which never fail. If, through fault of ours, however remotely or indirectly, by commission or omission, they are outcasts, let us now begin and try to bring them back to what once they were. The memory of their childhood is not dead within them; and if it be only a gleam of innocence long lost, it is also a throb of a higher life not yet extinct for ever.[24]

Manning's writings lack the charm and urbanity of Newman's. His letters, perhaps, can stand comparison. 'Even his shortest notes', G. W. E. Russell remarked, 'were exquisite in wording as in penmanship.'[25] In his prose writing, however, he could be very repetitive, and he had one or two little quirks – such as his liking for the ugly Hebraic phrase 'jot or tittle' – which jar in the ear.[26] It should be remembered, however, that whereas Newman drafted and redrafted his published works ('ten or fifteen times' over, with certain passages in the *Grammar of Assent*),[27] Manning lived the bulk of his life out of doors. Wilfrid Meynell expressed amazement at the actual quality of his output, written in such circumstances. 'I think he hardly ever rewrote a sentence in his life ...

He permitted himself no luxury of second thoughts.'[28]

The essence of effective apologetic is the conquest of one's readers through the engendering of sympathy both for the cause defended and for the apologist himself; and this requires more than just the manipulation of arguments by skilful rhetorical techniques. The more seductive the actual writing the more compelling the message, and the more irresistible the spell cast by the writer. This is where Newman excelled. He creates by the tone of his writing a frame of mind in his reader that will guarantee him a sympathetic hearing whatever cause he is choosing to defend. His literary style was recognized in his own lifetime as on a par with the greatest of nineteenth-century prose writers. In April 1869, *The Times* linked his name with those of De Quincey and Macaulay. On reading this, Newman was hard put to it to explain where he had acquired the skill.

> I never have been in the practice since I was a boy of attempting to write well, or to form an elegant style. I think I never have written for writing's sake; but my one and single desire and aim has been to do what is so difficult – viz., to express clearly and exactly my meaning . . . The only master of style I have ever had is Cicero.[29]

He was more forthcoming in one of his University lectures. He trained himself by imitation.

> When I was fourteen or fifteen, I imitated Addison; when I was seventeen, I wrote in the style of Johnson; about the same time I fell in with the twelfth volume of Gibbon, and my ears rang with the cadence of his sentences, and I dreamed of it for a night or two. Then I began to write an analysis of Thucydides in Gibbon's style.[30]

He learnt precision from Cicero, the flow and cadence of sentence structure from Gibbon; as for vocabulary, there can be little doubt that his intimate knowledge, from daily reading, of the Authorized Version left the deepest impression upon him. 'Except for a few semi-technical terms,' F. L. Cross has written, 'the whole of Newman's vocabulary is to be found in the Bible.'[31] Add to these his gifts from birth of a musical ear and a strong poetic sense, and a master prose-writer, combining exactitude with emotive power, was in the making. A perfect sentence, Matthew Arnold once observed, is one that passes the test of 'inevitability';[32] that is to say, the choice of words and their sequence are so patently right that, were one to change a single syllable, the magic would be lost. In the *Essay on Development*, the following passage occurs:

> One aspect of Revelation must not be allowed to exclude or to obscure another; and Christianity is dogmatical, devotional, practical all at once; it is esoteric and exoteric; it is indulgent and strict; it is light and dark; it is love, and it is fear.[33]

The effect of this sentence is heightened by the sensitive manipulation of the contrasts; not only the actual antitheses to illustrate his point, but also the contrast between the polysyllabic adjectives and the final sequence of fourteen consecutive monosyllables, falling on to the perfectly balanced phrase 'it is love, and it is fear'. A similar passage occurs later in the same book, falling on to the monosyllables 'It was Grace, and it was Truth'.[34]

Newman was well aware of the power of monosyllables in achieving a fitting climax. The Roman Church, he wrote, in his *Difficulties felt by Anglicans*, 'cannot help being strong, she cannot help being beautiful; it is her gift.'[35] The most perfect sequence of all is found in a climactic passage in the *Apologia*: three sentences of varying length, ranging from 18 words (including 15 monosyllables), via a highly complex but beautifully structured sentence of 67 words, to the four-word monosyllabic climax:

> All the logic in the world would not have made me move faster towards Rome than I did; as well might you say that I have arrived at the end of my journey, because I see the village church before me, as venture to assert that the miles, over which my soul had to pass before it got to Rome, could be annihilated, even though I had been in possession of some far clearer view than I then had, that Rome was my ultimate destination. Great acts take time.[36]

On two occasions in *Loss and Gain*, Newman breaks off his narrative, both to heighten the drama and to secure the sympathy of the reader for Charles Reding's agonizings over abandoning the Church of his baptism. To achieve the pathetic appeal, he uses two devices. The first is to become personal, by a direct appeal from the narrator to the heart of the reader; the second is to employ the enchanting effect of consecutive monosyllables at the close of each passage. 'Let us be patient with him, as his Master is patient, and bear that he should do a work slowly which he will do well.'[37] Then again, later: 'But we must indulge him, if, doing so great a work, he likes to do it in his own way; nor must we be hard on him, though it be not the best way.'[38]

There are times when the music of a sentence by Newman becomes sheer poetry. Towards the end of a short and pithy tract (Tract 3) on the somewhat unexciting subject of 'Alterations in the Liturgy', he betrays the identity of the anonymous author by this exquisite passage: 'Be practical, I respectfully urge you; do not attempt impossibilities.' Then follows the poetic line: 'Sail not as if in pleasure boats upon a troubled sea.'[39] In a famous passage in the *Idea of a University*, Newman laments: 'Alas, what are we doing all through life ... but unlearning the world's poetry, and attaining to its prose.'[40] He is writing figuratively, of course. But there are times when his prose translates easily into poetry; and some of his poetry achieves the dramatic effect of his prose-writing by the translation of a favourite technique. So, in the *Dream of Gerontius*, the pathos of some dim recollection by Gerontius of the moment of his actual death is conveyed by a combination of alliteration and the use of dominant mono-syllables:

> I had a dream. Yes, some one softly said
> 'He's gone', and then a sigh went round the room.[41]

Newman had the felicitous gift of rendering abstract ideas so much easier to grasp by his use of concrete images. This was frequently achieved by either analogies or metaphors. His most characteristic entrée into a picturesque analogy – the individuality of a man's shadow to demonstrate the personal quality of style, the distant spectacle of the village church to describe the last stages of his soul's journey to Rome – were the words 'As well might we say ... ' (or some such variation). In the *Lectures on Justification*, for instance, Newman argues that it is unmeaning to speak of 'living faith as being independent of newness of mind'. An analogy follows: 'As well might it be said that an arm or a foot can exist out of the body, and that man is born with only certain portions, head or heart, and that the rest accrues afterwards, as that faith comes first and gives birth to other graces.'[42] In a lecture on 'Christianity and Physical Science', Newman states that 'Theology and Physics cannot touch each other ... As well may musical truths be said to interfere with the doctrines of architectural science.'[43] So often does he use this construction,[44] that Henri Bremond unconsciously parodies Newman, when writing of his *Essay on Miracles*: 'As well might it be said of an invalid that he is partial to pills, of a penitent that he loves his punishment.'[45]

Coleridge, in *Aids to Reflection*, writes: 'Analogies are used in aid of conviction: metaphors, as means of illustration.'[46] The bounding-line between the two, however, can actually be very thin. Newman doubtless learnt the power of metaphor from his study of Aeschylus, whose writings he commended to his sister Jemima. 'You may feed on metaphors . . . for days together, since Aeschylus very seldom speaks without a metaphor.'[47] Nature metaphors had a special appeal to him. There are frequent sea-pictures, like the 'giant ocean' which 'snaps the cable of the smaller craft' occupied by Anglican divines. 'One vessel alone can ride these waves: it is the boat of Peter, the ark of God.'[48] In the *Lectures on Justification*, 'true faith' is depicted as something 'colourless, like air or water'.[49] He was particularly attached to the figure of the 'stream' and its source. 'In morals, as in physics, the stream cannot rise higher than its source', he wrote in one of his letters on 'The Tamworth Reading Room'. He then elucidated, consciously or unconsciously echoing the words of Lady Macbeth: 'Christianity raises men from earth, for it comes from heaven; but human morality creeps, struts, or frets upon the earth's level, without wings to rise.'[50] He repeats the metaphor in the second of his lectures on the *Present Position of Catholics*: 'The stream cannot rise higher than its source: if the well spring of the tradition is human, not divine, what profits its fidelity?'[51] The phrase occurs yet again in an essay on Biblical Inspiration in 1861.[52]

The Lady Macbeth passage quoted above ('creeps, struts or frets') illustrates another feature of Newman's style: his delight in qualifying statements by a series of words in parallel, each supplying some slight difference of nuance in meaning. In one of his earliest offerings, on 'Poetry, with reference to Aristotle's *Politics*', he describes how a writer 'selects, combines, refines, colours – in fact, poetizes'.[53] Sometimes these precise, parallel distinctions take the form of consecutive phrases. Writing of the frustration of Anglican High Churchmen, he depicts them observing their Church with 'ritual mutilated, sacraments defective, precedents inconsistent, articles equivocal, canons obsolete, courts Protestant, and synods suspended'.[54] The finest example of this, however, comes in Discourse IV of the *Idea of a University*: a whole paragraph of the most subtle distinctions and nuances of meaning, conveyed with such exact precision that the reader feels almost humbled by the exposure of his own woolliness of thought and facile use of words. Newman is describing the difference in the apprehension of sights and sounds between men and beasts:

> The intellect of man . . . seizes and unites what the senses present to it: it grasps and forms what need not have been seen or heard except in its constituent parts. It discerns in lines and colours, or in tones, what is beautiful and what is not. It gives them a meaning, and invests them with an idea. It gathers up a succession of notes into the expression of a whole, and calls it a melody; it has a keen sensibility towards angles and curves, lights and shadows, tints and contours. It distinguishes between rule and exception, between accident and design. It assigns phenomena to a general law, qualities to a subject, acts to a principle, and effects to a cause. In a word, it philosophizes.[55]

Equally incisive was Newman's command of epigram. 'When men have nothing to lose, they have nothing to fear.'[56] 'To be stationary is to lose ground, and to repose is to fail.'[57] 'To have recourse to physics to make men religious is like recommending a canonry as a cure for the gout.'[58] 'It is not the way to learn to swim in troubled waters, never to have gone into them.'[59] 'Ten thousand difficulties do not make one doubt.'[60]

This last example shows, however, how cleverly rhetoric can be concealed. It sounds much more convincing than it actually is. By using the term 'ten thousand' to express hypothetical magnitude, Newman diverts attention from the fact that a single difficulty, depending upon its nature, is capable of creating a doubt. As well might one say (to parody Newman) that ten thousand probabilities do not create a certainty. This is the device of graphic hyperbole which Newman employed time and time again. 'Doubtless Mr Simeon is ten thousand times more attractive than I.'[61] 'There is but one Atonement, there are ten thousand justifications.'[62] 'I have ten thousand claims upon me, urging me to stay where I am .'[63]

How well did Newman know himself? No better or worse than other men of complete integrity, is the probable answer. One piece of self-analysis, however, seems incontestable. His greatest service to his Church was as an apologist. Sometimes the very seductiveness of his prose defeated itself. To those, like Matthew Arnold and Walter Pater, who saw in Newman the very quintessence of good taste – everything that Philistinism was not – the beautiful sensitivity of his prose seemed to bear no acceptable relation to his uncongenial conclusions. Disciples they became – up to a point. As David Delaura has written, 'Arnold and Pater became the most influential advocates of an historic humanist consciousness, while at the same time rejecting the theological and metaphysical underpinnings of that heritage.'[64] This is the price that a consummate rhetorician may have to pay: unstinted admiration for his technique, with uneasy doubts about the motives of his seduction. It would nevertheless be true to say that no one of his day – perhaps no one since his day – has so signally succeeded in gaining for the causes dear to his heart, and for Roman Catholics above all, such goodwill, sympathy and understanding where there had been, before he brought his pen to their service, only ignorance, prejudice and an indifference not far short of contempt.

IV

An indoor life or an outdoor life: Manning really had no choice in the matter once he became Archbishop of Westminster. Not that he would have hesitated at all either in recognizing what suited his disposition better or in declaring which was the greater obligation upon a Christian. In the 1840s he had preached three sermons on the subject. In one, he had compared the ministry of John the Baptist with that of Christ. 'John lived out of the world, and Our Lord lived in it', he said. He lived in it 'for the sake of others'.[1] This did not mean, however, becoming worldly. 'To be in the world, and yet dead to it, is the highest reach of faith', he had declared in an earlier sermon.[2] In the last of the three on the same topic, he elaborated further on the two different aspects of the Christian life. 'A bishop ruling in the church . . . the saint in his closet . . . are serving their Father in heaven.' But, he added, 'a life of devotion does not mean a life of separation from active duties, but the discharge of all offices, high or low . . . in a devout spirit.'[3]

High office for Manning meant not only returning, although in a different capacity, to the world of ecclesiastical politics at the national level in which he had just been beginning to make his mark as a rising hope for the future in his latter days as an Anglican; it also inevitably involved renewing contact with certain former friends and associates whom he had thought, on becoming a Catholic, he had left for ever. One such was Gladstone, who, when Manning became Archbishop, was Chancellor of the Exchequer in Palmerston's second cabinet and destined within three years to form a ministry of his own. The first political issue which was bound to involve a resumption of relations between them was the notorious 'Irish Question' – how to redress the political and social grievances of that unhappy country? For the whole of his archiepiscopate, the possible and practical answers to this question were exercising Manning's mind; so too with Gladstone, for whom the resolution of Ireland's problems became the major preoccupation of the remainder of his political career. That the Archbishop of Westminster should take a lead in the conduct of Irish affairs was actually no part of Manning's inheritance. Wiseman had largely ignored them. 'He was a Tory without Irish sympathies, though himself an Irishman', Manning observed to Gladstone.[4] As a result, the Irish hierarchy had regarded him with distrust. Newman's lack of concern over Irish problems is equally surprising, in view of the number of visits he had paid to Dublin. He reckoned that, by the end of 1857, he had crossed the Irish Sea 54 times;[5] Manning, on the other hand, visited Ireland only once, to preach in Dublin in 1853.

Within months of his succession Manning announced his change of policy to Archbishop Cullen. There was between them, he said, 'such an identity of principles that we need only a fuller and more personal knowledge of each other to renew the union which once partially existed'.[6] He declared his readiness to use his personal influence with Gladstone, whenever possible, to assist with Irish grievances, on behalf of the hierarchy, and he began by extending an invitation to the Irish MPs to his Tuesday evening receptions at Archbishop House. He had chosen to fish in very troubled waters, as he was soon to realize. The essence of the Irish problem has been expressed memorably by G. M. Young:

> The Irish difficulty went deeper than the philosophy of the age could reach. The twin cell of English life, the squire administering what everybody recognizes as law and the parson preaching what everybody acknowledges to be religion, had no meaning in a country where the squire was usually an invader and the parson always a heretic.[7]

How to unscramble the complexities and injustices of centuries of history, then, admitted of no easy answer. The injustices were real enough, but so were the vested interests, and hopes of a calm and judicious appraisal of the country's needs were continually frustrated by the growing strength of those in Ireland who could see no hope of redress except by violent means. This movement, known as Fenianism, was a thorn in the flesh to both government and the Church. The problem for the government was to decide which should come first – coercion or concession, or perhaps both simultaneously; the problem for the Church was that, while conceding that their grievances were in the main entirely just, it could not condone the violence of malcontents. Cullen saw his duty as plain. Fenianism must be condemned, although he admitted privately to Manning that 'until something effectual shall be done for the country, it will be impossible to put down Fenianism or to establish order'.[8] To be one with Cullen, Manning had to adopt the same stance, and did so at a public meeting in Birmingham in 1867 when he made his widely-reported assertion: 'Show me an Irish Catholic who has lost his Faith, and I will show you a Fenian.'[9] He would tell the story that, on his return journey by train from Birmingham, he found himself sharing a compartment with an Anglican bishop who had just been handed a Fenian circular by one of his clergy. Shaking with rage, the bishop had said: 'Depend upon it, Manning is at the bottom of it', and vowed to wreak vengeance of some sort when he arrived in London. A solemn voice from the opposite corner interrupted his tirade. 'If you will give me that I will see that it is not given out at any Catholic church in the future; I am Manning.' At the next stop, he was left to continue his journey alone.[10] The story smacks of the anecdotal rather than reality, but at least there was this much truth in it. Manning felt keenly for the Fenians themselves, if he dissociated himself from their outrages. He had already said in public, at a previous meeting:

> No greater self-deception could we practice upon ourselves than to imagine that Fenianism is the folly of a few apprentices and shop-boys. Fenianism could not have survived for a year if it were not sustained by the traditional and just discontent . . . This feeling is to be found . . . amongst those who are in immediate contact with the land question . . . These are neither apprentices nor shop-boys, neither are they a handful, but a population in close kindred and living sympathy with millions who have tested the civil and religious equality, and are thriving under the laws of the United States.[11]

So what could he do? He could warn Gladstone, and duly did so. Republicanism, he said, 'is invading even the clergy, and if it establishes itself in the pastors you will have lost the people'.[12] He tried to fulfil his promise to Cullen to use his influence in high political circles, with an unfortunate sequel on his first attempt.

He succeeded in making the short period of Disraeli's minority government (at the beginning of 1868) even shorter, by venturing to advise him that he would be unopposed if he went ahead with his plans to make a gesture of concession to the Roman Church in Ireland by granting a charter to the Catholic University, albeit without any endowment. The measure was defeated in Parliament, and Disraeli found himself out of office, maintaining thereafter that Manning had 'stabbed him in the back'.

This was not the last occasion when a government fell in its attempts to regularize the position of the hapless Catholic University. Gladstone was ill-advised enough to make his Irish University Bill of March 1873 a vote of confidence, only to find that, in the end, the Irish MPs voted against him. There was no disguising Gladstone's bitterness in his letter to Manning. 'Your Irish brethren have received in the late vote of Parliament the most extravagant compliment ever paid them. *They* have destroyed the measure; which otherwise was safe enough.'[13] The received judgement has inclined to blame Manning again for this miscalculation on Gladstone's part. Edward Norman, while agreeing that in the earlier episode with Disraeli Manning 'gave assurances when he should not have done so because they had no foundation in the opinions of others',[14] exonerates him from misleading Gladstone. 'It is true', he writes, 'that after the collapse of the Bill, Manning and Gladstone ceased to communicate, but probably this did not relate to the Bill – as Manning had frankly admitted to Gladstone all along that the Irish bishops were going to be difficult – but to the publication in 1874 of Gladstone's *Vatican Decrees*.'[15]

The first significant service that Manning rendered to Ireland was the role he played in helping to secure the Disestablishment of the Irish Anglican Church. Cullen had made it clear that this was the first crucial measure to be achieved, and Manning needed no persuasion. Even before he became a Catholic he had told Samuel Wilberforce that the days of the Irish Establishment were numbered.[16] Accordingly, in March 1868 he published, in the form of a 'Letter to Earl Grey', an all-embracing indictment of the injustices inflicted upon Ireland. 'To our own hurt,' he wrote, 'we have made the English name hateful in the past, and we must bear the penalty till we have repaired the wrong.'[17] He enumerated the grievances to be rectified. There had, first of all, to be religious equality; second, the infamous land laws, which gave the tenants no protection against arbitrary raising of rents, no compensation for eviction, and no recognition of any improvements they had made to their holdings, called for immediate reform. When he touched upon the vexed question of Ireland being allowed to have its own parliament in Dublin, and the stock riposte that this would reduce the country to the status of a colony, he observed very pertinently that 'England treats its colonies, in education as well as in religious equality, better than it treats Ireland.'[18]

Perhaps on the primary issue of Disestablishment, as far as Gladstone was concerned, Manning was preaching to the converted. Fenian threats and pressure had convinced him of the urgency for action. The ticklish question of the transference of endowments was effectively decided by the Irish hierarchy, who refused to accept any form of state pensions or government gifts. When the Disestablishment Act received the Royal Assent on 26 July 1869, Manning heralded the event as 'the greatest act of the Legislature towards Ireland in our history'.[19] He had doubtless been aware that his 'Letter to Earl Grey' had supplied many of the arguments actually used in the parliamentary debate;[20] and Gladstone was unreservedly grateful to him. He wrote to Manning to acknowledge 'with what an accurate eye you have measured the situation . . . I am much indebted to you on behalf of the Govt. for the firm, constant, and discriminating support which you have afforded to our Bill during the arduous conflict now happily concluded.'[21]

Manning was determined that the matter should not rest there, however. The next objective must be the reform of the land laws – the achievement of the so-called 'Three Fs': Fair rents, Fixity of tenure, and Free sale. Gladstone had already turned his attention to this, and his first efforts bore fruit in his Land Act of 1870, which at least introduced protection against indiscriminate eviction. 'The circuitous road is really the only one practicable,' he explained to Manning, 'and is to be much preferred to scaling and descending precipices.'[22] Its concessionary effect was lessened, however, by an accompanying Coercion Bill; and when Manning pressed Gladstone not to be satisfied with half-measures, he received a rebuff. 'We might as well propose the repeal of the Union,' Gladstone replied.[23]

But Home Rule, of some complexion, was soon to be on the agenda. On this Manning and Gladstone rarely saw eye to eye. Manning had been much influenced by his reading of Isaac Butt's

Land Tenure in Ireland, which advocated a form of 'dominion self-government', but not total separation; and his letters to Gladstone in the early 1870s suggest that he was more sympathetic to the Home Rule movement than either the Prime Minister or his ecclesiastical colleagues.[24] Cullen was opposed to any suggestion of separation; so, indeed, was Newman. 'I have long thought that the Irish would gain Home Rule in some shape,' Newman wrote in 1881, '. . . but I am no advocate for such issue, rather it seems to me a blow on the power of England as great as it is retributive.'[25] Gladstone's views, as is well known, changed in the early 1880s, and possibly his resumption of reasonably cordial relations with Manning in 1885 signified his wish to carry the Cardinal with him.

Manning responded to Gladstone's olive-branch at once. 'Fifty-five years are a long reach of life in which to remember each other,' he wrote. 'We have twice been parted, but as the path declines, as you say, it narrows, and I am glad that we are again nearing each other as we near the end.'[26] His own view on concessions was more in harmony with Joseph Chamberlain's than with Gladstone's – a measure of self-government in Ireland while retaining Irish representation in the English parliament.[27] Gladstone, however, was now committed to a separate parliament in Dublin. On 8 April 1886, Manning was present in the gallery of the House of Commons to hear Gladstone's famous three-and-a-half-hour speech, and to witness his defeat by 30 votes. Ironically, only a year later Manning came round to Gladstone's way of thinking. He wrote to a friend in America, 'the time is come when Ireland shall be handed over to itself. Its people have attained their majority.'[28]

To many of his fellow Catholics, even to his once-devoted disciple Herbert Vaughan, Manning's friendship with Michael Davitt, the ex-Fenian recently released from jail, and with Charles Stuart Parnell, branded him as a dangerous Radical, especially when he befriended the Land League, founded in 1879. His stand was a consistent one, however. He would never support violence, or the 'boycotting' of those who acquired property from an evicted tenant, but – equally – he could never back the government line of coercion. Gladstone rectified the omissions of his 1870 Land Act when, in 1881, he at last granted the 'Three Fs', but yet again, what he gave with his left hand, he seemed to take away with his right, by continuing the policy of coercion. The atmosphere was becoming potentially explosive in the early 1880s; Parnell, Davitt and others had been imprisoned; then, in 1882, came the murder of Lord Frederick Cavendish and the Irish Under-Secretary in Phoenix Park (by extremists disowned by Parnell): a policy of appeasement became increasingly difficult to sustain.

In such an atmosphere the succession to the Archbishopric of Dublin in 1885 became something of a *cause célèbre.* Cullen had supported government policy; so had his successor, Archbishop McCabe. On McCabe's death in that year, the nationalist party were unanimous in their hopes that he would be succeeded by the President of Maynooth, Dr W. J. Walsh, whom they knew to be sympathetic to their cause. The government, on the other hand, was equally determined to secure a successor who would be seen to distance himself from nationalist fervour. Lord Granville therefore commissioned a Liberal Home-Ruler MP, Sir George Errington, to put diplomatic pressure on Leo XIII to nominate a successor who would support government policy. The situation provoked the first of three significant interventions by Manning, all designed to prevent the fomentation of nationalist indignation to fever pitch. Through his friendship with Sir Charles Dilke, and then in negotiation with the new Tory Viceroy of Ireland, Lord Caernarvon, he was able to frustrate the intentions of the 'Errington Mission'.[29] He then wrote personally to the Pope to explain the dangerous consequences in Ireland if Walsh were not to be appointed. Leo XIII took his advice.

Manning's second intervention was to attempt to forestall efforts to persuade the Pope to issue a direct papal condemnation of the Land League and the nationalist movement. As early as 1881 Gladstone had hoped that the Pope might achieve what the policy of coercion seemed unable to effect. He even wrote to Newman to enlist his support, only to receive a courteous disclaimer. 'I think you overrate the Pope's power in political and social matters,' Newman replied. 'It is absolute in questions of theology, but not so in practical matters.'[30] The Duke of Norfolk then lent a hand. He was fiercely antagonistic to Manning's sympathy for the nationalists, and thought he saw a way of severely limiting the Cardinal's authority and freedom of action. His plan was to open negotiations at Rome for the restoration of official diplomatic relations with the Holy See, in the expectation that the establishment of a papal nunciature in England would nullify Manning's influence at the Vatican. The Pope's response was to defer decision over the nunciature, but to dispatch a commission to Ireland, lead by Mgr Persico, to report on allegations that the Irish clergy were actively encouraging agrarian crime and violence.

It so happened that Persico was a long-standing friend of Manning, and he took his part (and also that of Archbishop Walsh) on the two most significant points. He emphatically endorsed Manning's view that the establishment of a papal nunciature was unnecessary and undesirable, and he satisfied himself that the Irish hierarchy were adopting a neutral stance over militant nationalism. It therefore came as much as a surprise to Persico as it did to Manning that Leo XIII chose not to wait until Persico's report had been submitted before issuing a condemnation of boycotting and the so-called Plan of Campaign. Manning again intervened, and succeeded in persuading the Pope to tone down his condemnation, and to admit that the extent of his inhibition had been misunderstood and misrepresented. This was duly publicised by Manning in the press.[31]

All along he had remained faithful to his pledge to Cullen that he would act as Ireland's champion. Some friendships suffered strain, as a result, and some old animosities were exacerbated. Michael Davitt turned his back on him, suspecting – quite wrongly – that Manning had played a part in obtaining the Pope's inhibition; estrangement from Parnell inevitably followed from Manning's conviction that he should renounce the leadership of the Irish parliamentary group after the scandal of his divorce. The most touching testimony to the depth of his personal feelings, however, has been given by Canon Arthur Ryan, who visited Manning at Archbishop House, shortly after the imprisonment of Parnell and others in 1881:

> When dinner was over and the visit to the Blessed Sacrament, the Cardinal drew me into the corridor and said: 'Oh, I fear every link of affection between the two countries is broken.' 'Yes,' I said, 'all but one.' 'What one is that?' said the Cardinal. 'Our love for you,' said I. I shall never forget how he looked me through when he answered: 'Do you mean that?' I said: 'You are the last man in England to whom I would say that if I did not believe it to be true.' And the dear old man burst into tears. After a bit, almost under his breath: 'It is what I have prayed for, it is what I have prayed for.' I don't think many men have seen Manning cry.[32]

V

Newman had prophesied correctly when he told R. W. Church and Frederic Rogers that Manning's first priorities would be the education of the poor and the training of the clergy. Within two weeks of his consecration Manning issued his first Pastoral Letter, in which he launched an appeal for help 'to gather in from the streets of this great wilderness of men the tens of thousands of poor Catholic children who are without instruction or training. It is our first appeal to you. But it will not be our last.'[1] He was true to his word. A year later, in his 1866 Pastoral, issued on the first anniversary of his consecration, he announced his establishment of a Central Diocesan Fund to finance parochial and mission schools, reformatories and orphanages. Catholic children were also to be reclaimed from workhouses, where such teaching as they received was exclusively Protestant. Within a year he had raised nearly £8,000 in his diocese and could report the opening of twenty new day schools. It was a beginning. With the help of T. W. Allies as Secretary of the Poor School Committee and Lord Howard of Glossop as chairman of a 'Crisis Fund', accommodation was eventually provided for 70,000 children, at a cost of £350,000.[2] Some of his bitterest battles were with the Poor Law Guardians; and in his closing years he had to resort to some delicate diplomacy to persuade Dr Barnardo to surrender his Catholic waifs and strays to the tender care of those whom the Doctor regarded as myrmidons of the Man of Sin.

The State, however, was moving too. Partly because of the necessity to 'educate our masters' after the Reform Act of 1867, and partly because of the advance of popular education in Germany, to its great advantage as a foreign competitor, a national system of education had to be devised. The result was the Forster Education Act of 1870, conceived in an atmosphere of intense conflict because of its creation of a Dual System, with the new strictly undenominational Board schools maintained by the rates, on the one hand, and the voluntary schools, on the other, financed by subscription with some assistance from government grants. Immediately the voluntary schools were placed at a direct disadvantage financially – the price they were obliged to pay for maintaining denominational teaching.

Manning was in Rome at the Vatican Council while Forster's Act was being piloted through Parliament, and he was criticized, both at the time and subsequently, for failing to defend the Catholic corner effectively. The Bill 'passed through all its stages', Christopher Howard has written, 'without his taking any step to protect the Catholic schools when vital interests were so closely affected.'[3] This was not true. Manning was in regular touch with Gladstone about the provisions of the Bill, objecting to the powers given to the local boards to set up schools where no voluntary schools existed, and protesting at the short time offered to the respective denominations to forestall such action by establishing schools of their own. Gladstone held out no hope on either count.[4] On the other hand, counsels of prudence and pragmatism seemed to dictate the advisability of accepting a *fait accompli* and co-operating with the local boards. Ullathorne, the most hostile of his episcopal colleagues, needed a deal of persuasion. 'It seems to me', Manning wrote to him, 'that our best course is to co-operate . . . and thereby to obtain a share in the treatment of questions which may affect us. If they should offer to include our clergy in any Boards, I think we ought to accept it.' Ullathorne was still unconvinced. Manning wrote to him again: 'By standing aloof', he said, 'we should be exposed to the danger of their hostility.'[5]

This was settling for second best, and he knew it. In an article in the *Nineteenth Century*, written in December 1882, he conceded the inevitability of a national education system, while steadfastly maintaining that 'Religion without doctrine is like mathematics without axioms, a tri-angle without bases or sides'.[6] When challenged by the Nonconformist R. W. Dale, that denominational teaching was best left to the home, he replied:

> It is now fifty years since I began to work among the poor; and I think I know their state. The home ought to be the best school, but it is not so. A Christian people can only be perpetuated by Christian education; but Christian education is not to be given in the unaided homes of England – no, not even of the rich, or of the middle class, or of the poor.[7]

He was fast becoming disillusioned by the actual workings of the Forster Act. In a pamphlet entitled 'The Future of the Primary Schools', he lamented that the voluntary schools were being forced to run 'an unequal race' against the Board schools, whose teachers were receiving 'salaries double in amount . . . armed with the attraction of costly buildings and ample playgrounds and all that public money can provide'. He concluded: 'We cannot gather grapes of thorns or figs of thistles.'[8]

In 1884 the Voluntary Schools Association was founded, to campaign for a more favourable settlement. In the following year, on the eve of a general election, Joseph Chamberlain announced his scheme for the complete abolition of school fees in all Board schools, with the ominous corollary that if the voluntary schools failed to follow suit they would be compelled to submit to the authority of the local boards. Manning was so outraged at this proposal that he took the unprecedented step of publishing in all the Catholic newspapers an article entitled 'How shall Catholics vote at the coming Parliamentary Election?', which included the key questions that all Catholics should address to their local candidates, with instructions to vote according to the degree of satisfaction afforded by their answers.[9] This prompted a letter from Manning's former Anglican companion on the Committee of the National Society, G. A. Denison, who expressed delight at his boldness in contrast to the 'grievous shortcomings of *our* Episcopate'.[10] The Liberals lost the election, although this may have been more Parnell's doing than Manning's. One bonus accrued, however. Manning had included in his 'questions to candidates' their acquiescence in the setting up of a Royal Commission to review the workings of the Forster Act; and this is precisely what Lord Salisbury did. Manning was invited to become one of the members of the Cross Committee. The majority report, which he signed, recommended that voluntary schools should enjoy parity with the Board schools, and be 'put on the rates'.

He did not live to see this realized. Complete parity was achieved by the Balfour Act of 1902. But in 1891 at least part of what he had worked for was obtained by the payment of a *per capita* grant for children in voluntary schools as compensation for the abolition of school fees. Manning's political expertise, together with the experience, during his long archiepiscopate of twenty-seven years, of constant lobbying of politicians, had taught him the lesson that, whether one is fighting against vested interests on behalf of the underdogs of Ireland, or seeking to advance sectional interests on behalf of one's Catholic flock, it is too much to hope that one will secure all that one sets out to achieve; and that such achievements as are gained must involve a long and arduous struggle. Gladstone knew this only too well himself. For all their differences and estrangements, he saluted

Manning as a fellow fighter, and a worthy one. He had once rebuked Acton for failing to realize that Manning was essentially 'a man of honour'.[11] Reflecting over their long and sometimes stormy relationship, he observed in 1896 that 'from my plane of thought and life, I can only look at him as a man looks at the stars'.[12]

VI

Manning's other educational ventures did not touch the English political scene. They were internal enterprises and both of them ended in either complete or relative failure. His ideal for the secular priesthood was an exalted one. In the first place, he objected to the word 'secular',[1] the long-standing designation for those of the priesthood who worked 'in the world' under the direct authority of the bishop, as opposed to the 'Regulars', members of religious orders and subject to a Rule. His preferred description was the word 'pastoral'. Second, he believed that the Church's health and the effectiveness of its mission depended on a disciplined army of priests (carbon-copies of his own Oblates) who while working in the world, were truly world-rejecting. He had never regarded the priesthood otherwise. In 1843, in a sermon preached at Oxford, he had delivered this warning to aspirants to Holy Orders: 'Truly I can advise no one to choose the pastoral office as one among many professions. It will be found a false coat for the man who loves quiet, or the world, or himself.'[2]

Exactly what this entailed, he elaborated years later in what became his most enduring literary work, *The Eternal Priesthood*. If all men had within them at least the potential to be saints, it must therefore be incumbent upon the priest to set the example of how to aspire to that goal. 'The priest is set *exercere perfectionem*', he wrote; 'that is, to manifest perfection in himself, and to form the souls of men to the same law and likeness. He must needs then be perfect himself.'[3] As an Anglican he had pointed the way. We must yearn to be crucified with Christ.[4] Time and time again he would return to this phrase in his Catholic writings. 'What sign of crucifixion is there in our blameless easy life?' he asked his priests. 'Who now takes as a rule of life the words . . . "with Christ I am nailed to the Cross; and I live, not now I, but Christ liveth in me"?'[5]

It was the ideal that he set for himself: too high an ideal, perhaps, to set for others; and his vision of a network of diocesan seminaries, modelled on the Tridentine prescription, from which would emerge this disciplined army of professionally-trained priests, proved equally unrealistic. In his own diocese, on the site of an old convent in Hammersmith, a new seminary was opened in 1869, and the theological students from St Edmund's, Ware, were duly transferred there. Eight further diocesan seminaries were opened during the course of his archiepiscopate. Few survived after his death; the expense involved was too great for some of the dioceses to shoulder, the numbers seeking training were too few, and the Tridentine pattern was too alien to the English seminary tradition, based on Douai. Under Herbert Vaughan, Manning's successor, even Hammersmith was closed down, and the master-plan was scrapped, to be replaced by the creation of a central seminary at Oscott which Vaughan hoped would become a much-needed centre of Catholic thought.[6]

The much-needed centre of Catholic thought, in Manning's ambitions, would have been a Catholic university on English soil. On 23 November 1875 he returned to Oxford to preach a sermon at the opening of the church of St Aloysius, and he mused aloud on both what might have been and what an ideal future might hold in store. Oxford had been the creation of the Catholic Church; but, following the onslaughts of the Reformation and the ensuing spirit of rationalism, what of today? 'We love it still but . . . the Divine Message has been mutilated and the Divine Method of its delivery has been inverted.' He pointed to the great Catholic universities of Louvain, Quebec, Paris and Lille. There 'the Catholic Church is laying down the foundations of universities on the same lines and base as that of Oxford in its glory, and with the same conditions of perfection and of permanence'.[7]

The Catholic University College at Kensington, which had opened that January, was of humbler pretensions. It was the first-fruit of discussions at the Fourth Provincial Synod of Westminster in the summer of 1873, when the bishops – after sifting through questionnaires addressed to a wide representation of Catholic opinion – responded to Propaganda's wish that urgent steps should be taken for the provision of Catholic higher education. They had proposed the formation of a federation of Catholic colleges, the nucleus of which would be a College of Higher Studies in London, situated in Kensington. The students would be prepared in a wide range of subjects with a view to taking London University degrees. A ruling body – the Academic Senate – would oversee the appointment of examiners and the award of prizes, and, in due course, perform the same function for such future colleges as would be established as part of the federation. This was not Paris or Lille, but it was better than nothing; and at least it was a start. Newman feared the worst. As early as 1865 he had suspected that Manning would, in his own good time, invite his co-operation in providing a substitute for the older universities. In that event, he told Richard Simpson, 'I should not undertake it – and have by anticipation thrown cold water upon any overtures that way. It would be a case of hot chestnuts – and chestnuts of his own heating.'[8]

To that resolve he firmly adhered. When invited to become a member of the Senate, he was one of only two of some fifty distinguished Catholics, clerical and lay, to decline. He wrote to Manning on 24 November 1873:

> I have read the Prospectus which you sent me with great and careful interest; and I hope that their Lordships and yourself will not deem it a presumption in me to say, that I feel an unsurmountable difficulty in giving my name to it. I hope they will so far throw themselves into my history and life-long opinions as to understand, that I could not without a great inconsistency take part in an institution which formally and 'especially' recognizes the London University, a body which has been the beginning, and source, and symbol of all the Liberalism existing in the educated classes for the last forty years.[9]

Newman had delivered snubs before to those in high places, and Manning had had his fair share of them; but in the past they had harmed no one but Newman himself. This, however, was a serious setback to Manning's hopes. Although the excuse given appeared somewhat feeble, leaving the impression of small-mindedness, a sort of calculated *quid pro quo* for the thwarting of his own Oxford plans, Newman's stand had a justification; perhaps even a sound one. The more that the attempt by Catholics to 'go it alone' over plans for a university came to naught, the more likely it was that the Church would in time concede that there was no practicable alternative to waiving their inhibition on Catholics going to Oxford or Cambridge (which it did, at last, in 1895). This may seem a little cynical; those who suffered were the parents who were determined to support

Manning, and their sons who went to Kensington (Wilfrid Ward was one) with high hopes that they would be well served by the experience.

The excellent credentials of the distinguished professorial staff should have guaranteed this; but there were other forces at work to doom the venture to failure. The most powerful was the Society of Jesus. Father Purbrick, Rector of Stonyhurst, had opposed the scheme from the beginning. The Jesuits had plans of their own to set up a college of higher studies at Richmond, and they asserted their traditional rights to supply the needs of Catholic higher education. On the advice of Father Alfred Weld, the Society's English Assistant, who was determined to challenge the bishops' Kensington scheme at Rome, pressure was put on the other religious orders to follow their example by refusing to supply the new College with youths from their own schools.[10] This proved a crippling blow, because the College could never acquire a sufficient number of students to pay the high salaries of the staff engaged. Practically everything went wrong thereafter. Mgr Thomas Capel, able man though he was, proved a disaster as Rector. He had private plans of his own to raise funds to found a Catholic public school; the financial situation, always precarious, soon became desperate, and Manning paid out £4,000 of his own money to try to stave off insolvency. Capel was a poor administrator and a lax disciplinarian. There were accusations of heterodoxy against the distinguished Professor of Biology, George Mivart, and damaging talk of immorality, extending even to Capel himself. By 1878 it became clear that Capel would have to go, and to avoid the publicity of litigation, the bishops were obliged to find a further £4,000 to buy him out (Manning again providing the lion's share). Although the College staggered on, in different premises, until amalgamated with St Charles College, Bayswater in 1882, its days were effectively over.

The whole sad venture brought to a head Manning's long-standing feud with the Jesuits. Ullathorne once observed that 'His Eminence was a typical Jesuit' himself, in his determination always to get his own way, and that he was therefore bound to clash with that equally authoritative body.[11] Manning's list of *gravamina* against them grew longer each year of his archiepiscopate. Fundamentally his opposition, as Shane Leslie rightly observed, had an ironical parallel with Errington's dislike and distrust of the Oblates: the Jesuits 'were not amenable to the Archbishop's control'.[12] Whatever they touched, they wanted to take charge of, and whatever they took charge of, they were determined never to abandon. They exercised through their schools the dominant influence in Catholic education, and their education – it seemed to Manning – was aimed, ultimately, at reproducing their own kind. In this way, priests whom Manning sought to draw into the secular clergy were persuaded to become members of the Society. 'A diocese cannot go upon crutches,' he complained to Father Galwey, the Jesuit Provincial, in 1876. '... The English Hierarchy could be helped but could not be made dependent on Religious Orders.'[13] Not only were priests being trained *ab initio* as Jesuit novices, but too many of the secular clergy were being seduced into their ranks. Manning's own private secretary, Canon Morris, succumbed to their blandishments; then one of his own Oblates; and – pouring vinegar into his wounds – his own nephew, William Anderdon, who then proceeded to presume upon his personal relationship by taxing Manning with unfair prejudice against the Society, arising from his misfortune of never having himself had to serve under a Superior.[14] A less worthy cause of complaint against the Society was his suspicion that they were inclined to favour Newman's stance, rather than his own, in the various issues that divided them.

In 1883, Manning poured out his woes to Ullathorne:

> I know there is a *praejudicium* against me, and I will tell you my whole mind. Before I was in the Church all my sympathies were with the Regulars. For the first four years after I was strongly drawn to the Passionists and to the Jesuits. The strong desire for rule and community life took me to Bayswater. But I came to see the divine institution of the Pastoral Office, and that no regular Order can meet this. I saw also that the pastoral clergy were at a disadvantage, depressed and lightly esteemed, but I saw that they were our Lord's own Order ... Regulars have authors, friends, preachers, books, prestige, tradition always working for their elevation. The pastoral clergy has none of these things ... I feel that our humble, hard-working, hard-worked, self-denying, unpretending, self-depressing pastoral clergy need and deserve to be encouraged, cheered, and told of their high and happy state. I confess that my heart is in the midst of them.[15]

This was Manning's most ardent testimony to the virtues of the 'outdoor' life. He erred only in his contention that the secular clergy received inadequate recognition. In the hundred years following the restoration of the hierarchy, all but seven of the 91 bishops were taken from their ranks.[16]

While Manning was smarting with frustration at seeing his efforts to build up his Catholic College at Kensington constantly blocked by the Jesuits, Herbert Vaughan was launching an attack upon the Society which culminated in the whole issue between the episcopate and the Regular clergy being referred to Rome. In 1875, in his diocese of Salford, Vaughan had imposed a restriction upon the number of schools run by the religious orders. The Jesuits defied the ban. Vaughan was so incensed that he went himself to Rome to inform Propaganda that unless he were supported, he would resign his See. He won his case; but the issue was then elevated from the particular to the general. In 1880 Manning, Clifford and Vaughan, together in Rome, made a concerted effort to obtain a permanent resolution of a long-standing conflict; and in 1881 Leo XIII issued the bull *Romanos Pontifices*, pronouncing in favour of the bishops.[17] In future, the religious orders would be obliged to obtain consent from their diocesan bishop (as well as from the Holy See) before establishing churches, religious houses, colleges or schools; and the same permission was required for any alteration in existing institutions.

Manning could not have hoped for more; the religious orders accepted the ruling with good grace; and the response of the episcopate was summed up by an exultant Ullathorne in a letter to Clifford, written immediately after he had heard the news. 'There is nothing left to be desired. The episcopal office is strengthened all through the document, and it gives a complete reply to the objections raised in the Vatican Council, that the infallibility would weaken the episcopate.' He concluded: 'The Birmingham Oratory has been with us through the whole case, and in complete sympathy with us.'[18] So, at least in one particular, in a conflict which Manning put almost on a par with his battle for infallibility at the Vatican Council, Newman and Manning found themselves on the same side.

VII

In the major issues that occupied Manning's attentions at home, seen so far, his score reads something like this: one triumph (over the religious orders) and one failure (his university plans); one partial success (his efforts to secure a satisfactory status for the voluntary schools) and one partial failure (his network of diocesan seminaries). As for Ireland, of no man yet in history can it be said that he was the saviour of that country's ills; but, in his own day, few men could equal Manning's contribution to the redress of Ireland's grievances. The problem of Ireland would never go away. Nor would another problem: that of the poor. They, too, are always with us, a fact that bothers some men more than others. It bothered Manning so much, during his archiepiscopate, that with a glad heart he chose to become a fool for Christ's sake in order to rouse his generation to a consciousness of the grievous nature of their plight.

The Anglican Archdeacon of Chichester lived on in the Catholic Archbishop in this as in other ways. In one of his sermons of the late 1840s, he had pointed to St Paul as the model of that 'boldness to be fools for Christ's sake';[1] his Lavington ministry had persuaded him to speak out for the dignity and the skills of working-men, and to dedicate himself to the alleviation of the miseries of the poor. As Archbishop he was in a position to do more than merely proclaim his priorities. He could now emulate what he had so much admired in George Selwyn, to whom he had dedicated his last volume of Anglican sermons, decribing him as one 'who in an age of softness taught us by living example that the Kingdom of Christ is not in word but in deed'.[2] So it was to be in his work for the labouring-classes, during his archiepiscopate, in which he was to become 'the lonely pioneer of social Catholicism in England'.[3] He had thought much about the problem in the intervening years; partly from his own observations; partly from his admiration for the French social reformer, Frederic Le Play, conceding – after his intervention in the London Dock Strike of 1889 – that 'whatever I may have done ... has been due to the counsels and teaching of my illustrious master, Le Play'.[4] His original manifesto, however, had been delivered in 1874, on the occasion of an address at the Mechanics' Institute in Leeds on 'The Dignity and Rights of Labour'.

'In the dim morning of society,' he said, 'Labour was up and stirring before Capital was awake.' Calling Adam Smith to witness, he asserted that: 'I claim for labour the right of property ... I claim for labour (and the skill which is always acquired by labour) the right of capital. It is capital in the truest sense ... Whatever rights, then, capital possesses, labour possesses.' It therefore followed that 'a labourer has a right to determine for whom he will work and where he will work . . . This carries with it also the right to say whether he can subsist on certain wages.' Labour, then, 'has a right to protect itself'. The indifference and apathy of successive governments in failing to redress the exploitation of labour and to improve the living conditions of the poor were the scandals of their day. 'These things cannot go on; these things ought not to go on . . . No commonwealth can rest on such foundations.'[5]

These were strong words; and if not unique from the lips of a dignitary of the Church (William Thomson, Archbishop of York, was to use similar language in an address in Sheffield in 1878),[6] they were not calculated to raise Manning's esteem in the eyes of many of the governing classes. They sounded suspiciously like Socialism. But Manning was prepared to go further than mere words. He had addressed public meetings at Exeter Hall in 1872 and 1874, in support of Joseph Arch's National Agricultural Labourers' Union. He then contributed to Union funds from his own pocket. He did his best to rouse Gladstone to action:

> Why cannot you do these things for the labourer [he asked]? Prohibit the labour of children under a certain age. Compel payment of wages in money. Regulate the number of dwellings according to the population of parishes. Establish tribunals of arbitration in counties for questions between labour and land.[7]

More controversial, and ultimately more decisive, was the support that he gave to the American organization called the Knights of Labour, which by the 1880s, under the leadership of T. V. Powderley, had expanded to such proportions in the industrial areas of North America and Canada that the Church began to take fright. This was more than a union to protect workers' rights; it was beginning to make radical proposals such as the nationalization of the railways and the mines. In 1886 the Archbishop of Quebec, Cardinal Tascherau, decided to take action. He excommunicated members of what he feared to be a secret society, tainted with Freemasonry, and sought Papal support. Cardinal Gibbons, Archbishop of Baltimore, was vehemently opposed to any official censure, and he enlisted Manning's support to persuade the Holy See to take no action. Manning did not hesitate, and gave expression to his convictions with almost prophetic fervour:

Up to the present [he wrote] the world has been governed by
dynasties; henceforward the Holy See must treat with the people, and
with bishops who are in close daily and personal relations with the
people. The more this is clearly and fully acknowledged, the more
firmly will the exercise of spiritual authority be established . . . This is
the opportunity of the present. The Church is the Mother, Friend,
and Protectress of the People. As our Divine Saviour lived among
persons of the people, so lives His Church.[8]

The point was taken at Rome. Leo XIII refused to condemn the
Knights of Labour and instructed Taschereau to lift the sentence
of excommunication. A crisis which threatened ugly confrontation had been averted, to the profound relief of, among others,
President Cleveland who, with the majority of the American
hierarchy, had been horrified at the prospect of a Papal condemnation.

The whole Western world in the later decades of the nineteenth
century was forced to grapple with the social, political and
economic consequences of industrialization on a hitherto unprecedented scale. Coinciding as it did with a vast extension of the
franchise in many countries, and first attempts to introduce
national systems of education, sooner or later the problems of the
organization of the labour force, the consciousness of the power
that it could wield through combination, and – as a concomitant –
the more confident assertion of workers' rights, had to be faced by
both Church and State. Manning saw the dangers arising from
secular, revolutionary or communist forces taking the initiative in
organizing the labour force; he saw also the advantages if such
movements could be guided and controlled under the aegis of the
Church.

He may have been almost the solitary advocate of social
Catholicism in England (Edward Bagshawe, Bishop of Nottingham, could be equally forthright), but his counterparts were
working for the same aims in Europe and overseas. One such was
Cardinal Moran in Australia. Ketteler, Bishop of Mayence, was
speaking similar language in his efforts to gain direction of a
centre party in Germany; and Cardinal Capecelatro in Italy, and
two French noblemen (Albert de Mun and René de le Tour du
Pin) who had been deeply influenced by the Society of St Vincent
de Paul, were all spokesmen, in their different ways, for the
alliance between the Catholic Church and the people. They all
acknowledged Manning's outstanding services to the cause. In his

book *Christ, the Church and Man*, Capecelatro testified that 'I know none among Catholic Socialists (let the name be permitted me) braver than my late beloved friend, Cardinal Manning, a social student fearless in speculation, effectual in enterprise'.[9] At a Catholic Congress at Liège in 1890, the third such assembly to discuss the Church's reaction to the social ills of the day, Manning – who had been invited to attend – caused something of a sensation among the more conservative elements by his declaration, in a letter addressed to the Congress, that:

> I do not believe that it will ever be possible to establish peaceful relations between employers and workers, until it is publicly acknowledged and established that there must be a just and fitting measure that will regulate profits and wages, a measure that will govern all the free contracts between capital and labour.[10]

There were some apprehensions about the response of the Holy See to these challenges. Leo XIII had given no promise at the beginning of his pontificate that he would be sympathetic, having issued an unequivocal condemnation of socialism and communism in one of his earliest encyclicals. By 1880 his attitude to social problems had changed. Of his encyclical of that year, condemning the practice of slavery, he was reported to have said, 'this last Encyclical is Manning's. It was he who put the idea into my head to do something for the slaves ... I have written this Encyclical in consequence of my conversation with him.'[11] Eleven years later he issued the important encyclical relating to workers' rights and conditions of labour, *Rerum Novarum*, parts of which could almost have been taken word for word from Manning's letter to the Congress of Liège. Leo XIII sent Manning a draft of the encyclical, asking him, in collaboration with Archbishop Walsh of Dublin, to prepare the English translation. Walsh, who was in Rome at the time, confirmed in a letter to Manning the extent of the Pope's sense of indebtedness. 'I think I trace your Eminence's influence', he wrote, 'in this as in many other things that I have noted here during this visit.'[12]

By that time, so near to the end of his own days, Manning's triumphant intervention in the crippling London Dock Strike of 1889 had been acclaimed beyond the confines of his own country. The dockers, under the leader of their union, Ben Tillett, had taken a determined stand to secure a better rate of pay, a fairer deal for casual workers and a reasonable settlement over hours of labour, believing the time to be propitious for a reassessment of their working conditions, as the country was emerging from a period of recession. On the refusal of the employers to meet their demands, the dockers went on strike on 14 August 1889. Neither the government nor the nation at large seemed to realize at the time the full seriousness of the situation, probably because they underestimated the determination of the dockers to stand firm. As the days passed, the crisis approached catastrophic proportions, with each side of the dispute threatening inflammatory measures to end the deadlock. The employers invoked the spectre of imported foreign labour; the dockers in return took steps to call for a general strike.

Manning, personally, was deeply alarmed. He had a sort of love–hate for London: fascinated by it, but also frightened. He knew enough of the appalling squalor of the rookeries, on the one hand, and of the frustrations of decent, honest working-men, on the other, whose efforts to gain a sympathetic hearing seemed impotent when confronted with the indifference of their employers. London was a powder-keg. The merest spark could ignite it, especially when thousands of men were roaming the streets idle, hopeful at one moment, desperate the next. He was haunted by the memories of the Paris Commune of 1871 and the dreadful murder of Archbishop Darboy. He had himself gone over to Paris to kneel on the very spot where Darboy died. What had overcome Paris could so easily happen in London. All the ingredients were there. Beneath the surface lay 'a power so ungovernable, a moral and spiritual power so terrible, that at any moment the justest and best laws may be scattered to ruin'.[13] He sensed the approach of Armageddon.

This tendency to view all human conflict in apocalyptic terms may have led him to exaggerate the catastrophic threat posed by the dockers' strike. But at least, in his handling of the issue, he buried his worst fears and acted with calmness and coolness. He had one great advantage: he knew Ben Tillett personally, and there existed between them a mutual respect. On one dark day for the strikers, when some of the men seemed disposed to drift back to work, in view of yet another deadlock in the talks, Tillett returned to his lodgings in Poplar to be told by his landlady that there was an old priest in the kitchen who had been waiting all afternoon to speak with him. Tillett found the 81-year-old Cardinal sitting there, reading the latest episode of Sherlock Holmes in the *Strand Magazine*. What could he do to help? – was the message he had brought; and he began his efforts at mediation on the following day.[14]

He duly visited the Home Office and the Mansion House; talked (without effect) to the Joint Committee of the Directors of the dock companies. Persistent badgering persuaded the Lord Mayor to invite him, with four others (including Frederick Temple, Bishop of London) to serve on a Committee of Conciliation. A compromise seemed to have been agreed upon, but the dockers' leaders refused to accept the date when the agreed wage of sixpence an hour should be paid. Further meetings followed; further compromises were proposed; then the talks collapsed altogether when the strike committee refused to back the concessions reluctantly accepted by their leaders. The Bishop of London resigned from the committee in disgust, to return to his interrupted holidays. Manning's response was to attend in person a meeting of the strikers at a local school in the East End. The mood was truculent and he risked a humiliating rebuff. Even Tillett opposed his suggested compromise at first. But Manning knew how to hold and to sway an audience; and he won in the end. He obtained the concessions he wanted, and then had the difficult task of persuading the Joint Committee of Directors to agree to the settlement he had negotiated. They eventually gave way. The London docks reopened in a matter of days.

Congratulations poured in from all quarters. Even the Pope sent a personal message of thanks. Newman, too infirm to write himself, dictated his message of gratitude, to which Manning replied on the following day. 'Your letter of this morning is as grateful to me, as it was unlooked for . . . Do not forget me in your prayers. Every day I remember you at the altar.'[15] The London dockers were so thankful that they had a whip-round and raised £160 to endow a bed at the London Hospital. The delegates of the London Trade Council agreed upon a resolution in the following terms:

> The Cardinal, by his tender sympathy for the poor, and his fearless advocacy of justice, especially for the poor, and by his persistent denunciation of the oppression of the workers, has endeared his memory to the heart of every true friend of Labour.[16]

VIII

Manning's 'tender sympathy for the poor' not only went back to his Anglican days, but also had about it a distinctly Anglican flavour. If the official policy of successive governments towards the 'condition of England' question was still what has been described as 'minimalist', shouldering only a 'last resort' responsibility in the areas of pauperism and public health,[1] there had never been lacking a succession of great philanthropists whose individual munificence and persistent pressure on politicians had in each generation served to inspire others to acts of charity and benevolence, partly from a sense of guilt, but primarily from a consciousness of religious duty. The Catholic attitude to poverty, however, was conditioned by a difference of situation and of theological standpoint. The sense of social guilt, for instance, was far less, because they had shared with the masses their portion of suffering at the hands of English society.[2] Furthermore, the doctrine of 'Holy Poverty' impressed upon them that poverty (in the words of Canon John Maguire) 'was the will of God ... It is profitable for our souls to see poverty and sickness and death.'[3] As for charity, this was a duty incumbent upon the rich, rather than any right that might belong to the poor. The Catholic gentleman, as Sheridan Gilley has observed, 'gave alms for his own sanctification, for a moral rather than a social end – and in obedience to divine command'.[4]

This was not good enough for Manning. To its great shame, the Catholic Church had much to learn from Protestants:

> All the great works of charity in England have had their beginning out of the Church, for instance, the abolition of the slave trade and of slavery ... Not a Catholic name so far as I know shared in this ... The Acts to protect children from cruelty were the work of Dissenters ... There are endless works for the protection of shop-assistants, over-worked railway and train men, women and children ground down by sweaters, and driven by starvation wages upon the streets. Not one of the works in their behalf were started by us ... It is not that our Catholics deliberately refuse, but partly they do not take pains to know, partly they are prejudiced ... unconscious that Lazarus lies at their gate full of sores.[5]

This was not quite fair to his fellow-Catholics. The Society of St Vincent de Paul had long been aware of the plight of Lazarus at the gate. But his remarks were chiefly directed to the Catholic laity, whose response to poverty and social injustice rarely went beyond alms-giving. This was all very well, but it was not enough. What Manning particularly disliked was the supposition that consciences could be salved and one's duty to the worthless in society could be satisfied by painless recreational fund-raising, like charity balls and bazaars.[6] More to the point, he regarded as so much facile evasion of one's Christian duty the contention that the salvation of the souls of the poor, not the amelioration of their social ills, was the all-important role of the Church. This was nonsense, in Manning's view. A human being was 'a soul–body', and 'a soul without a body was a spirit, whereas a body without a soul was a corpse'.[7]

He had a definite programme of 'practical Christianity' to set before his own flock and the whole nation; and the first priority was to tackle the evil of intemperance. 'Intemperance', he declared, was 'not a single sin, but the prolific cause of a whole progeny of vice and crime.'[8] It was England's 'national vice'.[9] It lay at the roots of the dissolution of family life, the collapse into pauperism of the worker, the creation of the brutal breed of 'English savage' whom drink drove to abuse his children;[10] it corrupted men, women and children, and – in the end – could prove the ruin of the nation as a whole. Although he was wont to contrast this national vice of the English with continental sobriety, he warned his fellow-countrymen to beware of the fate of Paris in 1871: 'I ask any man whether the drink that maddens and degrades this land is not a preparation for what we saw and wondered at in the drunken Commune of Paris?'[11]

Intemperance was to be fought on two distinct fronts. The first, dating from 1867, was the support that Manning gave to the United Kingdom Alliance, a powerful predominantly Nonconformist pressure group pledged to secure political intervention, by obtaining legislation to control the drink trade. Year after year he delivered forthright and increasingly militant speeches at the annual meetings of the Alliance. The second prong of his attack, dating from 1872 (when he himself became a total abstainer), was to work for moral persuasion in the founding of the League of the Cross, an organization with a network of branches throughout the country of those who had taken the 'pledge' and were committed to proselytize on behalf of total abstinence. On both fronts Manning was exposed to public odium and derision. On the political front he was battling against powerful vested interests as well as successive administrations, understandably nervous of the implications to their election prospects of unpopular sumptuary legislation. On the moral front, Manning's unashamed imitation of the successful techniques of the Salvation Army – with banners, processions and open-air meetings – exposed him both to ridicule and to accusations from many of his fellow-Catholics that he lowered the dignity of his office, encouraged his co-religionists to consort with Dissenters, and thereby exhibited disturbing symptoms of senility. Sadly, Herbert Vaughan left on record his own agreement with this view.[12]

Manning had no objection to sharing a platform with Bramwell Booth. He had reservations about the theology of the Salvation Army, their 'reckless language' about instant conversion and the like, but he believed that their objectives, ideals, devotion and discipline gave them a high ranking 'among the movements external to the Catholic unity'.[13] Bramwell Booth, for his part, regarded Manning as a saint.

> I do not think that outside the Salvation Army [he wrote] I ever met a man who more uncompromisingly brought his religion into everything he touched, into everything he wrote, into everything he planned. He did it with the most exquisite tact, and without the slightest suggestion of putting himself forward, but he did it.[14]

Specific social objectives were not Manning's sole concern. By his own example, he hoped to encourage Catholics to abandon their aloofness from English politics, and to persuade them that they constituted a significant and potentially influential pressure group. The time had come for them to enter into the mainstream of English political life. He would lead the way. He did so over the Temperance movement; he took his stand with the RSPCA over vivisection; he allied himself with Josephine Butler in her crusade against the Contagious Diseases Act, and with W. T. Stead in his courageous exposure of child prostitution. His services were recognized by the government in his appointment to the Cross Committee on elementary education, and by Sir Charles Dilke's invitation to him in 1884 to become a member of the Royal Commission on the Housing of the Working Classes. When, as a cardinal of the Roman Church, he was granted precedence on that Commission next below the Prince of Wales and above Lord Salisbury, it was a symbolic acknowledgement at least that the Catholic Church and its dignitaries, so reviled and rejected only some thirty years before, had now become a respected element within the English political scene.

It would not be quite true to say that Newman cared for none of these things, but he did not give the impression of caring very much. When appealed to, in 1860, on behalf of the poor children of London, he deflected the issue by pointing out to T. W. Allies that since most of them were Irish, the question should first be asked, 'What does IRELAND for them? Do any contributions come from the Bishops and clergy of Ireland?'[15] He was dismissive to the point of cynicism when his brother Francis wrote to him to enthuse over a speech by Manning at a Temperance meeting. 'I have heard that some also of our Irish bishops think that too many drink-shops are licensed. As for me, I do not know whether we have too many or too few.'[16] On the other hand, he had started off on the right track in his early days at St Clement's, showing genuine concern for his poor parishioners; he responded when the Oratory was appealed to for help during a cholera epidemic at Bilston in 1850, and did not hesitate to go himself.[17] He tried to overcome his distaste for bad smells and dirt in his dealings with his Irish penitents, but – being fastidious by nature – he found such contact a constant trial.

What is incontestable is that Newman differed fundamentally from Manning, in his conviction that the Church must always have regard for men's souls rather than for their bodies; and he was therefore inclined to question Manning's priorities. He was not unmoved by the contemplation of suffering. As J. H. L. Rowlands has observed, to Newman 'the Church's task was always to sanctify and yet to suffer with the world ... to redeem humanity and not reform society', and for the good reason that 'all the social reforms ever devised could not secure man's permanent, eternal happiness'.[18] So, in one of his lectures on the *Difficulties felt by Anglicans*, he resorted to polemical hyperbole in order to make this precise point. The Church, he wrote:

> holds that it were better for sun and moon to drop from heaven, for the earth to fail, and for all the many millions who are upon it to die of starvation in extremest agony, so far as temporal affliction goes, than that one soul, I will not say, should be lost, but should commit one single venial sin, should tell one wilful untruth, though it harmed no one, or steal one poor farthing without excuse. She considers the action of this world and the action of the soul simply incommensurate, viewed in their respective spheres.[19]

He was happy to repeat this passage in the *Apologia* in order to affirm that he did not retract a single word.[20]

But Newman was differently made from Manning. To him the two great realities had always been 'myself and my Creator'; and, as Douglas Woodruff observed, this meant that Newman was always 'so obviously more conscious of God than of other men'.[21] That is fair comment. What is far more questionable is the judgement of a more recent commentator who expressed the same idea thus: 'Men to whose minds the thought of the Last Judgment is ever present as a stupendous reality tend to have their enthusiasm less easily aroused by schemes of social betterment than those to whose minds the thought of it but rarely occurs.'[22] This is doubly presumptuous; first, because it suggests – by implication – that Manning's spirituality was somehow weaker than Newman's; second, because it assumes that one man's understanding of the obligations of a Christian was nearer to the will of God than the other's. Manning's reply to anyone who questioned his own priorities in having compassion for the multitude was to observe that 'I am very sure what Our Lord and His Apostles would do if they were in London'.[23]

It is not easy to define their respective political standpoints. Newman had some harsh things to say about democracy. 'When was a demos other than a tyrant?' he lamented in 1885.[24] 'What a dreadful thing this democracy is!' he wrote to R. W. Church in the same year. 'How I wish that Gladstone had retired into private life.'[25] Terence Kenny has suggested that Wilfrid Ward exaggerated Newman's hatred of democracy, reflecting both his own and his father's views.[26] In 1871, in correspondence with Matthew Arnold, Newman distinguished between democracy, as something which might not pose a threat to the Church, and communism and the spirit of rebellion, which undoubtedly did.[27]

The truth is that Newman was always happier with the few rather than the many. The very word 'demos' suggested crowds, which he detested. If Manning, while at home in a great city – London or Rome – was ever aware of its corruptions and potential for anarchy, Newman repeatedly wrote of cities with a sort of shuddering distaste. The city was a place of terrifying impersonality;[28] it was a dreadful reminder of the number of lost souls abroad in its streets ('A large town . . . is a fearful sight');[29] it was a place of cacophony, of 'ceaseless, importunate, monotonous din' with its 'canopy of smoke, shrouding God's day from the realms of obstinate sullen toil'.[30] The city mirrored the corruption of the world,[31] because – as Caecilius in *Callista* explained to Agellius – 'those who are shut up in crowded cities see but the work of man, which is evil'. [32] Translated into politics, these views are suggestive of a deep and enduring conservatism, but this did not necessarily mean that Newman never abandoned the ardent Toryism of his young days. Something of the same is seen in his attitude to liberalism. He loathed liberalism, if by that was meant the 'anti-dogmatic principle'; but he was not necessarily opposed to Liberalism as the description of a political party.[33]

Manning's Ultramontanism might suggest a definite leaning towards the right wing of politics, but in fact he was not a conservative, and never had been. The label that he chose for himself was 'a Mosaic Radical',[34] by which he meant a combination of deference to divine law and the divine will, and identification with the best interests of the people; a fusion of religion and humanity, Church and People bound indissolubly together, because – as he once remarked to the young Hilaire Belloc – 'all human conflict is ultimately theological'.[35] If the Radicalism was more evident in his advancing years, at least as early as 1864 he had written in an article on 'The Visit of Garibaldi in England': 'If I have any politics they are popular, learned in the School which teaches that princes are for the people, not the people for princes. This principle I accept from my heart with all its consequences and corollaries.'[36] Because the word 'Socialism' had a secular connotation, he shunned it; but he unhesitatingly upheld some of the basic tenets of that creed. He distrusted the power of capitalized industry; he rejected the *laissez-faire* doctrine that the State should adopt a neutral stance over economic bargaining and that the problems of poverty belonged to the sphere of morals as opposed to politics.[37]

The events of the 1870s bore witness to Manning's worst fears about the most imminent political dangers facing the Western world. The first was the Commune – people-power divorced from the guiding influence of the Church; the second was Caesarism, personified in Bismarck and his determination to effect complete State control of the Church in Germany and to crush all resistance by systematic persecution in the *Kulturkampf*, which began with the expulsion of the Jesuits in 1872 and revealed the full force of its anti-clerical animosity in the Falk and May Laws of 1873. It was the coming of Antichrist that Manning had long feared; and the apocalyptic language which came so easily to his pen fairly thundered from the pages of his published address to the Academy of the Catholic Religion in December 1873, entitled *Caesarism and Ultramontanism*, which has been described by Jeffrey von Arx as 'the most controversial public announcement that Manning ever made'.[38]

The main argument he advanced was that Caesarism constituted the complete defiance of the fundamental principle of the separation of powers. 'Christianity has confined the civil power within its own sphere as a delegation from God Himself; but by the same act Christianity has limited the sphere of its jurisdiction. It has withdrawn from its cognizance and control the whole inner life of man.'[39] Although he made it clear that Germany ('government of flesh and blood, or of blood and iron')[40] was the worst manifestation of Caesarism in modern times, and exempted England from the charge (merely because it could hardly any longer be described as an Establishment *de facto*), his description of the Reformation as 'the recrudescence of Caesarism' gave the impression that every assertion of that nationalistic spirit was a form of heresy.[41] The contrast that he was intending to draw was the displacement of the God-given international moral order by a form of ugly *Realpolitik*, which – to Manning – was (in Owen Chadwick's words) 'the harbinger of European suicide'.[42]

Perhaps because the *Kulturkampf* ultimately failed, and Bismarck was obliged, if only figuratively, to 'go to Canossa', Manning's language of an approaching Armageddon seemed exaggerated, even far-fetched. The examples that he cited were unashamedly medieval – the Gelasian principle, St Bernard, St Thomas, the bull *Unam Sanctam* (which 'contains no more, that the Vatican Council could define no less');[43] and the English press were not likely to subscribe to the paradoxical statement that 'Obedience to the Church is liberty; and it is liberty because the Church cannot err or mislead either men or nations'.[44] Newman did not approve. Surprisingly, his sympathies seem to have been pro-Prussian during the Franco-Prussian war. 'I am not at all sorry at the advance of the Germans,' he had commented to Frederic Rogers in September 1870.[45] He firmly believed that Manning had employed precisely the wrong tactics in his Academy address. 'I can't understand him,' he said to Lord Emly. '. . . I suppose he has a notion that Englishmen like outspoken men; and that they will respect Catholics, if they are bold – but that does not solve the difficulty to me.'[46]

There followed a series of open letters between Manning and Sir James Fitzjames Stephen, in the course of which Manning developed his views more fully, most particularly his conviction that an authoritative Church, far from being a tyranny, was actually the true protector of the people, who can be so vulnerable to the exploitation of secular forces. The monster which threatened to devour people's liberty was not the Pope, but the so-called 'German liberalism', which the *Kulturkampf* had un-masked. 'It is a compound of Antichristian hatred, inflated contempt of conscience in other men, with the bigotry of unbelief and the despotism of intolerance. Liberty of conscience exists no longer in Prussia, and where liberty of conscience is violated all liberty perishes.'[47] The vigour of Manning's attack is the more understandable when one appreciates that the Catholic clergy and Regulars who were being humiliated and imprisoned in Germany were – many of them – people whom he had known personally. He could not have watched unmoved while Earl Russell was drumming up support for Bismark at public meetings. The English people began to think again when the wreck of the *Deutschland* occurred off the coast near Harwich in December 1875, with the loss of 78 of the 213 passengers, including a party of nuns fleeing from Bismarck's persecution. Manning preached at their funeral at Leytonstone. On that occasion he forbore to inveigh against Caesarism: there was manifestly no need to. The tragedy, and what lay behind it, were self-evident.[48]

Nevertheless, the *Kulturkampf* enabled Manning to demonstrate what proved to be the most significant lesson that he endeavoured to convey to his posterity: that the strength, harmony and health of Christendom – both spiritual and temporal – depend upon an authoritative international Church securely established on a popular base. He had tried to impress this upon his clergy in one of his earliest Pastoral Letters in 1867:

> The tendency of political society is everywhere to the people. Of this we have no fear. The Church is nowhere more vigorous than when it is in closest sympathy with the people; as in Ireland, and Poland, in America, Australia, and in England.[49]

History abounds in ironies. Manning's message of the Church's essentially popular base made little lasting impression on English people as a whole, mainly because it was so often associated with unpopular causes: the maintenance of the Pope's temporal power and the doctrine of papal infallibility. It cut little ice with his successor, Herbert Vaughan, either, but for different reasons. He respected Manning's causes, but could never sympathize with his preoccupation with the interests of the people. Manning's deeds, and the compassionate heart that lay behind them, were saluted by his fellow-countrymen in his last days, but his vision for the future of the Catholic Church was quietly buried in his grave. It was as if those who came after him were at one with Newman, in this as in many other respects, and echoed his words: they could not truly understand him.

CHAPTER 7

The Two Cardinals

'If only we had stood side by side.' Autobiographical note by Manning, 1887

'What do you think Cardinal Manning did to me? He kissed me!' Newman to a fellow-Oratorian, 1883

I

On 15 MARCH 1875 Manning, who was in Rome at the time, received the official communication from Cardinal Antonelli informing him that at a consistory held that day he had been elevated to the 'sublime dignity of Cardinal'.[1] He had been kept waiting long enough, it must have seemed to many; perhaps because he was a convert, and was relatively young when he succeeded to Westminster; more likely because his active role at the Vatican Council had not endeared him to certain members of the Sacred College. E. S. Purcell has suggested that Cardinal Barnabò was the most hostile of all, and it is significant that Pio Nono proposed Manning's name, apparently a second time, immediately after Barnabò's death.[2] On this occasion the vote was unanimous, and his investiture took place on 29 March, when he was assigned as his title – to his great satisfaction – the priesthood of the very same church (the church of St Andrew and St Gregory on the Coelian Hill) that was attached to the monastery where Gregory the Great had lived and from which St Augustine of Canterbury had been dispatched on his mission to the heathen English. Twenty-five years earlier, Wiseman's reception in England in his new dignity had been one of uproar, admittedly to a

large extent provoked by his own indiscretions. Manning, by
contrast, deliberately avoided any controversial proclamation on
his return, and his recognition by the Holy See was greeted with
pride and almost universal satisfaction.

A letter from Newman awaited Manning when he arrived back
home, one among a huge pile of congratulations:

> My dear Lord Cardinal, I beg you to accept the congratulations of
> myself and this house on your recent promotion. It must be a great
> gratification to you to receive this mark of confidence placed in you by
> the Sovereign Pontiff. And it must be a source of true pleasure to your
> brother and his family and your other relatives and friends. And as
> regards the Protestant world it is striking to observe the contrast
> between the circumstances under which you return invested with this
> special dignity and the feelings which were excited in England
> twenty-five years ago ... That the temporal honours, to which you
> have attained, may be the token and earnest of those which come from
> God above, is the sincere prayer of, Yours affectly John H. Newman.[3]

Manning replied to this letter before any of the others; and
probably of all the letters, some effusive, some redolent of happy
memories (such as Odo Russell's, recalling with delight their walks
and talks at Rome),[4] it gave him the most satisfaction. What his
own feelings were can only be conjectured. In 1851 he had said to
Robert Wilberforce that he would sink to the bottom and disappear; now he was a member of the Sacred College, and within
three years was taking part in the conclave to elect Pio Nono's
successor. His own name came up in the course of discussions;
and, as Shane Leslie put it, 'for a glittering moment [he] stood on
the step of the Papal throne, the first Englishman since Wolsey
three centuries before'.[5] Manning was insistent, however, that the
political circumstances of Italy demanded that an Italian be
elected. Cardinal Bilio, who had refused to allow his own name to
go forward, pointed out that Manning 'had been so domesticated
in Rome as not to be a foreigner',[6] but eventually the wisdom of
appointing an Italian was accepted, and Cardinal Pecci, who
became Leo XIII, was duly elected.

What were Newman's true feelings during these years? There
were moments when it hurt to be seemingly out in the cold. 'I
wonder', he wrote to R. W. Church in October 1871, when
Church had became Dean of St Paul's and Frederic Rogers had
just been created Lord Blachford, 'whether it is because I am a
little man myself, that I feel melancholy to have associations

broken by the elevation of my friends.'[7] The newspapers rubbed
it in, a year later, when they published a story that Newman had
been turned out of St Paul's Cathedral by an officious verger who
thought the presence of 'a poorly clad, threadbare looking
individual' offensive to the dignity of the building.[8] This was only
partly true. Newman had slipped in to St Paul's to listen to the
chanting, and had been requested to leave, but the description of
him as a tramp was a piece of journalistic fancy. Two months after
Manning had been elevated to the cardinalate, Newman had to
cope with one of the greatest sadnesses of his life, the death on 24
May 1875 of his dearest friend and the closest companion of his
Catholic years, Ambrose St John. 'From the first he loved me with
an intensity of love, which was unaccountable,' he recalled to
Frederic Rogers;[9] and then to his friend, David Moriarty: 'My
present affliction is the greatest I have had in my life, but I cannot
really be surprised, and should be wicked to complain, that the
Mercy of God, after giving Fr St John to me for 32 years, at length
has reclaimed what is His own – and that, as I firmly believe to
warn me, that I must be prepared for His summons as my friend
was.'[10]

As 1877 drew to a close, however, the first signal that parties
were at work to accord him official recognition in his old age came
– appropriately enough – from Oxford. On 14 December he
received a letter from the President of Trinity College inviting
him to accept an Honorary Fellowship. Newman was as delighted
as a child. 'No compliment could I feel more intimately, or desire
more eagerly at once to seize and appropriate,' he replied on the
very next day, 'than that which is the subject of your letter just
received.'[11] Having obtained Ullathorne's permission, as a matter
of courtesy, he confirmed his acceptance of the honour on 20
December. He wrote to his friend Lord Emly: 'My affections have
ever been with my first College, though I have more and more
intimately personal Oriel friends. There was too much painful at
Oriel, to allow of its remembrances being sweet and dear; – hence
I rejoice that it is Trinity, not Oriel, that has reclaimed me.'[12] In
February 1878 he returned in honour to Oxford as the President
of Trinity's guest; he dined in Hall, and visited his old Tutor,
Thomas Short, aged 88 and nearly blind. It was a moment of
great happiness. He had not seen Oxford, except in the distance
from the windows of a train, since he left in February 1846.

One of his earliest converts, Sister Mary Gabriel Du Boulay, who had become a Dominican nun, wrote to him, on hearing the news: 'We hope it is the beginning of that full acknowledgement of all you have been ... which is certain to come hereafter, but which we *should* like you to receive before you go hence.'[13] Already rumours were beginning to circulate that Leo XIII had resolved to honour him by raising him to the cardinalate, and certainly the Pope himself did nothing to dispel the supposition that the intention had been long in his mind, when he assured Lord Selborne at an audience in 1888 that 'I always had a cult for him. I am proud that I was able to honour such a man.'[14] How well he actually knew his work and circumstances is somewhat doubtful, because when Wilfrid Ward, a student at the English College at Rome at the time, was granted an audience shortly after Leo XIII's election, they found themselves at embarrassing cross-purposes. Since he had been introduced to Leo as the son of an illustrious English convert, the Pope grasped the wrong end of the stick and conversed with Ward for several minutes under the impression that he was the son of Newman.[15]

The initiative to secure for Newman a cardinal's hat came from the two acknowledged leaders of the Catholic laity in England, the Duke of Norfolk and the Marquis of Ripon, who approached Manning in July 1878 with a formal request that he should take up the matter at Rome. If ever Manning was tempted to signify his disapproval with his characteristic sniff, it must surely have been on that occasion. But the record is otherwise. There was apparently a long silence, as the Cardinal bent his head in thought. Then came his reply, in three words: *Fiat voluntas Tua* (let Thy will be done).[16] It was a truly generous expression of his capacity to forgive personal slights, snubs and consistent opposition to his declared policies. If he had wished to stand in Newman's way, he could have refused then and there; and it is inconceivable that Rome would have acted without Manning's acquiescence. Having agreed to represent Newman's claims in Rome, he then did so with characteristic whole-heartedness. Lord Petre, to whom Manning showed his petition, thought that, if anything, the Cardinal had 'said too much'.[17]

The veneration for his powers [he wrote], his learning, and his life of singular piety and integrity is almost as deeply felt by the non-Catholic population of this country as by members of the Catholic Church. In the rise and revival of Catholic Faith in England there is no one whose name will stand out in history with so great a prominence ... No greater gratification to the Catholics of England could be given than by the elevation of Dr Newman into the Sacred College.[18]

On the receipt of this letter in Rome, events moved quickly. On 29 January 1879 Manning was able to dispatch to Ullathorne the official letter he had received from Cardinal Nina, asking him to ascertain confidentially whether Newman would accept the offer of a cardinalate if the Pope should propose his name. There was a certain urgency in obtaining Newman's reply, because Manning was due to leave for Rome on 6 February and had been requested to bring with him Newman's answer.[19] On 2 February Newman wrote to Ullathorne as follows:

> I trust that his Holiness and the most eminent Cardinal Nina will not think me a thoroughly discourteous and unfeeling man, who is not touched by the commendation of Superiors, or a sense of gratitude on the splendour of dignity, when I say to you, my Bishop, who know me so well, that I regard as altogether above me the great honour which the Holy Father proposes with wonderful kindness to confer on one so insignificant, an honour quite trancedent and unparalleled, than which his Holiness has none greater to bestow.
>
> For I am, indeed, old and distrustful of myself; I have lived now thirty years 'in my little nest' in my much loved Oratory, sheltered and happy, and would therefore entreat his Holiness not to take me from St Philip, my Father and Patron.
>
> By the love and reverence with which a long succession of Popes have regarded and trusted my St Philip, I pray and entreat his Holiness in compassion of my diffidence of mind, in consideration of my feeble health, my nearly eighty years, the retired course of my life from my youth, my ignorance of foreign languages, and my lack of experience in business, to let me die where I have so long lived. Since I know now and henceforth that his Holiness thinks kindly of me, what more can I desire?[20]

What was Newman actually saying? Ullathorne was quite clear in his own mind that although this letter read like a courteous refusal of the offer, Newman wanted to accept it, provided that he was not required, as a cardinal without specific office, to conform to the universal Roman rule of having to reside in Rome. He explained to Manning, by letter, that 'Dr Newman has far too humble and delicate a mind to dream of thinking or saying anything which would look like hinting at any kind of terms with the Sovereign Pontiff'.[21] Manning, however, took Newman's letter at its face value. He had expected all along that, when it came to the point, he would decline. After all, Newman had already assured Robert Whitty that he would do so, when rumours first began to circulate in March 1878. 'I trust nothing will come of it,' he had written. 'I am far from making light of dignities, but under the example and shadow of St Philip, I may be allowed to decline them.'[22] Why should he have changed his mind in less than a year, especially when he had – all through his Catholic career – steadfastly declined any honour divorced from duties? Furthermore, Manning was well aware of the Roman rule. To his knowledge, the Holy See had never made an exception to its ruling that a cardinal without office should take up residence in Rome; not, at least, since the seventeenth century,[23] and even then the cardinal so honoured (Cardinal de Berulle, in 1627) was serving as a Minister of State at the French court.[24]

Newman could and ought to have made his meaning more clear; and that would have put an end to the matter. Manning could and ought to have checked Ullathorne's interpretation by approaching Newman direct (he did in fact write to Newman, to send him a copy of his petition on behalf of the cardinalate, but made no request for further elucidation).[25] Ullathorne clearly felt uneasy about the situation when he learnt that Manning was sending Newman's reply to Cardinal Nina in Rome without his own explanatory letter. Doubtless Manning very reasonably thought that a reply to a letter of such importance as Cardinal Nina's did not call for an interpretation from a third party, especially when its meaning was so clear. Newman wrote himself to Manning on 5 February, on the eve of his departure for Rome. It was an extraordinary letter for its brusqueness and brevity. Newman must have read the eulogy that Manning had sent to Rome on his behalf, and one would expect him to have been overwhelmed by its generosity; but there is not a word of personal appreciation of Manning's labours, only a curt declaration that 'I could not be so ungracious, whether to the Holy Father or to the friends at home who have interested themselves in the matter, as to decline what was so kindly proposed, provided that it did not involve unfaithfulness to St Philip'.[26] This did not seem to Manning to change the situation. Newman was determined to stay where he was.

It has to be granted that Manning had jumped to a conclusion which happened to be the wrong one – possibly because this was the conclusion that he had anticipated and personally welcomed. He may also be forgiven for feeling a certain amount of exasperation over Newman's inability to give a straight answer to a very direct question. At this point, however, he made an inexcusable error. He informed at least two people that Newman had declined the cardinalate – the Duke of Norfolk, in a letter from Paris, and his own Vicar-Gencral, Daniel Gilbert, neither of whom had any need, or any right, to know. Furthermore, since he apparently imposed no condition of secrecy, the news leaked out.[27] On 18 February *The Times* reported that 'Dr Newman has excused himself from accepting the Sacred Purple';[28] and other papers soon followed with versions and comments of their own. This had at least one fortunate result, in spite of the temporary embarrassment caused to Newman. The Duke of Norfolk did what Manning ought to have done in the first place – he sought clarification from Newman direct. The reply he received was the one which Newman himself ought to have given in the first place: 'If so high an honour was offered me, I should not answer it by a blunt refusal.'[29] The Duke wrote at once to Manning in Rome to assure him that 'Father Newman did not mean the Pope to interpret his letter in the way in which it has been interpreted by the papers'. He pressed Manning to see the Pope personally to explain.[30]

Manning replied on 25 February: 'I have this moment received your letter, and write at once. This is the first moment that I have doubted the plain meaning of Dr Newman's letter to Cardinal Nina.' He then quoted Newman's letter of 5 February. 'I understood this note as saying that he had declined it. And the note so seems to say. The letter to Cardinal Nina assigned many reasons, and I never doubted of this meaning till your letter came. A fatality seems to hang over us.' The fact that he repeats himself in the course of four sentences is somewhat suggestive of 'protesting too much'. Nevertheless, he was genuinely aggrieved. 'This is the second time that I have acted as a true and old friend of Dr Newman's, and in both instances it has ended in misunderstanding – and the "rent is made worse". I will without fail . . . do all in my power to clear what has been misunderstood.'[31] He and Cardinal Howard saw the Pope together that same day, and Manning wrote again to Norfolk: 'We explained that Dr Newman was restrained by delicacy from saying all he meant. The Holy Father gave me leave to write and say that Dr Newman need not change his way of life nor leave the Oratory nor even come to

Rome, and that a letter in this sense will be sent to him.'[32]

On 8 March 1879 Manning wrote to Newman to explain what had happened. 'If I misunderstood your intention it was by an error which I repaired the instant I knew it.'[33] The ending had been a happy one, and Newman wrote to the Duke of Norfolk in gracious terms about Manning's letter. Manning

> has been so good as to explain all that took place at the time of his leaving England, and you will be glad to hear me say that I wish it all swept out of every one's mind and my own – and shall be sorry if it is not so. I wish it known that I am quite satisfied, and am grateful to him for the trouble that he has taken in my matters.[34]

Newman's own answer to the question, why had he accepted the cardinalate after having declined all previous offers of honours? was simply this:

> It puts an end to all those reports that my teaching is not Catholic or my books trustworthy, which has been so great a trial to me so long. Refusal too would have created a suspicion that it was true that I was but a half and half Catholic, who dared not commit himself to a close union with the Church of Rome, and who wished to be independent.[35]

Once the affair had been settled amicably, Manning was in his element in advising his brother cardinal-elect about his visit to Rome for the investiture in April. He arranged lodgings for him at the English College, ordered the necessary vestments and regalia, helped him to determine what were necessities and what might be described as optional extras. Newman duly set off on 17 April and arrived in Rome on the 24th. Although he was old and frail and Rome had never been his favourite place, it was an exciting time. There were details of his coat of arms to be decided; he needed to trace the precise source of his chosen motto – *Cor ad cor loquitur* (heart speaks to heart) – and actually got it wrong;[36] he had fittings for his 'red garments' and wondered 'what dear Dr Hawkins would have said if he had seen me in them'.[37]

On 12 May he received the *biglietto* (the official announcement of his elevation to cardinal) at the Palazzo della Pigna, the residence of Cardinal Howard, and – as was the custom – made a speech in reply, beginning with a sentence in Italian and then transferring to his mother tongue. In the course of the speech he noted how the Pope's generous honour had, as its intention, to 'give pleasure to English Catholics, and even to Protestant England, if I received some mark of his favour'.

In the long course of years [he continued] I have made many mistakes. I have nothing of that high perfection which belongs to the writings of the Saints, *viz.* that error cannot be found in them; but what I trust that I may claim all through what I have written, is this, – an honest intention, an absence of private ends, a temper of obedience, a willingness to be corrected, a dread of error, a desire to serve Holy Church, and, through Divine mercy, a fair measure of success. And, I rejoice to say, one great mischief I have from the first opposed myself. For thirty, forty, fifty years I have resisted to the best of my powers the spirit of liberalism in religion. Never did Holy Church need champions against it more sorely than now, when, alas! it is an error overspreading, as a snare, the whole earth . . . Liberalism in religion is the doctrine that there is no positive truth in religion, but that one creed is as good as another, and this is the teaching which is gaining substance and force daily . . . It teaches that all are to be tolerated, for all are matters of opinion. Revealed religion is not a truth, but a sentiment and a taste: not an objective fact, not miraculous; and it is the right of each individual to make it say just what strikes his fancy.[38]

It was his most powerful declaration of the conviction of a lifetime. At Oxford and thereafter, 'against the Anti-dogmatic principle I had thrown my whole mind'.[39]

Receptions, acclamations, gifts in profusion awaited his return to England in June. He discovered advantages in being a cardinal that had never occurred to him. He had the privilege of a brougham to travel in, 'a great comfort to me. I cannot walk much, and thus I am able to accept Sir Garnet W[olseley]'s dictum that mounted infantry are the military arm of the future – for my carriage takes me out for a mile or two and sets me down to walk as much as I choose, and picks me up.'[40] His fighting days were over, and so the unseemly spectacle of the two English Cardinals in conflict was rarely exhibited. They corresponded hardly at all. Occasional flickers of anger at past frustrations occur in Newman's letters to others, however. In November 1882 he wrote to Lord Braye, who had reopened the question of Catholics attending Oxford and Cambridge, deploring the state of Oxford after the death of Pusey and Liddon's decision to resign his Professorship to take up permanent residence in London.

The Undergraduates and Junior Fellows are sheep without a shepherd . . . The Liberals are sweeping along in triumph, without any Catholic or religious influence to stem them now that Pusey and Liddon are gone . . . Alas, it is only one out of various manifestations of what may be called Nihilism in the Catholic Body, and in its rulers. They forbid, but they do not direct or create. I should fill many sheets of paper if I continued my exposure of this fact.[41]

In the following year he and Manning took opposite sides in the controversy over Gladstone's Affirmation Bill, introduced in order to allow the atheist Charles Bradlaugh (elected MP for Northampton) to make an affirmation before taking his seat, instead of the customary oath. Manning took a strong line. On the first occasion of Bradlaugh's refusal to take the oath, he wrote three fierce articles in the *Nineteenth Century*, prophesying the collapse of the Christian State should atheists be allowed into Parliament, not for the first time somewhat overstating his case.[42] Monster petitions of outraged clergy were set in motion, and Newman shocked many of his co-religionists by refusing to sign. The reason he gave, when forced to speak out because of an incorrect report in the *Morning Post*, was that 'looking at the Bill on its own merit, I think nothing is lost to Religion by its passing and nothing is gained by its being rejected'.[43] The *Manchester Examiner* did its best to stir up old rivalries by comparing Newman's temperate views with Manning's fanaticism. 'Cardinal Newman shines far apart from the other great ecclesiastical luminaries, and offers especially a striking contrast to his English colleague of the Sacred College.'[44] To Manning this was yet another example of the way in which the press strove to exacerbate their differences, invariably taking Newman's side. In a sad recital of their conflicts over the years, compiled in 1887, Manning lamented how 'almost every newspaper in England abused and ridiculed me. My name was never mentioned, but his was brought in to condemn me; his name was never mentioned, but mine was brought in to despite me. If only we had stood side by side and spoken the same thing ... the unity of Catholic truth would have been irresistible. But it was not to be so.'[45]

Their meetings during the 1880s could be counted on the fingers of one hand. In March 1886 they both attended the Requiem Mass for the Dowager Duchess of Norfolk at the Brompton Oratory, Newman staying with R. W. Church at the Deanery of St Paul's. Purcell, who misdates the occasion by several years, records that they exchanged greetings in the porch after the service, Manning congratulating Newman 'on getting so well through the Absolutions'.[46] Five years earlier Newman had been in London to sit for his portrait by Millais. He paid a courtesy visit to Manning. On his return to Birmingham, he could – with a certain satisfaction – concede that Manning had done for him at least one deed which was in concert with his words. 'What do you think Cardinal Manning did to me?' he said to one of his Fathers. 'He kissed me!'[47]

II

They were both now in the grip of old age and Newman, being Manning's senior by seven years, was altogether more frail and infirm. Even in 1875, when James Bryce, then Regius Professor of Civil Law at Oxford, visited him at the Oratory, he realized that he was talking to a very old man.

> He looks very aged [he wrote], hair more white than silvery, body stooped, a very large and prominent nose and large chin, brow which seems good, though one can't see it for the tangled hair falling over it: an air of melancholy, as of one who has passed through terrible struggles, yet of serenity, as of one who has found peace. Not a priest in his manner – still an Englishman more than a R. Catholic.[1]

By 1883 Newman was conscious of declining powers – his memory frequently failing him, dimness of sight, increasing deafness, and he needed his brougham more and more because of his lameness. He had had to give up playing the violin, and decided to send his 'beautiful instrument', which Dean Church and Rogers had presented to him in 1865, to Church's daughter, Mary. 'I cannot count or keep time . . . One gets an affection for a fiddle, and I should not like to go without getting it a good master or mistress.'[2]

After he had seen his last published work through the press, in 1881, his *Select Treatises of St Athanasius*, he spent much of his time sorting out his papers, feeling the greater need to set the record straight for posterity as he witnessed the errors and misrepresentations in the reminiscences published by near contemporaries, especially his irresponsible brother-in-law, Tom Mozley. One final effort to secure an eminent convert, his former disciple Mark Pattison, on what proved to be his death-bed, sadly came to naught. Rather half-heartedly, one cannot but feel, he engaged in unwelcome controversy with the Congregationalist scholar A. M. Fairburn, who accused him of scepticism in an article in the

Contemporary Review in May 1885. Newman's reply, in October of that year, revealed that he was unwilling to the last to abandon his views on eternal punishment, insisting that he would have nothing to do with the 'corrosive effect of rationalistic first principles'. He accepted the Christian doctrine 'on the simple word of the Divine informant', and deplored the 'disintegrating consequences of letting it go'.[3] In one other respect, too, during these years, he indicated that nothing had changed. He was still unwilling to forgive the London Oratory for their treatment of him in the late 1850s. The Superior, William Philip Gordon, and the Duke of Norfolk entreated him to attend the opening of the new Oratory church in April 1884. He refused. Neither Father Gordon nor the Duke of Norfolk could make much sense of the somewhat circumlocutory explanations that Newman made in his letters of refusal, except that it was clear that old wounds had never healed. 'It is very sad,' the Duke commented to Gordon. 'What can one do with such an extraordinary mind?'[4]

Nevertheless, the prevailing note of Newman's last years was one of serenity. Two visitors to the Oratory in 1887 came away with the reflection that they had been speaking with a saint. One was Francis Palgrave, who visited him in January that year.

> There sat that aged man with his snow-white hair; he rose and thanked me for coming and for caring for him with a sort of young child's gracious simplicity. He was much changed, of course ... The look of almost anxious searching had passed into the look of perfect peace.

They talked of Oxford and of old friends; then his admiration for the great saints of the Counter-Reformation. 'This great and perfect humility was almost overwhelming in its strikingness ... What a strange and beautiful union of the saint and the poet.'[5]

In August, Ullathorne came over to visit him. It was one of their last meetings. After Newman had told him about the state of his eyes, following a visit to the oculist, the Bishop rose to leave. Then:

> an action of his caused a scene I shall never forget, for its sublime lesson to myself. He said, in low and humble accents, 'My dear Lord, will you do me a great favour?' 'What is it?' I asked. He glided down on his knees, bent down his venerable head, and said, 'Give me your blessing'. What could I do with him before me in such a posture? I could not refuse without giving him great embarrassment. So I laid my hand on his head and said: 'My dear Lord Cardinal, notwithstand-

ing all laws to the contrary, I pray God to bless you, and that His Holy Spirit may be full in your heart.'

It was on this occasion, as they were leaving, that Newman contrasted his indoor life with that of Ullathorne's battles for the Church in the world. 'I felt annihilated in his presence,' Ullathorne recalled. 'There is a Saint in that man.'[6]

Newman's mind had long been set on the end of his journey. In 1876 he had said to Anne Mozley, as he contemplated the onset of another spring: 'As life is waning, and friends dropping away, the extreme beauty of the ever-recurring triumphant spring seems to have something of young mockery in it, till one recollects that that beauty is an image and a promise of something more sweet and more lasting than itself.'[7] Four years later, he wrote to his brother-in-law, John Mozley:

> Looking beyond this life, my first prayer, aim and hope is that I may see God. The thought of being blest with the sight of earthly friends pales before that thought. I believe that I shall never die; this awful prospect would crush me, were it not that I trusted and prayed that it would be an eternity in God's Presence. How is eternity a boon, unless He goes with it?[8]

He died, following an attack of pneumonia, on 11 August 1890. Lord Rosebery was one among the many who came to see the Cardinal lying in state.

> The Cardinal just like a saint's remains over a high altar, waxy, distant, emaciated, in a mitre, rich gloves whereon the ring (which I kissed) rich slippers. With the hat at the foot. And this was the end of the young Calvinist, the Oxford don, the austere Vicar of St Mary's. It seemed as if a whole cycle of human thought and life were concentrated in that august repose. That was my overwhelming thought. Kindly light has led and guided Newman to this strange, brilliant, incomparable end.[9]

He was buried at Rednal on 19 August in the same grave as Ambrose St John, as he had requested. Manning delivered the oration at the Requiem held in the Brompton Oratory. His celebrated eulogy effectively became the judgement of Newman's posterity. Some wondered at so gracious a tribute from one who had so often been on 'the other side'. Perhaps he had just said what he had had to say, rather than what he truly felt. William Neville was emboldened to put this precise question to Manning afterwards. His reply was as follows:

What I said on Wednesday was weighed and written, and is pure truth. I have not failed to observe your words and their delicate meaning. But I hope you need no assurance that I knew him too well, to love him less because duty bound me to obey my conscience as he also obeyed his.[10]

III

There is no reason to doubt Manning's sincerity. It is almost true to say that, whereas he loved Newman, he did not actually like him very much. He respected his integrity, while disagreeing with many of his conclusions; he genuinely admired him, in the way that a man of totally different talents can admire his opposite. Very probably, the same was true of Newman's feelings for Manning. At the same time, neither displayed the slightest jealousy of the other. Each, however, thought he saw with painful clarity the other's faults; faults so much part of the other's temperament and nature that easy rapport could never be established. What Manning disliked in Newman was his evasiveness, his prickliness and his obstinacy. 'Shall I tell you, Wilfrid Ward,' Manning once said to Newman's future biographer, 'what has ruined that man's career? One thing and one thing only: Temper! temper!! TEMPER!!!'[1] Similarly, to G. W. E. Russell he observed, when Russell had commented to Manning on some unflattering sketches of Newman written by one of his Oratorians, that such assertions were indeed all very shocking; and then he paused: 'But', he added, 'if you ask me if they are like poor Newman, I am bound to say – a *photograph*.'[2]

A funeral oration is not the occasion to dwell on a man's shortcomings. Manning could genuinely salute Newman's unique stature as a religious thinker, because there was much in his writings that he applauded; but privately he believed, as – interestingly – Lord Acton did,[3] that some of his assertions were actually heretical, and on one occasion, to Bodley's amusement, he enumerated ten distinct examples from Newman's most widely-read works.[4] Influential as these writings were, and indisputably supportive to the Catholic cause, they nevertheless – it seemed to him – conflicted with the teaching of the Holy See. But Newman could never be other than his restless mind and his obstinate temperament had made him. As Bodley rightly observed: 'If they had both been born Catholics, both sent to a Roman seminary at an early age, and submitted to the same discipline for the priesthood – even then they would have fought, had they crossed one another's paths in the course of their pious ministry.'[5]

As it was, they lived very different lives in wholly different circumstances. At no time was this contrast more marked than in the closing years. Only in one respect was there a similarity. Manning, too, became very conscious of the fact that posterity would soon be judging him, and he began to compile his own version of the various conflicts in which he had been engaged; not surprisingly, they are very self-justificatory in tone; sometimes cantankerously so, especially when writing in his 'Reminiscences' about the most controversial episodes in his career. On the Vatican Council he indulged in what Ignatius Ryder described as 'an ecstasy of self-gratulation':[6] 'We, the ignorants, the fools, the flatterers, the empty pates, were right after all,' Manning wrote, crowing with triumph. 'An Oecumenical council justified us, and the Catholic Church believes and teaches what we said; and we said it because the Church taught us.'[7] He knew, just as Newman knew, that the penalty of living in the limelight was that pens would be poised to write, probably none too accurately, about his career on the moment of his death. They both did their best to put their papers in order and to try to ensure that their respective standpoints were properly understood.

The main point of contrast between the two cardinals in the last ten years of their lives was that Manning was active to the very end. More than that: the last decade of his life witnessed his greatest achievements. These were the years when he was so concerned with Irish affairs, when he was serving on Royal Commissions, when he was making an international name for himself as a champion of Social Catholicism, when he was campaigning most militantly on the Temperance platform, and when he took upon himself the task of mediator in the London Dock Strike. He never spared himself. From the moment that he became Archbishop, he never took a holiday. Right to the very end, although he was obviously ailing, he never relaxed his hold on the government of his diocese. On Sundays he would preach, sometimes on three occasions, very rarely fewer than two; and he usually chose a church in one of the poorest districts of his diocese, or some struggling distant mission. 'Even in his old age,'

Purcell noted, 'when his voice was too feeble to be heard at a distance, the presence of Cardinal Manning alone sufficed to fill the church of a Sunday afternoon as no other preacher could.' He 'was known, at least by sight, by every priest, secular and regular, in the diocese'.[8]

Such relaxation as he ever took was to attend meetings of the Metaphysical Society, that high-powered discussion group of diverse minds (including Browning, Tennyson, T. H. Huxley, Gladstone and W. G. Ward) at which he read at least five papers, holding his own against all comers, puzzling his co-religionists by his readiness to listen patiently to Huxley's refutation of the Resurrection, always able to gain an appreciative audience, partly because of the fascination of the incongruity of the ascetic figure in his Roman dress, with the lingering Oxford manner, and the shafts of humour that would spice his unashamedly dogmatic utterances. Often he would seek refuge in the Athenaeum, to read the papers, to recognize and to converse with acquaintances of his Anglican days, picking up the gossip of the day, because he always prided himself on being 'in the know'. He would occasionally attend public dinners, but would reserve his appearance to the end, having resolved to eat out as rarely as possible; and after 1872, he would never take wine.

The austerity of Archbishop House, during Manning's residence, soon became something of a legend. It was singularly comfortless. Before Manning acquired this barrack-like building, standing on the corner of Carlisle Place and Francis Street, it had been a club for private soldiers in the Guards. It was – in Shane Leslie's famous description – like 'a Dissenting chapel doing duty as a railway waiting-room'.[9] The meanest bedroom in a veritable warren at the top of the house was the Cardinal's own. Most of the rooms were carpetless, and the dominant feature of the vast downstairs reception room where Manning held his audiences was a large screen, behind which the Cardinal would be found sitting surrounded by a litter of papers and envelopes as he sorted through the day's correspondence. He probably hardly noticed its cheerlessness. A priest's mind should be set on higher things. Accordingly, he advised all his clergy to have nothing in their houses but plain and solid furniture, to exclude everything foolish and unseemly in the pictures on the walls, and to set an example to others of frugality of diet.[10] W. G. Ward, so ardent a supporter of all Manning's causes, always rather dreaded the occasions when the Cardinal called as a guest. His emaciation in his old age, in part the consequence of this self-imposed austerity, made him susceptible to cold, and he disliked fresh air. The first thing he would do, on entering a room, would be to close all the windows. But the prospect of having the Cardinal as a host was even more alarming. Once, when Ward told Manning that he had been suffering from depression, the kindly old man responded by saying, 'When you feel like that again, come and spend an evening with me at Archbishop House.' Wilfrid Ward recalled: 'The inextinguishable laughter with which my father repeated the remark told its own story.'[11]

Of course, stories like this grew in the telling. G. W. E. Russell agreed that Manning gave the appearance of having 'lived on biscuits and soda water', but in reality 'he had a hearty appetite for his midday meal, and, in his own words, "enjoyed his tea"'.[12] Bodley found him the best of companions. After the close friendship between the younger and the older man had been formed, from the days that they worked together on the Royal Commission for the Housing of the Working Classes, Bodley was a frequent visitor to Archbishop House, usually late in the evening, when the Cardinal would be allowing himself his solitary serious indulgence, huddled up close to a warm fire; and – as he was wont to say – warming old bones in the company of 'the only tongues that are silent and tell no fibs'.[13] On such occasions he could shed the cares of the day. Sometimes he would reminisce, one Oxford man to another, savouring together the lines of Matthew Arnold's *The Scholar Gipsy*. 'Ah! only Oxford men like you and me can understand that,' he would say. Then, 'nobody here understands Oxford; none of them have quite understood me ... It was always so from the first.'[14] With Bodley, probably because he was not of his own flock, he could laugh and joke. 'Forgive my togs,' he said on one occasion, when Bodley had dropped in when he was sitting at table arrayed in scarlet and lace. 'It's the Immaculate Conception and I have to go to Farm Street.'[15] He would pump the younger man for the latest gossip, and then pat him on the shoulder, saying, 'Well, well, it's a wicked old world, isn't it?'[16]

Although these evening *tête-à-têtes* with Bodley reveal that Manning sometimes felt very lonely and cut off from companionship in his last years, visitors were constantly calling on him; sometimes priests summoned for a dereliction of duty, when

Manning could be very imperious and strict; more often an extraordinary assortment would foregather in the ante-room, clerical and lay, some of whom would be dressed in rags, seeking counsel or petitioning for his charity, which was rarely refused. One such visitor every year, on the anniversary of Caroline's death, was a young girl (the eldest daughter of Reginald Wilberforce, the then squire of Lavington) who would come to see him bearing a rose from a bush by Caroline's grave. However distinguished the visitors might be, waiting for an audience, Dorothy Wilberforce was admitted first; and the Cardinal would take her up on his knee, and kiss the rose, often – she recalled – with tears in his eyes.[17] It seemed, as he grew older, that he wanted more and more reminders of this earlier happy time.

In 1890 Manning celebrated the jubilee of his archiepiscopate. An article in the *Tablet* saluted his achievements:

> To Cardinal Manning more than to any man is due that English Catholics have at last outgrown the narrow cramped life of their past of persecution, and stand in all things on a footing of equality with their fellow-countrymen ... An Englishman down to the marrow of his bones, he has always thrown himself into every movement which worked for the greatness and advancement of England ... No good cause, from Imperial Federation to Express Postage, ever appealed to him in vain.

Indeed, he was generous to the point of prodigality. When he was presented, at his jubilee, with lavish gifts by well-wishers and grateful organizations, he replied to one of the deputations:

> As I am rendering in all likelihood my last account to you, I will say two things: First, that I have never consciously or willingly wounded any man; secondly, that in many cases I have been bound by duty to act, not as my personal will but as my office compelled me ... Much has passed through my hands in these five-and-twenty years. Nothing has stayed under this roof; all has gone into the work which has been entrusted to me. My desire is to die, as a priest ought, without money and without debts.[18]

He had certainly lived as a priest. This was always the impression that lingered in the mind on meeting him. Bodley described it thus:

> Manning had none of that unctuous air with which some of the clergy, of all denominations ... seem to notify that they are agents of the unseen ... Yet in close contact with him one felt that he was always

living in the presence of an unseen Power, not as its pompous agent, but as its simple and humble messenger. It has been my lot to witness some of the most imposing religious ceremonies of modern Christendom; but nothing so impressive, so faith-inspiring has ever met my eyes as the sight of this noble old Englishman in his threadbare cassock kneeling alone before the altar of his bare chapel.[19]

But one also knew that one was in the presence of a Prince of the Church. G. W. E. Russell has given a memorable description of Manning in his last years:

He carried the irreducible minimum of flesh on his bones, and his hollow cheeks and shrunken jaws threw his massive forehead into prominence. His line of features was absolutely faultless in its statuesque regularity, but his face was saved from the insipidity of too great perfection by the imperious – rather ruthless – lines of his mouth and the penetrating lustre of the deep-set eyes. His dress – a black cassock edged and buttoned with crimson, with a crimson skull-cap and biretta, and a pectoral cross of gold – enhanced the picturesqueness of his aspect, and as he entered the ante-chamber where one awaited his approach, the most Protestant knee instinctively bent. His dignity was astonishing . . . He never put himself forward; never asserted his rank . . . Still, he always contrived to be the most conspicuous figure in any company which he entered.[20]

Nevertheless, the enduring impression that Manning made in any company was one of aloofness – a sort of calculated detachment, as of one who had resolved in his latter years to live out of the world, while at the same time missing nothing in the steady gaze of his penetrating eyes. One of his boy-attendants at Mass recalled how 'when he just turns his eye on you, oh my! don't you shiver!'[21] Mrs Adams-Acton, the wife of the great Victorian sculptor, observed him often when he came to her husband's studio for as many as twenty sittings. 'However friendly he might be,' she reflected, 'he was always aloof – a being apart . . . He never spoke till necessity for speech arose; and there was a peculiar movement, all his own, with that mobile mouth, which seemed to be forming well-considered words before they were uttered.'[22]

He was surely conscious of the effect of his physical presence; perhaps, also, an element of the thespian in him tempted him to play up to his image. G. K. Chesterton was a teenager when he first set eyes on him – a chance encounter in Kensington High Street in the 1880s – and he never forgot the experience. The boy had observed a crowd assembled by 'a rather dark and narrow entry on the southern side of that thoroughfare', and how, as a little dark carriage drew up, the whole throng subsided to their knees on the pavement. Out of the carriage came

> a ghost clad in flames [Chesterton recalled]. Nothing in the shilling paintbox had ever spread such a conflagration of scarlet, such lakes of lake; or seemed so splendidly likely to incarnadine the multitudinous sea. He came on with all his glowing draperies like a great crimson cloud of sunset, lifting long frail fingers over the crowd in blessing. And then I looked at his face and was startled with a contrast; for his face was dead pale like ivory and very wrinkled and old, fitted together out of naked nerve and bone and sinew; with hollow eyes in shadow; but not ugly; having in every line the ruin of a great beauty. The face was so extraordinary that for a moment I even forgot such perfectly scrumptious scarlet clothes.[23]

Manning died on 14 January 1892. The grief of the nation, and of London in particular, had no parallel, except perhaps at the passing of the great Duke of Wellington in September 1852. To cope with the crowds, the lying-in-state had to be extended by two days; and on the Sunday alone it was estimated that 100,000 mourners came to view his body. The four-mile route from the Brompton Oratory, where the Requiem Mass was celebrated, to Kensal Green cemetery was lined with mourners without any discernible gap. Forty years earlier, a cardinal seen in the streets of London might well have been pelted with mud.

Such was the passing of the greatest Roman of them all; and yet, for all his uncompromising claims for his Church, he was a man in whom the love of days far distant, when he served the tiny churches of Graffham and Lavington, never died. On his death-bed, with Herbert Vaughan beside him, he fumbled under his pillow and pulled out a small worn volume, saying: 'I know not to whom else to leave this – I leave it to you. Into this little book my dearest wife wrote her prayers and meditations. Not a day has passed since her death on which I have not prayed and meditated from this book. All the good I may have done, all the good I may have been, I owe to her. Take precious care of it.'[24]

Conclusion

'A saint is a peculiar being.' Newman to Henry Wilberforce, January 1849

GLADSTONE THOUGHT it rather odd that the nation went
into mourning over Manning's death on so vast a scale, when the
reaction to Newman's passing was relatively subdued. He could
not account for it.[1] But in 1892, Manning's stock was at its highest;
and if the responsibility for canonization had been the property of
the masses, there is very little doubt which of the two English
Cardinals would have been their choice. Such sublime accolades,
however, do not belong to the people, and – in any case – as
Newman rightly observed, 'Great saints ... like the everlasting
mountains, grow as we recede from them',[2] and 'Time is necessary, as the proof of things'.[3] It has been Manning's misfortune
that time has not served him well. The dirty work was done by his
original biographer; and as the years have passed the Church to
which he gave such devotion has tended increasingly to underrate
him, if not practically to disown him. Newman's reputation, apart
from a few hiccoughs during the Modernist controversy, has
waxed as his rival's has waned. The passage of time will always
favour the thinker rather than the doer of great deeds. Actions,
however admirable, retain only an historical interest, while words
endure, particularly words which have the prophetic quality and
seductive charm of Newman's.

Newman confidently believed that, given time, much of what
distressed him about the state of the Catholic Church of his own

day would be corrected under the guidance of the Holy Spirit; and the fact that the Second Vatican Council redressed the balance, or completed the unfinished work, of the First, at a time when the climate of Catholic thinking had so markedly changed, in so many ways in the direction to which Newman had been pointing, has led to the claim that Vatican II was 'Newman's Council', or 'Newman, come true'.[4] Vatican I, on the other hand, has come to be regarded, with at least a partial degree of truth, as 'Manning's Council', a label which he would not himself have been inclined to dispute. These respective designations, whether historical fact or not, tell their story of at least the acknowledged impact of the two great converts on the history of the Catholic Church in modern times.

The most far-reaching claims for the appropriateness of describing Vatican II as Newman's Council have come from Stephen Dessain:

> At the second Vatican Council the tides of clericalism, over-centralization, creeping infallibility, narrow unhistorical theology and exaggerated mariology were thrown back, while the things Newman stood for were brought forward – freedom, the supremacy of conscience, the Church as a communion, a return to Scripture and the fathers, the rightful place of the laity, work for unity, and all the efforts to meet the needs of the age, and for the Church to take its place in the modern world. Any disarray or confusion there may now be in the Church is the measure of how necessary this renewal was.[5]

This is perhaps a little *too* far-reaching, although there is a close affinity with Newman's teaching in four of the major issues discussed at Vatican II. Even Manning had conceded that the question of the *magisterium* of the Church had been left uncompleted in 1870. 'May we not unreasonably believe', he wrote, 'that the next time the Church meets in Council . . . the first duty will be to take up the work already prepared, and to define the Divine powers of the Episcopate and its relation to its Head?'[6] Where Vatican II went much further than Manning envisaged, and demonstrated a recognition of the insights of Newman, was in its decree *Lumen Gentium*, which at least suggested that Newman's seemingly heterodox 'On Consulting the Faithful in matters of Doctrine', and his teaching on the three-fold office of the Church in his Preface to the 1877 edition of the *Via Media*, had become sufficiently absorbed for the Council to define anew the primacy of the Pope within 'the larger context of the people of God who constitute the Church'.[7] John Coulson, for instance, states that 'the need for an educated laity . . . is now to be found expressed in the documents of the second Vatican Council . . . and it was Newman's achievement not only to anticipate but to explain how such views constituted important but neglected Catholic principles.'[8] Specific evidence of Newman's influence in the actual debates is scanty. The *Essay on Development* was quoted on a few occasions. Pope Paul VI's enthusiasm for Newman has prompted Nicholas Lash to suggest that it was 'on the margins of the Council, and on the coat tails of a friend, that Newman came nearest centre-stage'.[9] There is an interesting comparison here with Manning. Both men enunciated a theory of the popular base of the Church, while meaning entirely different things. Manning saw the alliance between Church and people in political and social terms; Newman's 'popular foundation . . . was a result of his reflection on the role of the laity in Church history',[10] and the integral part played by the laity within the *consensus fidelium.*

In the second place, John Coulson sees a clear anticipation of the decrees of Vatican II in Newman's writings on doctrinal development.[11] The fact that Newman was one of the pioneers of the historical approach to the study of doctrine does not necessarily mean, however, that the debates of a Council held over a hundred years later were echoing his voice. A number of scholars in recent years have issued warnings against assuming links between Newman's teaching and the conciliar resolutions when direct evidence is lacking.[12] The third affinity with Newman is again the subject of a bold claim by John Coulson – the Church's recognition of the role of Conscience, very much in the terms that Newman employed in his *Letter to the Duke of Norfolk* (Cardinal Heenan actually quoted Newman's famous remark about toasting conscience before toasting the Pope, in a speech at the fourth session of the Council).[13] 'The Church of Vatican II', Coulson writes, 'has declared where it stands on the matter, and it stands on the side of Newman and not against him. Conscience, and its inalienable rights, have been conceded in *Gaudium et Spes*, and in words, furthermore, which are strikingly reminiscent of Newman's own definition.'[14]

The fourth affinity between Newman's teaching and Vatican II is the common emphasis on biblically-inspired theology and the discarding of the strait-jacket of traditional scholasticism. In 1883 Newman wrote to Lord Emly, deploring the ignorance of the

Scriptures among his fellow-Catholics;[15] Manning, too, was wont to quote St Teresa, who had lamented that one of the chief causes of evil in her day was the ignorance of Holy Scripture. 'It is certainly so among us,' he wrote. 'It lowers the standard of Christian life and aspiration. The Scriptures are the voice of the Divine Spirit.'[16] Neither Newman nor Manning could claim that they were successful in injecting into the Catholicism of their day something that they both brought from their Evangelical heritage, but their common diagnosis of a failing in both the theology and the preaching of their own times was gradually appreciated by the Church, and firmly endorsed by the Council.

By these four developments or modifications of the Church's teaching, steps were being taken which rendered the prospects of fruitful ecumenical discussions very much more promising. It does not therefore follow, however, that either Newman (as is sometimes claimed) or Manning (whose influence in this direction has been largely ignored) should be described as pioneers of ecumenicism. Both made short shrift of Pusey's *Eirenicon*; neither would concede the validity of Anglican Orders; and Newman in particular – in the last years of his life – was emphatic in his rejection of overtures to enlist his support for gestures of union or reconciliation. When asked by G. A. Denison to use his influence with Gladstone to obtain a peerage for Antony Gibbs, a major benefactor of Keble College, he declined on the grounds that he could not 'as a Cardinal of the Holy Roman Church, allow myself to give a public sanction to a religious system, which in spite of the claims which many of its adherents have upon my love and esteem, does not, as I believe, come from God.'[17] To another hopeful Anglican correspondent, in December 1885, Newman wrote:

> As to the Church of England, I have no wishes just now for its destruction. I should rejoice to fancy the possibility of its reconciling itself to that Holy Catholic Church, whose boast it is that it concedes nothing: but I should not wish to purchase even the power and popularity of the Anglican Church at the price of surrendering one jot or tittle of Catholic Roman teaching. The Bishop of Durham with you speaks of the Disestablishment of the Ch of E as a great national sin. No – that sin was committed three centuries ago, when the State sent the true Church the right about and installed the Anglican in her place.[18]

This has a ring of Manning about it, but it is Newman writing.

The Ecumenical Movement, however, in its early stages expressed the hope that if Christians of different denominations agreed to work together in close co-operation, their divisions might gradually dissolve. Manning, in his creed of Practical Christianity and in his readiness to work in amity with Dissenters in the United Kingdom Alliance, and to share a platform with the Salvation Army, could claim to be the pioneer within his Church in this country of exactly that spirit of mutual co-operation that the first ecumenicists hoped to encourage. He never denied the workings of the Holy Spirit in the Church of England; where he offended Anglicans was in his insistence that they were no less in schism than Nonconformists. He recognized fellow Christians outside the Catholic unity; and he believed that his Church had much to learn from the Protestant ministry. 'Why then do we not draw men as Spurgeon and General Booth or Hugh Price Hughes? I am afraid that there are two obvious reasons. We choose our topics unwisely, and we are not on fire with the love of God and of souls.'[19] Even Manning's worst enemy could not accuse him of failing to practise what he preached. Bodley once expressed it thus:

> If there had been half-a-dozen Mannings, England would have run the risk of being converted – not necessarily to Roman Catholicism, for in all our years of close intercourse he never said a word to persuade me to join that religion, nor did he show forth its superiority except by his life and example – but to Christianity.[20]

Newman's claim to have any place in the development of ecumenicism is more elusive and indirect. It arises from the circumstance that insights which he had acquired as an Anglican came in time to exercise an influence on his own Church, so that as extreme positions were abandoned, dialogue between the two Churches could become possible and productive; and such has been the influence of his writings, both Anglican and Catholic, that members of both Churches have come to recognize a wider area of common ground than they had hitherto suspected. Probably Newman had neither the expectation nor the intention of bringing this about. After all, he was not to know that Anglicans would always continue to claim him as in part their own;[21] or that his fellow Catholics would come to realize that to understand his fertile mind fully imposed upon them the necessity of appreciating the extent to which his insights had been

formed outside the One True Fold. This being so, the mounting
enthusiasm for the bestowal upon Newman of the ultimate divine
accolade of canonization has almost as strong an Anglican backing
as a Catholic. Quite apart from the personal qualifications that
may be deemed necessary for such an honour, the act would
appear as some sort of symbolic gratification of the desire of the
two Churches to be more nearly one.

Fortunately it is no part of a historian's duty (and it is certainly
not his right) either to make or to unmake saints. He might,
however, be permitted to comment on some of the qualities that
would seem to be desirable, if not obligatory, for such an elevated
status, and to consider how the two convert cardinals measure up
to these criteria. If one attribute is the capacity to face heroic
suffering in the service of the Church, it would have to be
admitted that neither Newman nor Manning was ever exposed to
this test. They certainly suffered agonies of doubt and near
despair during the years leading up to their respective conversions, but so did all the converts; and at least both of them were so
circumstanced that they were not denied the privilege of priesthood when they became Catholics. Both had to cope with the
frustrations of either non-recognition or determined, sometimes
malicious, opposition as Catholics, but they eventually saw the
gratification of their respective ambitions (Newman was well
aware how considerable an influence he wielded in his writings,
and Manning gained the position of power he desired), and – in
the end – they received the highest honour that the Holy See
could bestow. The virtue of Christian fortitude impressed upon
them that – as Newman put it – saints should be 'forgetful of their
injuries',[22] or – in Manning's words – they should 'suffer and be
silent';[23] but neither passed this test at moments of deepest
frustration. If Newman complained rather more than Manning,
perhaps he had stronger reasons for so doing.

One of the hallmarks of a saint is the capacity to display a spirit
of Christian joyousness. Neither Newman nor Manning was an
exemplar of this virtue. The adjective that came most commonly
to people's lips in describing Manning was 'solemn'. He could be
witty as a public speaker, because this was all part of the
accomplished debater's armoury, but only in the complete privacy
of a *tête-à-tête* with a close friend could he drop the solemn and
stately manner. Spontaneous attempts to be light-hearted usually
flopped. Wilfrid Ward recalled a visit from him to St Edmund's,

when the mood among the students was hostile because Manning had replaced the popular 'old Catholic' President with 'a thorough Roman'. 'His solemn jokes, generally received with obsequious hilarity ... fell quite flat. The College band played dutifully to welcome him. He felt at once ... a want of cordiality, and tried to introduce a more genial atmosphere by taking the conductor's baton when the music was over and with a furtive smile beating the time himself, expecting much laughter ... Dead silence ensued ... and I think the Archbishop blushed.'[24]

Newman was a master of delicate irony, but – as has been observed by a sympathetic critic – this was almost his 'sole form of humour'.[25] When occasion demanded he could display effective satirical caricature, notably in *Loss and Gain* and his *Lectures on the Present Position of Catholics*. Once, and only once, he allowed himself to tell a joke in the course of his vast correspondence, a somewhat laboured one about an Irvingite and a keeper of a lunatic asylum.[26] Within his family circle, his humour tended to be facetious rather than funny. He needed the assurance of rapport and goodwill before he could relax. Like Manning, he loved children, and was easy with them, as the daughters of Dean Church fondly recalled. But he could be moody and shy with strangers. When von Hügel met him, he was surprised and disappointed. 'I used to wonder, in my intercourse with John Henry Newman,' he wrote, 'how one so good and who had made so many sacrifices to God, could be so depressing.' It was not at all what he had been led to believe was the character of a saint – no sign of 'deep spiritual joy'.[27] Wilfrid Ward blamed the Oxford Movement for this rather un-Catholic solemnity, which had left its mark on both men (but not his own father): 'an almost alarming gravity of outlook', not priggish exactly, but disturbingly scrupulous in religious temper and bearing.[28]

If it were demanded of a saint that he should exhibit in his character the sum of Christian virtues, which clearly it is not, neither Newman nor Manning would qualify. Humility was not Manning's natural state. He was proud by nature, and he knew it. Like Gregory VII, whom he so much admired, he had to fight a constant battle to suppress pride and ambition; and probably found it easier to be humble when he became Archbishop, as perhaps Newman did after he had become a cardinal. Neither man had anything more to prove. To apply this criticism to Newman may seem unfair, because the aura of humility about his person so often struck observers, who could be quite over-whelmed by it; and it would be wrong to suggest that this was a pose. Nevertheless the essence of humility is the determination to subjugate *self*, to be more conscious of one's own failings than the shortcomings of others. It is difficult to resist the conclusion that, if Manning's battle was with pride, Newman's chief temptation was self-will.

He had, he admitted, a 'morbidly sensitive skin',[29] which is itself a manifestation of self-absorption. His compulsion to speak out so often conflicted with his sense of duty to keep silent. As an Anglican he had regarded his bishop as his Pope, but only – in his heart of hearts – while his bishop was supportive and not restrictive. In the more authoritative Church that he joined, the dilemma became even more intense. Henry Scott Holland has summed up Newman's predicament memorably. With Newman, he wrote,

> always there is a little aloofness preserved; and you feel at last that Dr Newman must be Dr Newman; he cannot commit himself quite to anything outside his own intimate personality. And yet his loyalty to the Body is complete, and his desire to serve is passionately sincere, and his real humility is most touching. It is simply a sort of spiritual fastidiousness, that makes him conscious always of the personal element itself, to a degree that weakens action.[30]

Posterity has no cause to regret this. Newman's determination to follow his own line – in spite of the Persian lash of Propaganda – meant that he took risks in almost everything he wrote. Thankfully, the Church in the end came to recognize that the risks that he was prepared to take resulted in offerings, the value of which outweighed the occasional embarrassment that he may have caused. Less creditable to him, however, although it may have been the price that his genius had to exact of him, was the way in which his indomitable self-will coloured so many of his relationships. This was a fault which he either did not recognize in himself, or – if he did – could do nothing to amend. Almost all his friendships were far too personally self-directed. The value of a friendship tended to be calculated, with an almost mathematical exactness, according to the degree of unquestioning love towards himself, so that he gave the impression of elevating his own needs higher than a friend's. He therefore took the merest hint of a personal slight far too much to heart. This explains why he seemed continually to fail to come to grips with the concept of forgiveness as well as its practice. He nourished resentment far too deeply; he refused to take efforts at reconciliation at their face value; and a trust once broken was a trust destroyed.

So Newman had his faults, and the incapacity to forgive was by far the most serious. He had blind spots, too, the chief of which was his comparative indifference to poverty and social injustice. Nor was Manning by any means a paragon. His worst fault was his determination to get his own way, and to win his battles, some-times by ruthless means; and since he tended to see his various issues in black and white, his conviction of rectitude led him too often to translate his conflicts into apocalyptic terms, with his opponent cast in the role of Antichrist. Gladstone, for all his admiration for Manning, believed this to be his particular blind spot:

> I habitually considered Manning's faculties of action [he wrote], I mean in the management and government of men, to be far in advance of his faculties of thought. In polemical matters he was narrow and positive; he had not the power of looking all round a great subject; accordingly he was intensely satisfied with all his conclusions ... I think in short that his mind was not philosophical ... he arrived with extraordinary facility at broad conclusions; and held to them with a tenacity not less remarkable. He was not subtle, but he was always intensely clear; if he deceived anybody, the person taken in was alone responsible.[31]

Another fault that was sometimes alleged against Manning, and notably by Newman himself, was that he was insincere. He could say smooth and gracious things, while stabbing you in the back. It is perfectly true that his public remarks about people were sometimes contradicted by his private reflections; and it is prob-ably fair criticism that his propensity to offer olive-branches to those who opposed him was motivated more by his desire to win them to his side than by any sincere readiness to meet them half-way. He denied that he had ever consciously tried to wound any man, and probably believed that to be true. In the course of a conflict, however, in which – to him – crucial principles were at stake, the prosecution of his own concerns tended to take priority over personal consideration for others. He was not a spiteful man; and – to his great credit – he never bore grudges. He went out of his way to be forgiving to those who had tried to destroy everything he had worked for in his early years in the Catholic

Church – to Searle, to Maguire, and to Errington, above all. His efforts to vindicate Newman's reputation in Rome, both in 1875 and in 1878, were generous both in word and in deed. Of course, it is always easier to be generous in victory than in defeat; and Manning rarely lost his battles.

Although Newman constantly maintained that 'I have nothing of a saint about me',[32] he took a certain comfort from the fact that saints have been far from faultless. 'A saint is a peculiar being,' he had observed to Henry Wilberforce in 1849;[33] and in his introduction to his study of the early saints, in the second volume of his *Historical Sketches*, he had this to say: 'Their lingering imperfections surely make us love them the more, without leading us to reverence them the less, and act as a relief to the discouragement and despondency which may come over those, who, in the midst of much error and sin, are striving to imitate them.'[34] He could have been speaking both for himself and for Manning. Each, in his different way, was just such a man as Newman described in the first sermon of his *Discourses to Mixed Congregations* – one 'simply striving, in all he does, to please God';[35] and the one no less so than the other.

With Manning, this striving took the form of such a degree of unworldliness that he could not but strike awe in all who met him; and yet, although he always seemed to be governed 'by some mystical sense of the presence of unseen agencies guiding the corporate life of the Church',[36] he gave all his energies to the world, content to be a fool for Christ's sake, that he might heal its miseries and rescue its lost souls. It was an inspiring life; and its only sadness was that its legacy was relatively short-lived. Although he heralded the advent of democracy with such confidence, passionately believing that the Church of the future should gain its strength from, and give its heart to, the people, few have appreciated that in this appeal the great Ultramontane was perhaps more 'a man for our times' than any other churchman of his day. As Philip Hughes has put it:

> Alas, the leader of genius formed no school, left no Eliseus to catch his mantle as he sped from earth. But the memory of his universal sympathies, of his generous indignation, and of his virile public courage remained to animate a younger generation … and to strengthen the outspoken simplicities of the great cardinal of the war years, Arthur Hinsley. Nor are the echoes yet silent of Manning's mighty veracity.[37]

The services which Newman rendered to his Church have been universally acknowledged, but not always with the correct emphases. Books and articles in profusion have been written about his philosophical and theological perceptions, and a good many of them, one cannot but feel, would have been totally beyond Newman's comprehension, so enamoured was he of simple diction and so averse to technical verbiage. Besides, he knew where his strength really lay: he was first and foremost an apologist. In that capacity, none since his day (or during it) has remotely approached his stature. Through his writings, thousands of people, in his own lifetime and since his death, have been drawn to an appreciation of the beauty and the grandeur of Catholic truth; and thousands more will feel the same compulsion in years to come. Newman's influence will never die.

But there is something else besides, something even finer; something that comes from the heart of the man himself. When Dean Church had just published Newman's obituary in the *Guardian*, his friend E. S. Talbot, that great Anglican divine, wrote to share in Church's obvious sense of loss in the passing of his dear friend.

> Was there ever a life of more sweetly and gravely solemn power to thrill and touch one? What do we not owe him? and what might have been! It is wonderful to think of him *there*. I don't know whether you will like me to say it – but it is true that you have done more, so much more, than any one to carry on and convey to us the touch of his special spiritual and mental power: that indefinable thing.[38]

'That indefinable thing' – there is indeed no word for it; but whatever it may have been, it is surely something known to, and the property of, the saints. Perhaps, then, this special quality, when added to the incomparable influence for good in his writings, appreciated by Catholics and Anglicans alike, and helping – in mutual respect for their author – to bring them ever closer together, gives to Newman the stronger claim for the highest recognition that the Catholic Church can bestow; but this does not mean that he was necessarily the greater man.

Newman himself believed that there were two distinct classes of saints. There was St Ambrose, and there was St Basil. The 'majestic Ambrose' and the 'never-wearied Athanasius' were 'men of acute and ready mind, with accurate knowledge of human nature and large plans, and persuasive and attractive bearing, genial, sociable, and popular, endowed with prudence, patience, instinctive tact and decision in conducting matters, as well as boldness and zeal.' But then there was also

> the retired and thoughtful student, who remains years and years in the solitude of a college or a monastery, chastening his soul in secret, raising it to high thought and single-minded purpose . . . Such an one is often unsuccessful in his own day . . . he does his work, and so leaves it, and it seems to die; but in the generation after him it lives again, and on the long run it is difficult to say, which of the two classes of men has served the cause of truth more effectually.[39]

Such was Basil, this retired student indoors. Such might well be Newman, in contrast to the man with 'large plans' – a man like Manning, perhaps. Each will 'serve God according to the peculiar gifts given to him'.[40]

But will they recognize what each has to give, in their own lifetime? When, in 1864, Newman heard of the death of Bishop Bagot and how earnestly the bishop, as he lay dying, expressed the wish that he could see the former Vicar of St Mary's again, so that he could at least assure him of his enduring esteem, he felt a little guilty. He had not realized how much the other had felt for him. With this reflection, he wrote some very beautiful words; and, in reading them, one can easily transpose the aspiration for some ultimate reconciliation to the predicament of the two convert cardinals who, in their lifetime, found it so difficult to work together in mutual amity and trust:

> Alas, alas [Newman wrote] – in this world, how little we know each other – and how blessed will it be if we are by God's mercy brought together in a country where all is light and all is known.[41]

References

ABBREVIATIONS

The source most frequently quoted is *The Letters and Diaries of John Henry Newman*, edited by C. S. Dessain and others (London and Oxford, 1961–84), vols I–VI and vols X–XXXI. This source is abbreviated to the initials *LD*, followed by the volume number.

Place of publication throughout is London, unless otherwise stated.

Manning's works all carry the prefix [M], as under:

[M]	*Aem*	*Aemulamina Meliora*, 1880
[M]	*App*	*The Appellate Jurisdiction of the Crown in Matters Spiritual. A Letter to the Bishop of Chichester*, 1850
[M]	*CA*	'The Cathedral Act', in *British Critic*, LVII, 1841
[M]	*CES*	*The Child of the English Savage*, with B. Waugh, 1866
[M]	*CHA*	*Christ and Antichrist. A Sermon . . . for those who fell in defence of Rome*, 1867
[M]	*Charges*	*Charges delivered at the Ordinary Visitation of the Archdeaconry of Chichester*, 1841, 1842, 1845
[M]	*Dom*	'Dominus Illuminatio Mea' (Sermon at Oxford, 1875), in *Allen Review*, no. 6, 1992
[M]	*EC*	*The English Church: its Succession and Witness for Christ. A Sermon*, 1835
[M]	*EP*	*The Eternal Priesthood*, 1907 edn
[M]	*FPS*	*The Future of the Primary Schools*, 1886
[M]	*GOF*	*The Grounds of Faith. Four Lectures delivered at St George's Church, Southwark*, 1852
[M]	*HNNG*	*Help Nearest when Need Greatest. A Sermon preached at the Synod of Oscott, 11 July 1852*, 1852
[M]	*LGHS*	*The Last Glories of the Holy See Greater than the First. Three Lectures*, 1861
[M]	*LJP*	*The Love of Jesus to Penitents*, 1866
[M]	*Misc*	*Miscellanies*, 3 vols, 1877–88
[M]	*OUS*	*Sermons preached before the University of Oxford*, Oxford, 1844
[M]	*PCHS*	*The Present Crisis of the Holy See. Three Lectures*, 1861
[M]	*PO*	*The Pastoral Office*, 1883
[M]	*Ppap*	*Pastime Papers*, ed. W. Meynell, 1892
[M]	*PP*	*Petri Privilegium. Three Pastoral Letters*, 1871
[M]	*ROC*	*The Reunion of Christendom. A Pastoral Letter*, 1866
[M]	*ROF*	*The Rule of Faith. Appendix to a Sermon*, 1838

[M] *RV*   *Religio Viatoris*, 4th edn, 1890
[M] *Serm*   *Sermons*, 4 vols, 1845–50
[M] *Sin*   *Sin; and its Consequences*, 1874
[M] *SPP*   *St Peter's Pence. An Address to the Congregation of St Mary of the Angels*, 1861
[M] *TMHG*   *The Temporal Mission of the Holy Ghost; on Reason and Revelation*, 1892 edn
[M] *TPP*   *The Temporal Power of the Popes in its Political Aspect*, 1866
[M] *TSP*   *The Temporal Sovereignty of the Popes. Three Lectures*, 1860
[M] *TSVC*   *The True Story of the Vatican Council*, 1877
[M] *UC*   *The Unity of the Church*, 1842
[M] *VD*   *The Vatican Decrees and their bearing on Civil Allegiance*, 1875
[M] *WHS*   *The Workings of the Holy Spirit in the Church of England. A letter to the Rev. E. B. Pusey*, 1864

Newman's works all carry the prefix [N], as under:

[N] *Add*   *Addresses to Cardinal Newman, with his replies, 1879–81*, ed. W. P. Neville, 1905
[N] *Apol*   *Apologia pro vita sua*, 1864 and 1865 versions, ed. W. Ward, Oxford, 1913
[N] *Arians*   *The Arians of the Fourth Century, their Doctrine, Temper and Conduct*, 1833
[N] *AW*   *Autobiographical Writings*, ed. H. Tristram, 1956
[N] *Call*   *Callista. A Tale of the Third Century*, 1914 edn
[N] *CFD*   *On Consulting the Faithful in Matters of Doctrine*, ed. J. Coulson, 1986
[N] *CS*   *Catholic Sermons of Cardinal Newman*, ed. C. S. Dessain, 1957
[N] *DA*   *Discussions and Arguments on Various Subjects*, 1872 edn
[N] *Dev*   *An Essay on the Development of Christian Doctrine*, 1881 edn
[N] *Diff*   *Certain Difficulties felt by Anglicans in Catholic Teaching considered*, 2 vols, 1895 edn
[N] *Disc*   *Discourses addressed to Mixed Congregations*, 1849
[N] *ECH*   *Essays Critical and Historical*, 2 vols, 1872 edn
[N] *EOM*   *Two Essays on Biblical and Ecclesiastical Miracles*, 1873 edn
[N] *GA*   *An Essay in aid of a Grammar of Assent*, ed. I. T. Ker, Oxford, 1985
[N] *HS*   *Historical Sketches*, 3 vols, 1908 edn
[N] *Idea*   *The Idea of a University, defined and illustrated in Nine Discourses . . . and in Occasional Lectures and Essays addressed to Members of the Catholic University*, 1891 edn
[N] *Just*   *Lectures on Justification*, 1838
[N] *LBB*   *A Letter to the Bishop of Oxford on occasion of no. 90 in the series called the Tracts for the Times*, Oxford, 1841
[N] *LG*   *Loss and Gain. The Story of a Convert*, 1903 edn
[N] *LRWJ*   *A Letter to the Rev. R. W. Jelf . . . in explanation of no. 90 in the series called the Tracts for the Times*, Oxford, 1841
[N] *Med*   *Meditations and Devotions of Cardinal Newman*, 1893
[N] *OUS*   *Fifteen Sermons preached before the University of Oxford*, 1918 edn
[N] *PPC*   *Lectures on the Present Position of Catholics in England*, 1904 edn
[N] *PPS*   *Parochial and Plain Sermons*, 8 vols, 1868 edn
[N] *SE*   *Stray Essays on Controversial Points variously illustrated*, 1890
[N] *SN*   *Sermon Notes of John Henry Cardinal Newman, 1849–1878*, ed. Fathers of the Birmingham Oratory, 1913

[N] *SSD* *Sermons bearing on Subjects of the Day*, 1918 edn
[N] *SVO* *Sermons preached on Various Occasions*, 1870 edn
[N] *TPBI* *Theological Papers on Biblical Inspiration and on Infallibility*, ed. J. D. Holmes, Oxford, 1979
[N] *TPFC* *Theological Papers on Faith and Certainty*, ed. H. M. Achaval and J. D. Holmes, Oxford, 1976
[N] *UDIS* *Discourses on the Scope and Nature of University Education addressed to the Catholics of Dublin*, Dublin, 1852
[N] *VM1* *The Via Media of the Anglican Church*, ed. H. D. Weidner, Oxford, 1990
[N] *VM2* *The Via Media of the Anglican Church*, vol. 2, 1877
[N] *VVO* *Verses on Various Occasions*, 1868

NOTES

Prologue

1. G. M. Young, *Victorian England. Portrait of an Age* (1949), p. 150.
2. David Newsome, *The Parting of Friends. A Study of the Wilberforces and Henry Manning* (1966), pp. 381–2.
3. G. Kitson Clark, *The Making of Victorian England* (1962), p. 20.
4. G. K. Chesterton, *The Victorian Age in Literature*, p. 17.
5. *LD*, XXXI, p. 294.

INTRODUCTION: Abuse and Panegyric

SECTION I

1. H. I. D. Ryder, *Essays* (1911), p. 280.
2. J. E. C. Bodley, *Cardinal Manning, and other Essays* (1912), p. 21.
3. Maisie Ward, *The Wilfrid Wards and the Transition* (1934), vol. I., p. 20.
4. C. Butler, *The Life and Times of Bishop Ullathorne, 1806–1889* (1926), vol. II, p. 118.
5. Bodley, p. 15.
6. S. Leslie, *Henry Edward Manning. His Life and Labours* (1921), p. 273.

SECTION II

1. *LD*, XXVI, p. 200.
2. *LD*, XXX, p. 4; XXIX, p. 388.
3. *LD*, XXX, pp. 13–14.
4. *LD*, XXXI, p. 91 n.2.
5. *LD*, XXXI, p. 38.
6. *LD*, XXIX, pp. 343–4.
7. *LD*, XXXI, pp. 93–4.
8. *LD*, XXVIII, pp. 92–3; [N] *AW*, p. 24.
9. *LD*, XXII, p. 211.
10. *LD*, XXXI, p. 31.

11. *LD*, XX, pp. 442–4.
12. [N] *ECH*, vol. II, pp. 425–6.
13. [N] *HS*, vol. II, pp. 219–20.
14. *LD*, XXX, p. 303.
15. [N] *Apol*, p. 191.
16. *LD*, XV, pp. 164–5.
17. *LD*, XXVI, p. 375.
18. *LD*, XIX, p. 424.
19. *LD*, XX, p. 443.
20. E. E. Kelly, 'Newman's Reputation and the Biographical Tradition', in *Faith and Reason*, vol. XV no. 4 (1989), pp. 155–7.

SECTION III

1. V. A. McClelland, 'Gladstone and Manning: A Question of Authority', in P. J. Jagger (ed.), *Gladstone, Politics and Religion* (1985), p. 148.
2. Bodley, pp. 49–50.
3. For what follows, see S. Gilley, 'New Light on an old Scandal', in *Opening the Scrolls. Essays in Catholic History in honour of Godfrey Anstruther*, ed. A. Bellenger (Downside, 1987), pp. 166–95.

4. Butler, *Ullathorne*, vol. II, p. 17.
5. Gilley, *art. cit.*, pp. 171–2.
6. *Ibid.*, p. 173.
7. Quoted in *ibid.*, p. 175.
8. M. Ward, vol. I, p. 217.
9. Ryder, p. 274.
10. E. S. Purcell, *The Life of Cardinal Manning, Archbishop of Westminster* (1896), vol. I, pp. 415–17.
11. *Ibid.*, vol. I, p. 240.
12. *Ibid.*, vol. II, p. 96.
13. D. C. Lathbury, *Correspondence on Church and Religion of W. E. Gladstone* (1910), vol. II, p. 339.
14. W. Ward, *The Life and Times of Cardinal Wiseman* (1897), vol. II, pp. 321–2, 631–7.
15. Gilley, *art. cit.*, pp. 193–4.
16. Lytton Strachey, *Eminent Victorians* (1948 edn), p. 6.
17. F. A. Simpson, 'Max Beerbohm on Lytton Strachey', in *Cambridge Review*, 4 December 1943, p. 67.
18. Robert Gray, *Cardinal Manning. A Biography* (1985), p. 327.

SECTION IV

1. Owen Chadwick, *The Spirit of the Oxford Movement. Tractarian Essays* (Cambridge, 1990), p. 146.
2. A short biography can be found in G. Egner [P. J. Fitzpatrick], *Apologia pro Charles Kingsley* (1969), p. 221.
3. E. A. Abbott, *Philomythus: An Antidote against Credulity* (1891), p. 3.
4. E. A. Abbott, *The Anglican Career of Cardinal Newman* (1892), vol. II, p. 322.
5. *Ibid.*, vol. II, p. 428.
6. H. Bremond, *The Mystery of Newman* (1907), p. ix.
7. *Ibid.*, p. 62.
8. *Ibid.*, pp. 73–4.
9. *Ibid.*, p. 102.

10. *Ibid.*, pp. 196, 207–8, 319–23.
11. M. Ward, vol. II, pp. 172–3.
12. Chadwick, *op. cit.*, p. 181.
13. Bremond, p. 13.
14. G. Prevost (ed.), *The Autobiography of Isaac Williams* (1892), p. 49.
15. Bremond, p. 4.
16. M. Ward, vol. II, p. 334.
17. J. Coulson, 'Was Newman a Modernist?', in *Newman Studien*, vol. xiv, p. 74.
18. W. Ward, *Last Lectures* (1918), p. 169.
19. S. Gilley, 'An Intellectual Discipleship: Newman and the Making of Wilfrid Ward', in *Louvain Studies; John Henry Cardinal Newman 1801–1890*, ed. T. Merrigan (Louvain, 1990), p. 321.
20. E. Kelly, pp. 159–60.
21. M. Ward, vol. II, p. 349.
22. J. D. Holmes, 'Newman a Saint: Historical Perspectives', in *Newman Studien*, vol. xii, p. 31.
23. *LD*, XI, p. xx.
24. E. Kelly, p. 163 n.4.
25. Sheridan Gilley, *Newman and his Age* (1990), p. 416.
26. A. O. J. Cockshut, *Truth to Life. The Art of Biography in the Nineteenth Century* (1974), p. 199.
27. E. Kelly, pp. 161–2.
28. J. Altholz, 'Some Observations on Victorian Religious Biography: Newman and Manning', in *Worship*, vol. xliii, no. 7 (Minnesota, 1969), p. 412.

SECTION V

1. Owen Chadwick, *Michael Ramsey. A Life* (Oxford, 1990), p. 107.
2. [N] *PPS*, vol. III, pp. 321, 326.
3. David Mathew, *Catholicism in England. The Portrait of a Minority: its Culture and Traditions* (1955), p. 210.

CHAPTER 1 : Vocations

SECTION I

1. *LD*, II, p. 290.
2. Purcell, vol. II, p. 749.
3. *Ibid.*, vol. I, p. 67.
4. *LD*, III, pp. 95, 97.

5. Seán O'Faoláin, *Newman's Way* (1952), p. 9.
6. *LD*, XX, p. 23.
7. *LD*, XV, p. 396.
8. Purcell, vol. I, pp. 4–5.
9. F. W. Newman, *Contributions chiefly to*

the Early History of the late Cardinal
Newman (1891), p. 7.
10. *Ibid.*, p. 9.
11. [N] *AW*, p. 82.
12. A. Mozley (ed.), *Letters of the Rev.
J. B. Mozley* (1885), p. 59.
13. Purcell, vol. I, p. 7.
14. Gray, p. 14.
15. Purcell, vol. I, p. 9.
16. *Ibid.*, vol. I, p. 11.
17. J. H. Overton and E. Wordsworth,
*Christopher Wordsworth, Bishop of
Lincoln, 1807–1885* (1890), pp. 22–
3.
18. M. Ward, vol. I, p. 26.
19. Purcell, vol. I, p. 17.
20. Gray, p. 18.
21. A. P. Stanley, *The Life and
Correspondence of Thomas Arnold*
(1858), vol. I, p. 27.
22. Gray, p. 18.
23. [N] *AW*, p. 29.
24. Ian Ker, *John Henry Newman. A
Biography* (Oxford, 1988), p. 9.
25. Louis Bouyer, *Newman. His Life and
Spirituality* (1958), p. 5.
26. F. W. Newman, pp. 4–5.
27. *LD*, XIV, p. 78.
28. *LD*, I, p. 22.

SECTION II

1. [N] *Apol*, p. 107.
2. *LD*, I, p. 29.
3. Newsome, *The Parting of Friends*,
pp. 8–10.
4. Bouyer, p. 18.
5. [N] *Apol*, p. 108.
6. *Ibid.*
7. [N] *AW*, p. 150.
8. [N] *Apol*, p. 110.
9. *LD*, XXXI, p. 31.
10. C. S. Dessain, 'Newman's First
Conversion', in *Newman Studien*, vol.
iii, p. 37.
11. [N] *Apol*, pp. 105–6.
12. *Ibid.*, p. 106.
13. *Ibid.*, p. 108; cf. [N] *PPS*, vol. I,
p. 20, [N] *SSD*, p. 38.
14. [N] *Apol*, p. 291.
15. See [N] *AW*, p. 143.
16. [N] *Apol*, pp. 109–10.
17. Stephen Thomas, *Newman and
Heresy. The Anglican Years*
(Cambridge, 1991), p. 10.
18. *Ibid.*, pp. 46, 171.

19. *Ibid.*, p. 249.
20. [N] *GA*, pp. 259–60.
21. *Ibid.*, pp. 275–6.
22. *LD*, XIX, p. 66.
23. Robin Selby, *The Principle of Reserve
in the Writings of John Henry Newman*
(Oxford, 1975), p. 46.
24. [N] *PPS*, vol. I, p. 286.
25. [N] *Disc*, pp. 156–7.
26. G. Rowell (ed.), *Tradition Renewed.
Oxford Movement Conference Papers*
(1986), p. 71.
27. *LD*, XVIII, p. 81.
28. J. Walsh, 'Origins of the Evangelical
Revival', in *Essays in Modern Church
History in Memory of Norman Sykes*,
eds G. V. Bennett and J. D. Walsh
(1966), pp. 133–4.
29. [N] *AW*, p. 166.
30. [N] *Apol*, pp. 108–9.
31. Owen Chadwick, *Newman* (Oxford,
1983), pp. 9–10.

SECTION III

1. Purcell, vol. I, p. 25.
2. *Ibid.*, vol. I, pp. 13–14.
3. *Ibid.*, vol. I, p. 9.
4. *Ibid.*, vol. I, p. 10.
5. Gray, p. 19.
6. Purcell, vol. I, p. 23n.
7. *Ibid.*, vol. I, pp. 49, 57.
8. *Ibid.*, vol. I, p. 67.
9. *Ibid.*, vol. I, p. 49.
10. V. A. McClelland, 'Spiritual
Nemesis: Henry Edward Manning
and the Road to Rome', in *The Allen
Review*, 6 (1990), p. 5.
11. Purcell, vol. I, p. 48.
12. *Ibid.*, vol. I, p. 30 n.1.
13. T. Mozley, *Reminiscences chiefly of
Oriel College and the Oxford Movement*
(1882), vol. I, p. 424.
14. F. H. Doyle, *Reminiscences and
Opinions* (1886), pp. 105–6.
15. Purcell, vol. I, p. 30 n.1.
16. A. W. Hutton, *Cardinal Manning*
(1892), p. 10.
17. Leslie, p. 34.
18. Purcell, vol. I, p. 56.
19. *Ibid.*, vol. I, p. 55.
20. *Ibid.*, vol. I, p. 71.
21. *Ibid.*, vol. I, p. 77.
22. Christopher O'Gorman, 'A History
of Henry Manning's Religious
Opinions 1808–1832', in *Recusant*

History, vol. 21, no. 2 (October, 1992), p. 160.
23. *Ibid.*, pp. 159–61.
24. Leslie, p. 37.
25. *Ibid.*
26. O'Gorman, p. 161.
27. Purcell, vol. I, p. 89.
28. *Ibid.*, vol. I, p. 112.
29. Bodley, p. 30.
30. Richard Schiefen, *Nicholas Wiseman and the Transformation of English Catholicism* (Shepherdstown, 1984), p. 25.
31. *Ibid.*, p. 117.
32. [M] *LJP*, p. 83.
33. [M] *EP*, p. 85.
34. Leslie, p. 161.
35. [M] *RV*, p. 62.
36. Leslie, pp. 39–42.

SECTION IV

1. [N] *AW*, p. 30.
2. *LD*, XVI, p. 110.
3. *LD*, I, p. 40.
4. *LD*, II, p. 133.
5. *LD*, I, p. 99.
6. [N] *AW*, p. 47.
7. *LD*, I, p. 96.
8. [N] *AW*, p. 61.
9. *Ibid.*, p. 63.
10. H. P. Liddon, *The Life of Edward Bouverie Pusey* (1894–8), vol. I, p. 360.
11. [N] *AW*, p. 64.
12. *LD*, I, pp. 123–4.
13. [N] *AW*, p. 65.
14. *Ibid.*, p. 66.
15. Gilley, p. 43.
16. [N] *AW*, p. 66.
17. *LD*, I, p. 179; p. 183; p. 187; cf. *LD*, XV, p. 83; [N] *SN*, p. ix.
18. *LD*, I, p. 203 n.2.
19. *Ibid.*, I, p. 191.
20. [N] *Apol*, p. 111.
21. *LD*, I, p. 194 n.1.
22. [N] *AW*, p. 206.
23. [N] *Apol*, p. 111.
24. Günter Biemer, *Newman on Tradition* (Freiburg, 1967), p. 37.
25. *Ibid.*, p. 113.
26. [N] *ECH*, vol. II, pp. 56–7.
27. *LD*, I, pp. 219–20.
28. Alf Härdelin, *The Tractarian Understanding of the Eucharist* (Uppsala, 1965), p. 66.

29. [N] *Apol*, p. 113.
30. Härdelin, p. 66 n.33.
31. *Ibid.*, p. 67.
32. Gilley, p. 63; [N] *AW*, p. 211; Thomas, *Newman and Heresy*, pp. 15–19.
33. A. Dwight Culler, *The Imperial Intellect. A Study of Newman's Educational Ideal* (New Haven, 1955), p. 4.
34. *LD*, II, p. 37; [N] *AW*, pp. 212–13.
35. *LD*, II, p. 50.
36. Geoffrey Faber, *Oxford Apostles. A Character Study of The Oxford Movement* (1933), pp. 190–2.
37. Marvin R. O'Connell, *The Oxford Conspiracy: A History of the Oxford Movement 1833–45* (1969), p. 113.
38. *LD*, II, p. 55.
39. O. W. Jones, *Isaac Williams and his Circle* (1971), p. 25.
40. H. D. Weidner in [N] *VM 1*, p. xx.
41. *LD*, I, p. 285.
42. *Ibid.*, p. 309.
43. *LD*, XXX, p. 330.
44. Piers Brendon, *Hurrell Froude and the Oxford Movement* (1974), p. 37.
45. *Ibid.*, p. 71.
46. *Ibid.*, p. 68.
47. [N] *Apol*, p. 117.
48. *LD*, II, p. 173 n.1.
49. *LD*, II, p. 228; [N] *AW*, p. 78.
50. Liddon, vol. I, pp. 136–7.
51. [N] *Apol*, p. 118.
52. *LD*, II, pp. 117–18.
53. *Ibid.*, p. 122.
54. *Ibid.*, pp. 125–6.
55. *Ibid.*, pp. 127–8.
56. Peter Nockles, 'The Oxford Movement and the University', in *History of the University of Oxford*, ed. M. G. Brock, vol. vi (1991), p. 12.
57. *LD*, II, p. 367.
58. Newsome, pp. 94–5.
59. *LD*, II, p. 240.
60. R. D. Middleton, *Newman at Oxford. His Religious Development* (1950), p. 53.
61. *LD*, II, pp. 368–9.
62. Mark Pattison, *Memoirs* (1885), p. 87.
63. [N] *AW*, pp. 99–100.
64. *LD*, II, pp. 213–14.
65. *Ibid.*, p. 229.
66. [N] *AW*, p. 126.
67. Mary Church (ed.), *The Life and Letters of Dean Church* (1895), p. 36.

CHAPTER 2 : The Tractarian and the Churchman

SECTION I

1. *The Gladstone Diaries, with Cabinet Minutes and Prime-Ministerial Correspondence*, ed. H. C. G. Matthew (Oxford, 1982), vol. VII, p. 202.
2. *LD*, II, p. 128.
3. Newsome, p. 6.
4. *Ibid.*, p. 7.
5. Peter Toon, *Evangelical Theology 1833–56. A Response to Tractarianism* (1979), pp. 4–5.
6. Quoted in Boyd Hilton, *The Age of Atonement. The Influence of Evangelicalism on Social and Economic Thought, 1785–1865* (Oxford, 1988), p. 27.
7. William Palmer, *A Narrative of Events connected with the Publication of the Tracts for the Times* (1883), p. 99.
8. [N] *OUS*, p. 197.
9. [N] *DA*, pp. 27–8; [N] *ECH*, vol. I, pp. 269–70.
10. *LD*, VI, p. 256.
11. *LD*, XXXI, pp. 228–9.
12. *Ibid.*, p. 260 n.3.
13. J. W. Burgon, *Lives of Twelve Good Men* (1888), vol. I, pp. 158–9.
14. *LD*, III, p. 105.
15. *LD*, V, p. 399.
16. [N] *Apol*, pp. 127–8.
17. [N] *Arians*, p. 83.
18. Thomas, *Newman and Heresy*, p. 3; see also Maisie Ward, *Young Mr Newman* (1948), pp. 345–6.
19. *LD*, III, pp. 264–5.
20. Christopher Dawson, *The Spirit of the Oxford Movement* (1945), p. 19.
21. Selby, p. 44.
22. [N] *Arians*, p. 48.
23. Selby, p. 23.
24. [N] *Arians*, p. 79.
25. *Ibid.*, p. 81.
26. Walter Lock. *John Keble* (3rd edn, 1893), p. 48.
27. *LD*, III, p. 120.
28. [N] *ECH*, vol. I, p. 268.
29. *Ibid.*, vol. I, p. 272.
30. *LD*, III, p. 224.
31. *Ibid.*, p. 249.
32. E. Jane Whately, *Life and Correspondence of Richard Whately* (1866), vol. I, p. 229.
33. Terence Kenny, *The Political Thought of John Henry Newman* (1957), p. 121.
34. *Ibid.*, p. 142.
35. *LD*, II, p. 348.
36. William Robbins, *The Newman Brothers. An Essay in Comparative Intellectual Biography* (1966), pp. 33–4.
37. *LD*, III, p. 266.
38. *Ibid.*, p. 281.
39. *LD*, IV, p. 107 n.1.
40. *Ibid.*, pp. 107–8.
41. *Ibid.*, pp. 105–6; p. 110.
42. Ker, p. 87.
43. *LD*, III, p. 315.
44. [N] *Apol*, p. 135.
45. Dawson, p. 55.

SECTION II

1. Purcell, vol. I, p. 89.
2. *Ibid.*, vol. I, pp. 90–1.
3. O'Faoláin, p. 161.
4. Newsome, p. 116.
5. Leslie, p. 47.
6. Newsome, p. 122.
7. *Ibid.*, pp. 150–1.
8. *Ibid.*, p. 127.
9. [M] *Charges (1843)*, p. 35.
10. O'Gorman, p. 161.
11. Purcell, vol. I, p. 112.
12. Newsome, pp. 232–3.
13. *Ibid.*, pp. 200–1.
14. Purcell, vol. I, p. 107 n.1.
15. Text in *LD*, IV, pp. 66–7.
16. *LD*, IV, p. 91.
17. *Ibid.*, p. 68.
18. *Ibid.*, p. 308.
19. [N] *OUS*, p. 97.
20. [N] *VVO*, p. 78.
21. [N] *Call*, p. 215.
22. [N] *Apol*, p. 135.
23. *LD*, VI, p. 171.
24. *LD*, IV, pp. 116–17.
25. Brendon, p. 122.
26. Prevost, p. 63.
27. *The Remains of Richard Hurrell Froude* (1838), vol. I, p. 377.
28. *LD*, II, p. 365.
29. Härdelin, pp. 52–4.
30. Paul Misner, *Papacy and Development. Newman and the Primacy of the Pope* (Leiden, 1976), p. 24.
31. *LD*, IV, pp. 37–8.
32. *LD*, V, pp. 17–20.

33. *LD*, IV, p. 112.
34. *LD*, V, p. 263.
35. Rowell, *Tradition*, p. 41.
36. Palmer, pp. 137–8.
37. Purcell, vol. I, p. 218.
38. *LD*, IV, p. 92.
39. *Ibid.*, p. 97.
40. *Ibid.*, p. 317.
41. *LD*, V, pp. 6, 10.
42. [M] *EC*, pp. 5–7.
43. *Ibid.*, p. 18.
44. *Ibid.*, p. 11.
45. *Ibid.*, p. 26.
46. *Ibid.*, p. 29; cf. [M] *ROF*, pp. 55–6; [M] *UC*, p. 273; [M] *Serm*, vol. I, pp. 41–2; vol. IV, p. 374.
47. Purcell, vol. I, p. 116.
48. *LD*, III, p. 48.
49. *Ibid.*, p. 20.
50. James Pereiro, 'S. F. Wood and an early theory of Development in the Oxford Movement', in *Recusant History*, vol. 20 no. 4 (October 1991), p. 524.
51. J. G. Lockhart, *Charles Lindley Viscount Halifax* (1935), vol. I, p. 78.
52. Pereiro, pp. 530–1.
53. *Ibid.*, p. 534.
54. *Ibid.*, pp. 528, 533.
55. Purcell, vol. I, p. 119.
56. *LD*, V, p. 137 n.1.
57. *Ibid.*, p. 254 n.3.
58. *Ibid.*, p. 370.
59. *Ibid.*, p. 371 n.3.

SECTION III

1. O'Connell, p. 85.
2. *LD*, IV, p. 201.
3. *LD*, V, p. 83.
4. O'Connell, p. 180.
5. *Ibid.*, p. 194.
6. *Ibid.*, p. 206.
7. *Ibid.*, p. 204.
8. Whately, vol. I, pp. 353–9.
9. Newsome, p. 168.
10. [N] *ECH*, I, pp. 117–18.
11. J. B. Mozley, *Letters*, pp. 51–2.
12. Owen Chadwick, *From Bossuet to Newman. The Idea of Doctrinal Development* (Cambridge, 1957), p. 81.
13. Roderick Strange, 'Newman and Hampden', in *Newman Studien*, vol. xiv (1990), pp. 29–30.
14. Abbott, vol. II, pp. 44–50.

15. O'Connell, p. 199.
16. Nockles, *art. cit.*, pp. 48–9.
17. *LD*, IV, p. 270.
18. R. W. Church, *The Oxford Movement. Twelve Years 1833–1845* (1891), pp. 140–1.
19. W. Ward, *William George Ward and the Oxford Movement* (1889), p. 149.

SECTION IV

1. Middleton, p. 190.
2. Church, pp. 113–14.
3. *LD*, XIII, p. 99.
4. Anne Mozley (ed.), *Letters and Correspondence of John Henry Newman* (1891), vol. II, p. 322.
5. [N] *SN*, pp. vii–ix.
6. *LD*, XV, p. 284 n.2.
7. C. S. Dessain, *John Henry Newman* (1966), p. 43.
8. J. B. Mozley, pp. 110–11.
9. F. Bennett, *The Story of W. J. E. Bennett* (1909), pp. 63, 61.
10. *LD*, XVI, p. 75.
11. McClelland, 'Spiritual Nemesis', p. 6.
12. Dessain, p. 44.
13. Lathbury, vol. I, pp. 405–8.
14. [N] *LBB*, p. 40.
15. [N] *PPS*, vol. IV, pp. 286–7.
16. *Ibid.*, p. 147.
17. [N] *PPS*, vol. V, pp. 117, 136, 159–61.
18. Owen Chadwick, *The Mind of the Oxford Movement* (1960), p. 48.
19. F. L. Cross, *John Henry Newman* (1933), p. 84.
20. [N] *PPS*, vol. V, p. 315.
21. [N] *Idea*, p. 406, 413.
22. [N] *PPS*, vol. VI, p. 103.
23. Bremond, p. 324.
24. Ward, *Wiseman*, vol. II, p. 54.
25. Anne Mozley, vol. II, p. 408.
26. [N] *SN*, pp. 116, 147–51, 184, 262.
27. [N] *PPS*, vol. II, p. 322.
28. [N] *Idea*, p. 419.
29. [M] *Serm*, vol. I, p. 375; vol. III, p. 261; vol. IV, pp. 290, 298.
30. *Ibid.*, vol. II, p. 186; vol. IV, pp. 156, 163.
31. [N] *PPS*, vol. V, no. 11.
32. [N] *PPS*, vol. VIII, no. 16.
33. [N] *SSD*, no. 19.
34. Gilley, p. 126.
35. [N] *GA*, p. 252.

36. [N] *PPS*, vol. IV, p. 28.
37. [N] *PPS*, vol. IV, pp. 26–8; vol. V, p. 29; vol. V, p. 153; vol. V, p. 232; vol. V, p. 333; vol. VII, p. 196; [N] *SSD*, pp. 61, 337, 357, 374; *LD*, XXV, p. 355; XXVII, p. 374; [N] *Dev*, p. 103; [N] *Disc*, pp. 167, 386, 389; [N] *Diff*, vol. I, p. 337; [N] *Idea*, p. 66; [N] *HS*, vol. II, p. 107; [N] *GA*, p. 122; [N] *SN*, p. 143.
38. Geoffrey Rowell, *Hell and the Victorians. A Study of the nineteenth-century theological controversies concerning eternal punishment and the future life* (Oxford, 1974), p. 3; see also Hilton, p. 346.
39. [N] *PPS*, vol. VII, p. 214.
40. *Ibid.*, p. 9.
41. [N] *PPS*, vol. IV, p. 51.
42. [N] *Med*, pp. 469–70.
43. [M] *Serm*, vol. I, p. 134.
44. [M] *LJP*, pp. 34, 54.
45. [M] *Serm*, vol. I, p. 107.
46. [M] *OUS*, p. 37.
47. Rowell, *Hell and the Victorians*, p. 97.
48. Anthony Kenny, 'Newman as a Philosopher of Religion', in *Newman. A Man for our Times*, ed. D. Brown (1990), p. 61.
49. [N] *PPS*, vol. IV, p. 134.
50. [N] *PPS*, vol. VII, pp. 106–7.
51. [N] *Diff*, vol. II, p. 248.
52. Michael J. Allsopp, 'Conscience, the Church and Moral Truth: John Henry Newman, Vatican II Today', in *Irish Church Quarterly*, vol. 58, no. 3 (1992), p. 199.
53. [N] *GA*, pp. 251, 257–8.
54. [N] *PPS*, vol. I, p. 115; vol. IV, p. 134.
55. Dessain, pp. 60–1.
56. [N] *PPS*, vol. V, p. 271.
57. [N] *PPS*, vol. IV, pp. 37–8.
58. [N] *PPS*, vol. II, pp. 90–1.
59. [N] *PPS*, vol. V, p. 355.
60. [N] *PPS*, vol. I, p. 7.
61. [M] *UC*, pp. 305–6; cf. [M] *OUS*, p. 148.
62. [N] *Just*, pp. 214–15.
63. Y. Brilioth, *The Anglican Revival. Studies in the Oxford Movement* (1925), pp. 292–3.
64. [N] *PPS*, vol. V, p. 276.
65. [N] *Disc*, pp. 33, 40–2.
66. David Newsome, 'Justification and Sanctification: Newman and the Evangelicals', in *Journal of Theological Studies*, NS vol. XV, part I (1964), p. 28.
67. *Ibid.*, p. 40.
68. Newsome, *Parting of Friends*, p. 177.
69. *Ibid.*, p. 202.
70. [M] *Serm*, vol. III, p. 332.
71. [M] *Serm*, vol. II, p. 362.
72. *Ibid.* p. 392.
73. [M] *Serm*, vol. IV, p. 42.
74. *Correspondence of John Henry Newman with John Keble and others*, ed. Fathers of the Birmingham Oratory (1917), pp. 62–3.
75. [N] *PPS*, vol. V, p. 14.
76. Newsome, *art. cit.*, p. 41.
77. *Ibid.*, p. 45.
78. *Ibid.*, p. 49.
79. Palmer, p. 27.
80. [N] *Call*, p. 153.
81. [N] *SSD*, p. 141.
82. J. H. Walgrave, *Newman the Theologian. The Nature of Belief and Doctrine* (1960), p. 21.
83. F. Nietzsche, *Thus spake Zarathustra*, pt. 2 c. 29. I owe this reference to the Revd K. Harmon.
84. *The Times*, 22 April 1992.
85. Abbott, vol. II, p. 34.
86. See [N] *AW*, pp. 214–15.
87. [N] *LG*, p. 204.
88. [N] *Call*, p. 218.

SECTION V

1. *LD*, V, p. 241.
2. Birmingham Oratory MSS. Manning letters, no. 4.
3. *LD*, VI, p. 95.
4. Birmingham Oratory MSS. Manning letters, no. 5.
5. *Ibid.*, no. 7.
6. Newsome, *Parting of Friends*, p. 252.
7. *Ibid.*
8. *LD*, VI, p. 156.
9. Newsome, p. 253.
10. G. F. A. Best, *Temporal Pillars. Queen Anne's Bounty, the Ecclesiastical Commission and the Church of England* (Cambridge, 1964), p. 314.
11. Lathbury, vol. I, p. 41.
12. *LD*, VI, p. 175.
13. Purcell, vol. I, p. 148.
14. [M] *ROF*, p. 100.
15. *Ibid.* p. 128.
16. *LD*, VI, pp. 280–1.

17. Purcell, vol. I, p. 136.
18. [N] *VM1*, p. 71.
19. [N] *DA*, p. 18.
20. [N] *VM1*, p. 237.
21. *Ibid.*, p. 258.
22. *Ibid.*, pp. 64, 75.
23. *LD*, XI, p. 100. See also Thomas, *Newman and Heresy*, p. 186.
24. [N] *VM1* p. 268.
25. Biemer, pp. 46–7; Louis Allen, *John Henry Newman and the Abbé Jager. A Controversy on Scripture and Tradition 1834–36* (1975), p. 7.
26. Allen, pp. 17, 110.
27. Gilley, p. 166.
28. [N] *Just*, p. 348.
29. [N] *VVO*, p. 324.
30. *LD*, IV, p. 57.
31. *LD*, V, p. 77.
32. *Ibid.*, p. 108.
33. O'Connell, p. 227.
34. [N] *PPS*, vol. VIII, p. 121.
35. [N] *PPS*, vol. VI, p. 187.
36. [N] *HS*, vol. II, pp. 55–6.
37. Robbins, p. 83; D. Nicholls and F. Kerr, *John Henry Newman. Reason, Rhetoric and Romanticism* (Bristol, 1991), p. 6; [N] *LG*, p. 349.
38. Bouyer, p. 28.
39. *LD*, III, p. 70.
40. [N] *Call*, p. 122.
41. *LD*, IV, pp. 169–70.
42. Culler, pp. 89–91.
43. R. W. Church, *Occasional Papers* (1897), vol. II, p. 473.
44. [N] *Call*, p. 119.
45. *LD*, V, p. 314.

46. O'Faoláin, p. 187.
47. O'Connell, p. 237.
48. Prevost, p. 70.
49. *Tracts for the Times, by members of the University of Oxford* (1833–41), no. 82, pp. vi–vii; Liddon, vol. II, pp. 10–11.
50. *Tracts for the Times*, no. 71, pp. 9–13.
51. Allen, pp. 154–62; see especially *LD*, V, p. 174.
52. Thomas, *Newman and Heresy*, pp. 41–2.
53. *LD*, IV, pp. 230–1.
54. Burgon, vol. I, pp. 214–21; p. 242.
55. *LD*, V, pp. 302–3.
56. Burgon, vol. I, p. 264.
57. Jones, *Isaac Williams and his Circle*, p. 45.
58. [N] *VM2*, p. 193.
59. *Ibid.*, pp. 234–5.
60. *LD*, VI, p. 291.
61. *Ibid.*, pp. 150–1.
62. *Ibid.*, p. 307.
63. *Ibid.*, p. 347.

SECTION VI

1. *LD*, VI, p. 268.
2. [M] *ROF*, p. 48.
3. A. Chapeau, 'Manning the Anglican', in *Manning: Anglican and Catholic*, ed. J. Fitzsimons (1951), p. 9.
4. Birmingham Oratory MSS. Manning Letters, 25 January 1839.
5. *Ibid.*, 17 September 1839.
6. *Ibid.*, 23 October 1839.

CHAPTER 3 : Roads to Rome

SECTION I

1. Anne Mozley, vol. II, p. 287.
2. *Ibid.*, p. 286.
3. *W. G. Ward and the Oxford Movement*, p. 84.
4. *LD*, VI, pp. 285–6.
5. Anne Mozley, vol. II, p. 282.
6. *LD*, VI, pp. 349–50.
7. [N] *VM1*, p. 70 n.1.
8. [N] *Diff*, vol. I, p. 387.
9. [N] *LRWJ*, p. 5.
10. [N] *LBB*, p. 21.
11. Misner, pp. 8–9.
12. Gilley, p. 174.
13. *Ibid.*, p. 145.

14. Misner, p. 14.
15. Gilley, p. 187.
16. *LD*, IV, p. 258.
17. *LD*, VI, p. 10.
18. *Ibid.*, p. 150.
19. Anne Mozley, vol. II, p. 285.
20. *Ibid.*, vol. II, p. 292.
21. Birmingham Oratory MSS. S. F. Wood to J.H.N., 11 March 1840.
22. Anne Mozley, vol. II, p. 318.
23. [N] *ECH*, vol. II, p. 9.
24. *Ibid.*, vol. II, p. 32.
25. *Ibid.*, vol. II, p. 55.
26. *Ibid.*, vol. II, pp. 71–2.
27. Anne Mozley, vol. II, p. 295.
28. [N] *Apol*, p. 222.

29. Birmingham Oratory MSS. H.E.M. to J.H.N., 15 January 1840.
30. [N] *Just*, pp. 298–300.
31. *Tracts for the Times*, no. 90, p. 4.
32. *Ibid.*, pp. 81–2.
33. *Ibid.*, p. 80.
34. *Ibid.*, p. 24.
35. *Ibid.*, pp. 59, 63.
36. Anne Mozley, vol. II, p. 326.
37. *Ibid.*, p. 331.
38. [N] *LRWJ*, pp. 25–6.
39. [N] *Apol*, p. 235.
40. *LD*, XVIII, p. 102.
41. Brilioth, p. 155.
42. Lathbury, vol. I., p. 408.
43. *Newman. A Man for our Times*, p. 64.
44. *Correspondence with John Keble*, p. 77.
45. Burgon, vol. I, p. 420.
46. A. P. Perceval, *A Collection of Papers connected with the Theological Movement of 1833* (1842), p. 90.
47. *Correspondence with John Keble*, p. 85.
48. Whately, vol. II, p. 58.
49. *Ibid.*, vol. II, pp. 60–3.
50. [N] *LRWJ*, p. 29.
51. Anne Mozley, vol. II, p. 356.

SECTION II

1. Purcell, vol. I, p. 165.
2. [M] *CA*, p. 145.
3. Purcell, vol. I, p. 167.
4. Leslie, 59.
5. F. Maurice (ed.), *The Life and Letters of Frederick Denison Maurice* (1884), vol. I, p. 351.
6. Purcell, vol. I, p. 155.
7. *Ibid.*, vol. I, p. 169 n.1.
8. *Ibid.*, vol. I, p. 181.
9. *Ibid.*, vol. I, p. 184.
10. *Ibid.*, vol. I, p. 185.
11. *Ibid.*, vol. I, p. 186.
12. [M] *Charges* (1841), pp. 12–13.
13. *Ibid.*, p. 16.
14. *Ibid.*, pp. 46–7.
15. Purcell, vol. I, p. 202.
16. *Ibid.*, vol. I, p. 201.
17. *Ibid.*, vol. I, p. 201 n.1.
18. H. J. Burgess, *Enterprise in Education. The Story of the Work of the Established Church in the Education of the People prior to 1870* (1955), p. 146.
19. *Ibid.*, pp. 155–7.
20. Purcell, vol. I, p. 161.
21. [M] *Charges* (1845), pp. 25–6.
22. [M] *Charges* (1842), p. 21.

23. G. H. Tavard, *The Quest for Catholicity. A Study in Anglicanism* (1963), p. 166.
24. [M] *UC*, p. 19.
25. *Ibid.*, pp. 77, 85.
26. *Ibid.*, p. 158.
27. *Ibid.*, pp. 91–2.
28. *Ibid.*, pp. 159–60.
29. *Ibid.*, pp. 289–97; cf. [M] *WHS*, pp. 10–19; [M] *Sin*, pp. 14–15.
30. [M] *UC*, pp. 328–9.
31. *Ibid.*, p. 347.
32. *Ibid.*, pp. 152–3.
33. *Ibid.*, p. 290.
34. *Ibid.*, pp. 341, 361–2.
35. [M] *TMHG*, pp. 27–8.
36. [M] *WHS*, pp. 8, 21–3.
37. Purcell, vol. I, p. 233.
38. Lathbury, vol. II, p. 277.
39. J. Keble, *Occasional Papers and Reviews* (Oxford and London, 1877), pp. 360–1.
40. Keith Denison, 'Dr Pusey as Confessor and Spiritual Director', in P. Butler (ed.), *Pusey Rediscovered* (1983), p. 216.
41. Newsome, p. 233.
42. O'Connell, p. 301.
43. Ronald Chapman, *Father Faber* (1961), p. 97.
44. Mary Allies, *Thomas William Allies, 1813–1903* (1924), p. 49.
45. T. W. Allies, *A Life's Decision* (1880), p. 57.
46. Mary Allies, p. 66.
47. [N] *Disc*, p. 59.
48. [N] *Diff*, vol. I, p. 291.
49. [M] *Sin*, pp. 113–14, 131–4, 155; [M] *LJP*, p. 53.
50. [M] *Sin*, pp. 114, 137–41, 151, 174, 212, 236–8.
51. O'Connell, p. 359.
52. *Ibid.*, p. 360.
53. Leslie, p. 72.
54. *Correspondence with John Keble*, p. 155.
55. [N] *Apol*, p. 238.
56. *Ibid.*, p. 234.
57. R. D. Middleton, *Newman and Bloxam. An Oxford Friendship* (1947), p. 66.
58. *Correspondence with John Keble*, p. 242.
59. Anne Mozley, vol. II, pp. 393–4.
60. *Correspondence with John Keble*, p. 172.

61. *Newman and Bloxam*, p. 69.
62. *Correspondence with John Keble*, p. 224.
63. [N] *SSD*, p. 409.
64. *Correspondence with John Keble*, pp. 271–2.
65. *Ibid.*, p. 273.
66. Birmingham Oratory MSS. H.E.M. to J.H.N., 23 October 1843.
67. *Correspondence with John Keble*, p. 276.
68. Lathbury, vol. I, p. 283.
69. [M] *OUS*, p. 81.
70. *Ibid.*, p. 87.
71. *Ibid.*, p. 95.
72. J. B. Mozley, pp. 148–9.
73. Purcell, vol. I, p. 252.
74. *Correspondence with John Keble*, p. 280.
75. *LD*, XXX, pp. 437, 446, 448; XXXI, pp. 4–5.
76. *Correspondence with John Keble*, pp. 290–1.
77. *Ibid.*, p. 293.

SECTION III

1. [N] *Apol*, pp. 259–60.
2. *W. G. Ward and the Oxford Movement*, p. 31.
3. *Correspondence with John Keble*, p. 199.
4. [N] *Apol*, p. 261.
5. *W. G. Ward and the Oxford Movement*, p. 335.
6. Birmingham Oratory MSS. H.E.M. to J.H.N., 6 February 1845.
7. *W. G. Ward and the Oxford Movement*, p. 345.
8. *Correspondence with John Keble*, pp. 253–4.
9. *Tracts for the Times*, no. 71, p. 3.
10. Liddon, vol. II, p. 461.
11. Owen Chadwick, *Spirit of the Oxford Movement*, pp. 150–2.
12. F. L. Cross, pp. 54–6, 142.
13. *Correspondence with John Keble*, p. 211.
14. [N] *Apol*, p. 265.
15. [N] *LG*, p. 294.
16. *Ibid.*, p. 365.
17. [N] *Apol*, p. 264.
18. *Correspondence with John Keble*, p. 294.
19. Misner, p. 41.
20. Anne Mozley, vol. II, p. 445.

21. [N] *LG*, p. 348.
22. *LD*, VI, p. 83; [N] *VMI*, p. 105.
23. [N] *Just*, p. 380.
24. [N] *Apol*, p. 287.
25. *Correspondence with John Keble*, pp. 118–22, 168–9.
26. Biemer, p. 48.
27. [N] *OUS*, p. 323.
28. [N] *Dev*, pp. 5–6.
29. *Ibid.*, p. 7.
30. Walgrave, p. 3.
31. Stephen Prickett, *Romanticism and Religion. The Tradition of Coleridge and Wordsworth in the Victorian Church* (Cambridge, 1976), p. 153.
32. [N] *Dev*, p. 89.
33. *Ibid.*, p. 154.
34. [N] *VMI*, p. 102 n.1.
35. *LD*, XX, p. 308.
36. [N] *Dev*, pp. 97–8.
37. *LD*, XIII, p. 295.
38. [N] *Diff*, vol. II, p. 24.
39. [N] *Diff*, vol. I, p. 388.
40. [N] *Apol*, p. 132.
41. Anne Mozley, vol. II, p. 452.
42. Thomas Scott, *The Force of Truth* (1821), pp. 90–1.
43. [N] *Dev*, p. 445.

SECTION IV

1. *LD*, XI, p. 8.
2. Birmingham Oratory MSS. H.E.M. to J.H.N., 14 October 1845.
3. *LD*, XII, p. 154.
4. Prevost, p. 118 n.
5. J. F. White, *The Cambridge Movement. The Ecclesiologists and the Gothic Revival* (Cambridge, 1962), pp. 136–7.
6. Härdelin, p. 248 n.70.
7. *Ibid.*, p. 59 n.64.
8. Gertrude Donald, *Men who left the Movement* (1933), p. 205.
9. Liddon, vol. III, pp. 145–6.
10. Newsome, p. 316.
11. Purcell, vol. I, pp. 601–2.
12. Newsome, p. 268.
13. *Ibid.*, p. 310.
14. *Ibid.*, p. 313.
15. [M] *EP*, p. 191.
16. Ushaw MSS. Manning letters, 19 October 1845.
17. Ushaw, 14 July 1847.
18. Ushaw, 23 September 1848.
19. Ushaw, 'Feast of St John', 1848.

20. Ushaw, 2 October 1848.
21. Ushaw, 'Tuesday in Holy Week', 1849.
22. Purcell, vol. I, pp. 503–4.
23. G. C. B. Davies, *Henry Phillpotts, Bishop of Exeter, 1778–1869* (1954), p. 192.
24. Gray, p. 83.
25. Newsome, pp. 320–1.
26. Purcell, vol. I, p. 279
27. *Ibid.*, vol. I, p. 484.
28. Lathbury, vol. I, p. 353.
29. Purcell, vol. I, p. 338.
30. *Ibid.*, vol. I, p. 342.
31. *Ibid.*, vol. I, pp. 470–2.
32. *Ibid.*, vol. I, p. 382.
33. Leslie, p. 82.
34. *Ibid.*, p. 85.
35. Newsome, p. 337.
36. Purcell, vol. I, p. 511.
37. Newsome, p. 341.
38. Chapeau, p. 25–6.
39. Newsome, p. 326.
40. Purcell, vol. I, p. 701.
41. J. C. S. Nias, *Gorham and the Bishop of Exeter* (1951), p. 125.
42. Newsome, p. 349.
43. [M] *App*, p. 34.
44. Quoted in McClelland, 'Gladstone and Manning', in Jagger, p. 159.
45. Purcell, vol. I, p. 580.
46. *Ibid.*, vol. I, p. 617.
47. Newsome, p. 367.
48. Purcell, vol. I, p. 632.

CHAPTER 4 : Teething Pains

SECTION I

1. [N] *ECH*, vol. II, pp. 338–9.
2. Anne Mozley, vol. II, p. 318.
3. Michael Ffinch, *Cardinal Newman: The Second Spring* (1991), p. 133.
4. [N] *SVO*, pp. 172–3.
5. Josef Altholz, *The Liberal Catholic Movement in England: The Rambler and its Contributors, 1848–64* (1962), p. 17.
6. Butler, *Ullathorne*, vol. II, p. 152.
7. D. Mathew, 'Old Catholics and Converts', in G. A. Beck (ed.), *The English Catholics, 1850–1950* (1950), p. 232.
8. C. S. Dessain in [N] *CS*, p. 11.
9. For a sympathetic analysis of Faber's religious character, see Sheridan Gilley, 'Supernaturalized Culture: Catholic Attitudes and Latin Lands 1840–60', in *The Materials, Sources and Methods of Ecclesiastical History*, ed. D. Baker (Oxford, 1975), pp. 315–18.
10. John Bossy, *The English Catholic Community, 1570–1850* (1975), p. 298.
11. J. D. Holmes, *More Roman than Rome: English Catholicism in the Nineteenth Century* (1978), p. 22.
12. J. Bossy, p. 321.
13. *Ibid.*, p. 325.
14. W. Ward, *William George Ward and the Catholic Revival* (1893), p. 75.
15. Schiefen, p. 136.
16. S. Gilley, 'Roman Catholicism', in *Religious Traditions in the Nineteenth Century* (1991), p. 15.
17. Percy Fitzgerald, *Fifty Years of Catholic Life and Social Progress under Cardinals Wiseman, Manning, Vaughan and Newman* (1901), vol. I, p. 72.
18. Butler, *Ullathorne*, vol. I, p. 148.
19. Holmes, p. 83.
20. *LD*, XIV, pp. 108, 122.
21. Owen Chadwick, *The Victorian Church* (1966), vol. I, p. 306.
22. Fitzgerald, vol. I, p. 58.
23. Butler, *Ullathorne*, vol. II, pp. 299–300.

SECTION II

1. *LD*, XI, p. 47.
2. *Ibid.*, pp. 226–7.
3. *LD*, XII, p. 25.
4. *Ibid.*, p. 272.
5. Purcell, vol. I, p. 633.
6. *LD*, XI, p. 19.
7. *Ibid.*, p. 194.
8. *Ibid.*, p. 238.
9. *Ibid.*, p. 176.
10. *Ibid.*, p. 257.
11. *LD*, XII, pp. 24, 48.
12. *LD*, XI, p. 284.
13. *LD*, XV, p. 416.
14. Chadwick, *Bossuet to Newman*, pp. 48, 87; Biemer, p. 169; Kenny, p. 99.

15. *LD*, XI, p. 290.
16. *LD*, XII, p. 9.
17. A. E. Dingle and B. H. Harrison, 'Cardinal Manning as Temperance Reformer', in *The Historical Journal*, vol. XII, no. 3 (1969), p. 501.
18. Bodley, p. 14.
19. [N] *HS*, vol. II, p. 162.
20. F. J. Cwiekowski, *The English Bishops and the First Vatican Council* (Louvain, 1971), p. 55.
21. Chapman, p. 239.
22. Purcell, vol. II, p. 347.
23. *LD*, XII, p. 56.
24. Gray, p. 152.
25. Purcell, vol. II, p. 19.
26. [M] *GOF*, pp. 3, 6.
27. *Ibid.*, p. 46.
28. *Ibid.*, pp. 71–2.
29. J. G. Snead-Cox, *The Life of Cardinal Vaughan* (1910), vol. I, pp. 454–5.
30. *Ibid.*, vol. I, p. 455.
31. *LD*, XIII, p. 457.
32. *LD*, XI, pp. 143–4, 148.
33. *LD*, XIII, pp. 29–30.
34. *LD*, XII, p. 318.
35. *Ibid.*, p. 353.
36. *Ibid.*, p. 337.
37. *LD*, XIII, pp. 340–1.
38. *LD*, XVI, p. 104.
39. *LD*, XIII, pp. 307, 406; Michael Clifton, *The Quiet Negotiator* (1991), p. 29.
40. *LD*, XII, p. 239.
41. W. Ward, *The Life of John Henry Cardinal Newman* (1912), vol. I, p. 264.
42. *LD*, XIV, p. 206.
43. [M] *HNNG*, pp. 20–2, 30.
44. Bossy, p. 297.
45. [N] *SVO*, p. 177.
46. John Coulson, *Newman and the Common Tradition. A Study in the Language of Church and Society* (Oxford, 1970), p. 99.

SECTION III

1. Birmingham Oratory MSS. Manning letters, no. 31.
2. *LD*, XVIII, p. 49.
3. Beck, p. 235.
4. Aubrey de Vere, *Recollections* (1897), p. 329.
5. Purcell, vol. II, p. 79.
6. Leslie, p. 123.

7. Newsome, p. 402.
8. Gray, p. 153.
9. Purcell, vol. II, p. 17.
10. *LD*, XI, p. 295.
11. Purcell, vol. II, pp. 2–9.
12. Statistics in Fitzsimons, p. 54.
13. Purcell, vol. II, p. 75.
14. Leslie, p. 129.
15. Brian Fothergill, *Nicholas Wiseman* (1963), pp. 237, 240.
16. *Ibid.*, p. 232.
17. Schiefen, pp. 252–3; Fothergill, p. 234.
18. Fothergill, p. 247.
19. Ward, *Wiseman*, vol. II, pp. 354–65.
20. *Ibid.*, vol. II, pp. 631–7; Butler, *Ullathorne*, vol. I, p. 253.
21. Schiefen, p. 274.
22. Purcell, vol. II, p. 160; Fothergill, p. 253.
23. Ward, *Wiseman*, vol. II, p. 369.
24. Fothergill, p. 257.

SECTION IV

1. *LD*, XVII, pp. 38–9.
2. *Ibid.*, pp. 13–14; p. 54 n.2.
3. *Ibid.*, p. 72.
4. Chapman, p. 279.
5. *Ibid.*
6. John F. Quinn, 'Newman, Faber and the Oratorian Separation. A Reappraisal', in *Recusant History*. vol. 20, no. 1 (1990), pp. 106–26.
7. *LD*, XVII, pp. 129, 136–8.
8. *Ibid.*, p. 151.
9. *Ibid.*, p. 318.
10. Chapman, p. 276.
11. *LD*, XVII, p. 255.
12. Ker, p. 472; *LD*, XVIII, pp. 549–50.
13. *LD*, XIX, pp. 112–13.
14. *LD*, XVI, p. 31.
15. *Ibid.*, pp. 99–100.
16. Fergal McGrath, *Newman's University. Idea and Reality* (1951), p. 245.
17. *LD*, XVI, p. 116.
18. Schiefen, pp. 218–19.
19. V. A. McClelland, *English Roman Catholics and Higher Education, 1830–1903* (Oxford, 1973), p. 87.
20. *Ibid.*, p. 74.
21. *LD*, XVIII, pp. 562–3; XIX, pp. 265–6.
22. [N] *AW*, p. 290.
23. Roger McHugh, 'The Years in

Ireland', in *A Tribute to Newman: Essays on Aspects of his Life and Thought* (Dublin, 1945), p. 158.
24. *LD*, XXVI, p. 58.
25. *LD*, XIV, p. 389.
26. McGrath, p. 507.
27. *Ibid.*, p. 181.
28. Butler, *Ullathorne*, vol. II, pp. 312–13.
29. *LD*, XVI, p. 172.
30. McGrath, p. 189 n.3.
31. [N] *AW*, p. 320.
32. A. L. Smith, *Church and State in the Middle Ages* (Oxford, 1913), p. 135.
33. G. M. Young, *Today and Yesterday* (1941), p. 115.
34. *LD*, XVIII, p. 122.
35. Gilley, *Newman*, p. 299.

SECTION V

1. Altholz, *Rambler*, p. 39.
2. *LD*, XVIII, p. 406 n.1.
3. Altholz, p. 81.
4. *LD*, XVIII, pp. 559–62.
5. *LD*, XIX, p. 52.
6. *Ibid.*, p. 141.
7. *Ibid.*, p. 89.
8. [N] *Dev*, pp. 118–19.
9. [N] *Idea*, p. 178.
10. Christopher Hollis, *Newman and the Modern World* (1967), p. 66.
11. Coulson in [N] *CFD*, p. 2.
12. [N] *PPC*, Lecture IX, p. 22.
13. [N] *CFD*, p. 77.
14. *Ibid.*, p. 106.
15. *Ibid.*, p. 57.
16. *Ibid.*, p. 72.
17. Altholz, p. 109 n.37.
18. Butler, *Ullathorne*, vol. I, p. 316.
19. *LD*, XIX, pp. 289–90.
20. *Ibid.*, p. 282.
21. *Ibid.*, p. 290 n.2.
22. *Ibid.*
23. *Ibid.*, p. 333.
24. *Ibid.*, p. 359.
25. *Ibid.*, p. 333 n.2.
26. [M] *TMHG*, p. 124.
27. *LD*, XIX, p. 175 n.2.
28. Altholz, p. 111.
29. E. E. Y. Hales, *Pio Nono* (1956), p. 202.
30. Noel Blakiston, *The Roman Question. Extracts from the Dispatches of Odo Russell from Rome, 1858–70* (1962), p. 111.

31. John Morley, *The Life of William Ewart Gladstone* (1903), vol. II, p. 185.
32. Holmes, p. 121.
33. *LD*, XIX, p. 291.
34. *Ibid.*, pp. 299–300.
35. [N] *SVO*, p. 275.
36. E. R. Norman, 'Cardinal Manning and the Temporal Power', in D. Beales and G. Best (eds), *History, Society and the Churches* (Cambridge, 1985), p. 254.
37. *Ibid.*, p. 236.
38. [M] *PCHS*, p. vi.
39. [M] *TPP*, p. 7.
40. E. R. Norman, *art. cit.*, p. 240.
41. [M] *TPP*, p. 8.
42. E. R. Norman, *art. cit.*, p. 242.
43. *Ibid.*, p. 243.
44. J. P. von Arx, 'Manning's Ultramontanism and the Catholic Church in British Politics', in *Recusant History*, vol. 19 no. 3 (1989), p. 333.
45. [M] *Misc*, vol. II, p. 148.
46. [M] *PCHS*, p. 69.
47. Purcell, vol. II, p. 153.
48. Altholz, p. 176.
49. *LD*, XX, p. 325.
50. *LD*, XIX, p. 519.
51. Purcell, vol. II, pp. 348–9.

SECTION VI

1. *Gladstone Diaries*, vol. VII, p. 361.
2. J. P. von Arx, *art. cit.*, p. 333.
3. [M] *Misc*, vol. I, pp. 27–71.
4. *LD*, XX, p. 506; XXII, pp. 327–9.
5. E. Kelly, 'The Apologia and the Ultramontanes', in V. F. Blehl and F. X. Connolly (eds), *Newman's Apologia: A Classic Reconsidered* (New York, 1964), p. 28.
6. *LD*, XX, pp. 253–4.
7. *Ibid.*, pp. 215–17.
8. [N] *AW*, pp. 251–7.
9. *LD*, III, p. 9.
10. *LD*, VI, p. 348.
11. J. B. Mozley, *Letters*, p. 80.
12. M. Pattison, p. 171.
13. Chapman, p. 287.
14. *LD*, XX, p. 248.
15. *Ibid.*, p. 468.
16. Chapman, p. 337.
17. *Ibid.*, pp. 337–9.
18. *Ibid.*, p. 344; E. Bellasis, *Coram Cardinali* (1916), pp. 47–8.

CHAPTER 5 : A Case of Dr Fell

SECTION I

1. Fothergill, p. 270.
2. *Ibid.*, p. 260.
3. Scheifen, p. 317.
4. *LD*, XX, p. 512 n.2.
5. *LD*, XVIII, pp. 500–1.
6. *LD*, XX, p. 512.
7. *Ibid.*, p. 428.
8. Liddon, vol. IV, pp. 103–4.
9. *LD*, XXI, p. 343.
10. *Ibid.*, p. 84.
11. *Ibid.*, p. 319.
12. *Ibid.*, p. 388.
13. *LD*, XX, p. 518 n.1.
14. *LD*, XXI, p. 43.
15. Butler, *Ullathorne*, vol. II, p. 9.
16. McClelland, *English Roman Catholics*, pp. 203–5.
17. *LD*, XXI, pp. 308–9.
18. Gilley, *Newman*, p. 337.
19. *LD*, XXI, p. 79 n.2.
20. *Ibid.*, p. 87.
21. *Ibid.*, pp. 109, 127.
22. *Ibid.*, p. 73.
23. *Ibid.*, p. 260.
24. M. J. Svaglic, 'Why Newman wrote the *Apologia*', in Blehl and Connolly, *op. cit.*, pp. 10–11.
25. [N] *DA*, p. 293.
26. Walter Houghton, *The Art of Newman's Apologia* (New Haven, 1945), p. 40.
27. Abbott, vol. I, pp. 224–5; pp. 302–3; p. 308; vol. II, p. 79.
28. [N] *SE*, p. 78.
29. *LD*, XIX, pp. 289–90.
30. [N] *Apol*, p. 82.
31. *Ibid.*, p. 193.
32. A. F. Hort, *The Life and Letters of Fenton John Anthony Hort* (1896), vol. II, p. 35.
33. *LD*, XXI, p. 324 n.1.
34. Blehl and Connolly, *op. cit.*, pp. 34–6.
35. Snead-Cox, vol. I, p. 215.
36. [N] *Apol*, p. 351.
37. *LD*, XVI, p. 401.
38. *LD*, XIV, p. 360; cf. vol. XIII, p. 301.
39. *LD*, XXIII, p. 190.
40. *W. G. Ward and the Catholic Revival*, p. 227.
41. [N] *Idea*, p. 382.
42. *LD*, XXI, p. 344.

43. *Ibid.*, p. 191.
44. *Ibid.*, p. 167.
45. *LD*, XXIII, pp. 189–90.
46. [N] *Apol*, p. 265.
47. [N] *Dev*, p. 29.
48. [N] *Call*, p. 317.
49. [N] *TPBI*, p. 32.
50. [N] *GA*, p. 258.
51. *LD*, XXII, p. 44.
52. *LD*, XXVII, p. 270.
53. *LD*, XXI, p. 288 n.1.
54. *Ibid.*, p. 410.

SECTION II

1. *LD*, XXI, pp. 285–6.
2. Schiefen, p. 333.
3. *LD*, XXI, p. 426.
4. Ward, *Wiseman*, vol. II, pp. 524–9.
5. Purcell, vol. II, p. 209.
6. [M] *Serm*, vol. II, p. 145.
7. *LD*, XXIV, p. 167.
8. Purcell, vol. II, p. 206.
9. Leslie, p. 151.
10. Blakiston, p. 309.
11. Purcell, vol. II, pp. 215–17.
12. *Ibid.*, vol. II, p. 218.
13. *Ibid.*, vol. II, p. 244.
14. Fitzsimons, p. 58.
15. Purcell, vol. II, p. 218.
16. Leslie, pp. 162–4.
17. Purcell, vol. II, p. 223.
18. Butler, *Ullathorne*, vol. II, p. 125.
19. Leslie, p. 160.
20. *LD*, XXI, p. 466 n.1.
21. *Ibid.*, p. 466.
22. *Ibid.*, p. 471.
23. *Ibid.*, p. 471.
24. Leslie, p. 157.
25. Butler, *Ullathorne*, vol. II, p. 129.
26. V. A. McClelland, 'A Hierarchy for Scotland, 1868–78', in *Catholic History Review*, vol. 66, no. 3 (1970), pp. 474 *et seq.*
27. Birmingham Oratory MSS. H.E.M. to J.H.N., 30 May 1865.
28. Butler, *Ullathorne*, vol. II, p. 128.
29. *LD*, XXI, pp. 478–9.
30. Fitzsimons, p. 59.
31. Leslie, pp. 165–8.
32. *Ibid.*, p. 170.
33. *LD*, XXII, p. 5.
34. Mary Church, *The Life of Dean Church*, pp. 169–70.
35. Purcell, vol. II, p. 355.

SECTION III

1. Liddon, vol. IV, pp. 95–6.
2. [N] *Apol*, p. 396.
3. [M] *WHS*, pp. 8, 16.
4. *Ibid.*, p. 18.
5. *Ibid.*, p. 29.
6. Liddon, vol. IV, p. 108.
7. Butler, *Ullathorne*, vol. I, p. 346.
8. [M] *ROC*, pp. 16–17.
9. *Ibid.*, p. 73.
10. *LD*, XXII, pp. 165–72.
11. [N] *Diff*, vol. II, p. 7.
12. *Ibid.*, pp. 98–100.
13. *Ibid.*, pp. 113–14.
14. *Ibid.*, p. 81.
15. *Ibid.*, p. 22.
16. Purcell, vol. II, pp. 322–3, n.1.
17. *Ibid.*, vol. II, pp. 322–3.
18. [M] *Misc*, vol. I, p. 66.
19. [M] *VD*, p. 170.
20. Purcell, vol. II, p. 206.
21. *LD*, XXII, pp. 148–9.
22. *Ibid.*, p. 198.
23. *Ibid.*, p. 157.
24. *Ibid.*, pp. 189–91.
25. *Ibid.*, p. 227.
26. Butler, *Ullathorne*, vol. II, p. 14.
27. Ward, *Newman*, vol. II, p. 172;
    Butler, *Ullathorne*, vol. II, p. 14; M.
    Trevor, *Newman: Light in Winter*
    (1962), p. 387.
28. McClelland, *English Roman Catholics*,
    p. 220.
29. *Ibid.*, pp. 220–1.
30. Butler, *Ullathorne*, vol. II, pp. 15–16.
31. *LD*, XXII, pp. 276–9.
32. *Ibid.*, p. 331.
33. *LD*, XXIII, p. 129 n.1.
34. *LD*, XXII, p. 244.
35. *Ibid.*, p. 227; cf. vol. XXIII, pp.
    75–6.
36. *LD*, XXIII, p. 131.
37. *Ibid.*, p. 154.
38. *Ibid.*, p. 202.
39. *Ibid.*, p. 137 n.1.
40. *Ibid.*, pp. 90–1.
41. *Ibid.*, pp. 93–4.
42. *Ibid.*, p. 93 n.2.
43. *Ibid.*, p. 207.
44. *Ibid.*, p. 226.
45. *Ibid.*, p. 238 n.2; p. 209.
46. *Ibid.*, p. 17.
47. *Ibid.*, p. 119.
48. *Ibid.*, pp. 138–9.
49. Purcell, vol. II, pp. 318–19.

50. *Ibid.*, vol. II, p. 319.
51. *LD*, XXII, pp. 327–9.
52. *LD*, XXIII, p. 101.
53. *Ibid.*, pp. 277–8.
54. *Ibid.*, p. 307.
55. *Ibid.*, p. 329 n.1.
56. *Ibid.*, p. 290.
57. *Ibid.*, p. 322.
58. *Ibid.*, p. 328.
59. *Ibid.*, p. 329.
60. *LD*, XXIV, pp. 362–3.

SECTION IV

1. Purcell, vol. II, pp. 418–20.
2. Ward, *Wiseman*, vol. II, pp. 443–4.
3. Gilley, *Newman*, p. 364.
4. J. D. Holmes, *The Triumph of the Holy
   See. A Short History of the Papacy in the
   Nineteenth Century* (1978), p. 136.
5. Hales, p. 267.
6. *Ibid.*, pp. 255–6.
7. T. Capel, *A Reply to the Rt Hon W. E.
   Gladstone's 'Political Expostulation'*
   (1874), p. 44.
8. Hales, p. 273.
9. *LD*, XXI, p. 378.
10. *LD*, XXV, p. 24.
11. [N] *Idea*, p. 452.
12. [M] *RV*, p. 79; cf. [M] *Misc*, vol. II,
    pp. 346–8; [M] *TMHG*, pp. 214–16.
13. *LD*, XXV, p. 77.
14. [M] *PP*, p. 34; cf. [M] *TMHG*, p. 90;
    W. G. Ward and the Catholic Revival,
    p. 248.
15. [M] *TSVC*, p. 43.
16. Cwiekowski, p. 68.
17. [N] *TPBI*, p. 108.
18. *Ibid.*, p. 143.
19. *LD*, XXIII, p. 367.
20. [M] *TMHG*, p. 81.
21. *Ibid.*, pp. 202–3.
22. [M] *LGHS*, pp. 20–2, 33–8.
23. Owen Chadwick, *The Secularization of
    the European Mind in the Nineteenth
    Century* (Cambridge, 1975), p. 125.
24. *W. G. Ward and the Catholic Revival*,
    p. 187.
25. [M] *Misc*, vol. I, p. 299.
26. [M] *VD*, pp. 181–5.
27. M. Ward, vol. I, p. 209.
28. *W. G. Ward and the Catholic Revival*,
    p. 244 n.2.
29. *LD*, XXIV, p. 364.
30. *LD*, XIX, p. 167.
31. *LD*, XXV, p. 95.

32. *LD*, XXIV, p. 162.
33. Cwiekowski, p. 73.
34. *Ibid.*, pp. 52–3; M. Clifton, *The Quiet Negotiator*, pp. 165 *et seq.*, establishes Grant's infallibilist sympathies.
35. J. D. Holmes, *More Roman than Rome* p. 143.
36. Cwiekowski, pp. 169–70.
37. Hales, p. 290.
38. Purcell, vol. II, p. 418.
39. Hales, p. 152 n.1.
40. Blakiston, p. xxxv.
41. Purcell, vol. II, pp. 416–17.
42. C. Butler, *The Vatican Council: The Story told from inside in Bishop Ullathorne's Letters* (1930), vol. I, p. 167.
43. *Ibid.*, vol. I, p. 175.
44. *Ibid.*, vol. I, p. 169.
45. *Ibid.*, vol. I, p. 172.
46. Cwiekowski, p. 123.
47. *Ibid.*, pp. 121–3, 126–7.
48. Butler, *Vatican Council*, vol. I, p. 174.
49. Hales, p. 303 n.1.
50. Butler, *Ullathorne*, vol. II, pp. 56–7.
51. *LD*, XXV, pp. 18–19.
52. *Ibid.*, p. 54 n.1.
53. *Ibid.*, p. 55.
54. *Ibid.*, p. 61.
55. *Ibid.*, p. 63.
56. Purcell, vol. II, p. 436.
57. Blakiston, p. 3.
58. Purcell, vol. II, pp. 437–47.
59. Blakiston, pp. 396–7.
60. *Ibid.*, p. xxxv.
61. *Gladstone Diaries*, vol. VII, pp. 269–70, 277–8.
62. Butler, *Vatican Council*, vol. II, pp. 50–1.

63. Hales, p. 307.
64. Butler, *Vatican Council*, vol. II, pp. 49–50.
65. *Ibid.*, vol. II, p. 50.
66. *Ibid.*, vol. II, p. 133.

SECTION V

1. Purcell, vol. II, p. 553.
2. Hales, p. 329.
3. Purcell, vol. II, p. 74.
4. M. Ward, vol. I, p. 209.
5. *Gladstone Diaries*, vol. VII, p. 338.
6. W. E. Gladstone, *The Vatican Decrees in their bearing on Civil Allegiance: A Political Expostulation* (1874), p. 65.
7. *Ibid.*, p. 6.
8. [M] *VD*, p. 46.
9. *Ibid.*, pp. 135–7.
10. J. Fessler, *The True and the False Infallibility of the Popes. A Controversial Reply to Dr Schulte* (1875), pp. 70–5, 112.
11. [N] *Diff*, vol. II, pp. 193–4.
12. *Ibid.*, p. 198.
13. *Ibid.*, p. 280.
14. *Ibid.*, pp. 248–9.
15. *Ibid.*, p. 259.
16. *Ibid.*, pp. 311–12.
17. *LD*, XXVII, p. 192.
18. Nicholls and Kerr, *op. cit.*, pp. 146–8, 207–8; Ker and Hill, *op. cit.*, pp. 406–7.
19. [N] *Diff*, vol. II, p. 176.
20. *LD*, XXVII, p. 183 n.1.
21. [N] *Diff*, vol. II, p. 297.
22. Leslie, p. 281.
23. *Ibid.*, p. 232.

CHAPTER 6 : Indoor and Outdoor Lives

SECTION I

1. *LD*, XXI, p. 471 n.1.
2. Butler, *Ullathorne*, p. 284.
3. *LD*, XXII, p. 131.
4. *LD*, XXIV, p. 324.
5. *LD*, XXVII, p. 383.
6. Purcell, vol. II, pp. 750–2.
7. *LD*, XXII, p. 157.
8. *LD*, XXIII, p. 98.
9. *LD*, XXIV, pp. 212–13; cf. XXVIII, p. 216.
10. *LD*, XXI, pp. 170, 447.

11. [N] *HS*, vol. II, p. 217.
12. Nicholas Lash, *Newman on Development: The Search for an Explanation in History* (1975), p. 24.
13. T. Kenny, p. 33.
14. Lathbury, vol. II, pp. 300–1.
15. J. A. Froude, *Short Studies on Great Subjects* (1891), vol. IV, p. 280.
16. *LD*, XIX, p. 247.
17. *LD*, XXX, p. 391; XXXI, pp. 7, 57.
18. [N] *TPFC*, pp. 52, 65, 142 n.1.
19. *LD*, XXX, p. 391.
20. [N] *GA*, p. 198.

21. *LD*, V, p. 53.
22. J. D. Boulger, *Coleridge as Religious Thinker* (New Haven, 1961), p. 50; Prickett, pp. 38, 69.
23. [N] *ECH*, vol. I, p. 269.
24. [N] *Dev*, p. 40.
25. [N] *Idea*, pp. 109–10.
26. [N] *EOM*, pp. 14–18.
27. J. M. Cameron, 'The Night Battle: Newman and Empiricism', in *Victorian Studies*, December 1960, p. 102 n.4.
28. D. M. Mackinnon in introduction to *Newman's University Sermons* (1970), pp. 9–13.
29. *LD*, XXV, p. 35.
30. *LD*, XXX, p. 214.
31. *LD*, XXVI, pp. 158–9.
32. [N] *SSD*, pp. 263–4.
33. *Ibid.*, p. 242.
34. J. P. Migne, *Patrologia Latina*, vol. CXLVIII, Reg. VIII, Ep. XXI, columns 596–7.
35. [N] *Apol*, p. 335; Kenny, pp. 64–6.
36. [M] *UC*, pp. 29, 89, 189, 299–305.
37. [M] *TMHG*, pp. 23–5, 70.
38. *Ibid.*, pp. 87–8.
39. [M] *LJP*, pp. 57, 71.
40. [N] *Diff*, vol. II, p. 256; John Finnis, 'Conscience in the Letter to the Duke of Norfolk', in *Newman after a Hundred Years*, p. 413.
41. *LD*, XXVII, p. 383.
42. [N] *AW*, p. 18.
43. [N] *GA*, p. 42.
44. Roger Sharrock, 'Newman's Poetry', in *Newman after a Hundred Years*, p. 54.
45. Prevost, p. 67; Newsome, *Parting of Friends*, p. 189.
46. Sharrock, p. 55.
47. Rowell, *Hell and the Victorians*, p. 159.
48. Sharrock, p. 61.
49. [N] *VVO*, p. 339.
50. G. Rowell, 'The Dream of Gerontius', in *Ampleforth Journal*, vol. LXXIII, pt II (1968), p. 189.
51. T. Bokenkotter, *Cardinal Newman as an Historian* (Louvain, 1959), pp. 15–16.
52. [N] *ECH*, vol. II, p. 250.
53. Bremond, p. 9.
54. *LD*, XX, p. 477.
55. [N] *HS*, vol. I, pp. 110–11.
56. [N] *Call*, pp. 176–7, 257–64, 299–300.
57. [N] *DA*, p. 343.
58. *Ibid.*, pp. 252–3.
59. [N] *HS*, vol. I, p. 161.
60. *Ibid.*, p. 160.
61. *Ibid.*, p. 178.
62. S. Thomas, *Newman and Heresy*, p. 165.
63. [N] *EOM*, p. 229.
64. *Tracts for the Times*, no. 45, p. 5.
65. [N] *Dev*, p. 6.
66. [N] *GA*, p. 243.
67. [N] *TPBI*, p. 11.
68. Aubrey Gwynn, 'Newman and the Catholic Historian', in *A Tribute to Newman*, p. 295.
69. [N] *Dev*, p. 5; Lash, pp. 21–2, 27.
70. Quoted in Bokenkotter, p. 115.
71. McGrath, p. 287.
72. McClelland, *English Roman Catholics*, p. 14.
73. Gray, p. 294.
74. Coulson, *Newman and the Common Tradition*, pp. 88–9.
75. [N] *Idea*, pp. 19–20.
76. [N] *UDIS*, pp. 139, 142–3.
77. *LD*, XX, p. 426.

SECTION II

1. Cameron, *art. cit.*, p. 110.
2. Newsome, *Parting of Friends*, pp. 86–90.
3. *LD*, XV, p. 381.
4. [N] *GA*, p. 221.
5. B. M. G. Reardon, 'Newman and the Grammar of Assent', in T. R. Wright (ed.), *John Henry Newman: A Man for our Time?* (Newcastle, 1983), p. 51.
6. [N] *OUS*, pp. 226–7.
7. J. B. Mozley, *Lectures and other Theological Papers* (1883), p. 281.
8. *Ibid.*, p. 298.
9. [N] *GA*, pp. 228–9.
10. *Ibid.*, p. 206.
11. H. L. Weatherby, *Cardinal Newman in his Age: His Place in English Theology and Literature* (Nashville, 1973), p. 181.
12. [N] *Idea*, p. 28.
13. Weatherby, p. 164.
14. *Ibid.*, pp. 190–1.
15. *Ibid.*, pp. 194–5.
16. [M] *Misc*, vol. II, pp. 168, 174.
17. *Ibid.*, vol. II, p. 290.
18. M. J. Ferraira, *Doubt and Religious Commitment: The Role of the Will in*

Newman's Thought (Oxford, 1980), pp. 23–4.
19. [M] *RV*, introduction.
20. C. S. Dessain, 'The Reception among Catholics of Newman's Doctrine of Development', in *Newman Studien*, vol. VI, p. 179.
21. *Ibid.*, p. 189.
22. Ker, p. 300.
23. Chadwick, *Bossuet to Newman*, p. 98; F. L. Cross, pp. 103–4; Lash, p. 62.
24. *Newman. A Man for our Times*, p. 4.
25. e.g., [N] *PPS*, vol. II, p. 25; [N] *SSD*, p. 72.
26. *LD*, XIX, p. 251.
27. [N] *TPBI*, p. 18 n.1.
28. *LD*, XIX, p. 488.
29. [N] *SE*, p. 8.
30. *Ibid.*, p. 15.
31. [N] *VM I*, p. 23.
32. *Ibid.*, p. 29.
33. *Ibid.*
34. *Ibid.*, p. 36.
35. *Ibid.*, p. 35.

SECTION III

1. *LD*, XXIX, p. 206.
2. *LD*, V, p. 225.
3. *LD*, XXII, p. 157.
4. [N] *AW*, p. 18.
5. John Holloway, *The Victorian Sage: Studies in Argument* (New York, 1965), pp. 165–6.
6. [N] *Idea*, p. 276.
7. R. W. Church, *Occasional Papers* (1897), vol. II, p. 448.
8. M. Ward, vol. I, p. 220.
9. [M] *Misc*, vol. I, pp. 47–9.
10. [M] *TSVC*, pp. 101–113.
11. G. W. E. Russell, *Collections and Recollections* (1900), p. 45.
12. Church, *Occasional Papers*, vol. II, pp. 399–400.
13. [N] *Diff*, vol. I, pp. 241–2, 249–50.
14. *Tracts for the Times*, no. 1, p. 3.
15. Prickett, p. 158.
16. [N] *Apol*, p. 349.
17. *Ibid.*, pp. 363–4.
18. *Ibid.*, p. 404.
19. [N] *GA*, p. 273; cf. [N] *DA*, p. 294.
20. *Tracts for the Times*, no. 85, p. 73.
21. Robbins, p. 18.
22. Ward, *Last Lectures*, pp. 54–5.
23. [M] *Misc*, vol. II, pp. 74–7.
24. *Ibid.*, vol. III, pp. 274–5.

25. G. W. E. Russell, p. 45.
26. e.g., [M] *VD*, pp. 8–9; [M] *ROC*, pp. 16–17; [M] *TMHG*, p. 221; [M] *LJP*, p. 42; [M] *LGHS*, p. 25.
27. *LD*, XXIV, p. 389.
28. [M] *Ppap*, p. x.
29. *LD*, XXIV, pp. 241–2.
30. [N] *Idea*, p. 322.
31. F. L. Cross, p. 57.
32. J. Lewis May, 'Quis Desiderio', in *John Henry Newman Centenary Essays* (1945), p. 98.
33. [N] *Dev*, p. 36.
34. *Ibid.*, p. 357.
35. [N] *Diff*, vol. I, p. 239.
36. [N] *Apol*, pp. 264–5.
37. [N] *LG*, p. 207.
38. *Ibid.*, pp. 387–8.
39. *Tracts for the Times*, no. 3, pp. 4–5.
40. [N] *Idea*, pp. 331–2.
41. [N] *VVO*, p. 332.
42. [N] *Just*, p. 303.
43. [N] *Idea*, p. 435.
44. Other examples in [N] *PPS*, vol. VI, p. 169; vol. VII, p. 62; [N] *EOM*, p. 221; [N] *VM I*, pp. 84, 131, 218, 279; [N] *GA*, p. 110; [N] *Apol*, p. 150; *LD*, XII, p. 273; XXI, p. 48.
45. Bremond, p. 105.
46. S. T. Coleridge, *Aids to Reflection* (1854 edn), p. 158.
47. *LD*, I, p. 84.
48. [N] *Diff*, vol. I, p. 25.
49. [N] *Just*, p. 385.
50. [N] *DA*, p. 272.
51. [N] *PPC*, lecture 2, p. 8.
52. [N] *TPBI*, p. 23.
53. [N] *ECH*, vol. I, p. 13.
54. [N] *Diff*, vol. I, p. 16.
55. [N] *Idea*, pp. 74–5.
56. [N] *ECH*, vol. I, p. 113.
57. [N] *VM I*, pp. 48–9.
58. [N] *DA*, p. 299.
59. [N] *Idea*, p. 232.
60. [N] *Apol*, p. 322.
61. *LD*, V, p. 21.
62. [N] *Just*, p. 237.
63. [N] *Diff*, vol. I, p. 113.
64. David J. Delaura, 'Pater and Newman: The Road to the Nineties', in *Victorian Studies*, September 1966, p. 40.

SECTION IV

1. [M] *Serm*, vol. II, pp. 259–60.

2. *Ibid.*, p. 227.
3. *Ibid.*, p. 311.
4. V. A. McClelland, *Cardinal Manning: His Public Life and Influence* (1962), p. 161.
5. *LD*, XVIII, p. xiii.
6. E. R. Norman, *The Catholic Church and Ireland in the Age of Rebellion, 1859–1873* (1965), pp. 242–3.
7. G. M. Young, *Victorian England: Portrait of an Age* (1949), p. 44.
8. McClelland, *Manning*, p. 163.
9. Leslie, p. 195.
10. *Ibid.*, pp. 195–6.
11. McClelland, *Manning*, p. 165.
12. Norman, p. 111.
13. *Gladstone Diaries*, vol. VIII, p. 302.
14. Norman, p. 245.
15. *Ibid.*, pp. 457–8.
16. Leslie, p. 192.
17. [M] *Misc*, vol. I, p. 217.
18. *Ibid.*, p. 233.
19. Norman, p. 382.
20. *Ibid.*, p. 339.
21. *Gladstone Diaries*, vol. VII, p. 107.
22. *Ibid.*, pp. 238–9.
23. Gray, p. 225.
24. McClelland, *Manning*, p. 177; Leslie, pp. 206–7.
25. *LD*, XXX, p. 12.
26. Morley, vol. III, p. 281.
27. Alan O'Day, *Parnell and the First Home Rule Episode, 1884–87* (Dublin, 1986), p. 57.
28. McClelland, *Manning*, p. 190.
29. O'Day, pp. 48–9.
30. *LD*, XXX, p. 37.
31. McClelland, *Manning*, p. 196.
32. Leslie, pp. 431–2.

SECTION V

1. McClelland, *Manning*, p. 32.
2. Beck, pp. 158–9.
3. Fitzsimons, p. 103.
4. *Gladstone Diaries*, vol. VII, p. 205.
5. McClelland, *Manning*, pp. 70–1.
6. [M] *Misc*, vol. III, p. 7.
7. *Ibid.*, p. 43.
8. [M] *FPS*, pp. 4–5.
9. O'Day, pp. 104–5.
10. Fitzsimons, p. 106.
11. McClelland, 'Gladstone and Manning', in Jagger, *op. cit.*, p. 162.
12. *Ibid.*, p. 167.

SECTION VI

1. Leslie, p. 458.
2. [M] *OUS*, pp. 61–2.
3. [M] *EP*, p. 20.
4. [M] *Serm*, vol. III, p. 215.
5. [M] *EP*, p. 206.
6. Beck, p. 32.
7. [M] *Dom*, p. 27.
8. *LD*, XXI, p. 492.
9. *LD*, XXVI, p. 390.
10. McClelland, *English Roman Catholics*, pp. 284–97.
11. Butler, *Ullathorne*, vol. II, p. 159.
12. Leslie, p. 293.
13. *Ibid.*, pp. 294–5.
14. *Ibid.*, pp. 298–9.
15. Butler, *Ullathorne*, vol. II, pp. 155–6.
16. Beck, p. 187.
17. Snead-Cox, vol. I, pp. 320–57.
18. Butler, *Ullathorne*, vol. II, pp. 188–9.

SECTION VII

1. [M] *Serm*, vol. IV, p. 13.
2. *Ibid.*, Dedication.
3. Alec Vidler, *A Century of Social Catholicism, 1820–1920* (1964), p. 71 n.1.
4. *Ibid.*, p. 71.
5. [M] *Misc*, vol. II, pp. 74, 81–4, 91, 94–7.
6. K. S. Inglis, *Churches and the Working Classes in Victorian England* (1963), p. 22.
7. Fitzsimons, p. 141.
8. *Ibid.*, p. 142.
9. McClelland, *Manning*, p. 149.
10. Vidler, p. 143.
11. McClelland, *Manning*, p. 159.
12. *Ibid.*
13. Dingle and Harrison, p. 504.
14. Fitzsimons, p. 136.
15. *LD*, XXXI, p. 276 n.3.
16. McClelland, *Manning*, p. 148.

SECTION VIII

1. H. C. G. Matthew in *Gladstone Diaries*, vol. VII, p. xxvi.
2. Inglis, p. 134.
3. Sheridan Gilley, 'Heretic London, Holy Poverty and the Irish Poor', in *Downside Review*, vol. 89, no. 294 (January 1971), p. 66.
4. *Ibid.*, p. 67.

5. McClelland, *Manning*, pp. 20–1.
6. [M] *Aem*.
7. McClelland, *Manning*, p. 37.
8. Dingle and Harrison, p. 487.
9. [M] *Misc*, vol. III, p. 231.
10. [M] *CES*, pp. 4–5.
11. Dingle and Harrison, p. 506.
12. Snead-Cox, vol. I, p. 477.
13. [M] *Misc*, vol. III, p. 197.
14. McClelland, *Manning*, p. 215.
15. *LD*, XIX, p. 439.
16. *LD*, XXIII, p. 363.
17. Dermot Fenlon, 'The Aristocracy of Talent and the Mystery of Newman', in T. Merrigan (ed.), *Louvain Studies: John Henry Cardinal Newman* (Louvain, 1990), pp. 220–1.
18. J. H. L. Rowlands, *Church, State and Society: The Attitudes of John Keble, Richard Hurrell Froude and John Henry Newman, 1827–1845* (1989), pp. 157, 161.
19. [N] *Diff*, vol. I, p. 240.
20. [N] *Apol*, p. 339.
21. Douglas Woodruff, 'Newman and the Modern Age', in *Newman Centenary Essays*, p. 64.
22. Humphrey J. T. Johnson, 'Cardinal Newman', in Beck, p. 263.
23. Gray, p. 305.
24. *LD*, XXXI, p. 106.

25. Ward, *Newman*, vol. II, p. 513; cf. [N] *HS*, vol. I, p. 347.
26. T. Kenny, pp. 173–4.
27. *LD*, XXV, pp. 440–2.
28. [N] *PPC*, lecture IX, p. 15.
29. [N] *Disc*, p. 10.
30. *Ibid.*, p. 113.
31. [N] *CS*, p. 88.
32. [N] *Call*, p. 160.
33. T. Kenny, pp. 30–1.
34. Purcell, vol. II, p. 676.
35. Gray, p. 300.
36. [M] *Misc*, vol. I, p. 126.
37. Dingle and Harrison, p. 507.
38. Jeffrey P. von Arx, 'Archbishop Manning and the Kulturkampf', in *Recusant History*, vol. 21, no. 2 (1992), p. 255.
39. [M] *Misc*, vol. II, p. 134.
40. *Ibid.*, p. 148.
41. Arx, *art. cit.*, pp. 260–2; cf. [M] *PCHS*, p. 10.
42. Chadwick, *Secularization*, p. 134.
43. [M] *Misc*, vol. II, p. 141.
44. *Ibid.*, p. 135.
45. *LD*, XXV, p. 211.
46. *LD*, XXVII, p. 4.
47. [M] *Misc*, vol. II, p. 238.
48. Chadwick, *Secularization*, p. 260.
49. [M] *PP*, vol. I, p. 101.

CHAPTER 7: The Two Cardinals

SECTION I

1. Purcell, vol. II, p. 533.
2. *Ibid.*
3. *LD*, XXVII, p. 254.
4. Purcell, vol. II, p. 542.
5. Leslie, p. 252.
6. Purcell, vol. II, p. 551.
7. *LD*, XXV, p. 413.
8. *LD*, XXVI, p. 218 n.3.
9. *LD*, XXVII, p. 305.
10. *Ibid.*, p. 313.
11. *LD*, XXVIII, p. 279.
12. *Ibid.*, p. 290.
13. *Ibid.*, p. 291 n.1.
14. *LD*, XXIX, p. 426.
15. M. Ward, vol. I, p. 60.
16. Butler, *Ullathorne*, vol. II, p. 108.
17. J. D. Holmes, *More Roman than Rome*, p. 190.
18. *LD*, XXIX, pp. 423–4.
19. *Ibid.*, p. 17.

20. *Ibid.*, pp. 18–19.
21. *Ibid.*, p. 20.
22. *LD*, XXVIII, p. 335.
23. *LD*, XXIX, p. 53 n.3.
24. [N] *Add*, p. xv n.
25. *LD*, XXIX, p. 22.
26. *Ibid.*
27. *Ibid.*, p. 28.
28. *Ibid.*, p. 29 n.2.
29. *Ibid.*, p. 32.
30. *Ibid.*, pp. 46–7.
31. *Ibid.*, pp. 47–8.
32. *Ibid.*, p. 48.
33. *Ibid.*, p. 61.
34. *Ibid.*, p. 77.
35. *Ibid.*, p. 50.
36. G. Rowell, 'Cor ad cor loquitur: Newman's choice of his Cardinalatial Motto', in *Studies Urbanina*, no. 10 (Rome and Brescia, 1981), pp. 49–50.
37. *LD*, XXIX, p. 108 n.4.

38. [N] *Add*, pp. 62–4.
39. [N] *Apol*, p. 296.
40. *LD*, XXIX, p. 346.
41. *LD*, XXX, p. 143.
42. See especially [M] *Misc*, vol. III, pp. 101–2.
43. *LD*, XXX, p. 216.
44. J. D. Holmes, *More Roman than Rome*, p. 188.
45. Purcell, vol. II, pp. 351.
46. *Ibid.*, vol. II, p. 571 n.2; M. Trevor, *Light in Winter*, p. 613; *LD*, XXXI, p. 128.
47. Purcell, vol. II, p. 571 n.1.

SECTION II

1. *LD*, XXIX, p. 238 n.1.
2. B. A. Smith, *Dean Church: The Anglican Response to Newman* (1958), p. 302.
3. *LD*, XXXI, p. xiii.
4. *LD*, XXX, p. 337.
5. *LD*, XXXI, p. 184 n.5.
6. Butler, *Ullathorne*, vol. II, pp. 283–4.
7. *LD*, XXVIII, p. 55.
8. *LD*, XXIX, p. 241.
9. *LD*, XXXI, p. xv.
10. Birmingham Oratory MSS. Manning Letters, 24 August 1890.

SECTION III

1. M. Ward, vol. I, p. 227.

2. G. W. E. Russell, p. 49.
3. Bodley, p. 17.
4. *Ibid.*
5. *Ibid.*, p. 18.
6. H. D. I. Ryder, pp. 294–8.
7. Purcell, vol. II, p. 457.
8. *Ibid.*, vol. II, p. 804.
9. Leslie, p. 473.
10. [M] *EP*, pp. 238–9, 253–4.
11. M. Ward, vol. I, p. 24.
12. Russell, p. 41.
13. Leslie, p. 472.
14. Bodley, pp. 13–14.
15. *Ibid.*, p. 7.
16. *Ibid.*, p. 12.
17. This was recounted to me personally in 1963 by the rose-bearer herself, Mrs Dorothy Winkworth.
18. A. W. Hutton, *Cardinal Manning* (1892), pp. 238–9.
19. Bodley, p. 29.
20. Russell, p. 41.
21. A. M. W. Stirling, *Victorian Sidelights* (1954), p. 178.
22. *Ibid.*, pp. 176–8.
23. Sheridan Gilley, 'Manning and Chesterton', in *The Chesterton Review*, vol. XVIII, no. 4 (Saskatoon, 1992), p. 487.
24. B. Holland (ed.), *Baron Friedrich von Hügel: Selected Letters, 1896–1924* (1927), p. 256.

Conclusion

1. Gray, p. 3.
2. [N] *PPS*, vol. IV, p. 263.
3. [N] *PPS*, vol. IX, p. 26.
4. S. A. Grave, *Conscience in Newman's Thought* (Oxford, 1989), p. 1.
5. Quoted in N. Lash, 'Tides and Twilight: Newman since Vatican II', *Newman after a Hundred Years*, p. 460.
6. [M] *PO*, p. 218.
7. I. Ker, 'Newman and the Orphans of Vatican II', in *Louvain Studies*, p. 123.
8. Coulson, *Newman and the Common Tradition*, p. 50.
9. N. Lash, *art. cit.*, p. 449.
10. [N] *VM I*, pp. lxxvi–vii.
11. Coulson, 'Was Newman a Modernist?', in *Newman Studien*, vol. XIV, p. 82.

12. e.g., Chadwick, *Spirit of the Oxford Movement*, p. 165; Lash, *art. cit.*, p. 449; Grave, pp. 2–3.
13. Lash, *art. cit.*, p. 449.
14. Coulson, 'Conscience and Authority: Newman and the Two Vatican Councils', in *Newman Studien*, vol. IX, p. 169.
15. *LD*, XXX, p. 201.
16. Purcell, vol. II, p. 778.
17. *LD*, XXX, pp. 376–7.
18. *LD*, XXXI, pp. 104–5.
19. Purcell, vol. II, p. 777.
20. Bodley, p. 25.
21. Gladstone, *Vatican Decrees*, pp. 10–11.
22. [N] *Disc*, p. 108.
23. [M] *LJP*, p. 41.
24. M. Ward, vol. I, p. 39.

25. McGrath, p. 256.
26. *LD*, V, p. 380.
27. Quoted in Lord Elton, *Edward King and Our Times* (1958), p. 26.
28. M. Ward, vol. I, p. 143.
29. *LD*, XXX, p. 356.
30. H. Scott Holland, *A Bundle of Memories* (1915), pp. 114–15.
31. Cwiekowski, p. 57.
32. *LD*, XIII, p. 419.

33. *Ibid.*, p. 4.
34. [N] *HS*, vol. II, p. xiii.
35. [N] *Disc*, p. 5.
36. M. Ward, vol. I, p. 222.
37. Philip Hughes in Beck, pp. 27–8.
38. Mary Church, *Life of Dean Church*, p. 346.
39. [N] *HS*, vol. II, pp. 28–9.
40. *Ibid.*, p. 30.
41. *LD*, XXI, p. 86.

INDEX

Sub-headings within each entry are arranged in alphabetical order, except for entries of certain historical events (e.g. Oxford Movement), when they are arranged chronologically. Book titles are given separate entries, and do not appear under the entry for their authors. The abbreviations M for Manning and N for Newman are used within entries.